ZAGATSURVEY®

2003/04

PARIS
RESTAURANTS

Local Editors: Alexander Lobrano,
Mary Deschamps

Local Coordinator: Elizabeth d'Hémery

Editor: Troy Segal

Published and distributed by
ZAGAT SURVEY, LLC
4 Columbus Circle
New York, New York 10019
Tel: 212 977 6000
E-mail: paris@zagat.com
Web site: www.zagat.com

Distributed in France by
Flammarion
26, rue Racine
75006 Paris
Tel: 01 40 51 31 00

Acknowledgments

We would like to thank the following people for their support: George Balkind, Axel Baum, Odile Berthemy, Jean-Manuel Bourgois, Sabine and Patrick Brassart, Catherine Bret and Gilbert Brownstone, Mathilde Casimir, Frédéric Cassegrain, Erica Curtis, Jacques Dehornois, Denis Deschamps, Alexandra Ernst and Dean Garret Siegel, Barbara and Peter Georgescu, Jack D. Gunther Jr., Andrew Hibbert, Brigitte Jolly, Mark Kessel, M.L. Lewis, Vannina Maestracci, Anne Marsella, Anne and Gérard Mazet, Bruno Midavaine, Michelle Moss, Flore and Amaury de la Moussaye, Eleonare Nirat, Virginia and Jean Perrette, Anne de Ravel, Juliette Rey, Deirdre and Alfred J. Ross, Bibi Scuba, Robert J. Sisk, Anne Thomas, Robert C. Treuhold, Dagmar and François de la Tour d'Auvergne, Charlotte and Franck Ullmann, Yveline le Cerf Vaucher, Martine Vermeulen, Denise and Alexandre Vilgrain, Jennifer and Sebastien Vilgrain, Stanislas Vilgrain, Stephen R. Volk and Lawrence A. Weinbach.

This guide would not have been possible without the hard work of our staff, especially Reni Chin, Anna Chlumsky, Schuyler Frazier, Katherine Harris, Natalie Lebert, Mike Liao, Dave Makulec, Rob Poole, Robert Seixas and Sharon Yates.

Contents

About This Survey

For 24 years, Zagat Survey has reported on the shared experiences of diners like you. This *2003/04 Paris Restaurant Survey* is an update reflecting significant developments since our last edition was published. For example, we have included 88 places not in the previous edition, as well as indicating new addresses, phone numbers, chef changes and other key changes. All told, this guide covers some 986 restaurants.

By regularly surveying large numbers of avid local restaurant-goers, we hope to have achieved a uniquely current and reliable guide. For this book, more than 1,800 people participated. Since they dined out an average of 2.9 times per week, this *Survey* is based on roughly 273,000 meals annually. We sincerely thank each of these surveyors; this book is really "theirs."

Of course, we are especially grateful to our editors: Alexander Lobrano, European correspondent for *Gourmet* and a food and travel writer based in Paris for 16 years, and Mary Deschamps, a freelance writer in Paris. We would also like to thank *Le Figaro*'s François Simon for his help and advice along the way, and our coordinator, Elizabeth d'Hémery, who once again pulled this project together.

To help guide our readers to Paris' best meals and best buys, we have prepared a number of lists. See Most Popular (page 9), Top Ratings (pages 10–15) and Best Buys (page 16). To help the user find just the right restaurant for any occasion, we have also provided 43 handy indexes and have tried to be concise. Finally, it should be noted that our editors synopsized our surveyors' opinions, with their comments shown in quotation marks.

As companions to this guide, we also publish *Europe's Top Restaurants* and *Top International Hotels, Resorts & Spas* as well as maps and guides to 70 other world markets. Most of these guides are also on mobile devices and at **zagat.com,** where you can vote and shop as well.

To join our next ***Paris Survey*** or any of our other upcoming *Surveys,* just register at **zagat.com.** Each participant will receive a free copy of the resulting guide when it is published.

Your comments and even criticisms of this guide are also solicited. There is always room for improvement with your help. You can contact us at paris@zagat.com or by mail at Zagat Survey, 4 Columbus Circle, New York, NY 10019. We look forward to hearing from you.

New York, NY
April 7, 2003

Nina and Tim Zagat

What's New

Politically and economically, the world may look unsettled, but nothing comes between a Parisian and his restaurant. And while the average meal in the City of Light costs a relatively hefty 47.6 euros ($51.23), the *citoyens* are content to pay for their culinary pleasure – though here, as everywhere, they are demanding value for their money.

Tradition Triumphs: Perhaps that's why several pricey and high-profile fusion-menu places like Korova recently vanished in a puff of fashionable smoke, while traditional bistros have never been more beguiling. Not only are new addresses like Bistrot Paul-Bert in the 11th and De La Garde and La Grande Rue in the 15th thriving, but those eminently trend-aware restaurateurs, chef Alain Ducasse and Chez L'Ami Louis owner Thierry de la Brosse, have also skillfully renovated and updated the venerable Aux Lyonnais.

A La Mode: Not that the party's completely over for high-design, see-and-be-scene places. Several made splashy debuts this year, including two youth-oriented pre-clubbing addresses, B4 (it's a pun, get it?) in the 1st and La Maison Rouge in the Marais. Additional chic canteens for high-powered professionals include 6 New York, a slickly modern dining room overlooking the Seine, and R., whose penthouse premises offer the fabulous people a fabulous view of the Eiffel Tower.

Chefs on the Move: In this town, tracking the top toques is almost a spectator sport. Chef Alain Solivérès left Les Elysées du Vernet for Taillevent, filling the gap left by the departed Michel del Burgo (who's moved to Provence). Replacing Solivérès is Eric Briffard (ex Le Régence, the Hôtel Plaza-Athénée's old dining room). Other chefs on the go include Flora Mikula (ex Les Olivades), who opened a swanky, eponymously named establishment in the 8th, and Catherine Guerraz, who moved her popular Chez Catherine to more upmarket quarters in the 8th, upgrading her menu from homestyle bistro to New French in the process.

The Teething Tenth: Geographically, the most up-and-coming gastronomic grounds lie in the 10th, a long- neglected arrondissement being rejuvenated by the arty types moving into loft spaces. Their appetites are fueling the hottest table in town – Le Martel, a retro-chic bistro with a hybrid Franco-Algerian menu – along with such newcomers as Canal Café (Traditional French), Chaumière Massyle (North African) and Madonina (Italian).

As We Go to Press: Ever since he retired, chef Joël Robuchon has nurtured rumors of his return. This time it's for real, with the debut of his L'Atelier de Joël Robuchon in the Hôtel Pont Royal imminent. Finally, we would like to pay tribute to the late Bernard Loiseau, the renowned chef-owner of Burgundy's La Côte d'Or and Paris' three Tante restaurants.

Paris, France   Alexander Lobrano
April 7, 2003

Key to Ratings/Symbols

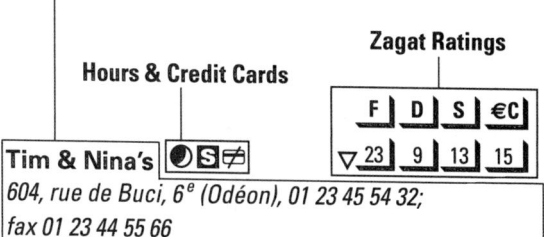

Name, Address, Métro Stop, Phone* & Fax Numbers

Hours & Credit Cards

Zagat Ratings

F	D	S	€C
▽ 23	9	13	15

Tim & Nina's 🌙 **S** ⊘

604, rue de Buci, 6ᵉ (Odéon), 01 23 45 54 32; fax 01 23 44 55 66

☑ *Jamais fermé*, this "crowded" 6th arrondissement cafe started the "Swedish-French craze" (e.g. herring or foie gras on tiny toasts with a choice of bordelaise sauces); though it looks like a "garage" and T & N "never heard of credit cards or reservations" – yours in particular – *les prix bon marché* and the "*merveilleuse* cuisine" draw demented "debit-account" diners to this "deep dive."

Review, with surveyors' comments in quotes

Restaurants with the highest overall ratings and greatest popularity and importance are printed in CAPITAL LETTERS.

Before reviews a symbol indicates whether responses were uniform ■ or mixed ☑.

Hours: 🌙 serves after 11 PM
S open on Sunday

Credit Cards: ⊘ no credit cards accepted

Ratings: Food, Decor and Service are rated on a scale of **0** to **30**. The Cost (C) column reflects our surveyors' estimate of the price of dinner including one drink and tip.

F	Food	D	Decor	S	Service	€C	Cost
23		9		13		15	

0–9	poor to fair	**20–25**	very good to excellent
10–15	fair to good	**26–30**	extraordinary to perfection
16–19	good to very good	▽	low response/less reliable

For places listed without ratings or a numerical cost estimate, such as an important **newcomer** or a popular **write-in**, the price range is indicated by the following symbols.

I	30€ and below	**E**	56€ to 75€
M	31€ to 55€	**VE**	76€ or more

* When calling from outside France, dial international code +33, then omit the first zero of the number.

Most Popular

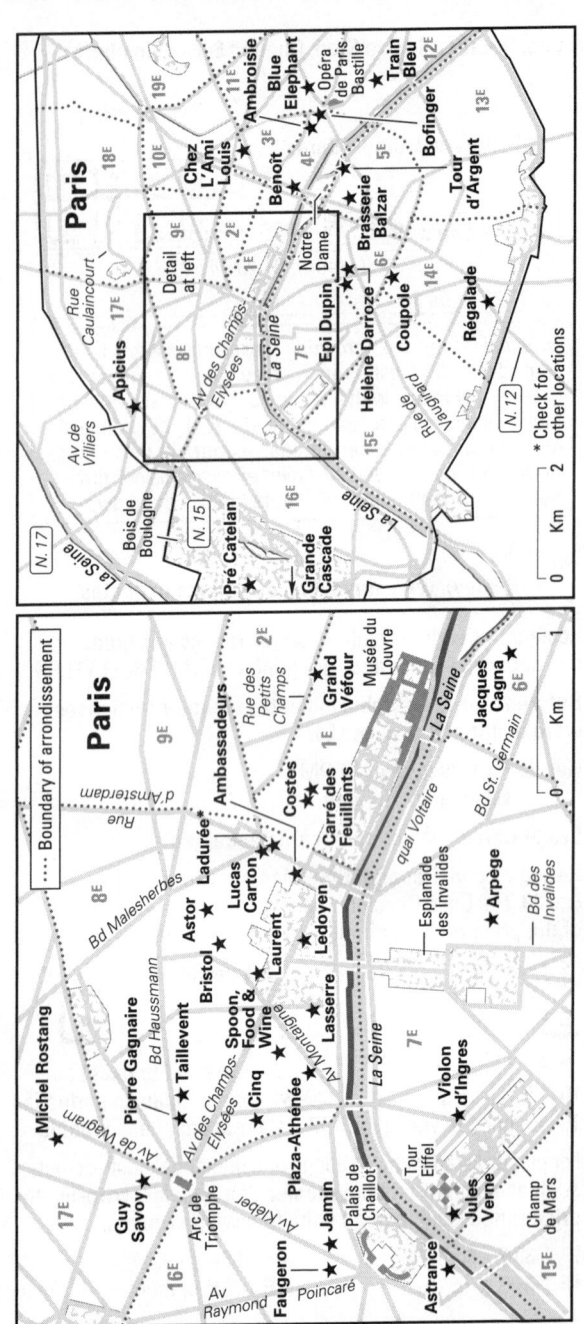

Paris

Apicius ★

Rue Caulaincourt

17E

Av de Villiers

8E Av des Champs Elysées

La Seine

19E

11E Ambroisie ★

Chez L'Ami Louis ★

10E

Benoît 3E ★

2E

1E

9E

Detail at left

Notre Dame

Blue Elephant ★

Opéra de Paris Bastille

Train Bleu ★

12E

Bofinger ★

13E

4E

5E

Brasserie Balzar ★

Tour d'Argent ★

Epi Dupin ★

Hélène Darroze ★

6E

Coupole ★

14E

Régalade ★

Rue de Vaugirard

N. 12

15E

* Check for other locations

La Seine

16E

Bois de Boulogne

N. 15

Pré Catelan ★

Grande Cascade ↓ ★

La Seine

N. 17

0   1   2
Km

Paris

Boundary of arrondissement

9E

Rue des Petits Champs

2E

Grand Véfour ★

Musée du Louvre

La Seine

Jacques Cagna ★

6E

Rue d'Amsterdam

Ambassadeurs ★

Costes ★

1E

Carré des Feuillants ★

Bd St. Germain

Ladurée ★ *

Lucas Carton ★

Bristol ★

Astor ★

Laurent ★

Ledoyen ★

quai Voltaire

Arpège ★

8E

Bd Malesherbes

Taillevent ★

Bd Haussmann

Spoon, Food & Wine ★

Lasserre ★

Esplanade des Invalides

Bd des Invalides

Michel Rostang ★

Pierre Gagnaire ★

Av de Wagram

Cinq ★

Av des Champs Elysées

Plaza-Athénée ★

7E

Av Montaigne

La Seine

Violon d'Ingres ★

Guy Savoy ★

17E

Arc de Triomphe

Av Kléber

16E

Jamin ★

Palais de Chaillot

Tour Eiffel

Champ de Mars

Jules Verne ★

15E

Faugeron ★

Av Raymond Poincaré

Astrance ★

0   1
Km

Most Popular

Each of our reviewers has been asked to name his or her five favorite restaurants. The places most frequently named, in order of their popularity, are:

1. Taillevent
2. Grand Véfour
3. Plaza-Athénée, Rest.
4. Lucas Carton
5. Arpège
6. Pierre Gagnaire
7. Tour d'Argent
8. Ambroisie
9. Guy Savoy, Rest.
10. Jules Verne
11. Bristol
12. Carré des Feuillants
13. Epi Dupin
14. Ambassadeurs
15. Benoît
16. Bofinger
17. Lasserre
18. Violon d'Ingres
19. Astrance
20. Blue Elephant
21. Apicius
22. Michel Rostang
23. Pré Catelan*
24. Chez L'Ami Louis
25. Costes
26. Hélène Darroze
27. Jacques Cagna
28. Cinq
29. Jamin
30. Laurent*
31. Astor
32. Faugeron*
33. Régalade*
34. Ledoyen
35. Ladurée
36. Coupole
37. Grande Cascade
38. Brasserie Balzar
39. Spoon, Food & Wine*
40. Train Bleu*

It's obvious that many of the restaurants on the above list are among Paris' most expensive, but if popularity were calibrated to price, we suspect that a number of other restaurants would join the above ranks. Given the fact that both our surveyors and readers love to discover dining bargains, we have added a list of 80 Best Buys on page 16. These are restaurants that give real quality at extremely reasonable prices.

---

* Tied with restaurant directly above it

Top Ratings

Top lists exclude restaurants with low voting. A restaurant followed by an asterisk is tied with the one directly above it.

Top 40 Food

28 Taillevent	Ostéria
27 Plaza-Athénée, Rest.	Espadon
Lucas Carton	Apicius
Grand Véfour	Isami
Pierre Gagnaire	Kinugawa
Michel Rostang	Marée
26 Guy Savoy, Rest.	**23** Divellec
Ambroisie	Violon d'Ingres
Bristol	Laurent
Arpège	Comte de Gascogne
Cinq	Duc*
25 Astrance	Pré Catelan
Carré des Feuillants	Nobu
Jamin	Tour d'Argent
Faugeron	Tastevin
Lasserre	Meurice
Ambassadeurs	Jacques Cagna
24 Chez L'Ami Louis	Muses
Astor	**22** Gérard Besson
Trois Marches	Ledoyen

Top by Cuisine (French)

Basque
18 Bascou
Pamphlet
Auberge Etchégorry
15 Casa Alcalde
Chez L'Ami Jean

Bistros (Contemporary)
22 Epi Dupin
Régalade
Relais Louis XIII
21 Petit Prince de Paris
Réminet

Bistros (Traditional)
24 Chez L'Ami Louis
22 Chez Michel
Benoît
21 Tire-Bouchon
Villaret

Brasseries
18 Café Runtz
16 Petit Lutétia
Bofinger
Terminus Nord
Brasserie Julien

Burgundy
20 Bourguignon du Marais
Récamier
18 Tante Louise
17 Tante Jeanne
16 Tante Marguerite

Haute Cuisine (Contemporary)
27 Pierre Gagnaire
26 Guy Savoy, Rest.
Bristol
Arpège
Cinq

Haute Cuisine (Traditional)
28 Taillevent
27 Plaza-Athénée, Rest.
Lucas Carton
Grand Véfour
Michel Rostang

Lyon
21 Bellecour
19 Moulin à Vent "Chez Henri"
18 Chez René
Rôtisserie du Beaujolais
17 Moissonnier

Mediterranean/Provence
21 Jardin
    Casa Olympe
    Fish La Boissonnerie
20 Petit Colombier
19 Bastide Odéon

Seafood
24 Marée
23 Divellec
    Duc
22 Petrossian
21 Taïra

Shellfish
20 Port Alma
    Marius et Janette
    Dôme
19 Pétrus
18 Pichet de Paris

Southwest
23 Violon d'Ingres
    Comte de Gascogne
22 Oulette
21 Trou Gascon
    Hélène Darroze

Steakhouses
19 Gavroche
    Rôtisserie d'en Face
18 Gourmets des Ternes
    Relais de Venise
    Rôtisserie du Beaujolais

Wine Bars/Bistros
20 Vin sur Vin
18 Willi's Wine Bar
17 Enoteca
    Dix Vins
15 Juveniles

Top by Cuisine (Other)

Asian
22 Tan Dinh
21 Tang
19 Village d'Ung et Li Lam
    Blue Elephant
18 Kambodgia

Chinese
21 Chen
19 Mirama
18 Chez Ngo
    Passy Mandarin
    Tsé-Yang

Italian
24 Ostéria
22 Sormani
    Chez Vincent
21 Grand Venise
20 Romantica

Japanese
24 Isami
    Kinugawa
23 Nobu
22 Benkay
    Isse*

Mediterranean/Middle Eastern
19 Délices d'Aphrodite
18 Fakhr el Dine
    Al Diwan
    Mavrommatis
    Byblos Café

North African
19 Oum el Banine
    404
    Atlas
    Timgad
18 Wally Le Saharien

Top by Special Feature

Breakfast†
18 Dalloyau
17 Ladurée
15 Deux Abeilles
    Bernardaud
14 Angelina

Caviar
22 Petrossian
21 Caviar Kaspia
19 Maison du Caviar
18 Flora Danica
14 Daru

---

† Other than hotels

Top Food

Hotel Dining

27 Plaza-Athénée, Rest.
Hôtel Plaza-Athénée
Pierre Gagnaire
Hôtel Balzac
26 Bristol
Hôtel Bristol
Cinq
Four Seasons George V
25 Ambassadeurs
Hôtel de Crillon

Late Dining

21 Caviar Kaspia
19 Maison du Caviar
Gavroche
18 Al Diwan
17 Livingstone

Newcomers/Unrated

Bistrot Paul-Bert
Chamarré
Cosi (Le)
Martel
Tonkinoise

Sunday Dining

27 Pierre Gagnaire
26 Cinq
25 Astrance
24 Chez L'Ami Louis
Astor

Tea & Desserts

18 Dalloyau
17 Ladurée
15 Deux Abeilles
Mariage Frères
A Priori Thé

Wine Lists

28 Taillevent
27 Plaza-Athénée, Rest.
Lucas Carton
Grand Véfour
Pierre Gagnaire

Top by Arrondissement

1st

27 Grand Véfour
25 Carré des Feuillants
24 Espadon
Kinugawa
23 Meurice

2nd & 3rd

24 Chez L'Ami Louis
22 Isse
Céladon
20 Drouant
19 404

4th

26 Ambroisie
24 Ostéria
Isami
22 Benoît
20 Bourguignon du Marais

5th

23 Tour d'Argent
21 Petit Prince de Paris
Réminet
Fógon Saint Julien
20 Palenque

6th

23 Jacques Cagna
22 Epi Dupin
Relais Louis XIII
21 Hélène Darroze
Fish La Boissonnerie

7th

26 Arpège
23 Divellec
Violon d'Ingres
22 Tan Dinh
Petrossian

8th

28 Taillevent
27 Plaza-Athénée, Rest.
Lucas Carton
Pierre Gagnaire
26 Bristol

9th & 10th

23 Muses
22 Chez Michel
21 Casa Olympe
20 Table d'Anvers
19 Alsaco

11th & 12th
22 Oulette
21 Trou Gascon
Villaret
C'Amelot
20 Repaire de Cartouche

13th & 14th
23 Duc
22 Montparnasse 25
Régalade
20 Dôme
Amuse Bouche
Avant Goût*

15th
22 Benkay
21 Tire-Bouchon
Os à Moelle
Chen
Grand Venise

16th
25 Astrance
Jamin
Faugeron
23 Pré Catelan
22 Relais d'Auteuil "Patrick Pignol"

17th
27 Michel Rostang
26 Guy Savoy, Rest.
24 Apicius
22 Faucher
Sormani

18th, 19th & 20th
22 Chez Vincent
20 Beauvilliers
19 Allobroges
18 Pavillon Puebla
17 Bœuf Couronné

Outside Paris
24 Trois Marches
23 Comte de Gascogne
Tastevin
21 Potager du Roy
19 Marée de Versailles

Top 40 Decor

28 Grand Véfour	**24** Ledoyen
Tour d'Argent	Lapérouse
Ambassadeurs	Maison de l'Amérique Latine
27 Taillevent	Blue Elephant
Jules Verne	**23** China Club
Cinq	Beauvilliers
Bristol	Elysées du Vernet
Train Bleu	Costes
26 Meurice	Brasserie Julien
Lucas Carton	Maison Blanche
Lasserre	Buddha Bar
Espadon	Pavillon Montsouris
Plaza-Athénée, Rest.	Altitude 95
Laurent	Chalet des Iles
25 Grande Cascade	**22** Cazaudehore La Forestière
Ambroisie	Livingstone
Pré Catelan	Orangerie
Georges	Coupe-Chou
Maxim's	Café Marly
Trois Marches	404

Outdoors

Cazaudehore La Forestière	Maison de l'Amérique Latine
Chalet des Iles	Pavillon Montsouris
Grande Cascade	Pré Catelan
Laurent	Trois Marches

Romance

Beauvilliers	Coupe-Chou
Blue Elephant	Georges
Brasserie Julien	Lasserre
Café Marly	Maxim's
China Club	Orangerie

Rooms

Ambassadeurs	Lapérouse
Ambroisie	Ledoyen
Bristol	Lucas Carton
Cinq	Meurice
Costes	Plaza-Athénée, Rest.
Elysées du Vernet	404
Espadon	Taillevent
Grand Véfour	Train Bleu

Views

Altitude 95	Quai Ouest
Benkay	R.
Cap Seguin	Rest. du Musée d'Orsay
Chez Francis	River Café
Georges	Toupary
Jules Verne	Tour d'Argent
Maison Blanche	Virgin Café

Top 40 Service

28 Taillevent
27 Plaza-Athénée, Rest.
26 Grand Véfour
   Cinq
   Ambassadeurs
   Bristol
25 Lucas Carton
   Pierre Gagnaire
   Espadon
   Lasserre
   Michel Rostang
   Guy Savoy, Rest.
24 Faugeron
   Arpège
   Tour d'Argent
   Ambroisie
   Meurice
   Laurent
   Jamin
23 Carré des Feuillants

   Elysées du Vernet
   Ledoyen
   Trois Marches
   Bel Canto
   Muses*
22 Astor
   Bar Vendôme
   Jardin
   Astrance
   Céladon
   Jacques Cagna
21 Grande Cascade
   Jules Verne
   Maupertu
   Pré Catelan
   Marée
   Obélisque
   Violon d'Ingres
   Relais Plaza
   Apicius

Best Buys

Top 40 Bangs for the Buck

List derived by dividing the cost of a meal into its ratings.

1. Chartier
2. Cosi
3. A Priori Thé
4. Rubis
5. Baron Rouge
6. Crêperie de Josselin
7. Lina's
8. Languedoc
9. Loir dans la Théière
10. Clown Bar
11. Petit Prince de Paris
12. Dix Vins
13. Ay!! Caramba!!
14. Perraudin
15. Trumilou
16. Chez Janou
17. Mariage Frères*
18. Coude Fou
19. Atlas
20. Deux Abeilles
21. Rest. du Musée d'Orsay
22. Lescure
23. Dame Tartine
24. Cave de l'Os à Moelle
25. New Jawad
26. Bistrot d'Henri
27. Cloche des Halles
28. Bistrot du Peintre
29. Café Véry
30. Dos de la Baleine
31. Sept Quinze
32. Filoche
33. Café Charbon
34. Temps des Cerises
35. Livingstone
36. Astier
37. Chez Prune
38. Cigale
39. Chez Paul
40. Relais de l'Entrecôte

Other Good Values

Agape
Ampère
Angelina
Auberge Aveyronnaise
Avant Goût
Baan-Boran
Babylone
Beaujolais d'Auteuil
Bernardaud
Biche au Bois
Bistro des Deux Théâtres
Bon Saint Pourçain
Bouillon Racine
Brasserie Munichoise
Byblos Café
Café du Commerce
Café Runtz
Caméléon
Chardenoux
Chez Gérard
Chez Marianne
Chez Omar
Chez Vincent
Cour de Rohan
Délices d'Aphrodite
Grenier de Notre Dame
Hangar
Maison du Jardin
Maupertu
Monde des Chimères
Paparazzi
Petite Sirène de Copenhague
Petit Lutétia
Petit St. Benoît
Pied de Fouet
P'tit Troquet
404
Saint Vincent
Studio
Troquet

Restaurant Directory

Abazu 🅂   _ | _ | _ | M
3, rue André Mazet, 6ᵉ (Odéon), 01 46 33 12 05
There's no sushi on the menu, but a generous side of showmanship accompanies the teppanyaki (fish, meat and vegetables cooked on a hot metal surface), the star dish at this cozy Japanese in Saint-Germain; opened last summer, it's already swarming with a stylish crowd of editors and politicians, as well as savvy tourists.

Absinthe (L')   14 | 14 | 14 | 42
24, pl du Marché St-Honoré, 1ᵉʳ (Tuileries), 01 49 26 90 04; fax 01 49 26 08 64
■ With "a great spot" in the Place du Marché Saint-Honoré, this "fun" – despite "snooty waiters" – French bistro serves up a "modern" version of "cuisine bourgeoise" that gets thumbs-up from those who find it a "good value"; and while epicures claim it's "a bit banal", all agree that the "charming terrace" in summer is "particularly pleasant."

A et M Le Bistrot   14 | 12 | 12 | 38
136, bd Murat, 16ᵉ (Porte de St-Cloud), 01 45 27 39 60; fax 01 45 27 69 71
■ Perhaps, like its fortysomething-plus clientele, it's "losing steam" a bit; but most still praise this bistro in the 16th as offering "great value for the money" with "trendy" yet "typically French" cuisine, plus "unbeatably priced wines"; and if the "service is sometimes casual", everyone "appreciates the valet parking."

Affriolé (L')   16 | 11 | 14 | 39
17, rue Malar, 7ᵉ (Ecole Militaire/Invalides), 01 44 18 31 33; fax 01 44 18 91 12
■ Near Les Invalides, this "cozy" Left Bank bistro serves up "typical New French fare with an atypical approach"; patrons willing to overlook its "kitschy" Pompeian red decor, "tight tables" and erratic service (ranging from "energetic" to "disagreeable") are rewarded with "exceptional food" at "easy prices" and a "bright and cheerful atmosphere."

African Grill ❶   _ | _ | _ | M
27, rue d'Enghien, 10ᵉ (Bonne Nouvelle/Strasbourg-St-Denis), 01 44 79 02 02; fax 01 44 79 02 02
Decorated with native art, this intimate eatery near Strasbourg-St-Denis attracts African expats and diplomats with Ivory Coast specials such as *kedjenou de poulet* (a traditional chicken stew) and banana tart; however, regulars find the food "decent" but "less inspired" of late.

Agape (L')   16 | 10 | 14 | 29
281, rue Lecourbe, 15ᵉ (Boucicaut/Convention), 01 45 58 19 29
■ "A neighborhood bistro that's worth paying attention to", this Traditional French in the 15th serves "original cuisine" that's "consistently delicious" and "prettily presented"; the "charming proprietor" may have upped the menu-

carte's prices (maybe to finance a "refreshed decor"), but supporters swear it's still a "great value."

Aiguière (L') ▽ 17 | 15 | 18 | 46

37 bis, rue de Montreuil, 11ᵉ (Faidherbe-Chaligny), 01 43 72 42 32; fax 01 43 72 96 36

■ This Gustavian-style inn in one of the "lonelier corners" of the 11th appeals to surveyors familiar with its "excellent tasting menus, including wine" and "sober but charming decor"; throw in "attentive service", and most agree this Classic French offers a "good deal" for the neighborhood.

Ailleurs ◗ 9 | 12 | 11 | 36

26, rue Jean Mermoz, 8ᵉ (Franklin D. Roosevelt), 01 53 53 98 00; fax 01 53 53 98 01

◰ Just off the Champs-Elysées, this "hipster" hangout offers "interesting cocktails" and, some say, a "decent" International menu (you "have to try the *kif au chocolat*", a molten chocolate cake); but serious diners who'd rather eat well than gape at "pretty girls, including the waitresses" advise "go *ailleurs*" (elsewhere).

Aimant du Sud (L') ◗ – | – | – | M

40, bd Arago, 13ᵉ (Glacière/Les Gobelins), 01 44 24 84 66; fax 01 43 31 61 86

"Original, high-quality Mediterranean cuisine" is what attracts sun-loving palates to this small bistro in the 13th, near Montparnasse; and if some feel it's "gone slightly downhill", "good wines" – mainly from the Southwest – "nice decor" and a large terrace keep most folks happy.

Alcazar ◗ S 12 | 18 | 12 | 46

62, rue Mazarine, 6ᵉ (Odéon), 01 53 10 19 99; fax 01 53 10 23 23

■ With "to-die-for" decor, this "noisy" brasserie (near the Odéon, though it feels more like "dining in London or New York" than Paris) attracts trendies who flock here "to be seen" and catch a seafood-oriented quick-fix dinner "before the club scene happens upstairs"; an outpost of designer/restaurateur Terence Conran's empire, its "high style is not matched by the food", which seems as "pricey as his furniture" – though most agree that the "excellent brunch" is perfect for a "rainy Sunday."

Al Dar ◗ S 16 | 11 | 14 | 37

8, rue Frédéric Sauton, 5ᵉ (Maubert-Mutualité), 01 43 25 17 15; fax 01 45 01 61 67

93, av Raymond Poincaré, 16ᵉ (Victor Hugo), 01 45 00 96 64

■ "Delicious" meze and other Middle Eastern delights draw diners and take-awayers to these "steady" Lebanese twins near the Place Maubert and the Place Victor Hugo; patrons praise "fresh" fare that's "simple and frank", though many are miffed at the "mediocre" service and "bland" decor.

Al Diwan ◐ S
18 | 13 | 15 | 42
*30, av George V, 8ᵉ (Alma-Marceau/George V), 01 47 23 45 45;
fax 01 47 23 60 98*
■ A "favorite" among fans for the most authentic food
"outside of Beirut", this "solid Lebanese" in the 8th serves
up "generously portioned" "royal feasts" amid a "crowded,
smoky" atmosphere and live music that converts consider
all part of the Middle Eastern experience; and while some
snipe at surroundings that are "a bit too cafeteria-feeling"
and prices "fit for an emir", they nevertheless reserve ahead
for "great fun."

Alivi (L') ◐ S
▽ 15 | 14 | 14 | 37
*27, rue du Roi de Sicile, 4ᵉ (Hôtel-de-Ville/St-Paul),
01 48 87 90 20; fax 01 48 87 20 60*
■ This "delightfully charming" Corsican off the Rue de
Rivoli in the 4th serves a "refreshing" and "exquisite mix
of flavors" that offer "a perfect antidote to the butter,
cream and cheese sauces" that abound in Classic French
cuisine; "young, fun waiters" make the place particularly
"congenial", as do wines from the mother island and the
"pleasant outdoor terrace."

Allard ◐
17 | 16 | 17 | 59
*41, rue St-André-des-Arts, 6ᵉ (Odéon), 01 43 26 48 23;
fax 01 46 33 04 02*
■ "A step back in time", this "quintessential Traditional
French bistro" in the 6th makes the "small portions of
Nouvelle Cuisine places" appear miserly indeed; patrons are
wooed by the "exceptional food" like the "superb duck
smothered in olives" in a setting that "causes Paris to feel
like Paris"; though locals lament it "caters to an American
clientele", admirers insist it's just what "one expects of a
proper Parisian restaurant" – "tight tables" and all.

Allobroges (Les)
19 | 13 | 17 | 40
*71, rue des Grands Champs, 20ᵉ (Maraîchers/Nation),
01 43 73 40 00*
■ "Consistently superior" Classic French cuisine is the lure
of this "charming neighborhood restaurant" "lost in the
20th"; enthusiasts appreciate the "subtle" play of flavors of
"beautifully presented food" at an "irreproachable price";
perhaps it's *un peu* "pompous", but most agree that this
one's "a must."

Al Mounia S
17 | 18 | 16 | 44
*16, rue de Magdebourg, 16ᵉ (Trocadéro), 01 47 27 57 28;
fax 01 41 44 73 63*
■ This traditional North African near the Trocadéro invites
diners to an "authentic" Moroccan experience replete with
leather poufs, low tables (those with weak backs, watch out)
and "delicious couscous" and "excellent" tagines; while
non-Maghreban mavens may not get it, most welcome
the "exotic" "change of pace."

Alsace (L') ●S
13 | 13 | 12 | 42

*39, av des Champs-Elysées, 8ᵉ (Franklin D. Roosevelt),
01 53 93 97 00; fax 01 53 93 97 09*

◪ "A place to be seen" right on the Champs, this around-the-clock Alsatian is perfect "après-clubbing" for "foie gras at 6 AM", shellfish platters ("if oysters are your game, this is the name") and "very good" choucroute, some surveyors say; antagonists argue this brasserie is "run like a factory", with "anonymous" staffers and "expensive" merchandise.

Alsaco (L')
19 | 10 | 15 | 35

*10, rue Condorcet, 9ᵉ (Anvers/Poissonnière), 01 45 26 44 31;
fax 01 42 85 11 05*

■ From choucroute that many hail as "the best in Paris" to a superb selection of regional wines, things are just "so Alsatian" at this "friendly" bistro in the 9th; the eccentric but "eager-to-please" owner manages to create a "convivial" ambiance in the "noisy, smoky" "chalet-like room"; his "excellent" efforts make the "long hike from the nearest Métro" worthwhile.

Altitude 95 S
14 | 23 | 15 | 39

*Tour Eiffel, Champ-de-Mars, 1st level, 7ᵉ (Champ de Mars),
01 45 55 20 04; fax 01 47 05 94 40*

◪ Sightseers come to this superbly situated spot for "the magic of the Eiffel Tower" and its "sumptuous" views; snide surveyors sniff "it's clear that the tourists keep this place open", but actually the score for the "decent" and "fairly priced" Classic French cuisine has risen since our last *Survey*; of course, the key is to "get a window table."

Ambassade d'Auvergne S
17 | 14 | 15 | 45

*22, rue du Grenier St-Lazare, 3ᵉ (Rambuteau), 01 42 72 31 22;
fax 01 42 78 85 47*

■ It's near the Pompidou Center, but "a taste of the countryside in Paris" describes this ambassador of "down-to-earth peasant food" from Auvergne, including its "famous *aligot*" ("cheesy mashed potatoes") that's "definitely not dietetic"; the "cozy, early-chalet" decor and "service that could not be friendlier" make it "perfect on a chilly, gray day."

Ambassade du Sud-Ouest S
16 | 9 | 13 | 40

46, av de La Bourdonnais, 7ᵉ (Ecole-Militaire), 01 45 55 59 59

■ Near the Ecole Militaire, this small Southwestern bistro wins hearts for its "very good" country cooking (especially "the excellent foie gras") and regional wines; a round of applause also goes to the "warm welcome", which enlivens the "cold" decor.

AMBASSADEURS (LES) S
25 | 28 | 26 | 113

*Hôtel de Crillon, 10, pl de la Concorde, 8ᵉ (Concorde),
01 44 71 16 16; fax 01 44 71 15 02*

■ Dining at this "royally classy" Contemporary French in the historic Hôtel de Crillon (once a noble's palace) makes its clientele "feel like kings", "even when being loaned a tie"; admirers acclaim the "imaginative cuisine that combines traditional ingredients in unexpected ways" and bow before the wine list that "you need to be physically fit to lift"; though the price for this treatment "is steep", the "sumptuous decor", "superb service" and "unforgettable" food leave regal diners with no regrets.

AMBROISIE (L')
26 | 25 | 24 | 140

9, pl des Vosges, 4ᵉ (Bastille/St-Paul), 01 42 78 51 45
■ "Still a stunner" say surveyors of this "delight on the Place des Vosges" where chef Bernard Pacaud's Haute Cuisine marries "classic elegance" with "modern inventiveness"; enthusiasts also hail the tapestry-laden "magnificent setting" in which service is performed "like a virtual ballet with zero excess movements" (though "somewhat frostily" to some Yanks); in short, "there's nothing to fault but the prices" – and maybe the fact that "reservations are almost impossible" to get.

Amici Mei ⌿
– | – | – | E

53, bd Beaumarchais, 4ᵉ (Chemin Vert), 01 42 71 82 62
Prices are steep and there's always a wait for a table, but this doesn't deter the hungry hordes of pizza lovers who aver that the best pies in town emerge from the brick bee-hive-shaped oven of this azure-colored, vest-pocket neophyte near the Bastille; other Italian offerings are on hand, so settle in over an antipasti before tucking into an imaginatively topped 'za, like the one with treviso, a bitter red lettuce.

Ami Pierre (A l') ☽
15 | 14 | 16 | 37

5, rue de la Main d'Or, 11ᵉ (Bastille/Ledru-Rollin), 01 47 00 17 35
■ "It's the France of the '50s" happily note nostalgists who feel like they've stepped back in time at this "familial" bistro à vins near the Bastille; "simple" Traditional French fare, numerous wines by the glass, a lively owner who loves to "celebrate birthdays" and a homey setting make it "ideal for an evening with good friends" ("timid lovers" might abstain).

Amognes (Les)
20 | 9 | 13 | 43

243, rue du Faubourg St-Antoine, 11ᵉ (Faidherbe-Chaligny), 01 43 72 73 05; fax 01 43 28 77 23
■ Behind the Bastille, this New French bistro earns nods from novelty-seeking palates on the lookout for "creative cuisine" that's a "sure value"; "flavorful" renditions of "country" favorites, including in-season game, lure fans who admit that "the food transcends the ambiance" and service is "a bit slow."

Ampère (L')
17 | 15 | 14 | 35

1, rue Ampère, 17ᵉ (Wagram), 01 47 63 72 05; fax 01 47 63 37 33
■ "Simple and good like a bistro should be" "with-it" surveyors say about this "unpretentious" Classic French in

the 17th near the Place Pereire; "tasty cuisine, nice wines" and "laid-back" ambiance that's "perfect for dinner with friends" are the lures here, along with "friendly service."

Amphyclès   20 | 16 | 17 | 105

78, av des Ternes, 17ᵉ (Porte Maillot), 01 56 68 08 00; fax 01 40 68 91 88

◪ "Sometimes great, sometimes not" sums up reviewers' reactions to this New French in the 17th; converts claim it "deserves more recognition" for its "subtle, refined" Haute Cuisine, but critics carp that the "once-seamless service has slipped" and while "the food is delicious", it's "expensive"; at least the "quiet, pleasant ambiance" appeals.

Amuse Bouche (L')   20 | 10 | 17 | 37

186, rue du Château, 14ᵉ (Gaîté/Mouton-Duvernet), 01 43 35 31 61; fax 01 45 38 96 60

■ Visiting this "very small" but "welcoming" New French is like "having dinner at the home of the best cook you know", and though the portion size may seem meager to some minds (or rather stomachs), the "creative cuisine" is "definitely a good buy"; only the "little-traveled location in the 14th" fails to amuse.

Anacréon   19 | 9 | 15 | 41

53, bd St-Marcel, 13ᵉ (Les Gobelins), 01 43 31 71 18; fax 01 43 31 94 94

■ "A slice of heaven a short walk from the Place d'Italie" is how loyalists laud this brainchild of chef-owner André Le Letty, a "talented Tour d'Argent veteran"; his ambition to "bring [Traditional French] cuisine to the people, not just to the few" is realized in his "consistently good food" that's served at a good value; the "service is warm" too, but "alas, that decor . . . ."

Anahï ●⧈   16 | 17 | 16 | 42

49, rue Volta, 3ᵉ (Arts-et-Métiers/Temple), 01 48 87 88 24; fax 01 42 77 41 65

■ This South American bistro with a "charming", "from-another-era" decor grills up "exceptional beef" for a "très hip" clientele whose jet-set quotient surges "during Fashion Week" with the arrival of "lots of models"; not far from the Place de la République, it's a little "too pricey for the quality", but most find it "enticing" anyway.

Anahuacalli ⧈   ▽ 18 | 12 | 17 | 31

30, rue des Bernardins, 5ᵉ (Maubert-Mutualité), 01 43 26 10 20; fax 01 42 53 06 82

■ Hailed by authoritative amigos as "the only real Mexican in Paris", this Latin Quarter Latino offers "authentic" dishes and "great margaritas" ("very potent – beware!") in a cozy, wood-beamed setting; "a wonderful change from typical Parisian Tex-Mex", it keeps enthusiasts coming with its "smiley service" and signature tequila mousse.

Androuet

_ | _ | _ | M

51, rue de Verneuil, 7ᵉ (Rue du Bac), 01 45 48 51 98;
fax 01 45 48 14 29

In Saint-Germain, this resurrection of a famous name among
fromageophiles has been an immediate success with
natives and tourists alike; the cheese-based Classic French
dishes include a variety of the old Androuet's classics, but
the real pleasure here are the tasting plates of farmhouse
fromages, amiably served in a beamed-wall dining room.

Andy Whaloo ●

_ | _ | _ | M

69, rue des Granvilliers, 3ᵉ (Arts et Métiers), 01 42 71 20 38

In an increasingly arty and trendy part of town – midway
between Les Halles and the Marais – this new North African
snackery is a runaway hit, thanks to its variety of *kemias*
(small dishes), served in a neo-hippie decor that conjures
up Bob Seger and the road-to-Katmandu; gentle prices and
a warm welcome add to the appeal.

Angelina 🅂

14 | 18 | 11 | 30

226, rue de Rivoli, 1ᵉʳ (Concorde/Tuileries), 01 42 60 82 00;
fax 01 42 86 98 97

◪ The once-"elegant" decor "may have seen better days",
but this "mythic tea salon" in the 1st still draws tourists
and "locals with their dogs" (the doggies get "water in a
fine china bowl") for its famous hot chocolate – "a thick
molten steaming cup of liquid pudding" that "remains
without equal" – and a "mont blanc from heaven"; fans
shrug off the "just ok" Classic French menu and the "lousy
service", saying this grande dame's a "must-visit landmark."

Angle du Faubourg (L')

18 | 15 | 16 | 59

195, rue du Faubourg St-Honoré, 8ᵉ (Charles de Gaulle-Etoile),
01 40 74 20 20; fax 01 40 74 20 21

◪ "Reeking of extreme trendiness", this Taillevent offshoot
in the 8th serves up Classic French food with a Med twist;
while there's praise for the "good choice of well-priced
wines", diners are divided on all else: cuisine ("inventive"
vs. "unoriginal"), decor ("gorgeous" vs. "glacial") and
service ("conscientious" vs. "neglectful").

Annapurna ●

17 | 17 | 15 | 50

32, rue de Berri, 8ᵉ (George V), 01 45 63 91 56

◼ Loyalists love to be lulled by the strains of live sitar music
while tasting tandoori at this 8th arrondissement Punjab
palace, which "may be the best Indian in Paris"; the "typical
decor" – i.e. sunken tables and chairs and "a view" of the
clay oven – adds "elegance" to the "hushed atmosphere."

Aoc (L')

_ | _ | _ | M

14, rue des Fossés St-Bernard, 5ᵉ (Cardinal Lemoine/Jussieu),
01 43 54 22 52; fax 01 43 25 80 16

If it was a tad cheeky to have co-opted the official French
designation for the highest quality, region-specific foods

(*Appellation d'Origine Contrôlée*), this Latin Quarter bistro lives up to its name: the open kitchen features rotisserie AOC meats, and also offers generous servings of other Traditional Bistro dishes; behind the bright yellow-and-red facade lies a relaxing dining room decorated with antique copper cookware and ceramic pots.

APICIUS | 24 | 18 | 21 | 98 |

122, av de Villiers, 17ᵉ (Pereire), 01 43 80 19 66; fax 01 44 40 09 57

■ Chef-owner Jean-Pierre Vigato continues to delight devotees at his Haute Cuisine haven near the Place Pereire; "you'll think you died and went to food heaven" after tasting the "exceptional" mix of "traditional" and "innovative" dishes – including a "most memorable pan-fried foie gras" – served by a "warm and welcoming" staff (which offsets the "slightly somber surroundings"); even adamant admirers admit the tariff's a tad "excessive" – but that's "the price you pay to taste talent."

Appart' (L') ● | 12 | 17 | 13 | 39 |

9, rue du Colisée, 8ᵉ (Franklin D. Roosevelt), 01 53 75 16 34; fax 01 53 76 15 39

■ A "warm welcome" by glam "hostesses in black dresses" wins points for this Classic French whose "show-biz ambiance" and "original", "perfect-for-people-in-love" setting (it's furnished to look like an apartment, hence the name) "make up for uneventful food" and often "so-so service"; if nothing else, it's a "good value" for the upscale neighborhood "near the Champs" and "convenient" for "late night, après-cinema" dining and scene-scoping.

A Priori Thé ⑤ | 15 | 17 | 13 | 23 |

35, Galerie Vivienne, 2ᵉ (Bourse/Palais Royal-Musée du Louvre), 01 42 97 48 75

■ Set in the "gorgeous" Galerie Vivienne, perhaps "Paris' most beautiful arcade", this Anglo-Saxon style tearoom is perfect for "lunch with the girls" or "a lazy Sunday brunch, watching the passersby"; service is a tad "slow", but nonetheless fans flock for "fresh salads", breakfast-lunch fare and "delicious sweets, washed down with a good selection of teas."

Arbre à Cannelle (L') | ▽ | 10 | 14 | 12 | 19 |

57, passage des Panoramas, 2ᵉ (Grands Boulevards), 01 45 08 55 87
14, rue Linné, 5ᵉ (Jussieu), 01 43 31 68 31

■ "The charm of Parisian arcades" draws a daytime clientele to this "tearoom from another era" – Napoleon III, to be precise – tucked away in the "superb Passage des Panoramas" (there's a twin in the 5th); food ratings for the "simple" but "filling" savories and desserts may not be brilliant, but it's a "perfect" "easy-on-the-wallet" spot "for a quick lunch with friends."

Arbuci (L') ◖ S   11 │ 12 │ 12 │ 34

25, rue de Buci, 6ᵉ (Mabillon), 01 44 32 16 00;
fax 01 44 32 16 09

■ "All-you-can-eat oysters" ("they'll give you a quizzical look after the fifth dozen – pay no mind!"), "good" rotisserie-grilled meats and "great jazz downstairs" Wednesday–Saturday are the lures at this "classic brasserie" in the heart of Saint-Germain; a few critics carp it's "bustling" with *beaucoup de* tourists (translation: "noisy"), but fin fans find it furnishes a "fun evening out"; N.B. a recent renovation may outdate the Decor score.

Ardoise (L') S   18 │ 10 │ 14 │ 38

28, rue du Mont Thabor, 1ᵉʳ (Concorde/Tuileries), 01 42 96 28 18

■ Just "moments from the Louvre", this "tiny" spot packs in the patrons for "generous portions" of "always reliable" Contemporary French bistro fare (including "delicious" market specials) chalked on an "informal blackboard menu" at "very reasonable prices"; despite a spike in the Decor score, the "think sardine" scene, plus "rushed and abrupt service", still depresses dissenters – though even they admit this is one of "the best deals in Paris."

Argenteuil (L') S   ▽ 21 │ 13 │ 17 │ 47

9, rue d'Argenteuil, 1ᵉʳ (Pyramides), 01 42 60 56 22;
fax 01 42 60 56 22

■ "This delightful little" New French in the 1st "deserves to be better known" for its "perfectly prepared" and "superbly inventive" dishes full of "complex but balanced flavors"; and if some find this "hidden jewel's" setting slightly "cold", a "great wine selection at good prices" does wonders to warm things up.

Aristide   ▽ 11 │ 11 │ 14 │ 41

121, rue de Rome, 17ᵉ (Rome), 01 47 63 17 83;
fax 01 47 54 97 55

■ "Perfect on a cold, rainy night", this small French bistro set in a century-old building in the 17th specializes in such classics as boeuf bourguignon, *confit de canard* and other duck-fat delicacies; husband-and-wife team Philippe and Vivianne Siegrist offset the "sad" decor with their "gracious and attentive" service.

Aristippe (L')   ▽ 22 │ 17 │ 18 │ 57

8, rue Jean-Jacques Rousseau, 1ᵉʳ (Palais Royal-Musée du Louvre), 01 42 60 08 80; fax 01 42 60 11 13

■ Chef-owner Gilles Le Gallès flaunts the flavors of his native Brittany in this "remarkable seafood restaurant" near the Louvre des Antiquaires that keeps supporters in the swim with "original, excellent" dishes and "utterly charming service"; the marine theme decor may strike some as "a bit cold", but most find the place "calm and pleasant" and, more important, "a good value" that "deserves more recognition."

Armand au Palais Royal
18 | 20 | 19 | 49

6, rue du Beaujolais, 1ᵉʳ (Bourse/Palais Royal-Musée du Louvre), 01 42 60 05 11; fax 01 42 96 16 24

■ Facing the elegant Palais Royal, this Classic French – replete with vaulted wood beam ceilings and duly decorated with antique furniture – is perfect for a "romantic dinner for two"; while most agree that the "magnificent decor" sets the stage for "memorable dining", the "impeccable service" (complete "with a verbal translation of the menu") and "terrific" food also "make the place worth visiting."

ARPÈGE (L')
26 | 22 | 24 | 129

84, rue de Varenne, 7ᵉ (Varenne), 01 45 51 47 33; fax 01 44 18 98 39

■ "A symphony of tastes" awaits at chef Alain Passard's "sublime" institution near Les Invalides, a "minimalist" pear-wood-and-glass setting that "reeks of Lalique"; the maestro's Haute Cuisine menu (which, after a Vegetarian experiment, carries a meaty dose of fish and fowl once more) makes most moan over "a legendary experience that elevates food to the realm of the spiritual"; some carp about "carrots for the price of caviar", still, a plurality proclaims "one of the best places in Paris."

Asian
13 | 21 | 12 | 43

30, av George V, 8ᵉ (Alma-Marceau/George V), 01 56 89 11 00; fax 01 56 89 11 01

◢ This "trendy" Right Bank "world-food factory" boasts an "exotic", "sumptuous decor" – the perfect backdrop for "watching the parade of pretty people" traipsing through in "fashion's latest"; unfortunately neither the "cool" ambiance nor the "magnificent hostesses can make you forget the mediocre", "pseudo-sophisticated" Pan-Asian cuisine (though the "good Sunday brunch" boasts some boosters).

Assiette (L') 🆂
20 | 10 | 12 | 62

181, rue du Château, 14ᵉ (Gaîté/Mouton-Duvernet), 01 43 22 64 86; fax 01 45 20 54 66

■ Located "in an old butcher shop" off the Montparnasse strip, this Traditional French bistro (patronized by the late president Mitterrand) serves up "very good homestyle cuisine", including specialties like salted duck; all the locals are in love with chef Lucette Rousseau ("when Lulu's there, it's the best food in Paris") but nevertheless wonder "how can they charge so much?"

Assiette Lyonnaise ◗🆂
11 | 9 | 12 | 25

21, rue Marbeuf, 8ᵉ (Franklin D. Roosevelt), 01 47 20 94 80; fax 01 47 23 53 94

◢ "You need to be hungry to eat" at this casual "familial" bistro serving up "simple", "filling" Lyonnaise fare near the Champs-Elysées; if some deem the cuisine just "ok" and "don't see the point", most agree it's at least "great value in an area not known for" such.

Assis au Neuf
− − − M

*166, bd Vincent Auriol, 13ᵉ (Nationale/Place d'Italie),
01 45 82 69 69; fax 01 45 82 68 69*

Reflecting the neighborhood around the Place d'Italie, this bistro has a friendly feel and a sort of rustic atmosphere; inspired by diverse Mediterranean cuisines, the kitchen produces dishes that are fresh and light, and the youthful service is all smiles; N.B. a large terrace overlooking the pretty Place des Alpes is ideal for al fresco dining.

Astier
19 12 15 32

*44, rue J.P. Timbaud, 11ᵉ (Oberkampf/Parmentier),
01 43 57 16 35*

■ For "good food, good wine and good spirit" diners cram in "cheek-to-cheek" at this "epitome of a bustling, good-value" Traditional French bistro in a hip pocket of the 11th near République; most are mum on the decor, which "hasn't changed" in a while, focusing instead on the "congenial" atmosphere, "a cheese tray that'll knock your socks off" and "unbeatable" prices for the quality.

ASTOR (L') S
24 19 22 97

*Hôtel Astor, 11, rue d'Astorg, 8ᵉ (Saint-Augustin), 01 53 05 05 20;
fax 01 53 05 05 30*

■ "Each meal is a discovery" at this "grand" New French in the Hôtel Astor in the 8th, where chef Eric Lecerf's "refined", "inventive" creations reflect consultant and mentor "Joël Robuchon's touch"; a mixed appraisal of the decor, ranging from "pretty" to "drab", is offset by "courteous service", a "wonderful wine selection" and "fair prices" that extend to a "marvelous bargain" prix fixe menu at lunch.

ASTRANCE (L') S
25 17 22 68

*4, rue Beethoven, 16ᵉ (Passy), 01 40 50 84 40;
fax 01 40 50 11 45*

■ "A gastronome's paradise" is how disciples describe this much-heralded Trocadéro-area New French table owned by "enthusiastic" Arpège alums Pascal Barbot, who turns out "delicious", sometimes "startling" dishes complemented by a "well-chosen" wine list, and Christophe Rohat, who oversees the "trendily" decorated room and "amiable" service; with a "one-month wait" for a table, the only question is "who do you need to know to get into this place?"

Atelier Berger (L') ◖
20 17 17 46

*49, rue Berger, 1ᵉʳ (Louvre-Rivoli), 01 48 28 00 00;
fax 01 40 28 10 65*

■ Like an artist in his atelier, Norwegian chef-owner Jean Christiansen concocts "exquisite", "creative" New French fare in an "'in'" duplex setting (complete with cigar bar) near Les Halles; additional accolades for his "interesting" wine selection, "affordable prices" and "efficient" service indicate this is definitely one "to watch."

F D S €C

Atelier Gourmand ▽ 17 | 14 | 16 | 38

*20, rue de Tocqueville, 17ᵉ (Villiers), 01 42 27 03 71;
fax 01 42 27 03 71*

■ "A true Parisian in the best sense" is the word on this spot in the 17th, where the chef-owner's "passion" is evident in "artisan"-quality New French dishes; those who "get past" the artist-studio and Napoleon III decor find it "fun."

Atelier Maître Albert 14 | 18 | 17 | 44

*1, rue Maître Albert, 5ᵉ (Maubert-Mutualité), 01 46 33 13 78;
fax 01 44 07 01 86*

■ For a whiff of Vieux Paris, ambiance-seekers head to this Classic French, fondly known for its "medieval" setting and large "open fireplace" – a sure draw in winter; it stands out among "the many, many places in the Latin Quarter" for its "honest" food, particularly the "roasted meats."

Atlas (L') S 19 | 16 | 18 | 35

*12, bd St-Germain, 5ᵉ (Maubert-Mutualité), 01 46 33 86 98;
fax 01 40 46 06 56*

■ "Flavorful", "original", "copiously" portioned tagines served in a "transporting" setting lure those looking to escape the workaday to this "white tablecloth" Moroccan near the Institut du Monde Arab in the 5th; while "you can find cheaper couscous in Paris, the service and quality make this place well worth the extra expense."

Auberge Aveyronnaise S 17 | 10 | 15 | 31

*40, rue Gabriel Lamé, 12ᵉ (Cour St-Emilion), 01 43 40 12 24;
fax 01 43 40 12 15*

■ This address in the 12th is convenient for a pre-Bercy-Palais-event supper and is especially "ideal for groups" who "can make noise and drink", all while tucking into "plentiful" portions of "simple", "filling" Aveyron fare, including a "very good *aligot*" (cheesy mashed potatoes); if the "rustic-kitsch" decor isn't everyone's cup of tea, the "good service" and low prices are more universally appreciated.

Auberge Bressane (L') S 16 | 15 | 16 | 39

*16, av de La Motte-Picquet, 7ᵉ (La Tour-Maubourg),
01 47 05 98 37; fax 01 47 05 92 21*

■ "You can't get more classic than this" circa-1945 bistro in the 7th that's perfect for a "meal among friends"; fans find the "medieval decor amusing", with a "congenial" ambiance well suited to the "heavy" bourgeois Bresse cuisine that hits the spot on a "cold night"; while some groan it "can get smoky" ("but where doesn't it in Paris?"), most maintain it's one of "the best values" around.

Auberge Dab (L') ●S 14 | 14 | 15 | 47

*161, av de Malakoff, 16ᵉ (Porte Maillot), 01 45 00 32 22;
fax 01 45 00 58 50*

■ Patrons count on this huge, "highly frequented" "honest brasserie" not far from the Porte Maillot for "classic" cuisine ("quality meats", "fresh *fruits de mer*") that's "consistent", if "conventional"; servers are "pushed but professional", and "despite the crush", "you can always go here" for "a seafood dinner after the movies."

Auberge du Champ de Mars   14 | 13 | 12 | 39
18, rue de l'Exposition, 7ᵉ (Ecole-Militaire), 01 45 51 78 08
■ "Very enjoyable" disciples declare this "neighborhood restaurant" near the Eiffel Tower, whose Classic French menu offers a variety of traditional meat and fish dishes (including a champagne-laced sole stew); the "pleasant prix fixe" is a "true value" at both lunch and dinner as well.

Auberge du Clou (L') ◑⑤⊅   ▽ 15 | 14 | 15 | 34
30, av Trudaine, 9ᵉ (Pigalle), 01 48 78 22 48; fax 01 48 78 30 08
■ "Cosmopolitan" cooking draws a trendy, globe-trotting clientele to this International; the "original" and "exotic" new world flavors (from grilled Uruguay beef to sautéed papaya with peanut ice cream), served in a "warm and friendly" Old Paris setting, make it definitely "worth a detour" to the 9th.

Auberge Etchégorry   18 | 15 | 14 | 37
41, rue Croulebarbe, 13ᵉ (Corvisart/Les Gobelins), 01 44 08 83 51; fax 01 44 08 83 69
◪ To its admirers, this "very rustic" veteran in the 13th is an "old classic" dishing up "very good" Basque eats, but detractors deem it "dusty" and "living on its past"; the "friendly atmosphere" and "well-priced" regional specials tilt the balance in its favor.

Auberge Nicolas Flamel   14 | 19 | 14 | 43
51, rue de Montmorency, 3ᵉ (Etienne-Marcel/Rambuteau), 01 42 71 77 78; fax 01 48 04 58 36
■ Set in what is allegedly the "oldest house in Paris" (1407), this Marais maven has fashionable fauna flocking to dine on an Eclectic array of, appropriately, Middle Ages specialties; the "exceptional historic setting" outshines the "pleasant" food, but nostalgists note this medievalist "finds a rare balance between value and atmosphere."

Auberge Pyrénées Cévennes (L')▽ 18 | 15 | 18 | 39
106, rue de la Folie-Méricourt, 11ᵉ (République), 01 43 57 33 78
■ Cassoulet lovers laud this Classic French in the 11th for its "authentic" Southwestern specialties served by "courteous" staffers in such "generous" amounts that it's "impossible to leave hungry"; the "surprising" setting – hams hang from the wooden-beamed ceiling – reeks of the provinces more than Paris, adding to the "all-around" charm.

Augusta   ▽ 19 | 12 | 15 | 69
98, rue de Tocqueville, 17ᵉ (Malesherbes/Villiers), 01 47 63 39 97; fax 01 47 63 33 97
■ Not far from Villiers, this small, 18-year-old fish specialist lures locals with "very good seafood", especially its

signature bouillabaisse; many suggest, however, that the owner "should think twice about his prices", particularly given the slightly "gloomy decor."

Avant Goût (L') — 20 | 13 | 17 | 38

26, rue Bobillot, 13ᵉ (Place d'Italie), 01 53 80 24 00; fax 01 53 80 00 77

■ "Exceptional, innovative food" and "outstanding service" keep this "out-of-the-way" "adorably stylish neo-bistro" in the 13th perennially "packed" with reviewers raving about the signature "pork pot-au-feu that gently surprises the palate" and the "original yet inexpensive" wine list; while renovations have lowered the noise level and boosted the Decor score, even die-hard devotees wish it was "less tight" and "more centrally located."

Avenue (L') ● S — 12 | 17 | 11 | 49

41, av Montaigne, 8ᵉ (Franklin D. Roosevelt), 01 40 70 14 91; fax 01 40 70 91 97

◪ "Beautiful People" are on the menu at this "chichi" New French ("yet another Costes" brothers production) where haute "attitude", not cuisine, prevails; indeed, many find the "overpriced" food rather "ho-hum" and (thanks to the "pretty, modish" low chairs) "practically served on your knees" by "slow, though sexy" staffers; clearly, the lure is the celeb and "upper-crust" 8th arrondissement scene – which even critics concede "is worth seeing once."

Ay!! Caramba!! ● S — 11 | 18 | 13 | 26

59, rue de Mouzaïa, 19ᵉ (Pré St-Gervais), 01 42 41 23 80; fax 01 42 41 50 34

■ "Just the place for a night out" say surveyors of this "festive" Mexican in the far stretches of the 19th, where live mariachi bands set the stage for savoring margaritas and south-of-the-border specialties; "the dancing's great, the eating less so", but all agree the "fun is guaranteed."

Baan-Boran ● — 18 | 14 | 17 | 36

43, rue de Montpensier, 1ᵉʳ (Palais Royal-Musée du Louvre), 01 40 15 90 45; fax 01 40 15 90 45

■ This "unpretentious", increasingly popular after-theater haunt near the Palais Royal offers an "extensive menu" of the "magical flavors" that characterize "true Thai cuisine" from the provinces; the "discretion" of the "smiling, traditionally clad waitresses" brings a "subtle, refined charm" to the small but "tastefully decorated interior."

Babylone (Au) ⌗ — ▽ 15 | 12 | 14 | 27

13, rue de Babylone, 7ᵉ (Sèvres-Babylone), 01 45 48 72 13

■ When shopping at the Bon Marché department store, this "relaxed" bistro in the 7th – a neighborhood fixture since the '50s – is "ideal for lunch" (the only meal it serves); it's especially "sunny in summer."

Bacchantes (Les) ◐ | 13 | 9 | 9 | 32 |
21, rue de Caumartin, 9ᵉ (Madeleine/Opéra), 01 42 65 25 35; fax 01 47 42 65 87

◪ Wine lovers come to this "always crowded" traditional bistro à vins not far from the Opéra Garnier for a variety of varietals (40 wines by the glass) and "filling" favorites, like pork confit and duck breast, from the Southwestern menu; but dissenters dis the "negligent" service of "ok" food, noting the "dumplike" decor is definitely "in decline."

Baie d'Ha Long (La)   ▽ | 16 | 8 | 12 | 42 |
164, av de Versailles, 16ᵉ (Porte de St-Cloud), 01 45 24 60 62; fax 01 42 30 58 98

■ "High-caliber Vietnamese cuisine" is on hand at this "hard-to-find" intimate locale in a "peripheral part" of the 16th; admittedly, it's "pricey for such a modest place", but "superbly flavored food" served by "discreet", "very nice people" makes all worthwhile.

Bains (Les) | 9 | 14 | 9 | 48 |
7, rue du Bourg l'Abbé, 3ᵉ (Etienne-Marcel/Réaumur Sébastopol), 01 48 87 01 80; fax 01 48 87 13 70

◪ The food is "surprisingly good for a nightclub" here at this famed hot spot in the 3rd, some say; but hard-core hipsters respond that the International menu may be "honest, but that's not why we come here" – "the real show is in the" disco below; if you do dine, be ready for "not great" service.

Ballon des Ternes (Le) ◐ | 15 | 14 | 15 | 41 |
103, av des Ternes, 17ᵉ (Porte Maillot), 01 45 74 17 98; fax 01 45 72 18 84

■ Not far from the Porte Maillot, this "brasserie par excellence" rates among regulars as a "dependable address" for its "superb shellfish" and "beautiful, circa-1900 decor"; naturally, there's "commotion and noise" ("hello, high decibels!"), but it's "ideal for a friendly business dinner with foreigners" or an "after-cinema" supper.

Bamboche (Le) | 19 | 16 | 17 | 55 |
15, rue de Babylone, 7ᵉ (Sèvres-Babylone), 01 45 49 14 40; fax 01 45 49 14 44

■ "A neighborhood jewel" is the tag patrons put on this New French off the Bon Marché store strip; "innovative cuisine" plus "great" (and greatly improved) service draws toned-down trendies who "always have a good time here"; "only the prices might scare you away" from a place that otherwise is "perfect for a romantic dinner."

Baptiste   ▽ | 16 | 13 | 16 | 35 |
51, rue Jouffroy d'Abbans, 17ᵉ (Malesherbes/Wagram), 01 42 27 20 18; fax 01 42 27 20 18

■ The 1930s-style setting of this Contemporary French near the Place Wagram may leave some "a bit cold", but its "talented young chef's" commitment to "creative" cuisine (including hare braised for 12 hours) has earned it a faithful following; it's especially good "for lunch with the girls."

Baracane ◗   16 | 10 | 16 | 35

38, rue des Tournelles, 4ᵉ (Bastille), 01 42 71 43 33

■ "A home away from home", this traditional regional bistro (a Marais offshoot of L'Oulette) woos urbanites with "good", "very Southwestern" comfort food, a "wonderful family-style atmosphere" and "friendly service"; despite the low Decor score, fans urge "don't hire a decorator – the Old French charm should not be modernized."

Bar à Huîtres (Le) ◗ S   13 | 13 | 13 | 40

33, bd Beaumarchais, 3ᵉ (Bastille), 01 48 87 98 92; fax 01 48 87 04 42
33, rue St-Jacques, 5ᵉ (Cluny-La Sorbonne/Maubert-Mutualité), 01 44 07 27 37; fax 01 43 26 71 62
112, bd du Montparnasse, 14ᵉ (Vavin), 01 43 20 71 01; fax 01 43 20 52 04

◩ These three "brasserie-style" seafooders are "not fancy", but the "wonderful oysters" – by many accounts "the most consistent around" – at "extremely reasonable prices" make them popular, particularly for "dining after the show"; skeptics sniff "the sea seems far away" and the staff can be a little too "efficient" ("they serve you as if you have to catch a train"), but fans say you'll do fine if you stick to the "ultra-fresh shellfish [and] forget the rest."

Bar des Théâtres ◗ S   11 | 11 | 13 | 37

6, av Montaigne, 8ᵉ (Alma-Marceau), 01 47 23 34 63; fax 01 47 50 72 23

◩ "You can't get more classic than this" 50-year-plus Avenue Montaigne institution that swells with a swish clientele when "the Théâtre des Champs-Elysées lets out"; although its "handy" location makes it "ideal after" or before the show, convenience is all it has, fume foes who find the Traditional French fare "overpriced" and the "service as snobby as the patrons"; but then most come here to "ogle the 'names', not for the food" (though some swear by "the best steak tartare in Paris").

Baron Rouge (Le)   13 | 15 | 13 | 22

1, rue Théophile Roussel, 12ᵉ (Ledru-Rollin), 01 43 43 14 32

■ This "classic" "neighborhood" bar à vins promotes good spirits, especially "on Sundays", when the nearby Marché d'Aligre is in full swing and patrons wash down "oysters and charcuterie served on the sidewalk" with "good wines"; it's best for "small bites" – appropriately, since the "popular" scene makes "Paris feel like a village."

Barramundi ◗   10 | 15 | 8 | 40

3, rue Taitbout, 9ᵉ (Richelieu-Drouot), 01 47 70 21 21

◩ It may be the site of a former hangout for "journalists from *Le Monde*", but few see a reason to stop the presses for this "trendy" spot that's here in the 9th now; while the "inventive setting", featuring furnishings from around the world, is "pretty", it "can't save" the "middling" International menu ("they confuse creativity with a mixture of no-matter-what"); since the "service is disorganized", "it's best for a drink" at the bar or cigar lounge.

Barrio Latino ●S

| 7 | 20 | 8 | 38 |

46-48, rue du Faubourg St-Antoine, 12ᵉ (Bastille), 01 55 78 84 75; fax 01 55 78 85 30

◪ This "gigantic" multi-level "late night dance and tapas place" a short walk from the Bastille "packs them in"; a "great place to see and be seen" insist enthusiasts wowed by the "stunning" "hacienda"-like decor and sultry salsa spun by the DJ; skeptics scoff at "mediocre, pseudo–Latin American cuisine" and "fake drinks" ("they wouldn't know a margarita if it bit them"), but amigos answer – maybe you "go here for the atmosphere, but definitely go!"

Barroco S

| – | – | – | M |

23, rue Mazarine, 6ᵉ (St-Germain-des-Prés), 01 43 26 40 24
Just steps from the Odéon, this restaurant-lounge-bar with a decor of Portuguese tiles cops a Latino attitude; a young crowd comes to sip well-mixed, mostly tropical cocktails before dining on a menu whose trans-Atlantic dishes run from the Iberian peninsula (Spain, Portugal) to South America (Brazil, Argentina) with a couple of side dips into Cuba and Mexico.

Bartolo ●◖S⌀

| 18 | 12 | 10 | 34 |

7, rue des Canettes, 6ᵉ (St-Germain-des-Prés), 01 43 26 27 08
■ "Great pasta" and "very good pizzas from a real [wood-burning] oven" encourage connoisseurs to choose this cozy Italian from among the "throng of restaurants" on the lively Saint-Sulpice strip; admittedly, "prices are bit high" ("might be preferable to fly" to Italy) and the service is frankly "unfriendly", but the "succulent spread" keeps the place "always full."

Bar Vendôme S

| 19 | 22 | 22 | 59 |

Hôtel Ritz, 15, pl Vendôme, 1ᵉʳ (Concorde/Opéra), 01 43 16 33 63; fax 01 43 16 33 75
■ A "top rendezvous" for "people-watching", this eatery in the Hôtel Ritz "works its magic" while you sip "tea or champagne" and enjoy an "interesting menu" (both Classic and New French) out on the terrace or in the "elegant" bar; the experience promises "sophisticated" exposure to a "magical little" realm – a pricey excursion, but "a joy."

Bascou (Au)

| 18 | 14 | 18 | 42 |

38, rue Réaumur, 3ᵉ (Arts-et-Métiers), 01 42 72 69 25; fax 01 42 72 69 25
▨ Near the Place de la République, this "authentically Basque" bistro wins more than a few points with its "warm

welcome", "wonderfully tasty dishes" and "surprisingly good wines" from the Southwest (both food and drink "reasonably priced" to boot); "what more can you ask for?" – well, a few wouldn't mind if they "changed the menu from time to time."

Basilic (Le) 🅂   14 | 15 | 12 | 41
2, rue Casimir Périer, 7ᵉ (Invalides/Solférino), 01 44 18 94 64; fax 01 47 53 77 96
■ "Hidden in a square behind the Assemblée Nationale", this intimate establishment is a "treasure, especially in summer", when its coveted "romantic" terrace caters to preppy locals; the Classic French cuisine rarely rises above "honest" (though the signature roasted lamb with guérande salt is "always good") and the "service is frosty", but it's still "a nice little address in the neighborhood."

Bastide Odéon (La)   19 | 16 | 18 | 43
7, rue Corneille, 6ᵉ (Odéon), 01 43 26 03 65; fax 01 44 07 28 93
■ "Terrific prices explain [why] the tables are full" (usually "with tourists") at this "nuevo bistro" near the Luxembourg Gardens where "food lovers will enjoy" the "wonderful Provençal cooking" full of "flavors of the South"; despite a rise in the score, some claim the "service is not up to par", but at least a renovation a while back means the "decor is much more beautiful now."

Bath's   22 | 17 | 20 | 68
9, rue de La Trémoille, 8ᵉ (Alma-Marceau), 01 40 70 01 09; fax 01 40 70 01 22
■ Patrons plunge happily into this "class act" off the Champs, which specializes in "marvelous" "neo – hence, lighter – Auvergnat cooking"; the "lovely father-and-son owners" provide "hospitable" service, and while some snap "there are better values out there", the consensus is that this regionalist fits "the ideal profile for a classy place: low-key, but tops."

Bauta (La)   16 | 12 | 13 | 46
129, bd du Montparnasse, 6ᵉ (Vavin), 01 43 22 52 35; fax 01 43 22 10 99
◪ To its friends, this "prettily decorated" Venetian near Vavin turns out "excellent cooking", including such signature dishes as spaghetti with cuttlefish ink; but while supporters sigh "ah, Venice!", foes fume that it's "pricey, pricey, pricey for food that isn't all that sumptuous" and they could do without the "arrogant" attitude as well.

Be   – | – | – | I
73, bd de Courcelles, 17ᵉ (Monceau), 01 46 22 20 20; fax 01 46 22 20 21
With a slick decor – including a giant wicker bread-rack – by interior designer Patrick Jouin, this long-awaited joint venture between baker Eric Kayser and super-chef Alain

Ducasse serves as a combo light-eats place and luxury bakery/grocery (or Boulangerie-Epicerie, as they say in France); soup, sandwiches, salads and pastries to go is one option, or you might BE happy eating at a stand-up counter on the premises.

Béarn (Le)   – | – | – | M

2, pl Ste-Opportune, 1er (Châtelet-Les Halles), 01 42 36 93 35; fax 01 45 08 59 12

No doubt the regulars – an eclectic mix of high-flying fashion and finance types and longtime locals, many of whom once worked in the old Les Halles nearby – would rather keep this vet confidential; but the combination of a cozy, clock-stopped atmosphere (tile floors and wood paneling), plus good-quality Classic French cooking, means that the word's getting out: this is one of the last of the old-fashioned, dyed-in-the-wool bistros in the heart of town.

Béatilles (Les)   18 | 14 | 18 | 52

11 bis, rue Villebois-Mareuil, 17e (Charles de Gaulle-Etoile/ Ternes), 01 45 74 43 80; fax 01 45 74 43 81

■ The husband-and-wife team of Christian and Catherine Bochaton add "a charming welcome" to "delicious cuisine" at this New French in the 17th; epicures praise the "serious", "gourmet" dishes but warn "it's a bit expensive" if you "stray from the menu"; though it's soothingly "calm", some say the "Zen-like" setting is "an acquired taste."

Beato   17 | 14 | 16 | 50

8, rue Malar, 7^e (Invalides), 01 47 05 94 27; fax 01 45 55 64 41

■ "Old-world charm" earns this "classic of Italian cooking" in the 7th a fashionable following; fans applaud the signature scampi and "melt-in-your-mouth" tiramisu; only service that can be "irregular" mars the "pleasure" of the experience.

Beaujolais d'Auteuil (Le) Ⓢ   14 | 13 | 15 | 31

99, bd de Montmorency, 16^e (Porte d'Auteuil), 01 47 43 03 56; fax 01 46 51 27 81

■ "Red-checked tablecloths" add "old-fashioned" charm to this 1920s-style bistro; "honest" "Traditional French cuisine "and "good wines" at "bargain prices" for the "costly" 16th make it "a good address" for a "simple dinner with friends" – even if the "tables are too tight."

BEAUVILLIERS   20 | 23 | 18 | 83

52, rue Lamarck, 18^e (Lamarck-Caulaincourt), 01 42 54 54 42; fax 01 42 62 70 30

■ "A Montmartre tradition" say surveyors who praise the "fabulous flowers", "sumptuous setting" (perhaps a tad "overdone") and "lovely service" of this Classic French; critics carp it's "crowded" and the "carefully executed" "bourgeois cuisine" could use some "lightening up", but most maintain this is the quintessential "big-night-out place" – perfect "for a romantic assignation."

Bel Canto
12 | 16 | 23 | 48

*72, quai de l'Hôtel de Ville, 4ᵉ (Hôtel de Ville/Pont-Marie),
01 42 78 30 18; fax 01 42 78 30 28*
*88, rue de la Tombe-Issoire, 14ᵉ (Alésia), 01 43 22 96 15;
fax 01 43 27 09 88*

■ "Incredibly nice" waiters serenade as they serve at this Italian duet in the 4th and the 14th; it's "a great concept" (especially "to seduce an opera fan"), even if the "middling" dishes simply "don't reach the high notes like the voices"; all the same, the lyrical dining experience is well "worth it."

Bélier (Le) 🆂
– | – | – | M

*L'Hôtel, 13, rue des Beaux-Arts, 6ᵉ (St-Germain-des-Prés),
01 44 41 99 01; fax 01 43 25 64 81*

"If you don't mind being stuffed like a *saucisson*" (it only seats 35), "this is the place" for the kind of "creative" New French cuisine – modish updates on traditional faves – that fashionable foodies crave nowadays; designed by the ubiquitous Jacques Garcia, this "cute", high-style haven is situated in a Saint-Germain boutique hotel that caters to celebrities both past (Oscar Wilde died here) and present.

Bellecour (Le)
21 | 15 | 20 | 59

*22, rue Surcouf, 7ᵉ (Invalides/La Tour-Maubourg),
01 45 51 46 93; fax 01 45 50 30 11*

■ In the 7th, this "unknown treasure" is the "sort of place that makes Paris" say fans who come for "excellent, sophisticated Lyonnaise food", "wait-on-you-hand-and-foot service" ("rare these days") and an "excellent value" prix fixe; some carp about the "claustrophobic" digs, but most deem this destination "a definite return."

Bellini
18 | 14 | 16 | 45

28, rue Lesueur, 16ᵉ (Argentine), 01 45 00 54 20; fax 01 45 00 11 74

■ Oh, "my little darling" coo regulars about this *bambina* that serves "superb" "classic Italian cuisine" ("ah, that pasta with parmesan") and "good wines" amid cozily "snug" surroundings in the 16th; throw in "constantly excellent" staffers and a "very reasonable" menu-carte at lunch, and small wonder folks keep "coming back."

Bellotta-Bellotta
– | – | – | M

18, rue Jean-Nicot, 7ᵉ (La Tour-Maubourg), 01 53 59 96 96

This simply decorated Spanish tapas bar in a swanky corner of the 7th offers classic Iberian small bites – mostly *jamon* and *queso* – and a variety of wines by the glass; convivial and reasonably priced, it's become very popular with a young crowd of well-heeled locals.

Benkay 🆂
22 | 17 | 19 | 72

*Hôtel Novotel Tour Eiffel, 61, quai de Grenelle, 15ᵉ
(Bir-Hakeim/Charles Michels), 01 40 58 21 26; fax 01 40 58 21 30*

■ "One of the best Japanese in Paris" proclaim patrons enchanted by the "magic" of seeing sushi, "extremely light tempuras" and the "best teppanyaki in town" "prepared right in front of your eyes" and delivered by "impeccable" servers; while lazybones lament its "strange location" in the Hôtel Novotel in the 15th, the "magnificent view over the Seine" makes up for it.

BENOÎT S | 22 | 19 | 20 | 73

20, rue St-Martin, 4ᵉ (Châtelet-Les Halles), 01 42 72 25 76; fax 01 42 72 45 68

■ "What tradition should always be" declare devotees of this "charming, classic bistro" (down to the "lace curtains on the windows") in the 4th, everyone's "favorite" for "excellent cassoulet", "true tarte Tatin" and other staples using ingredients "just caught or grown"; admittedly the "comfort food [comes] at Haute Cuisine prices", but when you factor in "friendly service" and a "sociable", "casual atmosphere" it's clear why fans (especially our American cousins) insist the "splurge" is "worth it."

Berkeley (Le) ◗ S | 12 | 15 | 12 | 43

7, av Matignon, 8ᵉ (Franklin D. Roosevelt/Miromesnil), 01 42 25 72 25; fax 01 45 63 30 06

◪ "Just off the rond-point Champs-Elysées", this haunt caters to a "fashionable" crowd with its "superb" auction-house decor (copies of Old Masters, bookshelves, striped tent ceiling, etc.); but while some style-spotters say the service and Classic French cuisine are surprisingly "good" for a "trendy restaurant", cynics shuck off the cost as "too much for too little"; still the terrace is tops for "having a drink – an expensive one – and watching the pretty people walk by."

Bermuda Onion ◗ S | 10 | 15 | 11 | 39

16, rue Linois, 15ᵉ (Charles Michels), 01 45 75 11 11; fax 01 40 59 92 94

◪ "A hip place for Sunday brunch", especially in "summer on the terrace", this "very, very noisy" Seine-side spot in the 15th has a "cult" following that for 15 years has flocked here for the "pretty view and pretty waitresses"; the trompe l'oeil "1980s decor" may come off as "kitsch" and the Classic French food rarely rises above "standardized", but "get a window table" and the scene may satisfy.

Bernardaud | 15 | 19 | 16 | 36

11, rue Royale, 8ᵉ (Concorde), 01 42 66 22 55; fax 01 47 42 60 06

■ For a "quiet break" in a "busy neighborhood" in the 11th arrondissment, reviewers recommend this "elegantly" decorated tearoom tucked away in the Galerie Royale arcade; nice "light lunches" and "delicious cakes" are proffered by "welcoming" servers, but what really wins "bravos" is that patrons select both the brew and their cup and saucer (guess which brand of "sumptuous china" is used).

Beudant (Le)
▽ 17 | 13 | 18 | 43

97, rue des Dames, 17ᵉ (Rome/Villiers), 01 43 87 11 20; fax 01 43 87 27 35

■ "An unbeatable value" patrons proclaim about this Classic French near Villiers; the reason is quite simple: "fresh", "sophisticated" seafood matched by "immensely professional" service, a combination that has admirers "thinking wistfully about coming back as soon as they step out the door."

Beurre Noisette (Le)
– | – | – | I

68 rue Vasco de Gama, 15ᵉ (Lourmel), 01 48 56 82 49

Hidden away in a remote corner of the 15th, this New French bistro is pulling crowds with a regularly changing market menu that runs to dishes like pumpkin soup with bacon and scallops with zucchini 'spaghetti'; the decor's not much, but friendly service and low prices mean you should book ahead.

B*fly ●S
9 | 15 | 9 | 41

49-51, av George V, 8ᵉ (George V), 01 53 67 84 60; fax 01 53 67 84 67

☑ "The concept's getting dated", "but there's always a crowd" at this '90s singles haunt/disco off the Champs; benevolent barflies find the "fabulously decorated" scene "fun and show-offy", though even they come more "for drinks" than for the "International cuisine"; the more wasp-tongued warn "avoid it": the food's like a "sophisticated McDonald's", the servers are "haughty" and it's "impossible to make yourself heard."

Biche au Bois (A la)
19 | 11 | 17 | 36

45, av Ledru-Rollin, 12ᵉ (Gare de Lyon), 01 43 43 34 38

■ "Hefty eaters" "thoroughly enjoy themselves" in the "convivial" (if "loud and smoky") dining room of this "typically Parisian" "institution" (established 1925) by the Gare de Lyon; it's "a must for game" and other Classic French "food that's terrific and a bargain" to boot; the "ownership has changed", but happily the "amicable service" remains intact.

Bistro 121 ●S
17 | 13 | 16 | 49

121, rue de la Convention, 15ᵉ (Boucicaut/Convention), 01 45 57 52 90; fax 01 45 57 14 69

☑ A "grand classic", this French bistro in the 15th may not reflect "high fashion", but regulars insist "you eat very well" for "a reasonable price"; stylistically, the room could use "a revision", but "warm service" makes this "a good place."

Bistro de Gala (Le) S
▽ 21 | 16 | 17 | 37

45, rue du Faubourg Montmartre, 9ᵉ (Grands Boulevards/ Le Peletier), 01 40 22 90 50; fax 01 40 22 98 30

■ "What a find!" say those who "luck upon this bistro" whose "simple" yet "original" New French fare (starring a foie gras that may be "the best of one's life") is a gala occasion in a part of the Faubourg Montmartre where good eats are rare; while it didn't take a designer to develop the decor (primarily posters), most find the digs "charming."

Bistro de la Grille ●🅂   14 | 13 | 13 | 37

14, rue Mabillon, 6ᵉ (Mabillon), 01 43 54 16 87; fax 01 43 54 52 88

■ This "true Parisian bistro" turns out "Traditional French cuisine" (plus Southwestern specialties) in a "convenient location" near Saint-Germain-des-Prés; there are "no frills" and "no surprises", but in between the "atmosphere" and the "good value", it "could easily become a habit"; P.S. it's "especially nice in summer with the outdoor tables."

Bistro de l'Olivier 🅂   16 | 15 | 15 | 43

13, rue Quentin Bauchart, 8ᵉ (George V), 01 47 20 78 63; fax 01 47 20 74 58

■ "Home cooking on a quiet corner" lures a "very stylish" clientele (and lunchtime suits) to this "chic" Mediterranean whose "gorgeous golden decor makes you feel you're in sun-drenched Provence"; a "welcome that's as warm as the room", fish that's "out of this world" and prices that get "slightly high" are all reminiscent of the Riviera, even though it's actually "in the heart of the 8th."

Bistro des Deux Théâtres (Le) ●🅂   13 | 13 | 14 | 31

18, rue Blanche, 9ᵉ (Trinité), 01 45 26 41 43; fax 01 48 74 08 92

◨ No standing ovations here, but "before or after the theater" this Classic French "near the Place de Clichy" can be a "practical" "standby for a prix fixe dinner"; while critics carp about crowds ("too many tour buses"), "overwhelmed waiters" and "formulaic" food, others insist it's a "good deal" and "great for [both] dining alone or with a group."

Bistro d'Hubert (Le) 🅂   19 | 17 | 17 | 42

41, bd Pasteur, 15ᵉ (Pasteur), 01 47 34 15 50; fax 01 45 67 03 09

■ "Not fancy but darn good" sums up this small but "sunnily decorated" New French in the 15th; "delicious, hearty portions" of "innovative cuisine" and the "cute atmosphere" help offset the "somewhat cool service", making it "a great place for a Sunday evening meal."

Bistro du 17ème (Le) 🅂   13 | 10 | 12 | 32

108, av de Villiers, 17ᵉ (Pereire), 01 47 63 32 77; fax 01 42 27 67 66

■ The goal is not gourmet at this "classic" French bistro near the Place Pereire, but its "all-inclusive formula of apéritif, three-course meal, wine and coffee" (the same patented prix fixe boasted by all of owner Willy Dorr's establishments) offers an operative option for those seeking a "good value"; a few grump it's "spoiled by the noise, tight tables and less-than-amiable service", but most find it fine for a "surprise-free" experience.

Bistro Melrose ●⑤   12 | 11 | 11 | 30

5, pl de Clichy, 17ᵉ (Place de Clichy), 01 42 93 61 34;
fax 01 42 93 76 45

■ "Created by Willy Dorr", this Traditional French bistro offers "the same thing" as its sister bistros: a "surprise-free prix fixe, from apéritif to coffee" (though there's "also an à la carte option"); perhaps it's "less good" than its siblings, but it still "fulfills its mission as an unpretentious business-lunch" spot, "a haven for Place de Clichy night owls" and an all-around dependable "choice for get-togethers."

Bistrot d'à Côté/   18 | 14 | 15 | 42
Bistrot . . . Côté Mer

16, bd St-Germain, 5ᵉ (Cardinal Lemoine/Maubert-Mutualité),
01 43 54 59 10; fax 01 43 29 02 08 ⑤
16, av de Villiers, 17ᵉ (Villiers), 01 47 63 25 61; fax 01 48 88 92 42
10, rue Gustave Flaubert, 17ᵉ (Pereire/Ternes), 01 42 67 05 81;
fax 01 47 63 82 75 ⑤
4, rue Boutard, Neuilly-sur-Seine (Pont-de-Neuilly),
01 47 45 34 55; fax 01 47 45 15 08

■ "Bistro food at its best" characterizes this Classic French quartet directed by chef Michel Rostang; "enjoyable" "products of the sea" are featured at the Saint-Germain and the Neuilly locales, while the "beef ribs are recommended" at the Villiers and Pereire sites; though grouches grumble about "cramped quarters" and "high prices for what you get", satisfied fans say they're "what you expect a bistrot to be": "warm, friendly", "relaxed."

Bistrot d'Albert   ▽ 21 | 12 | 20 | 40

150, bd Pereire, 17ᵉ (Pereire/Porte de Champerret),
01 48 88 93 68; fax 01 48 88 93 68

■ For "a real locals' spot off the tourist track", this *petit* place near the Place Pereire is an "exceptional price-performer" parsimonious patrons proclaim; "Traditional French bistro fare", with an emphasis on fish, is served in a "low-key but pleasant" setting by "very congenial hosts", while a "nice, quiet terrace" ensures it's "worth the trip."

Bistrot d'Alex   ▽ 17 | 13 | 14 | 42

2, rue Clément, 6ᵉ (Mabillon/Odéon), 01 43 54 09 53;
fax 01 43 25 77 66

☑ Drawing in Latin Quarter literati, this "cozy" Classic French puts a Southern spin on seafood and bistro staples; loyalists like the "good location" at Odéon and deem the dishes "decent", while antagonists argue against "adequate but uninspired food and decor"; service that's "polite but unbelievably slow" doesn't help the cause.

Bistrot d'André (Le)   12 | 13 | 14 | 31

232, rue St-Charles, 15ᵉ (Balard), 01 45 57 89 14; fax 01 45 57 97 15

■ Bargain hunters, unite: what was once a Citroën factory lunch room now serves French classics of a culinary sort at "astonishingly reasonable prices" to a very Parisian clientele; a "fun" spot in this otherwise "austere" quarter in the 15th, this bistro gets a big 'B' for "bon."

Bistrot de Breteuil (Le) S
15 13 14 33

3, pl de Breteuil, 7e (Duroc/Sèvres-Lecourbe), 01 45 67 07 27; fax 01 42 73 11 08

■ Now owned by prix fixe prince Willy Dorr, this "typically French bistro" in the 7th offers "unbeatable value" in its "traditional but good" "set-price menu" that goes from "apéritif to coffee"; a well-heeled clientele welcomes the "white tablecloths" and "greenhouse-like" decor; though "it's packed with locals" (which explains the "turbo"-speed service) visitors deem it "a must on all my trips."

Bistrot de l'Etoile Lauriston ●
16 12 15 47

19, rue Lauriston, 16e (Charles de Gaulle-Etoile/Kléber), 01 40 67 11 16; fax 01 45 00 99 87

■ Near the Etoile in the 16th lies this "cozy, contemporary French bistro" whose "unbeatably priced", "innovative menu" is capped by occasional "strokes of genius" in the kitchen; "low-key but efficient service" matches the "lively, relaxed" setting (despite a tendency to be a bit "too tight").

Bistrot de l'Etoile Niel ●
16 12 14 45

75, av Niel, 17^e (Pereire), 01 42 27 88 44; fax 01 42 27 32 12

☑ "The nice summer terrace" wins points for this off-the-Etoile option in the 17th; but while loyalists laud the Contemporary French bistro menu as "excellent and inventive", complainers carp the food "isn't what it used to be – and what's more, it's expensive!"; "disappointing" too are the "cramped quarters" and "service on the fly."

Bistrot de l'Université
16 11 16 37

40, rue de l'Université, 7e (Rue du Bac), 01 42 61 26 64; fax 01 42 61 26 64

■ In the 7th, this "quaint, family neighborhood spot" with vintage moldings fills up with Left Bank locals who enjoy the "honest" Traditional French bistro bill of fare; the parsimonious pout that "it's gotten pretty pricey", but still, it's a "nice little place for dinner with friends."

Bistrot de Marius (Le) ●S
16 13 13 45

6, av George V, 8^e (Alma-Marceau), 01 40 70 11 76

■ It's a "simpler version" of its next-door neighbor Marius et Janette, "but [there's] no loss in quality" at this 8th arrondissement bistro specializing in raw and "classically cooked" fish dishes that are "very good and affordable" and so fresh "you'll think you're at the seaside"; and though service can be a little "offhand", the majority is "never disappointed" in this "good address."

Bistrot de Paris (Le) S
15 15 14 44

33, rue de Lille, 7e (Rue du Bac), 01 42 61 16 83; fax 01 49 27 06 09

☑ Voters view this Traditional French bistro (founded by "formidable" chef Michel Oliver) near the Musée d'Orsay with mixed emotions: supporters call it a nice "neighborhood hangout", complete with a turn-of-the-century "Parisian setting"; holdouts harp that this "tourist-catering" place remains "far from what it was"; perhaps the recent post-*Survey* change in ownership will make a difference.

Bistrot des Capucins ▽ | 16 | 17 | 15 | 43 |
27, av Gambetta, 20ᵉ (Père Lachaise), 01 46 36 74 75; fax 01 46 36 74 89
■ Former Le Grand Véfour chef Gérard Fouché turns out Southwestern classics at this address across from Père Lachaise cemetery in the 20th; the signature duck breast fillet and other hearty dishes served amid cozy, "pleasant surroundings" make this a "regular haunt" for those craving a "family-like" dining scene.

Bistrot des Dames (Le) ●⑤ ▽ | 15 | 17 | 17 | 27 |
Hôtel El Dorado, 18, rue des Dames, 17ᵉ (Place de Clichy), 01 45 22 13 42; fax 01 43 87 25 97
■ The darling of young trendies in the Batignolles district, this "small, charming" Mediterranean bistro serves up innovative "excellent cuisine" (fried smelt, anyone?), accompanied by a "very good wine list" amid a "low-key" decor of moleskin banquettes and antique posters; patrons particularly praise the "pretty garden for summer dining."

Bistrot d'Henri (Le) ● | 19 | 14 | 17 | 33 |
16, rue Princesse, 6ᵉ (Mabillon/St-Germain-des-Prés), 01 46 33 51 12
■ "Good old-fashioned food and service" are the draws at this "great French" spot, "a refuge for real bistro cooking amid a touristy pocket" of Saint-Germain; what with the classic fare (think leg of lamb and chocolate mousse), "atmosphere" and "charming" staff, it's small wonder there's often "a line outside" formed by the "young" and restless.

Bistrot du Dôme (Le) ⑤ | 17 | 14 | 15 | 44 |
2, rue de la Bastille, 4ᵉ (Bastille), 01 48 04 88 44; fax 01 48 04 00 59 ●
1, rue Delambre, 14ᵉ (Vavin), 01 43 35 32 00; fax 01 48 04 00 59
■ "Forget Le Dôme" – the grande dame's two "little sisters" (one near Montparnasse, the other at the Bastille) serve the "same delicious seafood", only "at reasonable prices", and "beautifully presented" by an "accommodating if rushed" staff; perhaps the "insipid" decor leaves something to be desired, but the "exceptionally fresh" fish ensures these are the sort of places "you tend to dine at often."

Bistrot du Peintre (Le) ●⑤ | 12 | 17 | 12 | 28 |
116, av Ledru-Rollin, 11ᵉ (Bastille/Ledru-Rollin), 01 47 00 34 39; fax 01 47 00 34 39
◪ This attractive art nouveau–styled Traditional French bistro dishes up "good food" in a "congenial atmosphere"

that makes it popular among trendies in the 11th; and while naysayers gnash their teeth over the "uninteresting cuisine" and "mounting prices as it's gotten more modish", it's still easy enough on the wallet that most find it "very nice."

Bistrot du Sommelier
18 | 13 | 19 | 60

97, bd Haussmann, 8ᵉ (St-Augustin), 01 42 65 24 85; fax 01 53 75 23 23

■ "Dinners that turn into fascinating lessons in oenology" are common at this Classic French in the 8th, as owner and famous sommelier Philippe Faure-Brac invites you to "exceptional" wine-tasting menus with crus from his cellar "that make even the best pale"; if the "food doesn't quite match the excellence" of the varietals and prices are "globally expensive", "high-level service" ensures "an excellent experience."

Bistrot Mélac
11 | 12 | 15 | 39

42, rue Léon Frot, 11ᵉ (Charonne), 01 43 70 59 27; fax 01 43 70 73 10

◪ Well-known for its namesake proprietor, this bistro à vins in the 11th offers food "without fuss from the Auvergne"; foes fume the "Mélac folklore covers up" for "simple cooking, which could be better" – and less "expensive"; but it's a "don't-miss" for "lovers of wine and atmosphere" who find it "friendly" and "reliably fun."

Bistrot Papillon (Le)
▽ 22 | 20 | 20 | 37

6, rue Papillon, 9ᵉ (Cadet), 01 47 70 90 03; fax 01 48 24 05 59

■ "It gets better and better" say fans of this little-known establishment off the Square de Montholon in the 9th, loved for its "tasty" Traditional French cuisine (especially appetizers such as foie gras poached in a hand towel) and in-season game, served in a belle epoque setting that's not only "agreeable" but features a "real (and rare) non-smoking section."

Bistrot Paul-Bert (Le)
– | – | – | M

18, rue Paul Bert, 11ᵉ (Faidherbe-Chaligny), 01 43 72 24 01; fax 01 43 72 24 66

The traditional bistro is becoming an endangered genus in Paris, which is why this wine-oriented specimen deep in the 11th has been gaining a steady word-of-mouth following; founded by a former ad man, it provides relaxed atmosphere, friendly service, amusingly kitschy decor and, most of all, classic dishes and vinos (scrawled on the proverbial blackboard) for very reasonable prices.

Bistrot St. Ferdinand ●🅂
15 | 13 | 13 | 32

275, bd Pereire, 17ᵉ (Porte Maillot), 01 45 74 33 32; fax 01 45 74 33 12

■ "Very good prix fixe meals" – "everything included", "from apéritif to coffee" – make this Traditional French bistro (yet another from that sultan of the set-price, Willy

Dorr) in the 17th "a place to meet all year round", both for preppies and a lunchtime "business crowd from the Palais des Congrès"; "at night it gets a little lonely", but that, along with "quick service", makes it a good choice for a fast bite before or "after the show."

Bistrot St. James
16 | 12 | 18 | 36

2, rue Gén. Henrion-Berthier, Neuilly-sur-Seine (Pont-de-Neuilly), 01 46 24 21 06; fax 01 46 24 21 06

■ This Classic French bistro in Neuilly draws a devoted clientele by dint of its "consistent quality", "fine wines" and genial "welcome"; it's also "perfect for business lunches", particularly since the tabs can be a bit "pricey"; and though the decor might be "nothing special" and a few outsiders sniff that habitués get "better service", most vote it a "good address" for a weekday meal.

Bistrot Vivienne
– | – | – | M

4, rue des Petits Champs, 1er (Bourse/Palais Royal-Musée du Louvre), 01 49 27 00 50; fax 01 49 27 00 40

Tucked away in the covered arcade of the Galerie Vivienne, this vest-pocket bistro has quickly gained a varied following of antique dealers, fashion types and local shopkeepers thanks to its relaxed atmosphere, pretty decor (scarlet walls, sconces, mirrors) and moderately priced, old-fashioned French cooking.

BLUE ELEPHANT ●⑤
19 | 24 | 15 | 51

43-45, rue de la Roquette, 11^e (Bastille/Voltaire), 01 47 00 42 00; fax 01 47 00 45 44

▨ "Dining in the jungle is possible in Paris" via this Bastille-area Siamese whose fans are "transported" by some of "the finest Thai food"; others find the "decor better than" the "Europeanized" cuisine and wish it were "the other way around"; overall, though, an "exotic" experience is guaranteed, and while the tab can be "expensive", it's certainly "cheaper than" airfare to Asia.

Bœuf Couronné (Au) ●
17 | 13 | 15 | 46

188, av Jean Jaurès, 19e (Porte de Pantin), 01 42 39 44 44; fax 01 42 39 17 30

■ Carnivores lick their chops recalling the "exceptional meats" served at this Classic French "establishment" in the 19th that "upholds the tradition of the Villette" (site of the city's slaughterhouses until 1974); that it's a bit "far away" from central Paris doesn't keep 'em from "coming expressly for beef", and even those who chide the "blustery service" chalk it up to type, sighing "oh, these brasseries!"

Bœuf sur le Toit (Le) ●⑤
13 | 16 | 14 | 45

34, rue du Colisée, 8e (Franklin D. Roosevelt/ St-Philippe-du-Roule), 01 53 93 65 55; fax 01 53 96 02 32

▨ "Cozy", "crowded" and "noisy" Flo Group–owned classic brasserie whose "art deco" setting and "convenience" to the Champs-Elysées make it a "decent spot for visitors wanting something very 'French'"; despite the "formulaic" menu and "cafeteria"-like service, it's "reliable", especially for "late-night" dining on "raw bar" offerings; it's also mercifully "inexpensive", prompting the sentiment "chains aren't always a bad thing."

BOFINGER ●S
| 16 | 21 | 16 | 45 |
5, rue de la Bastille, 4ᵉ (Bastille), 01 42 72 87 82; fax 01 42 72 97 68

☑ "For an evening out of an Impressionist painting", "Opéra Bastille"-goers and "tourists" frequent this "very grand" brasserie, where "old-time" waiters ferry "gorgeous shellfish platters" ("everyone watches you make your way through them") and Alsatian specialties like a "super choucroute" amid "authentic art nouveau" decor; there might be room for "improvement" in the kitchen, but "noise" and "cramped" tables are tolerated for the "*so* Parisian" atmosphere; P.S. be sure to "reserve."

Bombis (Les)
▽ | 16 | 10 | 17 | 28 |
22, rue de Chaligny, 12ᵉ (Reuilly-Diderot), 01 43 45 36 32; fax 01 43 41 75 39

☑ "A real joy" says the pocketful of surveyors who've sampled the "tasty", "almost haute-gourmet" bistro fare at this small Traditional French "charmer" in the 12th; "amiable" owners, "friendly service" and reasonable prix fixes explain its appeal, and the "pleasant terrace" helps offset the low Decor score.

Bon ●S
| 10 | 22 | 10 | 49 |
25, rue de la Pompe, 16ᵉ (La Muette), 01 40 72 70 00; fax 01 40 72 68 30

☑ It's more the "fabulous", "very Starcky" (as in style guru and co-owner Philippe Starck) interior than the organic Vegetarian fare, now augmented by homey French classics, that lures "hipsters", "decorators" and "models" to the "sleepy 16th", but quizzical diners, who find the name incongruous with what's on their plates, ask: shouldn't "designer restaurants also be about food and service"?; still, they might admit that it's good "for a drink" and to check out the astonishing "rest rooms."

Bon Accueil (Au)
| 19 | 13 | 15 | 43 |
14, rue de Monttessuy, 7ᵉ (Alma-Marceau), 01 47 05 46 11

■ A "heart-stopping view" of the Eiffel Tower competes with "uncomplicated", high-"quality" Traditional French dishes and the "homey" setting at this "busy" "neighborhood bistro" in the 7th; service can be under "too much strain in good weather", when everyone – including "too many tourists" – wants a sidewalk table, and it's "more expensive than comparable" places; still, most agree it's a "great value" and a "quintessential Parisian experience."

Bon 2 ◐🅂
_— | — | — | M_

2, rue du Quatre Septembre, 2ᵉ (Bourse), 01 44 55 51 55; fax 01 44 55 00 77

The new branch of the enduringly trendy Philippe Starck–designed address attracts a mixed crowd of journalists and financial types with a masculine decor of tobacco-colored leather chairs and hassocks, a long bar, engraved mirrors and a rhinoceros head; as for the food – well, perhaps Contemporary French best characterizes the neo-brasserie menu (the scene, as much as the cuisine, is what counts here).

Bon Saint Pourçain (Le) ⌿
_19 | 14 | 19 | 39_

10 bis, rue Servandoni, 6ᵉ (Odéon/St-Sulpice), 01 43 54 93 63

■ It's like dining in a "postcard" say those besotted by this "charming" Classic French in the shadow of Saint-Sulpice church in the 6th; "good", "solid food", including a signature cassoulet, a "warm welcome" and a "friendly" staff that's "patient with non-French speakers" keeps the faithful "coming back and back" to this "gem."

Bons Crus (Aux)
_▽ 12 | 9 | 13 | 28_

7, rue des Petits-Champs, 1ᵉʳ (Bourse), 01 42 60 06 45

■ For a quick bite after work at the Bourse, this circa-1905 bistrot à vins near the Place des Victoires offers reliable, "simple" Lyonnaise fare that "complements" rather than competes with "the good wines" for which it's known; in this upscale pocket of town, it's also something of a bargain.

Bookinistes (Les)
_19 | 16 | 16 | 48_

53, quai des Grands-Augustins, 6ᵉ (St-Michel), 01 43 25 45 94; fax 01 43 25 23 07

■ "Pretty" and ever "trendy", this Guy Savoy–owned Seine-side spot in the 6th features "exalted" New French creations and draws a "good-looking" clientele heavily composed of tourists ("every concierge in town recommends" it); though some feel "there's too much hustle and bustle for a leisurely meal", others appreciate the "high energy" that makes it "the place to be seen on the Left Bank."

Boucholeurs (Les)
_— | — | — | M_

34, rue de Richelieu, 1ᵉʳ (Palais Royal-Musée du Louvre/Pyramides), 01 42 96 06 86

The handful of surveyors who know this Classic French not far from the Palais Royal in the 1st recommend its "excellent fish" for a pre–Comédie Française bite; the menu features fresh catches from Brittany and a selection of Loire valley whites; add to this an "intimate" maritime-themed setting and you have a near-seaside experience.

Bouchons de François Clerc (Les)
_15 | 12 | 14 | 45_

12, rue de l'Hôtel Colbert, 5ᵉ (Maubert-Mutualité), 01 43 54 15 34; fax 01 46 34 68 07

(continued)

(continued)
Bouchons de François Clerc (Les)
*7, rue du Boccador, 8ᵉ (Alma-Marceau), 01 47 23 57 80;
fax 01 47 23 74 54*
*6, rue Arsène Houssaye, 8ᵉ (Charles de Gaulle/Etoile),
01 42 89 15 51; fax 01 42 89 28 67*
*32, bd du Montparnasse, 15ᵉ (Montparnasse-Bienvenüe),
01 45 48 52 03; fax 01 45 48 52 17*
*22, rue de la Terrasse, 17ᵉ (Villiers), 01 42 27 31 51;
fax 01 42 27 45 76*
■ A "windfall" for "wine lovers", chef François Clerc's chain of bistrots à vins adheres to a "winning" formula: "wonderful wines" at "great prices" with "pretty good" New French food, including an "outstanding cheese course"; oenophiles consider them "the bargain of the city", and though critics note a "variance in quality between the different locations", they praise in particular the Boccador and Villiers branches.

Bouclard (Le)　　　　▽ 18 | 13 | 16 | 41
*1, rue Cavallotti, 18ᵉ (Place de Clichy), 01 45 22 60 01;
fax 01 45 22 60 01*
■ "You can't find bistros like this anymore" warn those who seek culinary comfort in the "filling", "country"-inspired fare at this "homey" Classic French near the Place de Clichy in the 18th; if the "friendly" service and decor featuring "pictures of a hefty grandmother in her old-style kitchen" don't tug at your heartstrings, it's "worth going just for the owner", who's "a real character" and part of the appeal.

Bouillon Racine 🆂　　　13 | 21 | 14 | 35
*3, rue Racine, 6ᵉ (Cluny-La-Sorbonne/Odéon), 01 44 32 15 60;
fax 01 44 32 15 61*
☑ The "gorgeous [art nouveau] interior and the beers are the real draws" at this Belgian brasserie in the 6th that's a favorite watering hole among Sorbonnites; but takes on the brew-based Flemish cuisine are mixed – "tasty and unpretentious" vs. "a disappointment" – and not up to the alluring decor; still, no one complains about the prices.

Boulangerie (La) 🆂　　▽ 16 | 12 | 17 | 28
*15, rue des Panoyaux, 20ᵉ (Ménilmontant), 01 43 58 45 45;
fax 01 43 58 45 46*
■ "Popular with the local media" and Ménilmontant hipsters, this Classic French bistro in an erstwhile bakery (hence the name) serves up "good" fare that's a "remarkably decent value"; fans have less to say about the "banal decor", though the mosaic floor catches the eye.

Bourdonnais (Le)/　　20 | 17 | 18 | 73
Cantine des Gourmets (La) 🆂
*Hôtel de La Bourdonnais, 113, av de La Bourdonnais, 7ᵉ
(Ecole-Militaire), 01 47 05 16 54; fax 01 45 51 09 29*
■ A well-heeled clientele salutes this New French "near the Eiffel Tower" as "a small culinary masterpiece" that's an

ideal place "to take guests"; chef Jean-François Rouquette has "real talent", turning out "delightful gourmet cuisine" in a "comfortable" setting complete with "professional" service; though a few wince at the prices and detect a bit of "snobbism", most maintain it's a "wonderful experience."

Bourguignon du Marais (Au) 20 | 17 | 16 | 45
52, rue François Miron, 4ᵉ (Pont-Marie/St-Paul), 01 48 87 15 40; fax 01 48 87 17 49
☑ "A real restaurant, not just a wine bar" say fans of this little Burgundian outpost "smartly situated" in the Marais; with an impressive cellar at his disposal, wine director Jacques Bavard "knows how to pair vintages with dishes" and "shares his passion" openly, so it's wise "to let him choose for you"; just be sure to "pay attention to the prices", as one glass easily leads to another, and another.

B4 ◑⑤ – | – | – | M
6-8, sq Ste-Croix de la Bretonnerie, 1ᵉʳ (Hôtel-de-Ville/ Rambuteau), 01 42 72 16 19
Owned by night-life impresarios David and Cathy Guetta (ex Les Bains), this wanna-be hip table near the Pompidou Center offers yet another take on the current local interior design trends – e.g. all-white walls, floors and furniture, punctuated with lots of plastic; the gently priced menu is equally fashionable, featuring a mostly Italian array of salads, pastas and grills.

Braisière (La) – | 13 | 18 | M
54, rue Cardinet, 17ᵉ (Malesherbes), 01 47 63 40 37; fax 01 47 63 04 76
■ "Excellent cooking" has earned this establishment "near the Parc Monceau" a coterie of devoted "regulars" who find it "great for lunch"; the "modest" setting is a tad too "sweet" and "flouncy" for tailored tastes, but "all you have to do is concentrate on your plate" and the "friendly" reception to enjoy yourself; N.B. new chef-owner Jacques Faussat and his New French menu arrived post-*Survey*.

BRASSERIE BALZAR ◑⑤ 14 | 17 | 16 | 42
49, rue des Ecoles, 5ᵉ (Cluny-La Sorbonne/St-Michel), 01 43 54 13 67; fax 01 44 07 14 91
☑ "The Latin Quarter old-time ambiance still works" at this traditional brasserie that "satisfies" a "bustling" crowd with "superb roast chicken" and "appears to be the real thing, even if it's owned by the Flo group"; nostalgists who sniff that it's suffering from a "midlife crisis" are countered by those who find it "always a pleasure" as a "Sunday refuge."

Brasserie de la Poste ⑤ 13 | 11 | 14 | 36
54, rue de Longchamp, 16ᵉ (Trocadéro), 01 47 55 01 31; fax 01 47 55 01 31
☑ Located near Trocadéro, this traditional brasserie turns out "well-executed" classic fare and beguiles with "stage

set" looks, leading some to call it the "quintessential Paris address"; while advocates note that "the owners have made a solid effort", cynics frown "it could do better", particularly with regards to the "slow service"; most agree, however, it's a "reasonable value" for the locale.

Brasserie de l'Ile St. Louis ⚫S 14 | 14 | 13 | 35

55, quai de Bourbon, 4e (Cité/Pont-Marie), 01 43 54 02 59; fax 01 46 33 18 47

☒ Thanks to a "panoramic" view of Notre Dame and "world-class people-watching" from its "marvelous" terrace, this traditional brasserie on the Ile Saint-Louis gets plenty of traffic, including bateau-loads of "tourists"; depending on your humor, the food might be either "run-of-the-mill" or "solid" and the room "noisy" or "convivial", but all agree it has "good value" and an "unparalleled site."

Brasserie du Louvre ⚫S 15 | 16 | 14 | 41

Hôtel du Louvre, place du Palais Royal, 1er (Palais Royal-Musée du Louvre), 01 42 96 27 98; fax 01 44 58 38 00

■ "Basic" but "surprisingly good" brasserie fare and a "great terrace for people-watching" make this "lively" Hôtel du Louvre restaurant a "must for museum visitors" or those on a Rue Saint-Honoré shopping trek; some might "expect more from such a grand hotel", but it's a "nice stop" with some of the "best scenery in Paris" as a backdrop.

Brasserie Flo ⚫S 15 | 19 | 15 | 43

7, cour des Petites-Ecuries, 10e (Château d'Eau), 01 47 70 13 59; fax 01 42 47 00 80

■ This "mythic" brasserie's inauspicious location in a "small alley" in the 10th belies a "lusty" art nouveau interior that creates the perception that "Toulouse-Lautrec could pop in at any minute"; there's suspicion that the kitchen resorts to "frozen and pre-prepared dishes" to handle the "crowds", but the "fresh" shellfish platters are "fabulous" and the "white asparagus could be a dessert", and if it's all become "too commercial", the "great ambiance" compensates.

BRASSERIE JULIEN ⚫S 16 | 23 | 15 | 44

16, rue du Faubourg St-Denis, 10^e (Strasbourg-St-Denis), 01 47 70 12 06; fax 01 42 47 00 65

☒ The "lovely" art nouveau interior of this "classic" 1889 brasserie makes it "a gem on a working-class street" in the 10th; not surprising, the "food and service don't compare to the beauty of" the interior (though sweet-tooths single out the signature "excellent profiteroles"), but it's good "noisy" "fun after midnight."

Brasserie Lipp ⚫S 15 | 19 | 14 | 50

151, bd St-Germain, 6e (St-Germain-des-Prés), 01 45 48 53 91; fax 01 45 44 33 20

☒ This "tired but true classic" brasserie stands firm as a Saint-Germain "monument" to a bygone era; first-timers are likely to be spirited upstairs to "Siberia", while "regulars and celebrities" swim in the ground floor "VIP aquarium"; though critics carp it's "a far cry from what it was" and wonder "is there a cook in the kitchen?", most nostalgists agree you "come for the ambiance" and leave "hoping it will be there forever."

Brasserie Lorraine (La) ◑🆂   13 | 13 | 12 | 50
2-4, pl des Ternes, 8ᵉ (Ternes), 01 56 21 22 00; fax 01 56 21 22 09
◪ "Remarkable oysters" are always a treat at this Frères Blanc–owned "institution" on the Place des Ternes, where the "classic" brasserie fare ranges from "industrial" to "improving"; scores suggest the "negligent" service could use some enhancement too, and cautious spenders wish it weren't so "expensive for what you get", but regulars "return with pleasure", particularly to the "nice terrace", and Salle Pleyel patrons find it a "lovely location" for a post-concert supper.

Brasserie Lutétia 🆂   14 | 15 | 14 | 49
Hôtel Lutétia, 23, rue de Sèvres, 6ᵉ (Sèvres-Babylone), 01 49 54 46 76; fax 01 49 54 46 00
◧ "Dependable" is how patrons describe this "busy" brasserie in the "landmark" Hôtel Lutétia, handily situated "close to the Bon Marché" store; the "food is very ordinary", but the "excellent shellfish platters" stand out for lunch, when "you might spot Catherine Deneuve", or for an "unrushed dinner"; although the "aging decor" could use a little "polish", fans appreciate the "calm" setting and "child"-friendly attitude.

Brasserie Mollard ◑🆂   12 | 20 | 13 | 47
115, rue St-Lazare, 8ᵉ (St-Lazare), 01 43 87 50 22; fax 01 43 87 84 17
◧ "Magnificent", "well-preserved" art nouveau decor is the bait at this "good, traditional" brasserie near the Gare Saint-Lazare, and while the menu options are admittedly "routine", the "oysters and shellfish platters" are among "the best" in town; a few still grumble about "hasty" service, but most consider this a "comfortable" and "typically Parisian" address.

Brasserie Munichoise ◑   ▽ 18 | 15 | 15 | 29
5, rue Danielle Casanova, 1ᵉʳ (Opéra/Pyramides), 01 42 61 47 16; fax 01 42 86 93 61
◪ The "robust" German cuisine made from "quality ingredients" "never disappoints" at this brasserie in the 1st arrondissement that's a "wonderland" for famished meateaters; while long-memoried alarmists attest the wursts "aren't as plump as before" and the "choucroute is losing its zing", they are outvoted by advocates who praise this "very honest" establishment for being easy on the wallet.

BRISTOL (LE) S   26 | 27 | 26 | 113

Hôtel Bristol, 112, rue du Faubourg St-Honoré, 8ᵉ
(Miromesnil), 01 53 43 43 40; fax 01 53 43 43 01

■ Kudos overflow for the "brilliant" New French cuisine of "master chef" Eric Fréchon, who "breathes new life into a classic space" in the luxurious Hôtel Bristol; it's "first class" "without the attitude", with an "impeccable" staff whose performance resembles a "ballet" as it moves from the "sumptuous" oak-paneled dining room in winter to the "beautiful" summer garden; while an "ample budget" is a must for dining here, acolytes await their "next decadent evening in this temple" of "delight."

Bûcherie (La) ◗ S   14 | 16 | 13 | 46

41, rue de la Bûcherie, 5ᵉ (Maubert-Mutualité/St-Michel),
01 43 54 24 52; fax 01 46 34 54 02

■ A "pretty view of Notre Dame" and a glowing "hearth" draw lovesome couples and "loads of tourists" to dine at this Classic French in the 5th; old-timers say it "lost its soul" during the "modern" redo, but the "romantic" ambiance is still intact and the "solid" if "unimaginative" fare unlikely to distract from any amorous overtures.

Buddha Bar ◗ S   11 | 23 | 10 | 51

8, rue Boissy-d'Anglas, 8ᵉ (Concorde), 01 53 05 90 00;
fax 01 53 05 90 09

■ "Not a Zen retreat" but a bi-level, "club"-like Asian in the 8th arrondissement "where the hip hang" to "see and be seen" in the shadow of a towering Buddha; most dismiss the cuisine as unfit for "foodies", coming "only for drinks" and to bask in "super ambiance" "pulsating" with "ethno-lounge tunes"; the "young, pretty" staff is generally deemed "rude enough for the entire nation", but if the place has already "peaked", that doesn't stem the "fun"-seeking "crowds."

Buffalo Grill S   6 | 8 | 8 | 22

15, pl de la République, 3ᵉ (République), 01 40 29 94 98;
fax 01 49 96 43 48 ◗

1, bd St-Germain, 5ᵉ (Jussieu), 01 56 24 34 49;
fax 01 53 10 85 94

3, pl Blanche, 9ᵉ (Blanche), 01 40 16 42 51; fax 01 44 91 81 24

36, bd des Italiens, 9ᵉ (Opéra), 01 47 70 90 45;
fax 01 53 24 19 16 ◗

9, bd Denain, 10ᵉ (Gare du Nord), 01 40 16 47 81;
fax 01 44 91 81 27

2, rue Raymond Aron, 13ᵉ (Quai de la Gare), 01 45 86 76 71;
fax 01 44 06 90 31

117, av du Général-Leclerc, 14ᵉ (Porte d'Orléans),
01 45 40 09 72; fax 01 56 53 70 16

154, rue St-Charles, 15ᵉ (Charles Michels/Courmel),
01 40 60 97 48; fax 01 40 60 17 46

6, pl du Maréchal-Juin, 17ᵉ (Pereire), 01 40 54 73 75;
fax 01 48 01 13 64

(continued)
Buffalo Grill S
29, av Corentin-Cariou, 19ᵉ (Porte de la Villette), 01 40 36 21 41; fax 01 53 26 88 17

▨ "One step up from McDonald's" and "good with young children" proclaim parents of this Old West steakhouse chain; critics dig in their spurs, contending these are simply "not restaurants" but propagators of a "grotesque parody of American cuisine", frugal "meat lovers" overlook even the "phantom" staff, saying they're a "quick", cheap fill-up – especially "after tax day."

Butte Chaillot (La) S   16 | 14 | 15 | 45
110 bis, av Kléber, 16ᵉ (Trocadéro), 01 47 27 88 88; fax 01 47 04 85 70

■ A "good place for casual dining" in the "chichi" 16th arrondissement, this Guy Savoy–owned Contemporary French bistro turns out "simpler cuisine" than at his eponymous restaurant, including such "comforting" dishes as a much-ballyhooed "roast chicken with mashed potatoes"; the international clientele is as "sleek" as the decor, which is more New York than Parisian, and the service is generally "pleasant", making this a "fair value" in a high-rent neighborhood.

Byblos Café S   18 | 12 | 17 | 35
6, rue Guichard, 16ᵉ (La Muette), 01 42 30 99 99; fax 01 42 30 54 54
■ "Refined" Lebanese fare earns high praise for this "small" family-owned Middle Eastern in the 16th that's among the "best" of its kind in Paris; enthusiastic patrons appreciate the "traditional hospitality" and "charming", "laid-back" atmosphere, not to mention the "reasonable prices", and say it "deserves wider recognition."

Ca d'Oro   ▽ 16 | 14 | 14 | 35
54, rue de l'Arbre-Sec, 1ᵉʳ (Louvre-Rivoli), 01 40 20 97 79
▨ "A real Italian" and a "very good" one say satisfied surveyors of this Venetian near the Louvre whose wine-bar decor inspires wistful travelers to sigh "we're still in Venice"; the less-transported claim the food is only "so-so", but they're outnumbered by locals who like this "unpretentious" place.

Café Beaubourg ◗S   11 | 17 | 11 | 34
100, rue St-Martin, 4ᵉ (Châtelet-Les Halles/Hôtel-de-Ville), 01 48 87 63 96; fax 01 48 87 81 25
▨ "Fun for a light meal" pre or post a Centre Pompidou visit, this Costes brothers split-level Contemporary French bistro still wows "tourists" and "certain Parisians" with its "fabulously" "modern" setting by designer Christian de Portzamparc; the "varied menu" of "cafeteria"-like fare is less interesting, however, and the "disagreeable" staff can be trying; still, there's "sure value" in brunching on the "pleasant terrace."

Café Bleu (Le)
10 | 11 | 13 | 38

*Lanvin, 15, rue du Faubourg-St-Honoré, 8ᵉ (Concorde),
01 44 71 32 32; fax 01 44 71 31 17*

■ "Practical during a day of shopping" on the Faubourg-Saint-Honoré, this Classic French nestled in the basement of the Lanvin boutique offers a decorous pit-stop for the Hermès-tote set, who can cool their heels and grab a "fast" lunch of "simple food" served with a side of fashion advice before heading back to do battle; N.B. lunch only.

Café Charbon S
10 | 18 | 11 | 27

*109, rue Oberkampf, 11ᵉ (Parmentier), 01 43 57 55 13;
fax 01 43 57 57 41*

■ "Young" locals and curious "foreigners" slide into the moleskin booths at this "cool" cafe in the "effervescent" 11th arrondissement whose "raffish" but "charming" looks score more points than the "authentic" but "nothing special" Traditional French bistro fare (though some say the food "is improving"); if you're not up for a full meal, come join the gang "for a drink", but note that it can get "too crowded on Saturdays."

Café d'Angel (Le)
20 | 11 | 16 | 38

*16, rue Brey, 17ᵉ (Charles de Gaulle-Etoile/Ternes),
01 47 54 03 33; fax 01 47 54 03 33*

■ "The warmest welcome" around the Etoile, backed by "excellent" and "elaborate" cuisine, impels patrons to salute this Contemporary French bistro with superlatives; perhaps the kitchen receives "angelic" inspiration to turn out such "inventive" takes on traditional favorites, with "gracious" service, "cozy" atmosphere and merciful prices contributing to make it a "first choice for casual dining."

Café de Flore ◗S
12 | 18 | 14 | 36

*172, bd St-Germain, 6ᵉ (St-Germain-des-Prés), 01 45 48 55 26;
fax 01 45 44 33 39*

■ "Come to be entertained" by the perennial parade of "fashionistas", tourists and "incognito celebrities" all steeping in Left Bank intellectual history at this Saint-German "biggie"; bearing in mind that the "ok" Traditional French bistro fare is "not why you're here", join the "party" for "Sunday breakfast" or an afternoon drink "with friends", either in the more "tranquil" upstairs or "on the terrace."

Café de la Jatte ◗S
14 | 17 | 13 | 44

*60, bd Vital Bouhot, Neuilly-sur-Seine (Pont-de-Levallois),
01 47 45 04 20; fax 01 47 45 19 32*

■ "Neuilly's golden youth" and "dynamic" white-collar workers get their kicks eating under the lee of "an immense dinosaur skeleton" (kind of like dining "in a museum of natural history") or on the garden-enclosed "pleasant terrace" at this "atypical" spot on the Ile de la Jatte; some find the Contemporary French bistro fare no better than "banal", but others claim it's "getting more refined."

Café de la Musique ●⑤   10 | 15 | 12 | 32
213, av Jean Jaurès, 19ᵉ (Porte de Pantin), 01 48 03 15 91; fax 01 48 03 15 18
■ This "elegant" Villette-area cafe seems to be "warming up" with age; the Contemporary French bistro fare is "fine", if "limited" in variety, and as with other Costes brothers ventures, "expensive for what it is", though the service "competent"; its real selling points are the large "open" terrace, off the street and "free of exhaust fumes", and convenience "after a concert" at the Cité de la Musique.

Café de la Paix ●⑤   13 | 18 | 12 | 45
Grand Hôtel Inter-Continental, 12, bd des Capucines, 9ᵉ (Auber/Opéra), 01 40 07 30 20; fax 01 40 07 33 86
■ This "landmark" traditional brasserie with "beautiful" fin de siècle decor near the Opéra Garnier is a "must for old time's sake" despite food that's "not the most exciting" and priced for "tourists" and service that's "haughty"; still, it's in a "prime" locale for "people-watching" and "drinks and dessert" after the ballet; N.B. closed for renovation at press time, it was scheduled to re-open in Spring 2003.

Café de l'Esplanade (Le) ●⑤   13 | 20 | 11 | 47
52, rue Fabert, 7ᵉ (Invalides/La Tour-Maubourg), 01 47 05 38 80; fax 01 47 05 23 75
■ A brasserie "with social aspirations" might describe this "'in' place" in the 7th from the "everything-we-touch-turns-to-gold Costes brothers", whose "chic clientele is almost as beautiful" as Jacques Garcia's "luxe" Empire-style decor ("plush velour", "rich colors"); outside, the "perfect" terrace affords a "stunning view of Les Invalides"; pensive patrons only wish the "good-looking" servers were less "smug" and the prices less "expensive for what you get."

Café de l'Industrie ●⑤   8 | 15 | 11 | 26
16, rue St-Sabin, 11ᵉ (Bastille/Bréguet-Sabin), 01 47 00 13 53; fax 01 47 00 92 33
■ "A cigarette-smoking, arty-intellectual" crowd creates an "amusing ambiance" at this "fun bar" in a "nice location" in the 11th; while a "limited choice" of Traditional French bistro fare ("served by students or would-be students") "isn't terrible", "Bastille hipsters" hightail it here "to have a drink and talk" – as indicated by the "noisy" scene.

Café de Mars ●⑤   13 | 13 | 16 | 34
11, rue Augereau, 7ᵉ (Ecole-Militaire), 01 47 05 05 91; fax 01 45 55 76 99
■ This "nice little" cafe run by a "pleasant team of women" near the Champs de Mars wins points for its "warm atmosphere" and "good, Traditional" French bistro cuisine; its Sunday brunch and "unpretentious" style make it a "meeting place for the golden youth" of the 7th; N.B. the decor received a boost post-*Survey*, outdating the score.

Café des Délices (Le) ◑   ▽ 20 | 7 | 13 | 44

87, rue d'Assas, 6ᵉ (Port-Royal/Vavin), 01 43 54 70 00;
fax 01 43 26 42 05

■ "The discovery of the year" deem the discerning who've located this world-beat Eclectic near the Luxembourg Gardens; chef-owner Gilles Choukroun daringly whips up "inventive" Med-inspired takes on classic bistro dishes, and the result is "delicious", even "memorable"; only the "curious" Orient-meets-Occident decor seems to be an acquired taste.

Café des Lettres ⑤   10 | 16 | 13 | 32

53, rue de Verneuil, 7ᵉ (Rue du Bac/Solférino), 01 42 22 52 17;
fax 01 45 44 70 02

■ Fans fill up this "calm, agreeable" place in the 7th arrondissement, not so much for the rather "average" "Scandinavian cooking" but for the "warm service" and the cobblestoned courtyard that's "ideal for Sunday brunch" or a drink (preferably aquavit); not surprising, "reservations are a must in the summer."

Café du Commerce (Le) ◑⑤   11 | 16 | 11 | 28

51, rue du Commerce, 15ᵉ (Emile Zola/La Motte-Picquet-Grenelle), 01 45 75 03 27; fax 01 45 75 27 40

■ "Incredible decor at incredibly low prices" sums up this "cheap and cheerful" 1920s-era brasserie in the 15th arrondissement; that the food is "perfunctory", perhaps even "just out of the freezer", few deny; but the "congenial setting" – three stories dominated by a bird-friendly atrium and a "roof that opens up in the summer" – makes it "worth the trip", especially at the "end of the month", when the money runs short.

Café du Passage (Le) ◑⑤   ▽ 18 | 16 | 18 | 38

12, rue de Charonne, 11ᵉ (Bastille/Ledru-Rolin),
01 49 29 97 64; fax 01 47 00 14 00

■ Considered a "peaceful haven at the Bastille" by the few surveyors who know it, this intimate wine bar offers some 350 bottles of Rhone Valley and Burgundy crus; the "pleasant setting" and signature *andouillette* (tripe sausage) are additional pluses.

Café Faubourg ⑤   17 | 18 | 16 | 46

Sofitel Le Faubourg, 11 bis, rue Boissy-d'Anglas, 8ᵉ
(Concorde/Madeleine), 01 44 94 14 24; fax 01 44 94 14 28

■ "As fashionable as ever and living up to its rep" say fans of this contemporary bistro housed in the Sofitel Le Faubourg hotel, where "Alain Dutournier [Carré des Feuillants] disciple" chef Fabrice Dubos turns out "sophisticated cuisine" amid the "hush-hush" ambiance of the stylish "Zen decor"; grumps gripe about the "heavy" Southwestern dishes and "ignorant service", but they're outvoted by enthusiasts who find it "reasonably priced" (maybe they mean for the area).

Café Flo
14 | 18 | 15 | 37

*Au Printemps, 64, bd Haussmann, 9ᵉ (Auber/Havre-Caumartin),
01 42 82 58 84; fax 01 42 82 51 88*

■ At this branch of the Flo Groupe chain on the top floor of the Au Printemps department store, the "best feature is the wonderful stained-glass ceiling"; perhaps the Traditional French cuisine boils down to "comfort food" (i.e. "mediocre in the nicest way"), but nevertheless this eatery remains a "worthwhile place" for "a shopping lunch."

Café Indigo ●Ⓢ
10 | 12 | 13 | 43

*12, av George V, 8ᵉ (Alma-Marceau), 01 47 20 89 56;
fax 01 47 20 76 16*

■ On the Avenue George V ("superb location"), this "trendy" bistro is a "people-watching place" where it's best to "have a drink, not dinner", since the Traditional French food is "rather average" and served in "skimpy portions"; but professionals protest it's "perfect for a business lunch", given the "pleasant welcome", which is surprisingly "unpretentious" for a stylish haunt.

Café Les Deux Magots ●Ⓢ
12 | 18 | 13 | 37

*6, pl St-Germain-des-Prés, 6ᵉ (St-Germain-des-Prés),
01 45 48 55 25; fax 07 45 49 31 29*

■ "A must-do in Paris", if only "for history's sake", this Saint-Germain cafe made legendary by literary figures is "excellent for people-watching"; "a nice mix of tourists and regulars" comes here "to drink eau-de-vie and reminisce about Hemingway" – perhaps the best idea, as the food is "only ok" (best bet: "nightcaps and desserts"); "Sartre would barf" at the prices, but who "can resist paying too much" for "street theater that may be the best in France" – seen from the "heated outdoor" terrace, *naturellement.*

Café Louis Philippe ●Ⓢ
▽ 13 | 15 | 16 | 29

*66, quai de l'Hôtel-de-Ville, 4ᵉ (Pont-Marie),
01 42 72 29 42*

■ "A local spot that's always reliable" is a typical take on this traditional bistro with "lots of charm" in the Marais; and while the cuisine is fairly "average", when added to the panoramic view ("watch the boats on the Seine from upstairs") and "nice summer terrace," it passes without problem; plus the price is right.

Café M Ⓢ
18 | 16 | 15 | 54

*Hôtel Hyatt, 24, bd Malesherbes, 8ᵉ (Madeleine/St-Augustin),
01 55 27 12 34; fax 01 55 27 12 35*

■ The decor's "seriously dark, but the food is bright" at this "stylish", "cozy" corner of the Hôtel Hyatt near the Madeleine; while some carp the New French kitchen's concepts can be "conventional, the execution is excellent" and there's "a good choice of wines from across the Atlantic" too; the only major regret is that the place is "way too expensive."

Café Marly ◑🅂 13 | 22 | 12 | 41
93, rue de Rivoli, 1ᵉʳ (Palais Royal-Musée du Louvre),
01 49 26 06 60; fax 01 49 26 07 06
◪ "What can beat dining in the courtyard of the Louvre?" –
not much, and that's why patrons put up with "lackluster
service" and "so-so food (for Paris)" to dine either on the
"exceptional" terrace that overlooks I.M. Pei's pyramid or
in the "sumptuous" Second Empire–style salon, with its
vistas of fashionistas, at what may be the "best of the
Costes" brothers' brasseries; "this cafe may be in love with
itself" – but why not, since "a trip to town is incomplete
without a visit."

Café Max ⊟ – | – | – | M
*7, av de La Motte-Picquet, 7ᵉ (Ecole Militaire/La Tour-
Maubourg), 01 47 05 57 66*
"Quirky" chef-owner Max Gerchambeau may "insult
you", but the food is "so good and typically Parisian that
you excuse his eccentricity" say surveyors of this tiny
traditional bistro in the 7th, which also serves Southwestern
favorites; the flea-market-style decor offers "a change of
scene" even for natives.

Café Ruc ◑🅂 11 | 13 | 11 | 39
159, rue St-Honoré, 1ᵉʳ (Palais Royal-Musée du Louvre),
01 42 60 97 54; fax 01 42 61 36 33
◪ Yet another brasserie in the brothers Costes constellation,
this velvety red spot is stationed across from the Louvre;
like its sister satellites, it remains popular among the "trendy
chic" set, who consider it a worthy place for "people-
watching" (some have spotted "Comédie Française actors
dining after the show" here), even as it draws dissent for its
"snobby service" and "disappointing" cuisine: "apparently,
one has to suffer to be seen."

Café Runtz ◑ 18 | 18 | 17 | 39
16, rue Favart, 2ᵉ (La Bourse/Richelieu-Drouot), 01 42 96 69 86;
fax 01 40 20 92 95
■ "Opposite the Opéra Comique" in the 2nd arrondissement,
this "authentic Alsatian" turns out "frank" fare including
"excellent sauerkraut" dishes, accompanied by many
"reasonably priced wines" from the region; a rise in the
Decor score confirms that the renovated surroundings
provide a "pleasant atmosphere."

Café Terminus 🅂 ▽ 14 | 14 | 16 | 41
Hôtel Concorde St-Lazare, 108, rue St-Lazare, 8ᵉ (St-Lazare),
01 40 08 43 30; fax 01 40 08 44 60
■ "A revelation" report reviewers of this Classic French
in the Hôtel Concorde Saint-Lazare; "big portions" of "good
brasserie cuisine and service to match" plus a warm,
"familiar ambiance maintained by its habitués" all add
up to "the only worthwhile restaurant around the Saint-
Lazare train station."

Cafetière (La)
| 15 | 14 | 15 | 42 |

21, rue Mazarine, 6ᵉ (Odéon), 01 46 33 76 90; fax 01 43 25 76 90

◼ "Intimate" and "off the beaten track", this Italian in the 6th near Odéon serves up "simple and succulent" eats; the "original decor" – walls decorated with the old-fashioned coffee pots for which it's named – makes an "adorable" addition to the "pleasant" ambiance, and "service could not be better", either.

Café Véry ⑤
| 7 | 19 | 8 | 23 |

Jardin des Tuileries, 1ᵉʳ (Concorde/Tuileries), 01 47 03 94 84; fax 01 47 03 94 84

◼ Dining "in the middle of the Tuileries Gardens, what a dream!" sigh surveyors of this shrubbery-surrounded cafe; unfortunately, the Classic French "cuisine and service are in need of an urgent upgrade" snipe skeptics left starving by the "skimpy servings" and "very slow service"; but if the food's "mediocre", at least the "prices are affordable", and of course there's always that "delightful setting" – just "pick a nice day to visit."

Caffé Toscano ⑤
▽ | 15 | 10 | 16 | 30 |

34, rue des Saints-Pères, 7ᵉ (St-Germain-des-Prés), 01 42 84 28 95; fax 01 42 84 26 36

◼ "Excellent Tuscan cuisine" and wine is the trademark of this Italian off the Saint-Germain strip; the offerings may "be few" (as the name suggests, it's closer to a cafe than a restaurant) but what is on the menu is "simple and fine and reasonably priced for the quality" and served by "pleasant" staffers; all told, "a good address for a light dinner."

Cagouille (La) ⑤
| 20 | 11 | 15 | 50 |

10, pl Constantin Brancusi, 14ᵉ (Gaîté), 01 43 22 09 01; fax 01 45 38 57 29

◼ This Montparnasse seafooder reels in reports of "rare flavors" and "remarkable fish"; too bad the service ("colder than the ocean") and the decor ("despairing") cast a shadow over the catch of the day, but "the pleasant garden terrace" makes up for it in summer; P.S. a special salon houses "the best collection of cognacs in town."

Cailloux (Les)
| 15 | 13 | 15 | 33 |

58, rue des Cinq Diamants, 13ᵉ (Corvisart), 01 45 80 15 08; fax 01 45 65 67 09

◼ In the heart of the "charmingly village-like" Butte aux Cailles, this Italian dishes up "excellent pasta" at easy prices: "it's a real find", but judging by the "constant deafening noise" level, too many have already found it.

Caméléon (Le)
▽ | 19 | 16 | 18 | 36 |

6, rue de Chevreuse, 6ᵉ (Vavin), 01 43 20 63 43; fax 01 43 27 97 91

◼ For 30 years, "excellent country cuisine" and "exquisite service" have kept connoisseurs coming to this Classic

French veteran in the 6th that boasts a "neighborhood bistro" feel and "reasonable prices"; a few anxious appetites might require larger servings, but for the majority it's "a jewel" that (to mix a metaphor) works like a "charm."

Camélia (Le) 🅂   17 | 15 | 16 | 52
7, quai Georges Clémenceau, Bougival (RER La Défense), 01 39 18 36 06; fax 01 39 18 00 25

▨ They "try hard to please" at this place in Bougival that sports a redone contemporary decor; but while partisans praise the "pleasant service" and "excellent" New French fare, critics carp the cuisine's "too conventional"; still, ratings side with those who feel this "constantly classy" site "deserves to be better known."

C'Amelot (Le) ⬤   21 | 11 | 18 | 38
50, rue Amelot, 11ᵉ (Chemin Vert), 01 43 55 54 04; fax 01 43 14 77 05

▧ Tucked away in the 11th between the Bastille and République, this "cozy" Contemporary French bistro gets a young, trendy crowd going with its "inventive" and "carefully executed" takes on classics; though a few lament the "restricted pick" of the daily changing, single prix fixe menu, most salute the "amazing freshness of the food"; add "easy prices" to the list and you have an "excellent value."

Camille ⬤🅂   12 | 12 | 14 | 34
24, rue des Francs-Bourgeois, 3ᵉ (St-Paul), 01 42 72 20 50; fax 01 40 27 07 99

▨ This "lovely neighborhood" bistro gets nods for "friendly service" and "decent" Classic French cuisine, but "there are so many others like it" jibe jaded surveyors; suffice it to say it's an "adequate" option when in the Marais and an even better one on days you can eat outdoors.

Canal Café   – | – | – | I
56, rue de Lancry, 10ᵉ (Jacques Bonsergent/République), 01 42 08 38 81

Just steps from the Canal Saint-Martin, this cafe has become a hang-out for the bobo (bohemian bourgeois) couples who are colonizing the up-and-coming 10th; gently priced Traditional French Bistro dishes, occasionally updated with imaginative garnishes, are the stars here, supported by friendly service and pretty stucco moldings on the wall.

Canard ⌖   – | – | – | M
36, rue Bayen, 17ᵉ (Pereire), 01 42 67 60 95; fax 01 42 67 60 95

"The food is as bourgeois as the clientele" at this Classic French in the 17th – obviously a good thing, since first-time visitors "happily return" for the "good", "high-quality" eats, proffered by "discreetly attentive servers" amid a "hushed ambiance"; a few lament the "very limited choice", but most find this presence in Pereire a "surprising" treat.

Cantine Russe (La)   _ | _ | _ | I
26, av de New York, 16ᵉ (Iéna), 01 47 20 65 17;
fax 01 47 20 08 06
Simple, traditional Russian fare is the attraction at this
picturesque Slavic enclave, adorned with musical
instruments (it once belonged to the Serge Rachmaninoff
Conservatoire) and portraits of famous artists, located
practically at the doorstep of the Palais de Tokyo; owner
Nicolas Novikoff always has a smile on his face as he
serves exceptionally reasonably priced pojarski (meat
patties) and other delicacies.

Cap Seguin (Le)   13 | 18 | 13 | 41
face au 27, quai le Gallo, Boulogne-Billancourt
(Pont-de-Sèvres), 01 46 05 06 07; fax 01 46 05 06 88
◼ The "unique" riverboat ambiance of this Seine-side
barge in Boulogne-Billancourt assures it a steady flow,
especially in summer, when the "remarkable terrace" makes
you feel "you're no longer in Paris"; but the barometer falls
when it comes to other elements, with mateys maintaining
the "Traditional French cuisine" is "simple and precise"
and the "service pleasant", and critics complaining the
cooking's "not exceptional" and "the staff leaves you with
plenty of time to admire the view."

Cap Vernet (Le) 𝕊   17 | 15 | 15 | 52
82, av Marceau, 8ᵉ (Charles de Gaulle-Etoile), 01 47 20 20 40;
fax 01 47 20 95 36
◼ "Cigar-smoking golden boys" gather at this "modern"
split-level brasserie, chef-restaurateur "Guy Savoy's
second restaurant", just off the Etoile; the upscale types
enjoy "irreproachable shellfish platters" and "simple,
reliable" seafood, but others grouse "it's a little expensive"
for cuisine that "never hits a bad note but never quite hits
the high ones either."

Caroubier (Le) 𝕊   _ | _ | _ | M
82, bd Lefebvre, 15ᵉ (Porte de Vanves), 01 40 43 16 12
Mavens who know this midsize, midpriced Moroccan
near the Porte de Vanves insist it's the place to come for
"classic North African cuisine", including couscous, tagines
and "certainly the best pigeon b'steeya in Paris"; the less
adventuresome acknowledge it's "nice, but you have to
be in a good mood."

Carpaccio 𝕊   ▽ 21 | 16 | 21 | 61
Hôtel Royal Monceau, 37, av Hoche, 8ᵉ (Charles de Gaulle-
Etoile), 01 42 99 98 90; fax 01 42 99 89 94
◼ This elegant, expensive Italian near the Arc de Triomphe
offers a "marvelous", "refined" menu that includes "the
best Parma ham to be found in Paris (even sons of Italy
think so)" and, during the season, white truffles in risotto;
perhaps it's "pricey for pasta", but the plush "setting and
the service help you forget" the cost.

Carpe Diem
16 | 11 | 16 | 51

*10, rue de l'Eglise, Neuilly-sur-Seine (Pont-de-Neuilly),
01 46 24 95 01; fax 01 46 40 15 61*

☑ "Homestyle cooking and a warm welcome" are why suburbanites seize the day when they can eat at this Traditional French in Neuilly; but critics carp it's best not to expect anything "exceptional" among the "overpriced" offerings (especially given the "frumpy" decor).

Carré (Le) ●
– | – | – | E

*12, pl St-Augustin, 8ᵉ (St-Augustin), 01 44 69 00 22;
fax 01 44 69 33 19*

A "pretty setting" – all brown velvet and dark woods – appeals to the well-heeled at this "fashionable" address in the 8th; fans also find that "a lot of attention" has gone into the New French fare; "too bad" the "service can be shaky."

CARRÉ DES FEUILLANTS
25 | 21 | 23 | 108

*14, rue de Castiglione, 1ᵉʳ (Concorde/Tuileries), 01 42 86 82 82;
fax 01 42 86 07 71*

■ "Bravo to the bearded" Alain Dutournier, the mastermind behind this New French in the 1st, whose "skillful balance between traditional Southwestern and inventive Haute Cuisine" "lifts the spirit"; the experience is "superb in all [other] respects" too, from the "divine wines" to "warm", "quietly efficient service" to the "modern" decor (though a few find the setting "without soul"); and while some opine it's overpriced, most "would go every day if we could get in."

Carr's 🆂
▽ 8 | 14 | 12 | 33

*1, rue du Mont Thabor, 1ᵉʳ (Tuileries), 01 42 60 60 26;
fax 01 42 60 33 32*

■ For a taste of "Irish ambiance" in the heart of Paris, this "laid-back" pub near the Tuileries is a good choice; the appeal is more Guinness than grub (it's really "not a place to eat"), but it's popular with "many expats", whose toes start tapping to the live Gaelic music on Fridays.

Cartes Postales (Les)
20 | 10 | 14 | 52

*7, rue Gomboust, 1ᵉʳ (Opéra/Pyramides), 01 42 61 02 93;
fax 01 42 61 02 93*

■ "A candy jar where you dine on sophisticated cuisine" sums up this "tiny" space; an Alain Dutournier–trained Japanese chef turns out "creative French-Asian fusion" fare that's "delicious" and "perfectly executed"; the modern decor gets mixed reviews (from "beautiful" to "sterile"), but the "practical half-portions" are a "good value", particularly for this part of the 1st.

Cartet Restaurant ⌗
▽ 18 | 10 | 21 | 43

62, rue de Malte, 11ᵉ (République), 01 48 05 17 65

■ Dining at this husband-and-wife-run "very classic" bistro behind the Place de la République is like "being fed by mom" sigh homesick surveyors; be sure to come early for the signature beef dishes and homemade tarts "to die for", as the kitchen closes at 9 PM (later on weekends); perhaps the eats are "a bit expensive", but "the generous servings" make this one a "favorite" nonetheless.

Casa Alcalde S | 15 | 11 | 14 | 38 |

117, bd de Grenelle, 15ᵉ (La Motte Picquet-Grenelle), 01 47 83 39 71

■ This "ever-packed" Spanish in the 15th is "just like being in the Basque country" swear fans who flock here for the "festive" ambiance, "genial" service and "good paella"; a few grumblers gripe it's "too expensive for a neighborhood restaurant", especially given the "squeezed" seating, but after a swig of the "super sangria", most don't mind.

Casa Bini S | 16 | 11 | 14 | 42 |

36, rue Grégoire de Tours, 6ᵉ (Odéon), 01 46 34 05 60; fax 01 40 46 09 71

■ Going into its second decade, this "most Left Bank of Italians" near the Odéon offers a "variety" of "very good food" and vino; perhaps it's a touch "pricey and pretentious for pasta", but most maintain it's "a fabulous find"; all agree, however, that the "straight-out-of-the-'80s" decor could use an update.

Casa Corsa ◐ | 18 | 14 | 15 | 39 |

25, rue Mazarine, 6ᵉ (Odéon), 01 44 07 38 98; fax 01 43 54 14 79

■ "Close your eyes and listen to Tino Rossi sing" (if only on tape) amid the "cheerful atmosphere" of this "underrated, authentic Corsican" near the Odéon; partisans proclaim it "can't be beat" for "tasty, inexpensive fare", with "a nice selection of [local] wines to boot."

Casa Olympe | 21 | 11 | 15 | 49 |

48, rue St-Georges, 9ᵉ (St-Georges), 01 42 85 26 01; fax 01 45 26 49 33

■ "The Queen of the 9th" is how surveyer-subjects refer to Olympe Versini, chef-owner of this Contemporary French bistro serving up "delicious and creative" "Provençal-inspired dishes in a rustic environment"; the "warm" ambiance and "sophisticated" fare that's an "excellent value" win it a royal following, even if a few dieting detractors deem the cuisine "heavy" and mutter about "morose", though "attentive, service."

Casa Tina ◐S | 13 | 12 | 12 | 33 |

18, rue Lauriston, 16ᵉ (Charles de Gaulle-Etoile/Kléber), 01 40 67 19 24

■ "The Gypsy Kings in yuppie-land" is how patrons evoke the ambiance of this Spanish near the Etoile; "typically Iberian cuisine" and wines plus an "innate congeniality" make the place popular amongst the young, well-heeled crowd that flocks to its bar for tapas and sangria; the only complaint from a few low-fueled billfolds is that it's "scandalously expensive" for such "unpretentious" eats.

Casa Vigata 🅂⌀   – | – | – | M
44, rue Léon Frot, 11ᵉ (Charonne), 01 43 56 38 66
Roberta Tringale, the friendly owner of this tiny trattoria near the Bastille, is a native of the Sicilian city of Catania determined to dispel stereotypes about her island's cuisine; though often considered good old home cooking, it can actually be quite sophisticated, as seen in dishes like penne with eggplant and ricotta in a light tomato sauce or swordfish with capers; but if the fare is cosmopolitan, the prices are provincially modest.

Catalogne, Maison de la   ▽ 14 | 16 | 13 | 30
4-6-8, Cour-du-Commerce-St-André, 6ᵉ (Odéon), 01 55 42 16 19; fax 01 55 42 16 33
■ With an "atmosphere that's beyond quaint – a stage set", this bi-level Spaniard offers "a bit of calm near the Odéon"; "good tapas" and "generous portions" appease the appetites of the "young, not too trendy" crowd in the bistro below, while a good-value "varied prix fixe" wins points with the finer diners in the restaurant upstairs; "from all points of view, very pleasant."

Catounière (La)   ▽ 13 | 9 | 12 | 35
4, rue des Poissonniers, Neuilly-sur-Seine (Pont-de-Neuilly), 01 47 47 14 33; fax 01 55 24 93 72
■ "Quality bourgeois cuisine" (think veal kidneys and chocolate desserts) is what lures locals to this Classic French, "one of the best values" in upscale Neuilly; the "simple but good" eats, served in a casual atmosphere, cause some to call it "a keeper" – while the possessive say keep it "confidential."

Caveau du Palais (Le)   14 | 15 | 13 | 46
17-19, pl Dauphine, 1ᵉʳ (Cité/Pont-Neuf), 01 43 26 04 28; fax 01 43 26 81 84
■ "For a bit of calm in the middle of Paris", "come here in summer for the terrace" of this "charming" Classic French on Ile de la Cité; the "tasty" wood-roasted meats are "rather expensive", but "the Place Dauphine is so beautiful, it'll make you forget" the bill.

Cave de l'Os à Moelle 🅂   18 | 14 | 15 | 32
181, rue de Lourmel, 15ᵉ (Lourmel), 01 45 57 28 28; fax 01 45 47 40 10
■ "Great concept" exclaim enthusiasts of the "congenial" communal-table format of this offshoot of the nearby Os à Moelle in the 15th; a prix fixe that offers "original" takes on "Traditional French food", "friendly service" and the chance "to meet some interesting people" are the draws; of course the "fun" all depends on your social skills (the shy say "only once").

Cave Drouot (La)   ▽ 18 | 13 | 18 | 42
8, rue Drouot, 9ᵉ (Richelieu-Drouot), 01 47 70 83 38;
fax 01 47 70 83 38

■ Perfect for "lunch before the auctions", this Traditional French bistro in the 9th caters to the staff and clients of the Salle Drouot nearby; the "very good cuisine" warms up the bidders-to-be with a selection of Beaujolais wines, but raise your paddle by midday – it's lunch only.

Cave Gourmande (La)   – | – | – | M
10, rue du Général Brunet, 19ᵉ (Botzaris), 01 40 40 03 30;
fax 01 40 40 03 30

This New French bistro in the 19th may be a hike from the city center, but foodies fawn over "creative young chef"-owner Mark Singer, who uses "fresh market fare" to create "new taste combinations"; perhaps the decor could use help, but the "thoughtful" service compensates.

Caves Pétrissans   14 | 12 | 14 | 43
30 bis, av Niel, 17ᵉ (Pereire/Ternes), 01 42 27 52 03;
fax 01 40 54 87 56

■ Near the Place des Ternes, terms of endearment abound for this "old-style bistro", a neighborhood "darling" that cooks up "simple" Classic French "country fare like we love it"; the patrons "generally speaking, are serious wine drinkers" attracted by the stellar selection of some 500 labels (which you can also get to go in the attached store).

Caviar Kaspia ◑   21 | 18 | 19 | 87
17, pl de la Madeleine, 8ᵉ (Madeleine), 01 42 65 33 32;
fax 01 42 65 66 26

■ Happiness is "a window table, caviar and more caviar followed by smoked salmon and blinis and non-stop vodka" rave roe-eaters at this "timeless and wonderful" "Parisian institution" (since 1927) that boasts "one of the great views of the Madeleine"; late hours make it "ideal for after the theater" or "a real celebratory dinner"; it's "clearly overpriced" but, "when you can afford it", "a treat."

Cazaudehore La Forestière 🅂   18 | 22 | 17 | 68
1, av Kennedy, Saint-Germain-en-Laye (RER St-Germain-en-Laye), 01 30 61 64 64; fax 01 39 73 73 88

■ The fact that reviewers rave first and foremost about the "beautiful setting" ("dining in the garden is delicious") of this hotel restaurant in upscale Saint-Germain-en-Laye suggests that the food alone doesn't hold the fort; still, "if not as good as the environs", the New French–Southwestern cuisine is "good" enough to ensure a "pleasant" overture to "a love night in the middle of the forest."

C . . . Comme Cochons ◑   – | – | – | M
135, rue de Charenton, 12ᵉ (Reuilly-Diderot), 01 43 42 43 36

"The only decent restaurant in the area" declare devotees of this spot near the Viaduc des Arts in the 12th; "inventive, original" takes on Classic French cuisine (braised chuck steak, for example) and a highly reasonable prix fixe make it a great place "to have dinner with friends."

Céladon (Le) S — 22 | 20 | 22 | 69
Hôtel Westminster, 15, rue Daunou, 2ᵉ (Auber/Opéra),
01 47 03 40 42; fax 01 42 60 30 66
■ Near the Place Vendôme, the Hôtel Westminster's Haute Cuisine haven treats takers to "a formal dining experience with attentive service and lovely food" (it's "hotel cooking – traditional, but seductive"); the plushly "beautiful decor" of the spacious dining room is "perfect for" both business-lunchers and evening romancers, and while "the bill can rival those of the Grand Restaurants, there is also a prix fixe" option; as a rise in scores suggests, it works "from all points of view."

Chai 33 S — – | – | – | M
33, cour St-Emilion, 12ᵉ (Cour St-Emilion), 01 53 44 01 01;
fax 01 53 44 01 02
Located on a cobbled pedestrian street amid the restored brick-and-stone warehouses of the up-and-coming Bercy quarter, this wine bar/restaurant pulls a young crowd with a menu of light eats (salads, cold-meat plates, sandwiches) plus a few Traditional French hot dishes, along with an ample assortment of pours by the glass.

Chalet des Iles (Le) S — 12 | 23 | 13 | 49
Lac du Bois de Boulogne, 16ᵉ (Av Henri Martin/
Rue de la Pompe), 01 42 88 04 69; fax 01 42 88 84 09
■ Boating over to this Classic French on an island in the Bois de Boulogne (the only means of getting there) is half the "fun"; but while the "sublime setting" is "well worth the crossing", the "cuisine leaves something to be desired", though a rise in the score reinforces reports of "progress"; at any rate, the "magical" environs may make this "the most romantic restaurant in Paris."

Chamarré (Le) — – | – | – | E
13, bd de la Tour-Maubourg, 7ᵉ (Invalides/La Tour-Maubourg),
01 47 05 50 18; fax 01 47 05 91 21
In a quiet corner of the 7th, this original newcomer evokes the tropical island of Mauritius with wooden blinds and rich colors and a menu co-designed by maitre d'hôtel Antoine Heerah (a Mauritian chef); the hybrid cuisine, a mixture of French, Indian and African, is executed by Jerome Baudreau, an Arpège veteran.

Champ de Mars (Le) S — 17 | 14 | 15 | 42
17, av de La Motte-Picquet, 7ᵉ (Ecole-Militaire/
La Tour-Maubourg), 01 47 05 57 99; fax 01 44 18 94 69
■ This "familial" Classic French is near the Ecole Militaire but "like dining in the provinces", with its "well-executed" veal dishes (including the specialty calf's liver) and "warm

welcome"; while there's concern "it's becoming touristy", "good food and good value" still sum up the scene; N.B. closed at press time, it was scheduled to re-open May 2003.

Chantairelle ▽ 19 | 18 | 19 | 33
17, rue Laplace, 5ᵉ (Maubert-Mutualité), 01 46 33 18 59; fax 01 46 33 18 59

■ "Real country cuisine" served by a "considerate staff" at "reasonable prices" is what makes this 5th arrondissement Auvergnat popular with academics and other budget-watchers; the village-like decor (including a well) and sound effects (of birds) recreate a "convincing" Massif Central milieu; N.B. there's a grocery stocked with regional products.

Chardenoux S 18 | 18 | 16 | 38
1, rue Jules Vallès, 11ᵉ (Charonne/Faidherbe-Chaligny), 01 43 71 49 52; fax 01 45 62 04 07

■ An "out-of-the way Paris treasure", this "historic" site in the 11th recently reopened under new ownership and with a careful renovation of the "charming" belle epoque decor; a new kitchen team has spruced up the Traditional French menu, but favorite "first-rate" dishes like the *blanquette d'agneau* (lamb stew) remain, so this "classic" is still "a must."

Charlot - Roi des Coquillages ●S 14 | 12 | 12 | 51
12, pl de Clichy, 9ᵉ (Place de Clichy), 01 53 20 48 00; fax 01 53 20 48 09

◪ This self-styled "King of Shellfish" reigning over the Place de Clichy remains on his throne but gets mixed votes: loyalists love the "irreproachable" Marseilles-style bouillabaisse and "excellent raw platters", while detractors express "disappointment" over "average" fare ("King of the Microwave") at "high prices" and knock the "overly sumptuous and outdated decor."

Charpentiers (Aux) ●S 13 | 13 | 13 | 38
10, rue Mabillon, 6ᵉ (Mabillon/St-Germain-des-Prés), 01 43 26 30 05; fax 01 46 33 07 98

◪ The "nostalgia can't be beat" at this very Traditional French bistro (established 1856) near the Marché Saint-Germain; "solid fare at a fair price" makes this "working man's cafe" a popular Left Bank haunt – though more among tourists than locals, carp critics who also complain about the "appallingly" "rough-and-ready service" and call the food "mediocre"; but whether or not it's "worth all the hype", most agree it's "a good value" for "a bit of old Paris."

Chartier S 9 | 19 | 13 | 21
7, rue Faubourg-Montmartre, 9ᵉ (Cadet/Grands Boulevards), 01 47 70 86 29; fax 01 48 24 14 68

■ "An exceptional 1900 decor" and "the cheapest dishes in Paris" are why diners line up outside to get into this cafeteria-like, immense "institution" that's the *Survey*'s Top

Bang for the Buck; "go to satisfy your curiosity, not your appetite", since the Classic French fare is "not pricey [but] not good" either; still, "you don't come here for the food but for the performance" that recreates a "classic belle epoque" dining experience – right down to the "waiters adding up the tab on the paper tablecloth."

Chaumière Massyle (La)   _ | _ | _ | I

52, rue de Chabrol, 10ᵉ (Poissonnière), 01 47 70 30 62
This new North African makes a welcome alternative to the Alsatian brasseries that dominate the dining scene around the Gare de l'Est; the lighting is a bit intense and the decor rather minimal, but this doesn't stop fans of first-rate couscous and tagines, who also appreciate the low prices and cheerful waiters.

Chavignol (Le)   _ | _ | _ | M

135, av de Villiers, 17ᵉ (Porte de Champerret), 01 43 80 40 65
Don't be fooled by the neon script on the facade or the Formica-heavy decor – this bistro à vins has become an insider's address with bon vivants, including many famous chefs, who recognize the AOC-pedigreed produce used by the kitchen here; the Traditional French Bistro fare is well priced, with no extra charge for the convivial atmosphere.

Chen   21 | 14 | 16 | 87

15, rue du Théâtre, 15ᵉ (Charles-Michels), 01 45 79 34 34; fax 01 45 79 07 53
☑ "Excellent but exorbitant" diners declare of this entry, aka "the best Chinese in Paris"; most get over the "shock of the commercial decor" (it's located in the underpass of a building in the 15th) when they taste "extraordinary", "artistically presented" specialties such as "frog's legs to die for" and "a marvel of a Peking duck"; however, a vocal minority maintains that the "uptight service" and "hardly copious" helpings "ruin the experience."

Cherche Midi (Le) ◑⑤   15 | 11 | 13 | 39

22, rue du Cherche-Midi, 6ᵉ (Sèvres-Babylone/St-Sulpice), 01 45 48 27 44
■ Perhaps "people come here to be seen, but the pasta is exceptional" at this popular "reservations-are-a-must" Saint-Germain Italian; and while the chic-appeal means the tab's a tad more expensive and the "tightly spaced tables" result in considerable noise, habitués hail it as "irresistible", and "after all these years" too.

Chez Albert ◑   ▽ 16 | 10 | 14 | 36

43, rue Mazarine, 6ᵉ (Odéon), 01 46 33 22 57
■ An "excellent Portuguese table" is always set at this small spot near the Odéon, where "very warm" servers keep you supplied with "delicious" fish dishes and "marvelous wines and ports"; there are problems with the "lame decor

and lighting that kills" any hope of a romantic mood, but "it remains a favorite, even so."

Chez André ●⑤   16 | 12 | 15 | 44

12, rue Marbeuf, 8ᵉ (Franklin D. Roosevelt), 01 47 20 59 57; fax 01 47 20 18 82

■ Get ready to "rub elbows with your neighbors" at this "bustling neighborhood hot spot" off the Champs; the Traditional French bistro fare is "nothing fancy, but it all tastes good", plus the "service is friendly"; true, it tends to be "noisy and crowded" and a few feel its "uniqueness has suffered" since its acquisition by the Gérard Joulie group, but by most accounts it's "still amusing."

Chez Catherine   – | – | – | E

3, rue Berryer, 8ᵉ (George V/St-Philippe du Roule), 01 40 76 01 40; fax 01 42 80 96 88

Chef Catherine Guerraz, one of Paris' top female toques, has moved to an elegant new setting, featuring Moroccan-style waxed walls in gray and turmeric, tables smartly dressed in contemporary china and silver, and lots of orchids scattered through the two dining rooms; her menu retains some of the Traditional Bistro fare that made her renown, but also includes a variety of New French dishes, so that this place is now a decidedly modern address, attracting bankers in a blue-blooded business precinct of the 8th.

Chez Clément ●⑤   11 | 14 | 11 | 30

17, bd des Capucines, 2ᵉ (Opéra), 01 53 43 52 00; fax 01 53 43 82 09
21, bd Beaumarchais, 4ᵉ (Bastille), 01 40 29 17 00; fax 01 40 29 17 09
9, pl St-André-des-Arts, 6ᵉ (St-Michel), 01 56 81 32 00; fax 01 56 81 32 09
19, rue Marbeuf, 8ᵉ (Franklin D. Roosevelt), 01 53 23 90 00; fax 01 53 23 90 09
123, av des Champs Elysées, 8ᵉ (Charles De Gaulle-Etoile), 01 40 73 87 00; fax 01 40 73 87 09
106, bd du Montparnasse, 14ᵉ (Vavin), 01 44 10 54 00; fax 01 44 10 54 09
407, rue de Vaugirard, 15ᵉ (Porte de Versailles), 01 53 68 94 00; fax 01 53 68 94 09
47, av de Wagram, 17ᵉ (Ternes), 01 53 81 97 00; fax 01 53 81 97 09
99, bd Gouvion St Cyr, 17ᵉ (Porte Maillot), 01 45 72 93 00; fax 01 45 72 93 09
98, av Edouard Vaillant, Boulogne-Billancourt (Marcel Sembat), Boulogne, 01 41 22 90 00; fax 01 41 22 90 09

◪ With numerous outposts in and around Paris, it's normal that there's a "big variance among the establishments" of this "well-organized" Classic French chain that's "famous for shellfish"; on average, it's "adequate at best", dishing up standards "without surprises", and the rural-themed decor is either "fun" or "faux" depending on your taste; given that, it's "a sure value", so "if there's nothing else around, go ahead and try it."

Chez Denise
20 | 17 | 17 | 44

5, rue des Prouvaires, 1er (Châtelet-Les Halles),
01 42 36 21 82

■ It's "smoky, noisy and crowded", but this "monument of a bistro" is "about as fun as Paris gets"; "go late for the festivities" (it's open 24 hours) and sit down to such Classic French delights as "big slabs of foie gras and huge ribs of beef" when the "party" begins; if this "always packed" Les Halles hot spot can afford to "close on weekends, you know it works!"

Chez Diane ◑
▽ 19 | 18 | 22 | 59

25, rue Servandoni, 6e (St-Sulpice), 01 46 33 12 06;
fax 01 43 25 96 55

■ "Tiny and charming", this "cozy" Classic French across from the Luxembourg Gardens wins hearts with candlelight ambiance and "yummy" food; the "intimate", "romantic setting" and "warm welcome" by the husband-and-wife team make it a "pleasant" dining experience.

Chez Diep ◑ S
16 | 14 | 14 | 50

55, rue Pierre Charron, 8e (Franklin D. Roosevelt),
01 45 63 53 76; fax 01 42 56 46 56

■ "A change of pace" pronounce patrons of this "high-class Thai"-Vietnamese off the Champs; and while "factory-like" service makes some feel they're eating "fast food at 500 francs", the "expensive" fare is "succulent", particularly the signature duck; indeed, the "stylish clientele" seems happy "to pay for it."

Chez Fabrice
▽ 18 | 13 | 17 | 33

38, rue Croix des Petits-Champs, 1er (Palais Royal-Musée du Louvre), 01 40 20 06 46

■ "Wow!" exclaim awed advocates of this Classic French near the Place des Victoires where chef-owner Fabrice Wolff is "to be encouraged" for his "good food at remarkably low prices"; "opt for the main dining room and avoid the cellar (cold in winter)" advise the initiated.

Chez Francis ◑ S
13 | 15 | 13 | 47

7, pl de l'Alma, 8e (Alma Marceau), 01 47 20 86 83;
fax 01 47 20 43 26

■ At the Place de l'Alma, this "comfortable, slow-paced" brasserie "par excellence" "does honor to the genre" with its "great view of the Eiffel Tower" and "elegant" seafood; "go here for the excellent oysters after the theater" say habitués; just be forewarned that "it's expensive."

Chez Françoise ◑ S
15 | 14 | 14 | 44

Aérogare des Invalides, 7e (Invalides), 01 47 05 49 03;
fax 01 45 51 96 20

■ Seated in the *aérogare* of the Invalides, this Classic French draws in deputies from the nearby Palais Bourbon; long-standing patrons and politicos vote their approval for "traditional" dishes like duck confit and crêpes suzette that "haven't changed in 40 years"; and though a dissenting faction claims this "1950s club" "has aged", most find it "pleasantly consistent", especially if you're situated on the "beautiful terrace."

Chez Fred ▽ 18 | 12 | 17 | 39

190, bis bd Pereire, 17ᵉ (Porte Maillot), 01 45 74 20 48; fax 01 45 74 20 48

■ "A neighborhood classic" say 17th arrondissement fans of this traditional "little bistro specializing" in Lyonnais cuisine; "very good meat", an impressive selection of Beaujolais and Bordeaux wines and sidewalk tables have kept the faithful flocking since 1945.

Chez Gégène S⊉ 6 | 16 | 9 | 33

162 bis, quai de Polangis, Joinville-le-Pont (Joinville-le-Pont RER), 01 48 83 29 43; fax 01 48 83 72 62

■ You'd better like "the smell of fries" and the strains of the accordion (the "ambiance *musette*") say *guinguette*-goers who flock to this restaurant/music hall along the Marne river in Joinville; the Classic French food "leaves a lot to be desired", but don't fret if fried smelt's not your thing – "you don't come here to eat (happily)" but "to dance, people-watch" or simply bask in the pre–World War I atmosphere of the place.

Chez Georges 19 | 18 | 17 | 49

1, rue du Mail, 2ᵉ (Bourse), 01 42 60 07 11

■ "For the feel of Paris as it used to be", "rather stylish" regulars head to this "truly traditional bistro"; "it's the real thing" and it "never disappoints" with its "simple, honest" French eats, "generous portions" and "smiling servers"; tucked behind the Place des Victoires, "it's worth the hunt" for "old-fashioned fun."

Chez Georges-Porte Maillot ●◗S 15 | 13 | 15 | 46

273, bd Pereire, 17ᵉ (Porte Maillot), 01 45 74 31 00; fax 01 45 74 02 56

■ Dining at this 1920s Classic French brasserie near the Porte Maillot is like "having dinner at someone's home"; the "excellent leg of lamb" and other country fare "carved in front of you" suits "big appetites", and while there's some report tradition can be taken too far ("they're afraid to change anything, except the prices"), most agree this is a good, if slightly "austere", option.

Chez Gérard S 16 | 12 | 15 | 33

10, rue Montrosier, Neuilly-sur-Seine (Porte Maillot), 01 46 24 86 37; fax 01 46 37 21 72

■ "Not very original but good" is the skinny on this humble "Classic French bistro", a dying breed in upscale Neuilly; supporters insist the "congenial ambiance" makes it the right choice "for dinner with friends or family", especially since the wines are "quality" merchandise ("after a few glasses you forget the decor").

Chez Germaine ⌿   ▽ 14 | 11 | 18 | 18
30, rue Pierre Leroux, 7ᵉ (Duroc/Vaneau), 01 42 73 28 34
■ Get infused with the "Paris bistro spirit" at this Traditional French example in the 7th arrondissement, whose main drawing cards are its "just-like-at-home" feel and "fresh, seasonal" classics at "prices that can't be beat"; small wonder patrons get packed "elbow to elbow" in the "tiny, busy" space.

Chez Gildo   16 | 9 | 12 | 53
153, rue de Grenelle, 7ᵉ (La Tour Maubourg), 01 45 51 54 12; fax 01 45 51 54 12
■ "A marvel of Italian cooking" is embodied in this sophisticate in the 7th, where chef-owner Gianfranco Ugolini – a "monument in his own right" – turns out "sublime stuffed fried olives" and pastas; only complaint is that it seems a tad "pricey", especially given the "dressed-down 1950s-style decor."

Chez Jacky   ▽ 19 | 14 | 19 | 49
109, rue du Dessous-des-Berges, 13ᵉ (Bibilothèque François Mitterand), 01 45 83 71 55; fax 01 45 86 57 73
■ Were it in central Paris, this "intimate" French near the Bibliothèque Nationale might be just "another classic bistro", but with an overflow of Chinese eateries in the 13th, it strikes locals as almost exotic; the "excellent cuisine" and "intimate" atmosphere earn applause, and though the prices are "shocking", regulars want to keep this lone ranger around.

Chez Janou ◑⧅⌿   15 | 17 | 15 | 31
2, rue Roger Verlomme, 3ᵉ (Chemin Vert), 01 42 72 28 41; fax 01 42 72 96 12
■ Everyone agrees that "in summer, dining [outside] on the little square is a delight" at this contemporary Provençal bistro near the Place des Vosges; some skeptics sniff "without the terrace, it's overrated" (especially given the "not very nice service"), but sympathetic souls say the "tiny kitchen turns out consistently good food" with "a Southern accent" and admire an atmosphere that's "hip without being youthfully pretentious."

Chez Jean   ▽ 16 | 12 | 13 | 44
8, rue St Lazare, 9ᵉ (Notre-Dame de Lorette), 01 48 78 62 73; fax 01 48 78 35 30
■ "A perfect Parisian bistro" surveyors sum up this New French in the 9th; both business types at noon and the mix of tourists and locals at night enjoy the "interesting" eats and the "excellent value", but the 1950s-era decor of red-velvet booths and wood paneling garners a mixed response: "beautiful" vs. "lacking warmth."

Chez Jenny ◐ S
13 | 15 | 13 | 43

*39, bd du Temple, 3ᵉ (République), 01 44 54 39 00;
fax 01 44 54 39 09*

■ Despite a drop in the Decor score, this "big, buzzy" brasserie off the Place de la République lures a constant crowd with its "fabulous setting" featuring "sculpted wood and marquetry"; although the ambiance is "better than the food", Alsatian advocates attest that "for choucroute garnie this is the place to be" – even as grumpsters gripe "the sauerkraut has lost its soul" since the acquisition by the Frères Blanc group; P.S. fair-weather Parisians proclaim the flowering patio "real nice in summer."

Chez L'Ami Jean
15 | 12 | 16 | 36

27, rue Malar, 7ᵉ (Invalides), 01 47 05 86 89

■ "Honest Southwestern cuisine and the high spirits that befit it" reign at this "wonderful" Basque bastion in the 7th; a "warm welcome" and a "convivial ambiance" make fans feel they're dining in a veritable country auberge; the market-based menu (three specials per day) and live regional music certain evenings ensure "it's always packed."

CHEZ L'AMI LOUIS ◐ S
24 | 14 | 18 | 95

32, rue du Vert-Bois, 3ᵉ (Arts et Métiers), 01 48 87 77 48

■ Pleasing politicos "from Chirac to Clinton", this classic bistro near the Place de la République fills up serious foodies ready to feed and fork out for "Pantagruelesque portions" of "French versions of meat and potatoes" (plus "copious foie gras") at "enormous prices"; as with every success story, there are carps ("too many Americans", "dingy" decor, sometimes "snobbish" service), but the majority swears this "hole-in-the-wall" is "worth the experience, at least once in a lifetime."

Chez la Vieille
19 | 15 | 17 | 50

1, rue Bailleul, 1ᵉʳ (Louvre-Rivoli), 01 42 60 15 78

■ "Don't miss this one" rave reviewers of this Classic French daytimer (open Thursdays only for dinner) at Les Halles; the generous portions of "simple and delicious" "bourgeois cuisine" encourage patrons to protract the pleasure into a "four-hour lunch", and while the decor seems "a little sad", the place maintains its "charm" by most accounts; so what if it's "a little expensive", you'll "save money by digesting – hence not eating – for the next three days."

Chez Léon
13 | 11 | 14 | 40

*32, rue Legendre, 17ᵉ (Villiers), 01 42 27 06 82;
fax 01 46 22 63 67*

◪ Old-timers may lament it's "a pale replica" of its past self, but an across-the-board rise in scores, following the arrival of a new chef, sides with those who hold this decades-old French in the 17th to be the "symbol of a true Parisian bistro", with a "very nice menu" that emphasizes escargots and such classics as *tête de veau*; Bordeaux is a strength of the wine list.

Chez Livio S
13 | 12 | 14 | 35

6, rue de Longchamp, Neuilly-sur-Seine (Pont de Neuilly), 01 46 24 81 32; fax 01 47 38 20 72

■ In between the "businessmen at noon and families at night", seems like "all Neuilly and the 16th arrondissement end up" at this "noisy", "popular" Italian "institution" that pushes pasta "in an indoor/outdoor setting"; antagonists argue it's an "overrated" "pizza factory" and even admirers admit that ambiance outweighs the "ordinary" eats, but "there's the garden" ("enclosed in winter") and a "warm welcome for regulars", and that carries the *giorno.*

Chez Maître Paul S
19 | 14 | 18 | 46

12, rue Monsieur-le-Prince, 6ᵉ (Odéon), 01 43 54 74 59; fax 01 46 34 58 33

■ "The grand tradition of the Franche-Comté" region draws everyone from literati to well-heeled locals to this Left Bank locale; the "marvelous food" – especially the "wonderful chicken dishes" cooked in wine and flecked with morels – are "a bargain given the quality"; and while opinions split on the stone-walled and wood-beamed decor ("clean and sparkling" vs. "a little much"), "amiable service" and "cozy ambiance" cause jurists to judge this Jura specialist favorably.

Chez Marcel
– | – | – | M

3, rue Stanislas, 6ᵉ (Notre-Dame-des-Champs), 01 45 48 29 94

Near Montparnasse, this classic "bistro for buddies" is "one of those places they don't make anymore", offering a "marvelous welcome", "traditional Lyonnais" "food that's not expensive" and "old-fashioned decor"; "at night it gets packed and noisy", so some fans find "lunch is our favorite."

Chez Marianne S
12 | 11 | 10 | 24

2, rue des Hospitalières St-Gervais, 4ᵉ (St-Paul), 01 42 72 18 86; fax 01 42 78 75 26

■ "The lines might discourage you", but this is "a very good Marais address for Eastern European–Jewish cuisine"; the "laid-back" atmosphere has "lots of personality", even if the staff doesn't ("service is deplorable"); still, it's such "an excellent value" that you better "think of reserving."

Chez Michel ●
22 | 13 | 18 | 41

10, rue de Belzunce, 10ᵉ (Gare du Nord/Poissonière), 01 44 53 06 20; fax 01 44 53 51 31

■ "Offbeat" and "original" is how a "stylish crowd" sums up this New French that boasts "sophisticated yet traditional cuisine" from Brittany; chef Thierry Breton "succeeds in marveling diners" with "exceptional" fare proffered by "caring servers"; near the Gare du Nord, it may "not be easy to find" (so take your map) but "it's definitely worth it."

Chez Nenesse
▽ 15 | 12 | 16 | 34

*17, rue de Saintonge, 3ᵉ (Filles du Calvaire/République),
01 42 78 46 49; fax 01 42 78 45 51*

▣ Enthusiasts encourage this Classic French "pearl" in the Marais, saying "it deserves better recognition" for its "original recipes" and "nice" welcome, while dissenters deem the "average quality" food "disappointing" and the setting "banal"; "too bad, because it's a good value."

Chez Ngo ◑⑤
18 | 17 | 14 | 42

*70, rue de Longchamp, 16ᵉ (Trocadéro), 01 47 04 53 20;
fax 01 47 27 81 06*

▣ It's in the 16th, but this "Chinese-Thai is off the well-beaten path" of standard Asian fare, thanks to its "very good" cuisine served in an "original" and "sublime" setting (the "private salons are much appreciated"); prices are rather "luxurious" too, but the lunch prix fixe is "a real deal."

Chez Omar ◑⑤⇆
16 | 11 | 14 | 29

*47, rue de Bretagne, 3ᵉ (Arts et Métiers/République),
01 42 72 36 26*

▣ Sit back and roll with the "joyful jostle" at this "hip" North African, a sort of "couscous-joint-meets-brasserie" presided over by "glib owner" Omar; sure, it's "noisy and crowded", but since it's one of the "Marais' cheaper options", diners "go back again and again."

Chez Paul ◑⑤
16 | 14 | 15 | 32

*22, rue Butte-aux-Cailles, 13ᵉ (Corvisart/Place d'Italie),
01 45 89 22 11*

▣ "The only good restaurant in Butte-aux-Cailles" declare devotees of this small Traditional French bistro in the 13th, which attracts a "young crowd", often after-theater, with hearty helpings of such classics as pot-au-feu and chocolate marquise with an orange coulis; reservations are highly recommended, as the vaguely art deco space fills up fast; N.B. no relation to the same-named place in the 11th.

Chez Paul ◑⑤
16 | 14 | 15 | 32

*13, rue de Charonne, 11ᵉ (Bastille/Ledru-Rollin),
01 47 00 34 57; fax 01 48 07 02 00*

▣ This "bustling" century-old establishment "looks, tastes and acts like a real French bistro", which is to say, it's "smoky, noisy but festive" – so much so, it's "quasi-impossible to get in"; snobs scoff it's "amusing for the tourists", but most find it's "great for a late, post–Opéra Bastille supper" of steak *au poivre* and "copious" amounts of other traditional eats at "reasonable prices."

Chez Pauline
20 | 17 | 18 | 60

5, rue Villedo, 1ᵉʳ (Pyramides), 01 42 96 20 70; fax 01 49 27 99 89
▣ "A marvelous class act" applaud audiences of this "very traditional" French bistro at an "exquisite location"

in the 1st near the Palais Royal; "consistently delicious food", "remarkable service" and the somewhat sumptuous mirrored decor of red banquettes and wood paneling make this "'Chez' better than most"; skeptics sniff it's a bit "stiff" and "too expensive", but the majority rules "it meets all expectations."

Chez Prune ⑤   10 | 13 | 13 | 25
*36, rue Beaurepaire, 10ᵉ (République), 01 42 41 30 47;
fax 01 42 00 32 28*
■ "Life is sweet" at this "hip" place along the Platane tree-lined Canal Saint-Martin, where "pleasant" "little plates" (maybe "too little") of International eats suit the young trendies who take over the terrace on warm days; sure it's "loud", but the ambiance is "so laid-back, so good, that you'll feel right at home."

Chez René   18 | 14 | 18 | 44
14, bd St-Germain, 5ᵉ (Maubert-Mutualité), 01 43 54 30 23
■ "You change eras" when you walk into this Saint-Germain spot, a traditionalist in its "nice old-fashioned service" (get ready to "be doted on"), "pretty decor" ("nothing ever alters but the paint job") and menu, which constitutes "the best Lyonnaise cooking north of Lyon" (think coq au vin and boeuf bourguignon); "despite the presence of a celeb or two", the atmosphere is "unpretentious"; small wonder that reviewer after reviewer calls it "my favorite bistro."

Chez Savy   ▽ 17 | 13 | 19 | 50
*23, rue Bayard, 8ᵉ (Franklin D. Roosevelt), 01 47 23 46 98;
fax 01 47 23 46 98*
◪ "A rare find in the 8th", this "pleasant neighborhood bistro" puts an Auvergnat twist on such "good, solid" fare as the roasted shoulder of lamb, which washes down well with a bottle of Morgon; but critics contend you'll need "a rich wallet" for such "rich cuisine" – "it's really too expensive for what it is."

Chez Toutoune ⑤   16 | 14 | 14 | 45
*5, rue Pontoise, 5ᵉ (Maubert-Mutualité), 01 43 26 56 81;
fax 01 40 46 80 34*
■ In the 5th, this long-running Left Banker is "warm and homey" like the first course of "great soup" served to all diners; the Traditional French cooking with a Southern slant is "simple but good", and with flowered tablecloths and "paintings on the walls", the decor creates "a vacation atmosphere"; some lament the "limited menu choice", but most agree life here "is very pleasant."

Chez Vincent   22 | 10 | 19 | 40
*5, rue du Tunnel, 19ᵉ (Botzaris/Buttes-Chaumont),
01 42 02 22 45*
■ A location in the "faraway 19th" arrondissement and a dining room that's "noisy and crowded" don't discourage

disciples of this "excellent" establishment, "*the* Italian restaurant to know in Paris"; a clientele that's "*so* bobo" (the French equivalent of 'yuppie') and a sprinkling of "stars" gather nightly for a "tasting menu that's first-rate" and – given that "you leave really full" – a "good value" as well.

Chez Vong 19 | 18 | 17 | 52

10, rue de la Grande Truanderie, 1ᵉʳ (Etienne-Marcel), 01 40 26 09 36; fax 01 42 33 38 15
■ "Welcoming and exotic", this "classy" Chinese in Les Halles offers "excellent traditional cooking" against the backdrop of a Buddha-bedecked, "magnificent decor"; try the Peking duck, but be prepared to pay for your pleasure.

Chiberta 21 | 18 | 20 | 84

3, rue Arsène Houssaye, 8ᵉ (Charles de Gaulle-Etoile/ George V), 01 53 53 42 00; fax 01 45 62 85 08
■ This "elegant" "expense-account restaurant" is "perfect for a business lunch", not only because it offers "very refined", "inventive" Contemporary French cuisine, but also because "nothing is too much trouble" for the staff and "the cushy atmosphere is so relaxing"; "the best [off] the Champs-Elysées", "it's not exactly cheap, but it's a sure value"; N.B. a renovation post-*Survey* may outdate the Decor score.

Chicago Pizza Pie Factory ●⑤ 8 | 10 | 9 | 26

5, rue de Berri, 8ᵉ (George V), 01 45 62 50 23; fax 05 45 63 87 56
☑ "Industrial pizza" is the specialty at this "very American", "very noisy" "hanger" in the 8th; because it's "inexpensive", "portions are Pantagruelian" and service is "smiling" (if not always efficient), it's "perfect for family dining" – even if, to quote one surveyor, "my 8-year-old daughter loves it, my wife and I don't."

Chieng Mai ●⑤ 19 | 9 | 12 | 33

12, rue Frédéric Sauton, 5ᵉ (Maubert-Mutualité), 01 43 25 45 45
■ The food's "spicier than usual" at this "terrific Thai" just off Maubert-Mutualité that's widely appreciated for its "authentic" cooking, even if many find the decor "a little ugly" and the service "mediocre" ("it's rapid at the beginning and then becomes very slow"); "go at least once for a change of scene."

Chien qui Fume (Au) ●⑤ 15 | 16 | 14 | 41

33, rue du Pont-Neuf, 1ᵉʳ (Châtelet-Les Halles), 01 42 36 07 42; fax 01 42 36 36 85
■ "A happy exception" in Les Halles, this "reliable", "traditional brasserie" is "a multi-room establishment filled with paintings of sophisticated dogs smoking pipes, which gives it a warm, clubby atmosphere amidst gleaming brass and white table linens"; the kitchen serves up "superb pig's

feet" and other "decent" "classics", including what some deem "the best oyster bar" in town.

CHINA CLUB ◗S
12 | 23 | 13 | 41

50, rue de Charenton, 12ᵉ (Bastille/Ledru-Rollin), 01 43 43 82 02; fax 01 43 43 79 85

◪ While everyone loves the "exceptional atmosphere" and "superb decor" of this Bastille hot spot – a mix of "colonial" and "opium den" that "recalls China during the '20s" – critics club the "uninteresting" cuisine ("good Chinese for those who don't normally like Chinese"); "it's best to come here just for a drink" at the "magnificent bar" and maybe a cigar "in front of the fireplace in the *fumoir*"; add in some "good music" and you've got "a perfect romantic rendezvous."

China Town Olympiades ◗S
– | – | – | I

44, av d'Ivry, 13ᵉ (Porte d'Ivry), 01 45 84 72 21; fax 01 45 84 74 52

"One of the bastions of Chinatown", this 400-seat Asian is "amusing if you know how to order right" among the "huge choice" of dishes (special mention: the "marvelous fish"); but foes find the "cuisine variable – the best and the worst" at once – and deem the "enormous" environs "rather noisy" as well.

Christine (Le) ◗
∇ 16 | 17 | 18 | 42

1, rue Christine, 6ᵉ (Odéon/St-Michel), 01 40 51 71 64; fax 01 42 18 04 39

◼ "Just lovely" everyone exclaims about this "small and charming" spot set in a pretty space with exposed stone walls and views over a courtyard garden in Saint-Germain; the "always gracious personnel" serve "consistently good" Classic French staples like "excellent rack of lamb with smoking thyme", accompanied by a "superior wine list"; all told, a "terrific neighborhood restaurant" – and a "very good value" as well.

Cigale (La)
20 | 14 | 18 | 37

11 bis, rue Chomel, 7ᵉ (Sèvres-Babylone), 01 45 48 87 87; fax 01 45 48 87 87

◼ The "excellent variety of soufflés" ("the best in town – maybe even the best ever") swells the ranks of the "exotic 7th arrondissement" crowd at this "good little" stop near the Bon Marché department store; "too bad" "the tables are so tightly spaced", but what really matters here is that "the soufflés never fall", and there's "friendly service" too.

CINQ (LE) S
26 | 27 | 26 | 125

Four Seasons George V, 31, av George V, 8ᵉ (George V), 01 49 52 71 54; fax 01 49 52 71 81

◼ For an "outstanding", "over-the-top" experience, come to this "sumptuous", "beautiful room (especially the flowers)" with "high ceilings and gilt" at the George V; "the pleasure for the eyes is equaled by pleasure for the palate", since

Philippe Legendre, "formerly of Taillevent", "is a great chef" who provides "amazing meals"; "impeccable, unpretentious service" further ensures this New French is "the perfect place to seduce an important client" or to treat yourself – provided you can "throw financial caution to the wind."

59 Poincaré   18 | 19 | 18 | 76

Hôtel Le Parc, 59, av Raymond Poincaré, 16ᵉ (Boissière/Trocadéro), 01 47 27 59 59; fax 01 47 27 59 00
◪ Occupying the elegant art nouveau mansion near the Place Victor Hugo that once housed Alain Ducasse (who consults here), this New French with a modish "modern decor" offers an "interesting idea" – "beef or lobster prepared in a variety of different ways"; while fans find it "chic but fun", this Gallic take on surf 'n' turf makes doubters declare there's "too much concept" and too little "soul" – "next to the beautiful vegetables in the showcase, you're just another one" – and it's "too expensive" to boot.

Clémentine   ▽ 16 | 12 | 15 | 36

5, rue St-Marc, 2ᵉ (Bourse/Grands Boulevards), 01 40 41 05 65; fax 01 45 08 08 77
◼ With a big zinc bar and a pattern of ivy and clementines stenciled on the walls, this cozy little Classic French bistro near the Bourse is popular at noon with financial types who appreciate "a really good buy"; it's quieter in the evenings, when locals come to try the "inventive, varied and light cooking", including chicken breast with goat cheese.

Cloche des Halles (La) ⊘   14 | 11 | 12 | 25

28, rue Coquillière, 1ᵉʳ (Les Halles/Louvre-Rivoli), 01 42 36 93 89
◼ "More French than the Eiffel Tower" rave reviewers about this "atmospheric" bar à vins named after the bell that once rang the opening and closing hours of Les Halles; a "friendly welcome and nice service" make it easy to enjoy "the best ham roasted on the bone in Paris", "well-chosen wines" and "yummy fruit tarts, made in-house", for gentle prices.

Cloche d'Or (La) ◕⑤   – | – | – | M

3, rue Mansart, 9ᵉ (Blanche/Pigalle), 01 48 74 48 88; fax 01 40 16 40 99
Parisians must be turning in earlier, since very few know this long-running "late-night" bistro in the 9th; those who do come for "solid Classic French favorites", like the signature rack of lamb – even if they can sometimes be "uneven" – and appreciate a lively clientele of showbiz and media types, amid an old-fashioned atmosphere created by white tablecloths and vest-wearing waiters (a good show in itself).

Clos des Gourmets (Le)   20 | 11 | 15 | 49

16, av Rapp, 7ᵉ (Alma-Marceau/Ecole-Militaire), 01 45 51 75 61; fax 01 47 05 74 20
◪ If chef Arnaud Pitrois' Contemporary French cooking has myriad admirers – "truly sensuous", "amazing flavors" –

many also find "the service has a hard time keeping up" (and in fact has fallen in the ratings) in the "cramped" and "tempestuous" dining room; still, it's "the best buy in the 7th", and "the terrace is pleasant" during the summer.

Closerie des Lilas (La) ◑ⓢ 　　15 | 19 | 15 | 57

171, bd du Montparnasse, 6ᵉ (Raspail/Vavin), 01 40 51 34 50; fax 01 43 29 99 94

☑ Steeped in literary legend, this Montparnasse "classic" is especially "charming in the spring" and summer with its "lovely garden", but there's also "marvelous ambiance" in the piano bar where Hemingway slugged them back; if some snap it's a "highly hyped" "tourist trap", nostalgists loyally note the Traditional French "food's better than average"; of course, it's "expensive" ("you pay for the name"), but "the brasserie is cheaper than the restaurant."

Clos Morillons (Le) 　　　　20 | 13 | 15 | 54

50, rue des Morillons, 15ᵉ (Porte de Vanves), 01 48 28 04 37; fax 01 48 28 70 77

■ Throughout the 15th, this New French is renowned for its "inventive kitchen" that "uses spices creatively and intelligently" to produce "an out-of-the-ordinary culinary experience"; surveyors who found the surroundings "sad" will be happy to know the dining room's been refurbished (which may outdate the Decor score).

Clos Saint-Honoré (Le) ◑ 　　－ | － | － | E

3, rue St-Hyacinthe, 1ᵉʳ (Tuileries), 01 40 15 09 36; fax 01 40 15 09 56

Perhaps because it's hidden in a handsome, arched 17th-century cellar near (or should we say under?) the Tuileries, very few have yet discovered this rather confidential Classic French, which has made a name for itself with dishes like sea bass with fresh coriander; prices are steep, but service is attentive, the atmosphere's warm and there's even occasionally a small orchestra for ambiance.

Clovis ◑ 　　　　　　▽ 14 | 14 | 14 | 58

33, rue Berger, 1ᵉʳ (Châtelet-Les Halles), 01 42 33 97 07; fax 01 42 33 97 07

■ This "bistro the way we like them" dates from the days when Les Halles was the proverbial belly of Paris, and it still serves up the sturdy, "copious" old-fashioned French dishes like veal stew that made it a favorite with the market workers pictured in framed photos on the walls; if it's become a tad pricey, well, authenticity doesn't come cheap.

Clovis (Le) 　　　　　　　▽ 23 | 21 | 21 | 70

Sofitel Arc de Triomphe, 2, av Bertie Albrecht, 8ᵉ (Charles de Gaulle-Etoile/George V), 01 53 89 50 53; fax 01 53 89 50 51

■ "Imaginative, always successful cooking" and "polished, somewhat dramatic service" are winning fans for this "continuously improving" Contemporary French "in the Sofitel Arc de Triomphe"; if many specify that it's ideal "for business", perhaps because of the "space between the tables" and "the pleasantly calm atmosphere", others insist it's so "truly amazing" that it warrants a visit under any circumstances, personal or professional.

Clown Bar ●⑤⊅   15 19 16 31
114, rue Amelot, 11ᵉ (Filles-du-Calvaire), 01 43 55 87 35
■ "The unique decor" – landmarked art nouveau tiles depicting circus scenes – of this little bar à vins next door to the Cirque d'Hiver may "incite childhood dreams", but the "surprisingly good" "comfort food", including hearty bistro classics like poached eggs in bacon-wine sauce, makes it perfect "for dinner with friends during the week", especially when accompanied "so wonderfully by a glass of wine."

Coco de Mer   14 13 13 38
34, bd St-Marcel, 5ᵉ (Les Gobelins/St-Marcel), 01 47 07 06 64; fax 01 47 07 41 88
■ It's like "the Seychelles in Paris – but this food's better than what you find there!" exult enthusiasts of this "exotic" Indian Ocean–influenced outpost in the 13th, which even has a white-sand beach in front; along with "excellent [native] fish prepared in delightful ways" there are authentically "lukewarm cocktails", served by a "really pleasant", if "too slow", staff; it may well "make you want to go to the islands the next morning."

Coco et sa Maison   12 13 14 47
18, rue Bayen, 17ᵉ (Charles de Gaulle-Etoile/Ternes), 01 45 74 73 73; fax 01 45 74 73 52
◪ Run by Coco Couperie and his sister Virginie, the wife of singer Julien Clerc, this trendy Contemporary French–Med in the 17th pulls a stylish "showbiz", celebrity-studded crowd; foes fume not only is the "cooking very far from good", it's "expensive, without a soul and for outdated yuppies", but fans insist you get a "warm welcome" and "generous portions"; maybe it depends on your own degree of star quality; N.B. a recent decor change may outdate the above score.

Coconnas ⑤   16 20 16 51
2 bis, pl des Vosges, 4ᵉ (Bastille/St-Paul), 01 42 78 58 16; fax 01 42 78 16 28
◪ Proprietor Claude Terrail, who also owns the Tour d'Argent, has installed a different chef and a moderate prix fixe in this Classic French that boasts a "memorable setting in the Place des Voges" (it's under the vaulted, circular arcade); critics still carp it's "a tourist trap" and "hardly at the height of its reputation" but an across-the-board rise in ratings indicates that most surveyors approve, saying "after the change", there's now relatively "affordable excellence" in this tony part of town.

Coffee Parisien ●S
12 | 11 | 10 | 29

4, rue Princesse, 6ᵉ (Mabillon), 01 43 54 18 18;
fax 01 43 54 94 96
7, rue Gustave-Courbet, 16ᵉ (Trocadéro), 01 45 53 17 17;
fax 01 43 54 94 96

■ "Young, bourgeois types" with "portable phones" find these "cozy, trendy" "perpetually packed" Yankee-themed coffee shops in the 6th and 16th "pleasant" for their "good burgers" and "Sunday brunch with eggs Benedict" ("almost like home" sigh "those homesick U.S. expats"); the main drawback is "service with an attitude" ("so bad we can't go anymore").

Coin des Gourmets (Au) S
▽ 18 | 8 | 14 | 33

5, rue Dante, 5ᵉ (Cluny-La Sorbonne/Maubert-Mutualité),
01 43 26 12 92

■ "Delicious Cambodian cooking" and "wonderful" service pull "the locals" and the odd fashion designer or movie star to this vest-pocket-size dining room in the Latin Quarter; the decor may be "pathetic" – just a few framed prints and a vase of flowers on the bar – but it doesn't deter the accolades for a place converts call "the best Indochinese in Paris" and a good buy to boot.

Colette
12 | 15 | 12 | 35

213, rue St-Honoré, 1ᵉʳ (Tuileries), 01 55 35 33 93;
fax 01 55 35 33 99

■ "The only reason to stop here is for sustenance after intensive shopping in the trendiest boutique in Paris" fashionistas figure about this lunch option occupying a "hip, minimalist setting" in the Colette store; augmented by a "water bar" serving H_2O from all over the world, the "healthy" Italian cuisine offers "perfect food if you're a top model" but might be deemed "disappointing" by those not slated to appear on the cover of *Vogue*; still, the service is "astonishingly nice" and "it's not too expensive."

Comédiens (Les) ●
▽ 16 | 13 | 11 | 46

7, rue Blanche, 9ᵉ (Trinité), 01 40 82 95 95; fax 01 40 82 96 95

◪ If no one faults the "decent" food at this Classic French bistro near the 9th arrondissement theaters, many regret the "slow" service and judge it "too expensive", asking "have the actors ['comédiens'] been spoiled by success?"; still, the occasional presence of showbiz denizens creates a pleasantly "noisy" atmosphere amid the exposed-brick walls.

Communautés (Les)
▽ 19 | 14 | 18 | 53

CNIT, 2, pl de la Défense, Puteaux (La Défense-Grande Arche),
01 46 92 10 30; fax 01 46 92 28 16

◪ "The one and only real restaurant in La Défense" say fans of this New French fish specialist, noting that its "modern and luxurious" setting makes it "good for a business lunch" but "even better in the evening"; however, the unimpressed sniff it's "rather expensive for the average food quality";

N.B. closed for renovation at press time, it was scheduled to re-open in May 2003.

Comptoir du Saumon
10 | 8 | 9 | 31

60, rue François Miron, 4ᵉ (St-Paul), 01 42 77 23 08; fax 01 42 77 44 75
61, rue Pierre Charron, 8ᵉ (Franklin D. Roosevelt/George V), 01 45 61 25 14; fax 01 45 63 47 04
116, rue de la Convention, 15ᵉ (Boucicaut), 01 45 54 31 16; fax 01 45 54 49 68
3, av de Villiers, 17ᵉ (Villiers), 01 40 53 89 00; fax 01 40 53 89 89
☑ If some think this chain of Scandinavian specialists in smoked fish and caviar offers "a good compromise for a light lunch" or dinner ("especially during the all-you-can-eat promotions"), skeptics shrug "except for the salmon, avoid it" – the service is often "manic-depressive", and the atmosphere is as "glacial" as a refrigerated counter.

Comptoir Paris-Marrakech ●🅂 ▽
11 | 17 | 8 | 31

37, rue Berger, 1ᵉʳ (Les Halles/Louvre-Rivoli), 01 40 26 26 66; fax 01 42 21 44 24
■ At this Moroccan in Les Halles (sister to an eatery in Marrakesh), "great atmosphere and attractive decor" combine with "healthy and inventive" North African fare to provide an "agreeable" "change of scene"; some carp about the "slow service" of "miniscule portions."

COMTE DE GASCOGNE (AU)
23 | 20 | 20 | 84

89, av Jean-Baptiste Clément, Boulogne-Billancourt (Pont-de-St-Cloud), 01 46 03 47 27; fax 01 46 04 55 70
■ An "expensive" but "exceptional restaurant" is the consensus on this "oasis of greenery", a "lovely courtyard" of palm trees and "murmuring fountains" in suburban Boulogne; famed for its "unforgettable tasting menu" and "sublime foie gras", this New French comes across as "cozy and romantic" with "refined service" that's pretty "perfect" if a bit "pretentious"; one would say it "merits its reputation" – except it "isn't well-known enough!"

Congrès (Le) ●🅂
13 | 10 | 12 | 43

80, av de la Grande-Armée, 17ᵉ (Porte Maillot), 01 45 74 17 24; fax 01 45 72 39 80
☑ Conveniently located at the Porte Maillot, this "honest brasserie" is "amazingly consistent" claims its "habitual clientele", especially for the "extremely fresh shellfish"; but adversaries attest that given the "mediocre" meals, vintage '70s decor with "too small and tightly spaced" tables and often "inefficient service", being "open all night is its main advantage."

Conti
19 | 14 | 16 | 64

72, rue Lauriston, 16ᵉ (Boissière), 01 47 27 74 67; fax 01 47 27 37 66
■ "Another 16th arrondissement standby", this "excellent Italian" ("the best Italian handled by a Frenchman", namely

ex Orient-Express chef Michel Ranvier) offers "original" pastas served by a "pleasant staff"; some feel the setting "puts you at ease", but for others, it's a little too restful, reminding them of "a retirement home."

Contre-Allée (La) **S** | 15 | 13 | 15 | 41 |
83, av Denfert-Rochereau, 14ᵉ (Denfert-Rochereau), 01 43 54 99 86; fax 01 43 25 05 28
■ The constantly "changing menu is always wonderful" (not to mention "very good value for the money") at this Contemporary French in a "restaurant-deprived section" of the 14th; "service that's attentive and efficient" augments the "imaginative cooking in an appealingly calm ambiance", but what really pulls in the stylish, young Montparnasse crowds is "the terrace, perfect on summer evenings."

Copenhague | 18 | 15 | 16 | 63 |
142, av des Champs-Elysées, 8ᵉ (Charles de Gaulle-Etoile/George V), 01 44 13 89 44; fax 01 42 25 83 10
■ This Nordic "institution" has had a complete renovation, so the '70s-vintage Slavic decor that many found "icy" now sports red-leather chairs, floor-to-ceiling windows and an interior garden "that makes you feel miles away from the Champs-Elysées"; fans of the "fabulous fish" and other "good Danish food" will be glad to hear that the menu remains basically the same, as does the "fine" if "slightly frosty service"; alas, it's "rather expensive."

Coq de la Maison Blanche (Le) | 18 | 13 | 17 | 54 |
37, bd Jean Jaurès, Saint-Ouen (Mairie de St-Ouen), 01 40 11 01 23
■ "One has the impression of being in a '50s film" (the interior dates from that era) at this Classic French, a "good business restaurant" in suburban Saint-Ouen; the "excellent bourgeois cooking" (house specialty: coq au vin) is dished out by "friendly servers"; although some say "it's the boss who makes this *maison*", others gripe he "only recognizes the regulars", leaving them to contemplate the faded decor.

Corte (La) | – | – | – | E |
320, rue St-Honoré, 1ᵉʳ (Tuileries), 01 42 60 45 27
Though few know this "very good and authentic Italian" near the Tuileries, it's vaunted by its regulars, who have followed the chef's Neapolitan creations from Da Mimmo; compared with that trendy spot, the setting here is as refined as the clientele, a mix of business types and well-heeled locals who appreciate the relaxing atmosphere and Sicilian and Tuscan wine list – if not always the stiff prices.

Cosi **S** ⊘ | 15 | 11 | 12 | 19 |
54, rue de Seine, 6ᵉ (Odéon/St-Germain-des-Prés), 01 46 33 35 36; fax 01 46 33 48 40
■ "The perfect stop during a stroll through Saint-Germain" supporters synopsize this "original, pleasant" *sandwicherie/*

wine bar a few steps from the Odéon; "the sandwiches are large, fresh and good" and the "musical ambiance" – the owner's an opera buff – "aids the digestion"; though "very casual", the setting's enhanced by the "awkward but pleasant English-speaking waitresses."

Cosi (Le)

– | – | – | M

9, rue Cujas, 5ᵉ (Cluny-La Sorbonne/Luxembourg), 01 43 29 20 20

On a quiet street behind the Sorbonne, this Corsican serves hearty portions of the Mediterranean island's hearty food to an international crowd that's also garnished with students and professors; sweet-tempered servers operate within a setting decorated with warm Pompeian red walls and the same charming art deco lighting fixtures which have been in place since the '30s, when the site housed the legendary Chez Pento bistro.

COSTES ●⬛S

13 | 23 | 12 | 56

Hôtel Costes, 239, rue St-Honoré, 1ᵉʳ (Concorde), 01 42 44 50 25; fax 01 42 44 50 01

⬛ This "watering hole for the chic" in the 1st elicits extreme opinions: most "feel absolutely wonderful" about the "tented dining room" whose "subtle lighting and fantastic music make" this "the sexiest restaurant in Paris"; but while friends find the Classic French–International fare "often original" and "want to take some of the cute staff home", foes fume "the food's too cool for its own good", deem the service almost "painful" and utter the fatal words "beginning to be a has-been."

Cottage Marcadet (Le)

– | – | – | E

151 bis, rue Marcadet, 18ᵉ (Lamarck-Caulaincourt), 01 42 57 71 22

Only a handful of surveyors know this cozy cottage, perhaps because it's "a little out of the way" in the 18th arrondissement, but those who do call it "one of our favorite restaurants in Paris", thanks to such "superb" New French specialties as lobster fricassee, as well as "wonderful times with the owner"; even if it falls into pricey territory for most (despite several reasonable prix fixes), regulars recommend it as "good value for the money."

Coude Fou (Le) ●⬛S

15 | 14 | 15 | 29

12, rue du Bourg-Tibourg, 4ᵉ (Hôtel-de-Ville), 01 42 77 15 16; fax 01 48 04 08 98

⬛ It would "be difficult to make things any cozier" at this "nice and relaxed" beamed bistro tucked away in the Marais; maybe the "menu is always the same", but fans don't mind when the Contemporary French cooking is so "very good" and supplemented by "efficient service"; some go so far as to say "it's one of the rare acceptable restaurants in this neighborhood", which may explain why it's "always full."

Cou de la Girafe (Le) ◑ | 12 | 11 | 11 | 40 |

*7, rue Paul Baudry, 8ᵉ (Franklin D. Roosevelt/
St-Philippe-du-Roule), 01 43 59 47 28; fax 01 42 25 06 62*

☑ A "stylish, young clientele" likes to do "dinner with friends" at this fashionable address just behind the Champs-Elysées, citing the "sophisticated cuisine" and "sensual service" from "charming waitresses"; critics carp the Classic French–International menu's "hardly memorable", resulting in an "expensive and disappointing" evening; still, many go for the "subtly lit, lively atmosphere" (just "don't forget your earplugs").

Coupe-Chou (Le) ◑ 🅂 | 16 | 22 | 16 | 49 |

9, rue de Lanneau, 5ᵉ (Maubert-Mutualité), 01 46 33 68 69; fax 01 43 25 94 15

■ The "enchanting interior" at this old house in the Latin Quarter, blessed with stone walls and a big fireplace ("especially great in cold weather"), is more delicious than either the "decent", "slightly expensive" "Classic" French food or the service that can range from "gracious" to "indifferent"; despite its being "a bit on the tourist beat", the "very romantic and charming" atmosphere makes it "the ideal place to propose."

COUPOLE (LA) ◑ 🅂 | 14 | 20 | 14 | 46 |

102, bd du Montparnasse, 14ᵉ (Vavin), 01 43 20 14 20; fax 01 43 35 46 14

☑ If there's any consensus on this "mythic" brasserie in Montparnasse with an "art deco extraordinaire" decor, it might be "go for the atmosphere, not the food"; otherwise, reviewers fall into two herds – those who chide it as a "noisy" factory "living on a faded reputation" and "sloppy" staffers, and loyalists who say it remains a "lively, fun place" with "service that's prompt and gracious despite the crowds"; it's "worth a detour" at least once, if only for "champagne and oysters at midnight."

Cour de Rohan (La) 🅂 ▽ | 14 | 17 | 14 | 34 |

59-61, rue St-André-des-Arts, 6ᵉ (Odéon), 01 43 25 79 67

■ "The cakes" (nearly 30 varieties), "the best soft-boiled eggs in the world" and the "intimate place" make this "nice little" tea salon on a pedestrian-only lane near the Odéon "a delicious place"; it's "super for lunch and Sunday brunch", though – depending on one's budget – the prices can range from "low" to "expensive."

Crêperie de Josselin (La) ◑ 🅂 ⌿ | 17 | 10 | 14 | 22 |

*67, rue du Montparnasse, 14ᵉ (Edgar Quinet/
Montparnasse-Bienvenüe), 01 43 20 93 50*

■ Bare-bones decor and occasional "waits at the door" don't stop anyone from flocking to this Montparnasse "institution" for "the best crêpes in Paris", which are not only "delicious" but "enormous"; once seated, the service is also "quick" and "efficient", making this "a wonderful place for a simple meal", but try to come off-hours to avoid the dinner or "lunch crowds."

Crus de Bourgogne (Aux) `12` `10` `12` `40`
3, rue Bachaumont, 2ᵉ (Les Halles/Sentier), 01 42 33 48 24; fax 01 40 28 66 41

🔲 Surveyors split on this 71-year-old vet near Les Halles: "lobster lovers" call it a "terrific traditional bistro" for its reasonably priced "quality" crustaceans and find the tiled-and-red-checked-tablecloth setting "full of charm"; but sliding scores side with the skeptics, who snap that the French menu and the decor "need to be dusted off" and the "irregular service" could use straightening out.

Dagorno ◐🆂 `16` `12` `12` `46`
190, av Jean Jaurès, 19ᵉ (Porte de Pantin), 01 40 40 09 39; fax 01 48 03 17 23

⬛ A relic of the day when the slaughterhouses of Paris were located in Villette, this rather off-the-beaten-path 19th-century brasserie remains a reliable "good buy" to its loyal crowd of carnivores with "tasty" Classic French and Southwestern fare; though the decor has been redone, no one pays much attention to it, preferring instead to banter with the friendly, if leisurely, waiters.

Dalloyau `18` `14` `15` `41`
5, bd Beaumarchais, 4ᵉ (Bastille), 01 48 87 89 88; fax 01 48 87 73 70 🆂
2, pl Edmond Rostand, 6ᵉ (Cluny-La Sorbonne/Odéon), 01 43 29 31 10; fax 01 43 26 25 72 🆂
63, rue de Grenelle, 7ᵉ (Rue du Bac), 01 45 49 95 30; fax 01 42 84 04 75 🆂
101, rue du Faubourg-St-Honoré, 8ᵉ (Miromesnil/ St-Philippe-du-Roule), 01 42 99 90 00; fax 01 45 63 82 92 🆂
Galeries Lafayette, 48-52, bd Haussmann, 9ᵉ (Opéra), 01 53 20 05 00; fax 01 53 20 02 21
69, rue de la Convention, 15ᵉ (Boucicaut), 01 45 77 84 27; fax 01 45 75 27 99 🆂
65-67, av J.B. Clément, Boulogne-Billancourt (Boulogne-Jean Jaurès), 01 46 05 06 78; fax 01 46 03 90 30 🆂

⬛ "Perfect at teatime", this old-fashioned and well-mannered string of tea salons gets high marks for what's possibly "the best pastry in Paris" ("sweets lovers and chocoholics – this is your place"), as well as "great quiches" and salads; "the take-away box lunches are also terrific"; yes, they're "extremely expensive", but that doesn't seem to stop folks from "wanting to eat the entire menu."

Dame Tartine 🆂 `9` `11` `10` `20`
2, rue Brisemiche, 4ᵉ (Hôtel-de-Ville), 01 42 77 32 22; fax 01 42 77 32 22
59, rue de Lyon, 12ᵉ (Bastille), 01 44 68 96 95; fax 01 44 68 95 50

🔲 These two sandwich shops in the 4th and the 12th offer open-face *tartines*, which make them convenient "for a quick bite"; critics scold "bizarre combinations" of ingredients on dishes that are often "skimpy and dried out" ("you're better off having a sandwich at home"); still, "it's a decent alternative to McDonald's when you're broke", and it's pleasant to overlook the "fountain next to the Centre Pompidou" if you frequent that branch.

Da Mimmo ◑   16 | 8 | 13 | 41
39, bd de Magenta, 10ᵉ (Jacques Bonsergent/Gare de l'Est), 01 42 06 44 47
☑ "Typical trattoria spirit" guides this Neapolitan near the Gare de l'Est say score-supported surveyors who salivate over the "delicious dishes" and Tuscan wine list; but it's a big "nullissimo" to naysayers who find the "dried-out pizzas" "very disappointing"; at least everyone agrees about the "excessive prices" and decor that resembles "that of a lousy pizzeria" ("the seat covers could use recovering").

Daru (Le)   14 | 10 | 15 | 54
19, rue Daru, 8ᵉ (Courcelles), 01 42 27 23 60; fax 01 47 54 08 14
☑ "The place to bring a melancholy Slav" says one habitué of this "discreet Russian" restaurant behind the Russian Orthodox Church in the 8th, the idea presumably being to cheer him up with "salmon and caviar" and other "quality" dishes; but while the "atmosphere's pleasant and the service is good", some think "it was better under the former owner"; certainly it's "much too expensive" now.

Dauphin (Le) 🅂   16 | 13 | 12 | 45
167, rue St-Honoré, 1ᵉʳ (Palais Royal-Musée du Louvre), 01 42 60 40 11; fax 01 42 60 01 18
■ Chef/co-owners Didier Oudill and Edgar Duhr of Biarritz's celebrated Café de Paris helm this Classic French offering "unbeatable", "inventive" Southwestern cuisine just across the street from the Comédie Française; the "simple" dining room with a few art deco touches pleases most, as does "the good value for the money"; however, as a slide in the score suggests, service can be "inconsistent."

Davé ◑🅂   15 | 13 | 16 | 45
12, rue de Richelieu, 1ᵉʳ (Palais Royal), 01 42 61 49 48
☑ "Models go" to this pricey, clubby Chinese that, after years on the quiet Rue Saint-Roch, now occupies the busy Rue de Richelieu; if the fashion-crowd following finds the food "very good", non-runway types warn "if you know the owner it's great – otherwise, beware."

D'Chez Eux   17 | 14 | 18 | 59
2, av Lowendal, 7ᵉ (Ecole-Militaire), 01 47 05 52 55; fax 01 45 55 87 79
■ "Skip lunch" if you plan to dine at this traditional bistro in the 7th arrondissement turning out huge portions of "excellent" Southwestern eats ("if you leave hungry, you

have an eating disorder"), "paraded by a helpful staff"; the "*auberge* ambiance" with red-and-white-checked tablecloths adds "authenticity" to this "exceptional", if "slightly expensive", foray into French "regional specialties."

Dédicace Café (Le) 🇸   – | – | – | E

7, rue St-Benoît, 6ᵉ (Mabillon/St-Germain-des-Prés), 01 42 61 12 70; fax 01 42 61 22 04
This newcomer has transformed the space once occupied by the brasserie Le Muniche using a literary theme, with banners of book dedications fluttering from the ceiling and famous quotations framed on the walls; editors as well as local shopkeepers, tourists and fashion types appreciate the cozy atmosphere and fish-oriented New French fare by chef Francisco Merino (ex Bristol), who's overseen by Philippe Groult of L'Amphyclès.

De La Garde   – | – | – | M

83, av de Ségur, 15ᵉ (Ségur), 01 40 65 99 10
Occupying the premises of a former butcher's shop in the 15th, this new Traditional French bistro is named after chef-owner Yohann Marraccini's (ex Arpège) home village in the central Auvergne region; the place offers reasonably priced prix-fixes to a diverse but contented crowd of locals who appreciate the excellent quality of the produce, organic beef and veal and free-range chicken.

Délices d'Aphrodite (Les) ◗   19 | 12 | 14 | 34

4, rue de Candolle, 5ᵉ (Censier-Daubenton), 01 43 31 40 39; fax 01 43 36 13 08
■ Run by the Mavrommatis brothers, who also own the pricier, dressier Mavrommatis a few doors down, this "friendly" eatery is "more laid-back than its sister"; but its "very good Greek" fare valiantly defends Hellenic culinary tradition, and in a part of the Latin Quarter overrun with mediocre, tourist-trap "rip-offs", "it's a very good buy"; furthermore, it makes you "feel like you're there."

Délices de Szechuen 🇸   17 | 12 | 14 | 39

40, av Duquesne, 7ᵉ (St-François-Xavier), 01 43 06 22 55
■ "Slightly pricey" but greatly appreciated ("my favorite Chinese in Paris"), this "7th arrondissement classic attracts a very stylish clientele" for its "deliciously spicy" Szechuan fare (unlike the timid seasoning of many of the city's Asians); a "lovely", "calm" summer terrace highlights an atmosphere that's "peaceful", despite "unsmiling" service.

Dell Orto ◗   – | – | – | M

45, rue St-Georges, 9ᵉ (St-Georges), 01 48 78 40 30
Pass through the heavy velvet drapes in the doorway of this corner shopfront Italian and you'll find yourself in the attitude-heavy preserve of the trendy young things who've been gradually turning the 9th into one of the most discreetly stylish parts of town; originally from Milan, the young chef-

owner previously cooked at Fellini and Paolo Petrini before setting up shop here.

Dessirier ● S
17 | 12 | 14 | 64

9, pl du Maréchal Juin, 17ᵉ (Pereire), 01 42 27 82 14; fax 01 47 66 82 07

☑ A mixed catch of comments characterizes this "brasserie de luxe" on the Place Pereire: advocates applaud the "nicely prepared", "superb fish and shellfish", while opponents insist the "dishes lack muscle"; views on the service vary from "efficient" to "awful", but all agree "you pay too much for the Michel Rostang label" (the chef took over three years ago); P.S. (and S.O.S.) from non-smokers: this place is "like eating in an ashtray."

Deux Abeilles (Les)
15 | 13 | 14 | 28

189, rue de l'Université, 7ᵉ (Alma-Marceau), 01 45 55 64 04

■ The "cozy" atmosphere and "wholesome, honest" food at this "cute", well-mannered and well-heeled tearoom near the Alma make this Gallic version of the "old-time Schraffts" perfect for "lunch with your girlfriends"; "the apple crumble is to die for" and the "cakes are excellent" too; a few find the "atmosphere sad" and the management "crabby" – but "you always return" anyway.

Deux Canards (Aux)
▽ 18 | 14 | 19 | 44

8, rue du Faubourg-Poissonnière, 10ᵉ (Bonne Nouvelle), 01 47 70 03 23; fax 01 47 70 18 85

■ On the Grands Boulevards in the 10th, this rustic spot is "the best place in Paris to take foreigners, since the boss puts on such a show" explaining the menu; "amusing owner" aside, the Classic French "food's very good", with specialties like duck à l'orange and crêpes with chocolate sauce; late hours on weekends make it ideal after a movie at the landmarked art deco Rex cinema nearby.

DeVèz (Le) ● S
– | – | – | M

5, pl de l'Alma, 8ᵉ (Alma-Marceau), 01 53 67 97 53; fax 01 47 23 09 48

Though they dis the Brits as 'beefeaters', the French have always loved their red meat, too, as evidenced by this new steakhouse that's become an instant hit with the media, ad and fashion people who work in the fashionable 8th; the menu stars Aubrac beef from the Auvergne served several ways in a slick, minimalist and masculine setting – suede-covered stools at a bare wooden table d'hôte and open wine racks.

Diable des Lombards (Au) ● S
▽ 10 | 10 | 11 | 25

64, rue des Lombards, 1ᵉʳ (Châtelet-Les Halles), 01 42 33 81 84; fax 01 42 33 28 22

☑ It's "always the best place for Sunday brunch, and what's more, the prix fixes are among the cheapest in town" at this U.S.-inspired spot in Les Halles; "nice service", "a large terrace" and the "good atmosphere" created by a young crowd (including many gays) are other attributes cited by converts; but beyond brunch, the "so-called American food" doesn't generate a lot of enthusiasm – "cholesterol paradise" huff the health-conscious.

Diamantaires (Les) ●⑤   ▽ 16 | 10 | 18 | 41
60, rue La Fayette, 9ᵉ (Cadet/Le Peletier), 01 47 70 78 14; fax 01 44 83 02 73

■ Though it's pushing 75 years, few know this Armenian-Greek in the 9th; those who do say it offers "affordable, quality" eats and advise "drinking ouzo with your meal"; if no one pays much attention to the generically Middle Eastern decor, it could be because they're distracted by the live music and the lively atmosphere, provided by members of Paris' substantial Franco-Armenian community, for whom this functions as an unofficial clubhouse.

DIVELLEC (LE)   23 | 17 | 20 | 104
107, rue de l'Université, 7ᵉ (Invalides), 01 45 51 91 96; fax 01 45 51 31 75

☑ If "sublime turbot" and "warm lobster and foie gras that absolutely melts in your mouth" are your thing, head for this "mecca for seafood" in the 7th; critics contend that the "good food is destroyed by the arrogance" of the staff, "crazy prices" and an interior that "urgently needs to be redecorated", but that doesn't stop the schools of supporters swimming over for what may be "the best *poisson* in Paris."

Dix Vins (Le) ●⊟   17 | 11 | 15 | 26
57, rue Falguière, 15ᵉ (Pasteur), 01 43 20 91 77

■ "One is never disappointed" by this "very nice little neighborhood restaurant"; there's "varied" Traditional French bistro fare, but what really pleases is the "unbeatable and easily devoured" prix fixe and "reasonable wine prices"; "the absence of real lighting" makes this place "a dark sardine tin", but with "charming service" you always come back.

Djakarta Bali ⑤   ▽ 13 | 14 | 14 | 36
9, rue Vauvilliers, 1ᵉʳ (Châtelet/Louvre-Rivoli), 01 45 08 83 11; fax 01 44 26 31 64

☑ Since it's run by a native brother-and-sister team – he serves, she cooks – "authentic" accurately describes this quiet little corner of Indonesia in Les Halles; if foes find it "expensive for simple food", enthusiasts appreciate the "good rijsttafel" and other "interesting dishes."

Domaine de Lintillac ⑤   – | – | – | M
54, rue Blanche, 9ᵉ (Blanche), 01 48 74 84 36

Just on the edge of Pigalle, this yearling serves as the Paris showcase of a top-quality producer of foie gras, preserved duck and various other traditional dishes from Southwestern

France, where the Lintillac firm is based; the white-painted '50s decor is an ideal setting for a hearty feast.

Dôme (Le) ●Ⓢ   20 | 17 | 17 | 66

108, bd du Montparnasse, 14ᵉ (Vavin), 01 43 35 25 81; fax 01 42 79 01 19

■ "Been there three times and can't wait to return" sums up the superlatives lavished on this Montparnasse historic cafe (once frequented by Trotsky and other '20s intellectuals) turned "very expensive" eatery – specifically, a "seafood heaven", staffed by "attentive" servers; a "lively crowd" animates the "art nouveau interior", composed of a "series of terraced salons."

Dôme du Marais (Le)   – | – | – | M

53 bis, rue des Francs-Bourgeois, 4ᵉ (Hôtel-de-Ville/ Rambuteau), 01 42 74 54 17; fax 01 42 77 78 17

Located in a historic church – hence, the gorgeous cupola over the dining room – this handsome edifice has a popular new lease on life as a restaurant with a Breton accent; Nantes native chef Pierre Lecoutre skillfully reinterprets the region's traditional dishes, as well as offering an appealing range of French classics; N.B. it also boasts a terrace for summer dining – a rarity in the Marais.

Dominique ●   17 | 14 | 15 | 51

19, rue Bréa, 6ᵉ (Vavin), 01 43 27 08 80; fax 01 43 27 03 76

■ It's a "Russian holiday every night" at this Montparnasse old-timer, known for "very good smoked fish" and, of course, vodka (50 different varieties); a few communists complain it's "too expensive", but most luxuriate in the "plush interior" that re-creates "the ambiance of another era" (presumably a pre-1917 one).

Doobie's ●Ⓢ   9 | 13 | 9 | 38

2, rue Robert Estienne, 8ᵉ (Franklin D. Roosevelt), 01 53 76 10 76; fax 01 42 25 21 71

◪ "One of the most animated Sunday brunches in Paris" is the main reason many visit this Contemporary French–Eclectic just off the Champs-Elysées; "no longer trendy", it still has "a nice decor and atmosphere" that's popular with singles; but "don't come for dinner", since "only the bar counts" here at night; P.S. billiard players note: there's a "free table" on the premises.

Dos de la Baleine (Le) Ⓢ   17 | 16 | 17 | 34

40, rue des Blancs-Manteaux, 4ᵉ (Hôtel-de-Ville/Rambuteau), 01 42 72 38 98; fax 01 42 71 40 59

■ "Good cooking and a warm welcome" join to make this "charming" little Traditional French bistro in the 4th popular with a young crowd, including many gays; a kitchen that sends out "refined" dishes and a "cozy" setting are topped off by what's perhaps "the best value in the Marais."

Driver's ◑   ▽ 16 | 15 | 15 | 27

6, rue Georges Bizet, 16ᵉ (Alma-Marceau), 01 47 23 61 15; fax 01 47 23 80 17

■ Though few surveyors have felt driven to discover this "pleasant Traditional French bistro" in the 16th, those who have appreciate the "home cooking" that's "not expensive"; the automotive-racing theme of the decor makes it "a good place to invite car lovers."

Drouant   20 | 20 | 20 | 84

18, rue Gaillon, 2ᵉ (Opéra/Quatre Septembre), 01 42 65 15 16; fax 01 49 24 02 15

☑ Famed as the annual meeting place of the Prix Goncourt (France's most prestigious book award), this historic institution has reawakened with the return of chef Louis Grondard and a renovation of the Classic French kitchens, which offer "fine food now"; the refreshed decor remains "refined and cozy" and the "irreproachable" staff wins many kudos; but despite these changes, some still say it's "stuffy" and the literary effect "has its limits", especially since this "old lady" continues to be "quite expensive."

DUC (LE)   23 | 14 | 18 | 87

243, bd Raspail, 14ᵉ (Raspail), 01 43 20 96 30; fax 01 43 20 46 73

■ "Excellent but very expensive" is the chorus on this Montparnasse *poisson* palace that pioneered the current culinary "religion of quality seafood prepared with complete simplicity"; the crowd also agrees that the porthole decor "needs to be redone" and a few infidels mutter about "stuffy" servers, but for most fin fanatics it's "still one of the best."

Durand Dupont ◑ ⑤   12 | 13 | 11 | 39

14, pl du Marché, Neuilly-sur-Seine (Les Sablons), 01 41 92 93 00; fax 01 46 37 56 79

☑ The "nice Sunday brunch" buffet, "amusing decor" and "large", "lovely terrace" are the main attractions at this "trendy" Neuilly New French bistro that's frequented by local singles and young couples, plus "fashion victims and the stars of the M6 television station"; still, skeptics scold service that's "a joke, or a nightmare", and swear that the place charges "slightly expensive" prices for singularly "uninteresting cuisine."

Ebauchoir (L')   15 | 10 | 12 | 30

43-45, rue de Citeaux, 12ᵉ (Faidherbe-Chaligny), 01 43 42 49 31

■ "Pleasantly authentic" "Classic French" cooking "contrasts with the [trendy] clientele" at this bistro near the Bastille; "young professional servers" and "good value for the money" ensure it's "worth going out of your way to find" this "slightly hidden" "neighborhood place" in the 12th arrondissement.

Ecluse (L') ◐ S
12 | 12 | 13 | 35

15, quai des Grands-Augustins, 6ᵉ (St-Michel),
01 46 33 58 74; fax 01 44 07 18 76
64, rue François 1er, 8ᵉ (George V), 01 47 20 77 09;
fax 01 40 70 03 33
15, pl de la Madeleine, 8ᵉ (Madeleine), 01 42 65 34 69;
fax 01 44 71 01 26
13, rue de la Roquette, 11ᵉ (Bastille), 01 48 05 19 12;
fax 01 48 05 04 88
1, rue d'Armaillé, 17ᵉ (Charles de Gaulle-Etoile),
01 47 63 88 29; fax 01 44 40 41 91

◪ This "simple little chain" of "pleasant bistros à vins" offers "an alternative to a cafe"; fans find the combination of "light meals" ("good charcuterie") and "lots of wines by the glass" a "long-lasting formula" that's "more than serviceable", while skeptics snort it's a "nice place for a drink but the food is nothing special" – and "rather expensive" as well; perhaps the best plan is to think of the experience as being "all about the wine, with some tasty accompaniments."

Editeurs (Les) ◐ S
– | – | – | M

4, carrefour de l'Odéon, 6ᵉ (Odéon), 01 43 26 67 76;
fax 01 46 34 58 30

The management has "completely redone" this reliable neighborhood fixture in the 6th, replacing the old hearty Alsatian fare with "unpretentious brasserie dishes" like salmon tartare, carpaccio and rack of lamb; the name and "nice library-like setting" (tome-filled bookshelves and authors' portraits line the walls) render homage to the publishing houses and stores traditionally associated with Saint-Germain.

El Mansour
17 | 16 | 17 | 55

7, rue de La Trémoille, 8ᵉ (Alma-Marceau), 01 47 23 88 18;
fax 01 40 70 13 53

■ Off the Avenue George V in the 8th, this "refined address" serves "excellent" North African eats – "especially the lamb tagine" and "the best couscous" – in large quantities; and though they deem it "a bit expensive", aficionados appreciate the "attentive" service and "understated atmosphere"; all told, there's "very good hospitality" for those in a Moroccan mood.

ELYSÉES DU VERNET (LES) S
– | 23 | 23 | VE

Hôtel Vernet, 25, rue Vernet, 8ᵉ (Charles de Gaulle-Etoile/
George V), 01 44 31 98 98; fax 01 44 31 85 69

■ "Perfection from start to finish" proclaim patrons of this "elegant" establishment in the Hôtel Vernet, whose landmarked dining room bears a "glass-domed" ceiling (designed by Gustave Eiffel, of tower fame); the cuisine's now under the control of chef Eric Briffard (ex Plaza-Athénée), whose luxurious Classic French dishes arrived post-*Survey*; but they are "impeccably served", and for slightly lower prices, so *sans doute*, "stunning" still sums up the experience here.

Elysées Hong Kong 🔲   _ | _ | _ | M

80, rue Michel-Ange, 16ᵉ (Exelmans), 01 46 51 60 99
The red dining room of this newcomer has become an instant institution for fans of fine Asian fare in this plush corner of the 16th; aside from the gentle prices, what pleases the regulars is the solicitous service of the hardworking Chinese family that owns and runs the restaurant.

Emporio Armani Caffé   15 | 15 | 13 | 41

149, bd St-Germain, 6ᵉ (St-Germain-des-Prés), 01 45 48 62 15; fax 01 45 48 53 17
■ Since it's located in the Emporio Armani boutique in Saint-Germain, this "chic, modern" cafe naturally makes "a perfect pit stop while shopping"; but "surprise – it's good" as well, offering Italian "food that's tasty and fresh" (if as "expensive" as the designer's duds); though the "people-watching's a plus", some fashion victims pout "if you're not dressed in the latest, they treat you like an interloper."

Enoteca (L') ◑🔲   17 | 15 | 13 | 41

25, rue Charles V, 4ᵉ (St-Paul/Sully Morland), 01 42 78 91 44; fax 01 44 59 31 72
■ "Warm Italian atmosphere" and a "bellissima" vino list make this wine bar/bistro in the Marais popular with a stylish young crowd that appreciates the beamed ceiling, Murano-glass lighting and cosmopolitan buzz as much as they do the "decent and simple" – if sometimes "uneven" – food; just be braced for an "incredibly bad-mannered staff."

Entoto   _ | _ | _ | M

143-145, rue L.M. Nordmann, 13ᵉ (Glacière), 01 45 87 08 51
Come to this "amusing", "transporting" Ethiopian in the 13th for "the pleasure of eating with your fingers" – mainly "vegetable purees and meat" – that you scoop up with "traditional Ethiopian bread"; despite nonexistent decor, the service is friendly and fans say "it's maybe even better than what you find in Addis Ababa."

Entracte (L')
(Chez Sonia et Carlos) 🔲   _ | _ | _ | M

44, rue d'Orsel, 18ᵉ (Abbesses/Anvers), 01 46 06 93 41
Few outside the neighborhood know this Classic French not far from Sacré-Coeur, but those who do say it offers "a warm welcome", "superb produce-oriented cuisine", and "charming decor"; since it has "many regulars" but only 20 seats, you better "think of reserving your table."

En Vue ◑   _ | _ | _ | M

39, rue Boissy-d'Anglas, 8ᵉ (Concorde/Madeleine), 01 42 65 10 49; fax 01 40 17 09 28
Flanking the new Cartier HQ building and just up the street from Hermès, this hip address in the swank 8th pulls in a

slickly dressed young crowd hungry for New French fare; soft lighting, lounge music and bird's-eye maple paneling suggest that style reigns supreme here, but friendly service and reasonable prices are also part of the smart package.

Epicure 108
∇ 19 | 11 | 18 | 43

108, rue Cardinet, 17ᵉ (Malesherbes), 01 47 63 50 91

■ "The marriage of Alsatian cooking and the chef's native Japan is a true marvel" at this "excellent address" near the Square des Batignolles in the 17th; the dining room itself is "very ordinary", but the "welcome is delicious", the service is "delicate" and the "interesting", "innovative" cooking is also "a good buy"; the only complaint is that "portions are small, like they are in Japan."

Epi d'Or (L')
18 | 17 | 19 | 43

25, rue Jean-Jacques Rousseau, 1ᵉʳ (Louvre-Rivoli), 01 42 36 38 12; fax 01 42 36 46 25

■ "Constant in both quality and kindness", this "wonderful bistro" between the Palais Royal and Les Halles is treasured for its "good", "traditional family-style cooking", including "real [French] classics, such as marinated leeks", "lentil salad, cold beef salad and roast leg of lamb"; the "friendly welcome" and "charming service" add to the allure of this "sentimental favorite" that's also, wonder of wonders, "a sure value."

EPI DUPIN (L')
22 | 13 | 17 | 44

11, rue Dupin, 6ᵉ (Sèvres-Babylone), 01 42 22 64 56; fax 01 42 22 30 42

◪ Many know this "very popular" bistro in the 6th where chef-owner François Pasteau serves up "delicious" food ("the cod with gravlax was a revelation – I thought only I could make my girlfriend's face look like that") as one of "Paris' biggest bangs for the buck"; but this "price-performer" may be "getting arrogant", as several snarl over "the difficulty of making reservations", long waits and "snippy", "overwhelmed" service in the "small, frenetic" dining room; to decide for yourself, be sure to "book early."

Erawan
18 | 14 | 15 | 40

76, rue de la Fédération, 15ᵉ (La Motte Picquet-Grenelle), 01 47 83 55 67; fax 01 47 34 85 98

■ Although "it hardly ever changes", "a vast menu" makes this a "good address" for "nice traditional Thai fare" in the 15th; enthusiasts endorse "the astonishing mixture of flavors – sweet/sour, sharp/subdued – and textures"; "smiling servers" make up for "drab decor."

Escargot Montorgueil (L')
14 | 18 | 13 | 53

38, rue Montorgueil, 1ᵉʳ (Les Halles), 01 42 36 83 51; fax 01 42 36 35 05

◪ "It has to stop living on its reputation" a majority says about this Les Halles Classic French bistro, a 19th-century escargot expert now managed by the Terrail family of La Tour d'Argent; some still smile on the "splendid decor" and advocate the "always good cuisine", but critics carp "the kitchen is becoming more and more mediocre" ("hunting for snails with a shotgun") and the "tourist-trap" ambiance resembles "a Vincente Minnelli vision of Old Paree where the French wear berets and carry baguettes."

Espace Sud-Ouest/Chez Papa ◗ ⑤   12 | 6 | 9 | 25
29, rue de l'Arcade, 8ᵉ (St-Lazare/Madeleine), 01 42 65 43 68
206, rue La Fayette, 10ᵉ (Louis Blanc), 01 42 09 53 87
6, rue Gassendi, 14ᵉ (Denfert-Rochereau), 01 43 22 41 19
101, rue de la Croix Nivert, 15ᵉ (Commerce), 01 48 28 31 88
■ "Good" and "hearty Southwestern fare" is the lure at this "fun", "no-frills" quartet; sure, they're "crowded" and "very noisy", but this makes for a "convivial" atmosphere if you know what you're getting into, and since most find the "gargantuan portions" of "honorable cassoulet" and "huge salads" "a great buy", it's no wonder "getting a table is tough."

ESPADON (L') ⑤   24 | 26 | 25 | 111
Hôtel Ritz, 15, pl Vendôme, 1ᵉʳ (Concorde/Opéra),
01 43 16 30 80; fax 01 43 16 33 75
■ What with "harp and violin background" music, "Limoges china" and "real flowers abloom everywhere", this "has to be the most romantic spot in Paris" rave reviewers about the "formal" showpiece set "in the classic elegance of the Ritz"; the homecoming of chef Michel Roth (ex Lasserre) has resulted in an "exquisite" Haute Cuisine menu, accompanied by near-"perfect service"; this "glamorous" baby means a "maximum bill" – but most think the "money's well spent."

Espadon Bleu (L')   17 | 17 | 16 | 52
25, rue des Grands-Augustins, 6ᵉ (Odéon/St-Michel),
01 46 33 00 85; fax 01 43 54 54 48
◣ A "baby bistro by chef Jacques Cagna and one of the best buys in Paris" crow converts about this "delightful" seafooder in Saint-Germain, just across the street from the man's eponymous main table; but while the owner "often stops by", unconsoled cynics complain about "haphazard, somewhat ungracious service" and "basically cheap fish that's badly cooked."

Etienne Marcel ◗ ⑤   – | – | – | M
34, rue Etienne Marcel, 2ᵉ (Pyramides), 01 45 08 01 03;
fax 01 42 36 03 44
The main thing that distinguishes this year-old Costes Frères address is its '60s decor – think white plastic armchairs that vaguely evoke Courrèges; otherwise, it's the brothers' usual formula par excellence – New French fare, a central location (in the 2nd), an attractive, style-conscious clientele and equally attractive – and don't they know it – servers.

Etoile (L') ● S 16 | 22 | 15 | 58
12, rue de Presbourg, 8ᵉ (Charles de Gaulle-Etoile),
01 45 00 78 70; fax 01 45 00 78 71

■ Maybe you "thought it was only a nightclub", but this "comfortable and sophisticated" Classic French offers a "delicious, inventive menu" – an "agreeable surprise" that augments the "dream decor" with its "great view" of the Arc de Triomphe; the presence of a "young rich-kid crowd" attests to the "very expensive" prices, but folks still return to what's "inarguably the best trendy restaurant in Paris."

Etoile Marocaine (L') S ▽ 16 | 15 | 15 | 41
56, rue Galilée, 8ᵉ (George V), 01 47 20 44 43; fax 01 47 20 69 85

■ Not far from the Champs, this Moroccan impresses with warm, Arabian Nights–style decor that creates "a handsome setting" in which to sample "classic", "exceptional roast lamb couscous" and other "interesting" traditional dishes made from "fresh ingredients"; although it's not the *Survey*'s highest-rated North African, it's "maybe the best when you consider the prices elsewhere in this neighborhood."

Etrier (L') – | – | – | M
154, rue Lamarck, 18ᵉ (Guy Moquet), 01 42 29 14 01

The enormous popularity of the film *Amélie,* which is set in this Montmartre neighborhood, might induce discoveries of this cozy (28-seat) bistro full of Classic French "food and service that's always charming"; "the midday prix fixe is the best buy in Paris."

Excuse (L') ▽ 21 | 15 | 18 | 45
14, rue Charles V, 4ᵉ (St-Paul), 01 43 14 32 32; fax 01 42 77 88 55

■ Regulars rave about this "very precious" "little gem", whose "fantastic" New French food includes langoustine-filled ravioli and shortbread with sheep's-milk ice yogurt; "good service" and the "great, intimate setting" in an old house in the 4th make it quite "a romantic hideaway."

Fabrique (La) ● S 10 | 12 | 11 | 33
53, rue du Faubourg St-Antoine, 11ᵉ (Bastille), 01 43 07 67 07

■ "An unusual mixture of techno music and Alsatian cooking" sums up the scene at this microbrewery/nightclub in a "trendy location" near the Bastille; "not as bad as you would expect, the food" features *flammenküche* (a cream, onion and bacon pie) that goes well with the freshly drawn brews, and a "very good vegetarian menu too"; "sit with a bunch of friends" at the large tables.

Fakhr el Dine ● S 18 | 14 | 17 | 49
3, rue Quentin Bauchart, 8ᵉ (Charles de Gaulle-Etoile),
01 47 23 44 42; fax 01 53 70 01 81
30, rue de Longchamp, 16ᵉ (Trocadéro), 01 47 27 90 00;
fax 01 53 70 01 81

■ Head for these two addresses in the 8th and the 16th for "authentic", "high-level Lebanese" fare proffered by "discreet" and "efficient, if slightly impersonal", servers in "refined" dining rooms; though "expensive, very expensive", they're among "the best in Paris."

Faucher
22 | 17 | 20 | 78

123, av de Wagram, 17ᵉ (Ternes/Wagram), 01 42 27 61 50; fax 01 46 22 25 72

■ Chef-owner Gérard Faucher's "very fine", "inventive" "New French cooking", backed by "personalized service", makes this "plush" table in the 17th "always very, very successful", especially as a "good expense-account restaurant" – although some have doubts about the renovated "decor that's not in harmony with the classicism of the kitchen"; P.S. "the terrace behind the pine trees is quite agreeable during the summer."

FAUGERON
25 | 20 | 24 | 105

52, rue de Longchamp, 16ᵉ (Trocadéro), 01 47 04 24 53; fax 01 47 55 62 90

■ Run by Henri (winner of the Légion d'Honneur) and Gerlindé Faugeron, this "small, sparkling" restaurant in the 16th is "certainly one of the best tables in Paris", offering "consistently superb" Classic French–Corrèze region cooking, like the "celebrated soft-boiled egg with pureed truffle"; "professional, discreet service", plus "well-spaced tables", makes it an "absolute favorite", and while it's "on the expensive side", most find prices "fair" for "such an elegant", "unforgettable" place.

Fellini
19 | 13 | 17 | 49

47, rue de l'Arbre-Sec, 1ᵉʳ (Louvre-Rivoli), 01 42 60 90 66; fax 01 42 60 18 04 S
58, rue de la Croix Nivert, 15ᵉ (Commerce/Emile Zola), 01 45 77 40 77; fax 01 45 77 22 54

■ A lot of entries from Italy have opened in Paris recently, but this pair in the 1st and the 15th arrondissements still get "recommended" as "real trattorias" serving "very good", "surprisingly authentic" food; perhaps the "settings are modest", but the staff ("true Italians, accent and all") is "really nice."

Ferme (La)
– | – | – | M

55-57, rue St-Roch, 1ᵉʳ (Opéra/Pyramides), 01 40 20 12 12; fax 01 40 20 06 06

Located in an organic food shop in the 1st, this cafe carries salads and sandwiches that are "delicious, original and reliable"; although it boasts an attractive bare-wood and wicker-chair decor, it's also "great for a picnic lunch to go."

Ferme de Boulogne (La)
∇ 17 | 18 | 18 | 51

1, rue de Billancourt, Boulogne-Billancourt (Pont-de-St-Cloud), 01 46 03 61 69; fax 01 46 04 55 70

◪ Reminiscent of a "little provincial" place, "the setting is worth a detour" (especially when "the weather's good

and warm") at "one of the prettiest restaurants in Paris"
fans say; but skeptics shrug off this Traditional French
near the Porte de Saint-Cloud: although "nice", the food's
"not memorable", and it seems "a little pricey for what it is."

Ferme des Mathurins (La) ▽ 13 | 9 | 15 | 41

17, rue Vignon, 8ᵉ (Havre-Caumartin/Madeleine),
01 42 66 46 39; fax 01 42 66 00 27
■ "You can't get much more French" than this traditional
1945 "classic" that generously ("what portions!") serves
"honest", "good-quality Burgundian" homestyle cooking
near the Madeleine; "go there with good company, which
might help you forget" the faded, old-fashioned dining room.

Ferme St-Hubert (La) 17 | 12 | 14 | 36

21, rue Vignon, 8ᵉ (Madeleine), 01 47 42 79 20; fax 01 47 42 46 97
■ "If you crave cheese", this "small and cozy" address
"near the Madeleine" "is the place to go", since it offers
36 – count 'em 36 – "original dishes" featuring *fromage*
(special mention: the "excellent soufflé and Camembert
croquettes"); perhaps the decor needs "dusting off", but
most moan "what a way to get a heart attack!"

Ferme St-Simon (La) 20 | 17 | 18 | 60

6, rue de St-Simon, 7ᵉ (Rue du Bac/Solférino), 01 45 48 35 74;
fax 01 40 49 07 31
■ "Very recommendable" sums up this "Classic" French in
the 7th, whose "bourgeois" crowd includes politicians ("it's
excellent for a business lunch"); the "traditional" cuisine
"makes no attempt at fusion" but is "very consistent" in
its "nice chicken dishes" and "succulent hare"; though
"strange", the "beamed ceiling" and "mirrored decor
manages to stay just on the right side of good taste" and
the "service is good, even if you aren't a minister."

Fermette du Sud-Ouest (La) – | – | – | M

31, rue Coquillière, 1ᵉʳ (Les Halles/Palais Royal-Musée
du Louvre), 01 42 36 73 55
Though it's been serving up "hearty" Southwestern classics
like cassoulet and foie gras for ages, few have found their
way to this cozy spot in Les Halles with a rustic decor of
16th-century exposed-stone walls and beams; adherents
appreciate the staff's "niceness", as well as the "small bill."

Fermette Marbeuf 1900 (La) ●🅢 14 | 21 | 15 | 51

5, rue Marbeuf, 8ᵉ (Alma-Marceau), 01 53 23 08 00;
fax 01 53 23 08 09
◪ Many find the "stunning", "superb 1900 vintage" decor
the most alluring thing about this "fading" "chain" link (it
belongs to the Frères Blanc) that, foes fume, serves "bland
food" "for tourists" off the Champs; supporters say the
Classic French fare is "better than you would think";
generally, though, "if you don't sit in the little dining room
with the glass ceiling, it's not worth bothering with."

Fernandises (Les)   ▽ 16 | 8 | 13 | 37

*19, rue de la Fontaine-au-Roi, 11ᵉ (Goncourt/République),
01 48 06 16 96*

■ "Too bad there aren't more restaurants like this one around" attest admirers of this slightly "rough" "traditional Norman" in the 11th; what pleases is the gently priced, made-on-the-premises menu, which features "perfect house-aged, flavored Camemberts"; the odd hand-painted mural on the wall and rather automatic service don't distract.

Feuilles Libres/Entrées Libres   – | – | – | M

*34, rue Perronet, Neuilly-sur-Seine (Les Sablons),
01 46 24 41 41; fax 01 46 40 77 61*
*49, rue Madeleine Michelis, Neuilly-sur-Seine (Les Sablons),
01 46 24 00 84; fax 01 46 40 77 61*

Husband-and-wife team Emmanuel and Nathalie Laporte have created a dual culinary delight in this quiet, residential area of Neuilly; their small Feuilles Libres – which resembles a house, with silver candelabras and colorful linens on wood- topped tables – serves a moderately priced New French menu, while the younger brick-walled bistro (located kitty-corner to the restaurant) offers an even less-expensive alternative; both share a terrace under the linden trees, a delightful destination during the dog days of summer.

Filoche (Le)   20 | 13 | 19 | 35

*34, rue du Laos, 15ᵉ (Cambronne/La Motte-Picquet-Grenelle),
01 45 66 44 60*

■ Tucked away in the 15th, Danielle and chef Serge Filoche's Traditional French bistro offers "very good" cooking, especially when it comes to fish – "the best fillet of grilled John Dory in Paris" – and heartier specialties like the "braised sweetbreads"; what's more, the "gracious" service is nearly "perfect", and even if the "decor could use a jolt of imagination", ultimately "this is the type of restaurant you want to find and then not let anyone else discover."

Findi ●⑤   13 | 14 | 12 | 43

*24, av George V, 8ᵉ (Alma-Marceau/George V), 01 47 20 14 78;
fax 01 47 20 10 08*

◪ For a bit of "*La Dolce Vita* in Paris", folks head to this "fashion Italian" in the 8th; but while advocates applaud the "handsome" setting ("especially the widely spaced tables, so rare nowadays") and "great fresh pasta", antagonists argue against the "average food for scenesters" that's "expensive for the quantities" served; P.S. it resides in the 'Golden Triangle' near couturiers, but "is it necessary to note on the menu that the waiters are dressed by Smalto?"

Fins Gourmets (Aux) ⌿   16 | 14 | 16 | 36

*213, bd St-Germain, 7ᵉ (Rue du Bac), 01 42 22 06 57;
fax 01 42 22 06 57*

■ This "very good address" in the 7th is "one of the rare surviving [traditional] bistros in Paris", so "let's hope it lasts"; the "old-fashioned atmosphere" and service, plus "hearty quantities" of Southwestern vittles, make it "a place to bring foreigners", especially since it's also a "good buy"; perhaps it could use "a paint job", but for most it's an "authentic" "classic" with "timeless cooking."

Finzi ◐ S   15 | 11 | 12 | 42
182, bd Haussmann, 8ᵉ (St-Philippe-du-Roule), 01 45 62 88 68; fax 01 45 61 41 05
☑ Frequented by a "bourgeois crowd and businessmen", this Italian on the Boulevard Haussmann "disappoints" many pasta lovers, who lament its being "a very poor buy for the money" and are sick of "being squeezed in" the "busy, noisy" dining room; *amici* insist it's a "solid" bit of "Little Italy" – but maybe they're just hungry for "all the handsome guys" here.

Fish La Boissonnerie S   21 | 13 | 18 | 40
69, rue de Seine, 6ᵉ (Odéon), 01 43 54 34 69; fax 01 46 34 63 41
■ Co-owned by an American, Juan Sanchez from Miami, this wine-and-fish-oriented contemporary bistro not far from the Odéon offers "simple" but "oh-so-scrumptious" French-Med food and "interesting wines at reasonable prices"; it's a "great place" for "casual dining", if you don't mind that the "funky bilingual staff's" service gets "spotty when busy."

Flamboyant (Le) S   ▽ 19 | 11 | 17 | 31
11, rue Boyer-Barret, 14ᵉ (Pernety), 01 45 41 00 22; fax 01 45 41 00 22
■ "Recommended for anyone on a small budget", this "intimate" long-running spot in the 14th sets "one of the best Creole tables in Paris", though actually the menu includes items from Francophone islands all around the world; the place has "the simplest of decors", but "the service is excellent."

Flandrin (Le) ◐ S   11 | 14 | 12 | 46
80, av Henri Martin, 16ᵉ (Rue de la Pompe), 01 45 04 34 69; fax 01 45 04 67 41
☑ Set in an old train station, this brasserie seems almost "a caricature of the 16th", which is to say "pricey" ("avoid it at lunchtime so that you won't feel lost among the Porsches") and trendy ("practical for learning the latest model of whatever"); a facelift has boosted the Decor score, and the beautiful people praise the "gorgeous sidewalk terrace here during the summer"; but this institution gets derailed when it comes to the service ("disinterested") and cuisine ("insipid").

Fleurs de Thym   – | – | – | I
19, rue François Miron, 4ᵉ (Hôtel-de-Ville/St-Paul), 01 48 87 01 02; fax 01 42 76 08 38
A former chef of Fakhr el Dine runs the kitchen at this cozy, good-value Lebanese in the Marais; the high-quality

cuisine, the attractive setting – the exposed stone walls of a 17th-century house – and friendly service have already won this newcomer a following among antique dealers.

Flora   – | – | – | E

36, av George V, 8ᵉ (George V), 01 40 70 10 49; fax 01 47 20 52 87
Fashionable decor (tone-on-tone wallpaper, plum-colored furnishings, glass sconces), amiable service and an eclectic collection of dishes inspired by the cuisines of Provence, Tunisia, India and other sultry locales distinguish this latest project from Flora Mikula (ex Les Olivades); the convenient location on the Avenue George V is an added bonus.

Flora Danica ⑤   18 | 15 | 16 | 54

142, av des Champs-Elysées, 8ᵉ (Charles de Gaulle-Etoile/ George V), 01 44 13 86 26; fax 01 44 13 89 44
■ Re-opened after a renovation, this "modest" sibling of Copenhague on the Champs-Elysées delights Dane-lovers with its "delicious Nordic dishes" – "above all the salmon", "not that the marinated herring should be ignored"; a few find it "too expensive", especially given what they claim are "newly shrunken portions"; still, "it's good for lunch", especially on "its very pretty terrace."

Flore en l'Ile (Le) ◑⑤   12 | 16 | 12 | 35

42, quai d'Orléans, 4ᵉ (Hôtel-de-Ville/Pont-Marie), 01 43 29 88 27; fax 01 43 29 73 54
■ At this Ile Saint-Louis brasserie, "the decor is really the view, and the view is divine", offering a "marvelous" look at Notre Dame; the "food is fine" (if "nothing more"), and it offers one of "the best little breakfasts in Paris."

Florimond (Le)   ▽ 18 | 14 | 19 | 36

19, av de La Motte-Picquet, 7ᵉ (Ecole-Militaire), 01 45 55 40 38; fax 01 45 55 40 38
◪ The stylish 7th arrondissement professionals who patronize this "perfect neighborhood place" love it for its "seriously good food" ("*chou farçi* forever!" cry the stuffed-cabbage connoisseurs), "irreproachable service" and "friendly prices"; all in all, a "very comfortable" corner.

Foc Ly ⑤   17 | 13 | 15 | 41

79, av Charles de Gaulle, Neuilly-sur-Seine (Les Sablons), 01 46 24 43 36; fax 01 46 24 48 46
◪ A suburban "institution" since 1976, this Chinese is "not very special" say Asian aficionados (the "welcome is wanting"), but proponents protest that, while "unoriginal", the "dependable food and service" "never disappoint"; just be warned it's "priced for Neuilly" (i.e. "expensive").

Fogón Saint Julien ◑⑤   21 | 12 | 18 | 40

10, rue St-Julien-le-Pauvre, 5ᵉ (Maubert-Mutualité/St-Michel), 01 43 54 31 33; fax 01 43 54 07 00
■ "The best paella in Paris" along with other "Spanish dishes of great finesse" receive a resounding ole! from

fans of this "crowded" "little" spot with slightly "sad decor" but "friendly service" in the Latin Quarter; some pout about paying too many pennies, but most are enthused about this way to "discover cuisine español."

Fontaine d'Auteuil (La) ▽ 17 | 13 | 15 | 46
35 bis, rue La Fontaine, 16ᵉ (Jasmin), 01 42 88 04 47; fax 01 42 88 95 12
■ "An excellent surprise in a gastronomic desert" (the Auteuil district of the 16th arrondissement) declare discoverers of this small Contemporary French that offers "fair value for the money"; just be aware that "while the food is good, the decor is sad."

Fontaine de Mars (La) 🅂 17 | 16 | 17 | 42
129, rue St-Dominique, 7ᵉ (Ecole-Militaire), 01 47 05 46 44; fax 01 47 05 11 13
■ A combined "local and tourist crowd makes for a nice mix" at this "charming" old-style bistro in the 7th; regulars recommend its "succulent bourgeois cuisine", along with Gascon and other Southwestern specialties; the only debate is over "what makes this place more inviting: the warm smile of co-owner Christiane Boudon" or the "nice country decor" ("love those red-checked tablecloths"); N.B. for those into group dining, L'Auvergne Gourmande, its new little annex next door, offers two tables d'hôtes.

Fontaines (Les) 20 | 7 | 14 | 35
9, rue Soufflot, 5ᵉ (Cluny-La-Sorbonne), 01 43 26 42 80; fax 01 44 07 03 49
■ "Large portions – large even for Americans" explain the enduring popularity of this Traditional French bistro near the Panthéon, "one of the best buys for the money in Paris"; "the decor could drive you to suicide", it's "so ugly" (think a 1970s French version of a New York City coffee shop), but "the meat's so delicious" that "it must be tried", along with "the grilled lobster"; all told, you'll have a "crowded but fun" time.

Fontanarosa 🅂 15 | 13 | 13 | 43
28, bd Garibaldi, 15ᵉ (Cambronne), 01 45 66 97 84; fax 01 47 83 96 30
■ "Step out of the 15th and into Italy" at this "neighborhood place" with "charming Latin waiters" and a "magnificent little terrace"; most find the "simple cooking" "good every time", although some snipe that this spot is a bit "too pricey for pasta."

Forge (La) – | – | – | I
63, bd de Vaugirard, 15ᵉ (Montparnasse-Bienvenüe/Pasteur), 01 43 20 87 10
Few surveyors have heard of this modest Alsatian that specializes in *flammenküche* (open-faced cream tarts with either savory or sweet garnishes) and regional wines;

those who have call it "the best bistro in the area" around the Gare Montparnasse, with "great prices, friendly service and super decor."

Foujita
20 | 8 | 13 | 28

41, rue St-Roch, 1er (Pyramides), 01 42 61 42 93

■ "Honest and authentic", this "little neighborhood Japanese" near the Tuileries gardens in the 1st offers "irreproachable quality" and a variety of maki that is literally "a fresh delight"; service is "rapid" and prices are "reasonable", constituting perhaps "the best buy among all Paris sushi bars", which makes it easy to ignore that "there's not much originality in the decor."

Fouquet's (Le) ◑⬛
14 | 19 | 15 | 62

99, av des Champs-Elysées, 8e (George V), 01 47 23 50 00; fax 01 47 23 50 55

◪ No one argues that this "mythic" cafe on the Champs isn't "a fun place to meet", with its "old-fashioned decor of dark wood and red velvet", but otherwise, it's "overpriced" and "touristy", with "snobby" service ("if you speak English you're placed in Siberia, if you speak French things go a little better") and "mediocre" Classic French cuisine – though these thoughts (and ratings) may not reflect the arrival post-*Survey* of chef Gérard Salle (ex Plaza-Athénée).

Fous d'en Face (Les) ◑
13 | 12 | 13 | 31

3, rue du Bourg Tibourg, 4e (Hôtel-de-Ville), 01 48 87 03 75; fax 01 42 78 38 03

◪ If some say this bistro à vins near the Hôtel de Ville makes "a good effort" with its Classic French dishes that go with "well-chosen and well-explained wines", others retort that it's "living on its reputation" and is "expensive for what it is"; at least there's "a pleasant terrace in summer."

Frégate (La)
– | – | – | M

30, av Ledru Rollin, 12e (Gare de Lyon), 01 43 43 90 32; fax 01 43 43 90 32

A "nautical setting for generous seafood-oriented cuisine" characterizes this small fish house tucked away in the 12th; "much improved since its renovation", it remains "a good value", given the "friendly staff" and "nice view" of the Seine.

Fumoir (Le) ◑⬛
9 | 18 | 11 | 38

6, rue de l'Amiral-de-Coligny, 1er (Louvre-Rivoli), 01 42 92 00 24; fax 01 42 92 05 05

◪ "Poor food, poor service, pretty good atmosphere" sums up this "chic" New French–International with "a great view of the Louvre" across the street; the "attractive setting", featuring a book-filled "library room", appeals to the "intellectual, hip" hordes who say the place isn't "bad for brunch"; otherwise, it's "best for having a drink while reading the papers" or meeting folks in the "nice bar."

Gallopin ◐

15 | 17 | 16 | 42

40, rue Notre-Dame-des-Victoires, 2ᵉ (Bourse), 01 42 36 45 38; fax 01 42 36 10 32

■ "More Parisian than this and you die" surveyors say about this "traditional brasserie" across the street from the old stock exchange; the "rich wood paneling" and antique brass lamps (circa 1876) create a nice backdrop for "classic and correct", "rich" cooking, "professionally" served; overall, "you get your money's worth" – so no wonder it's historically been "beloved by brokers."

Gamin de Paris (Au) ◐S

14 | 12 | 11 | 35

51, rue Vieille du Temple, 4ᵉ (Hôtel-de-Ville/St-Paul), 01 42 78 97 24

■ "Right in the heart of the Marais", this "favorite" candlelit Classic French glows with "warm atmosphere" and "consistently good", "affordable" fare – though even supporters sigh over the "lamentable service"; regulars recommend you "make a reservation" and "avoid Saturday nights, when anarchy reigns."

Gare (La) ◐S

9 | 17 | 10 | 39

19, chaussée de la Muette, 16ᵉ (La Muette), 01 42 15 15 31; fax 01 42 15 15 23

◪ Frequented by a stylish young crowd, the "superb", "very original" setting of this "trendy" restaurant – an old train station in the 16th arrondissement – is more appealing to most than the "mediocre" Traditional French cooking; "very slow", even "deplorable", service is another drawback, though it seems less so when seated "in the open air" on the "pleasant terrace."

Garnier ◐S

17 | 16 | 16 | 59

111, rue St-Lazare, 8ᵉ (St-Lazare), 01 43 87 50 40; fax 01 40 08 06 93

■ Everyone's always loved the "excellent oysters and shellfish" at this seafood-oriented brasserie across the street from the Gare Saint-Lazare in the 8th arrondissement, and many of those who have been here since it was renovated find the revamped menu of "fish dishes quite good"; the updated look – kind of a mixture of art deco and contemporary – is likewise "a success", although a few find it "kitsch"; "too bad the prices have almost doubled" since the redo.

Gastroquet (Le)

▽ 17 | 11 | 17 | 46

10, rue Desnouettes, 15ᵉ (Convention/Porte de Versailles), 01 48 28 60 91; fax 01 45 33 23 70

■ This "tiny little bistro is quite nice": there's "a jovial welcome" at the beginning, an "acceptable tab" at the end and in the interim, "excellent Traditional French cooking"; it's especially a "good place to bear in mind if you're visiting a show" at the convention center at the Porte de Versailles.

Gauloise (La) S
14 | 13 | 12 | 49
59, av de La Motte-Picquet, 15ᵉ (La Motte-Picquet-Grenelle), 01 47 34 11 64; fax 01 40 61 09 70
☑ "Still good" some say about this "reasonably priced" "Traditional French bistro" with "celeb clients" (the late president Mitterrand was among them) in the 15th near Le Village Suisse antiques center; but opponents opine "it's living off of, but not up to, its reputation", offering "absentee service in a mediocre ambiance."

Gavroche (Le) ◐
19 | 14 | 18 | 41
19, rue St-Marc, 2ᵉ (Bourse/Richelieu-Drouot), 01 42 96 89 70
■ In the 2nd, this "unpretentious" Traditional French bistro has "loads of atmosphere, very good Beaujolais wines" and a kitchen that features "fresh" ingredients, including the "best prime rib in Paris" and a great "steak au poivre"; it's "very Parisian at lunchtime" and – since it "serves until 1 AM" – "always a party" at night.

Gaya, L'Estaminet
17 | 14 | 14 | 57
17, rue Duphot, 1ᵉʳ (Madeleine), 01 42 60 43 03; fax 01 42 60 69 35
■ Though it's not cheap, this seafooder with "simple decor" behind the Madeleine is "a favorite" for "excellent fresh fish"; it's also "one of the best places in the area for a business lunch", since "you can sit and talk and not be rushed" (to put a positive spin on "indifferent" service).

Gaya Rive Gauche
20 | 14 | 17 | 67
44, rue du Bac, 7ᵉ (Rue du Bac), 01 45 44 73 73; fax 01 45 44 73 73
☑ Stylish fin fans find the "fish irreproachably fresh" and even "magical" at this little Left Bank seafooder that operates "without the pretension of other establishments" – though the "best" fare comes "at the highest prices", which not all feel are "justified"; rather minimalist decor also creates a "lack of atmosphere", though "very friendly service" helps make up for it.

GEORGES ◐S
14 | 25 | 12 | 53
Centre Georges Pompidou, 19, rue Beaubourg, 4ᵉ (Rambuteau), 01 44 78 47 99; fax 01 44 78 16 80
☑ "A view worth fighting for" of "the cathedrals and rooftops of Paris", a "superb" modern interior and a "trendy with a capital T" atmosphere have made this International on the top floor of the Centre Pompidou popular despite the fact that it's "just another Costes brothers place foodwise" ("unremarkable") and servicewise ("gatekeepers of chic who could use a lesson in grace"); but hey, with such a "priceless setting, who needs to eat" anyway?

GÉRARD BESSON
22 | 17 | 20 | 104
5, rue Coq Héron, 1ᵉʳ (Louvre-Rivoli/Palais Royal-Musée du Louvre), 01 42 33 14 74; fax 01 42 33 85 71
☑ Though many find chef-owner Gerard Besson's "calm", "refined home" for Haute Cuisine in the 1st "still a great

classic", with "excellent, if not very innovative" fare, a slide in the Food score sides with iconoclasts who insist it's become "mediocre" and "labored"; still, the "service is high quality", and happy hunters insist you should "run here when game's in season."

Gildas Delamer ⑤   – | – | – | M
24, rue de Montorgeuil, 2ᵉ (Les Halles), 01 42 21 12 11
285, rue St-Jacques, 5ᵉ (Port-Royal), 01 43 54 71 70
Tucked away in the mostly pedestrian, increasingly trendy Montorgeuil neighborhood and also near the Port-Royal, these popular pearls feature the famed Breton oysters of Gildas Le Gall; cheerful service enlivens the anodyne rust and ochre–colored decor, and a catch-of-the-day menu of contemporary, modestly priced fish dishes makes reservations a must.

Gitane (La)   14 | 11 | 13 | 34
53 bis, av de La Motte-Picquet, 15ᵉ (La Motte-Picquet-Grenelle), 01 47 34 62 92; fax 01 40 65 94 01
■ "What a find – Southwestern and typically Classic French food at affordable prices" attest admirers of this bistro near the Champ-de-Mars, whose "nice, relaxed atmosphere" is enhanced by a particularly "pleasant terrace"; although the "warmth of the welcome depends upon which waiter seats you", service is usually "rapid."

Giulio Rebellato ⑤   19 | 14 | 15 | 51
136, rue de la Pompe, 16ᵉ (Victor Hugo), 01 47 27 50 26
■ Despite its "slightly sad decor", this "very good Italian" not far from the Place Victor Hugo pulls a "clientele of Parisian regulars" who create a rather "chic" atmosphere; "a very warm welcome" and "pleasant service" add to its allure, and though "prices are a bit high", "this is real cooking from the North and the South."

Glénan (Les)   ▽ 19 | 13 | 17 | 45
54, rue de Bourgogne, 7ᵉ (Varenne), 01 45 51 61 09; fax 01 45 51 27 34
■ Though it's actually been around a while, this "friendly fish joint" in the 7th seems like "a surprising discovery" since chef and co-owner Emmanuel Jerz (ex Guy Savoy) took over – now "the cooking's ambitious, like" its creator; perhaps "the prix fixe menus are less advantageous than they used to be", but the "soothing atmosphere" and "good service" remain the same.

Gli Angeli ●⑤   15 | 12 | 15 | 35
5, rue St-Gilles, 3ᵉ (Chemin Vert/St-Paul), 01 42 71 05 80
■ Not far from the Place des Vosges, this "pretty trattoria" pulls an arty local crowd that debates its growing popularity: the hostile huff it's "too bad success has caused them to raise prices and cut portions in half"; still, for most it's a "relaxed", if "noisy", neighborhood place "run by Italians"

and featuring "very good cooking, value for the money" and "super-nice staffers."

Goumard 🆂   21 | 16 | 19 | 86

9, rue Duphot, 1ᵉʳ (Madeleine), 01 42 60 36 07; fax 01 42 60 04 54

◪ Though it has recently changed owners and chefs, this veteran establishment "close to the Place de la Madeleine" continues to please with "extraordinary seafood and excellent service" in a dining room with "lovely decor complete with Lalique lighting fixtures and a faux fish tank" (the fishies are made of glass); antagonists argue it lacks "that 'something special' quality – only the [high] prices hold that honor" – but the predominant school says you "should splurge" on "food to die for in a bright happy room."

Gourmet de l'Isle 🆂   18 | 16 | 18 | 43

42, rue St-Louis-en-l'Ile, 4ᵉ (Pont-Marie), 01 43 26 79 27

◪ "Located on the Ile Saint-Louis", this "somewhat romantic" Traditional French has a wonderful setting – a beamed and vaulted 17th-century cellar – but opinions vary on the cooking, ranging from "classic and well-prepared" to "an overall disappointment" (maybe "simple and old-fashioned" dishes like "guinea hen with lentils" don't leave a major "memory"); still, this islander's worth a bridge crossing for its "marvelous, playful staff" and the fact that it's a "great bargain."

Gourmets des Ternes (Les)   18 | 10 | 12 | 43

87, bd de Courcelles, 8ᵉ (Ternes), 01 42 27 43 04

■ Its devoted following declares this "real bistro" near the Place des Ternes "chic, authentic and sincere", with a Traditional French menu that emphasizes "very good meat", including what many claim is the "best prime rib in Paris", and "great baba au rhum"; many would also agree that "the setting and the hospitality are mediocre"; be sure to book, since it's always "packed, and deservedly so."

Graindorge   17 | 12 | 16 | 51

15, rue de l'Arc-de-Triomphe, 17ᵉ (Charles de Gaulle-Etoile), 01 47 54 00 28; fax 01 47 54 00 28

■ "Inventive cooking" that features "the culinary specialties of Northern France" and Belgium, plus "rare beers" from Flanders, leads loyalists to this locale "a few steps from the Etoile"; "it lacks a scene", but the "attentive" service and "pleasant art deco" setting make it a "favorite for quiet business lunches."

Grand Café (Le) ●🆂   14 | 20 | 15 | 46

4, bd des Capucines, 9ᵉ (Opéra), 01 43 12 19 00; fax 01 43 12 19 09

◪ "The Boulevard des Capucines location and the belle epoque decor are the draws" of this Frères Blanc–chain brassiere, since the cuisine is at best "correct" (though "now much better than fast food") and the "service is spotty"; still, it's "a sure value for shellfish", especially "after an Opéra Garnier" evening.

Grand Colbert (Le) ◐Ⓢ | 13 | 20 | 15 | 44 |

2, rue Vivienne, 2ᵉ (Bourse/Palais-Royal), 01 42 86 87 88; fax 01 42 86 82 65

◪ Located in the beautiful Passage Vivienne, this landmark locale is "one of the prettiest grand brasseries in Paris"; but while everyone says "yes to the very attractive decor", plenty say "no to the mediocre cooking and the prices"; but even if "it could do better", it's still recommended for "people-watching" (just be aware the "fun starts at 11 PM with the post-theater crowd; earlier, and it's all tourists").

Grande Armée (La) ◐Ⓢ | 11 | 16 | 10 | 43 |

3, av de la Grande-Armée, 16ᵉ (Charles de Gaulle-Etoile), 01 45 00 24 77; fax 01 45 00 95 50

◪ "Another Costes restaurant with a decor by Jacques Garcia" jeer jaded surveyors who hiss the "insipid" food, "mediocre value for the money" and "catastrophic" staff ("for service, McDonald's is better") at this large Classic French; on the other hand, optimists enjoy the "pretty" Napoleon III–style interior, the "nice terrace" and the "great location" near the Etoile, even calling the "cold shellfish platters excellent."

GRANDE CASCADE (LA) Ⓢ | 21 | 25 | 21 | 96 |

Bois de Boulogne, allée de Longchamp, 16ᵉ (Porte Maillot), 01 45 27 33 51; fax 01 42 88 99 06

■ Everyone loves the "sumptuous", "magical, romantic setting" – a Napoleon III pavilion – and "superb decor" of this New French in the Bois de Boulogne, and a cascade of compliments also falls on the "almost-perfect service"; if a majority admires the "fine food", a few feel it's "not up to the prices", but overall, this is a midsummer night's "dream"; N.B. the departure of chef Jean-Louis Nomicos may outdate the Food score.

Grande Rue (La) | – | – | – | I |

117, rue de Vaugirard, 15ᵉ (Vaugirard), 01 47 34 96 12
Though the dining room is simple to the point of being austere and the location in the 15th is a bit off the beaten track, the good-value prix fixes have made this young bistro a grand hit with thrifty bon vivants; chef-owner Emmanuel Billaud, who worked with Alain Ducasse and Joël Robuchon, does hearty Classic French cooking, which pleases the stylish young types who've become regulars here.

Grandes Marches (Les) ◐Ⓢ | 15 | 16 | 16 | 48 |

6, pl de la Bastille, 12ᵉ (Bastille), 01 43 42 90 32; fax 01 43 44 80 02
◪ This brasserie with a "chic and slightly cold" decor by star architect Christian de Portzamparc and his wife Elizabeth is "the perfect place for pre– and post–Opéra"

Bastille dining confirm culture-vultures who applaud its "wonderful seafood platters" and "professional" service; but critics call the cooking "boring", suggesting that its "unusual location" is its main plus.

Grand Louvre (Le) ⑤   ▽ | 16 | 19 | 21 | 56 |

Musée du Louvre, under the Pyramide, 1er (Palais Royal-Musée du Louvre), 01 40 20 53 20; fax 01 42 86 04 63

■ "One wonders why this spot isn't better frequented" – in the midst of the busy Louvre, it's an "elegant", "nice quiet place to sit down and have a good meal" of Classic French fare surrounded by modern decor by Jean-Michel Wilmotte; "probably it's the location" under the famed pyramid that keeps it hidden, but at least it's also a "best-kept secret" for value too.

GRAND VÉFOUR (LE) | 27 | 28 | 26 | 123 |

17, rue de Beaujolais, 1er (Palais Royal-Musée du Louvre), 01 42 96 56 27; fax 01 42 86 80 71

■ "One of the glories of France", this "exquisite", "elegant" and "very expensive" Haute Cuisine haven makes a diner "feel like a grand duchess" or Napoleon, since it's "so beautiful and full of history" in its "gorgeous", Directoire-decorated (and No.1-rated) dining room overlooking the gardens of the Palais Royal; "the superb creations" of chef Guy Martin leave everyone scrambling for superlatives such as "sublime", and the "impeccable service" rounds out the pleasure of a trip to the "height of luxe."

Grand Venise (Le) | 21 | 16 | 19 | 84 |

171, rue de la Convention, 15e (Convention), 01 45 32 49 71; fax 01 45 32 07 49

■ "It's the Venice of Casanova" crow conquests of this long-running "festival" in the 15th that offers "a typically Italian avalanche" in its "gigantic portions" of "excellent" food and "generous welcome"; yes, "the bill tends to run away", but the cost is "justified."

Grange Batelière (A la) | 17 | 14 | 17 | 49 |

16, rue de la Grange-Batelière, 9e (Richelieu-Drouot), 01 47 70 85 15; fax 01 47 70 85 15

■ "Inspired cooking" and "old-fashioned bistro decor" (carefully restored since a post-*Survey* fire) are the attractions at this New French in the 9th, near many a bank HQ and the Drouot auction rooms (hence, "no ambiance at night"); despite that, it's such a "pleasant spot" that it "makes you want to become a regular"; P.S. there's "good game in season."

Grenadin (Le)   ▽ | 19 | 16 | 17 | 50 |

44, rue de Naples, 8e (Villiers), 01 45 63 28 92; fax 01 45 61 24 76

■ "Always enjoyable" and "very good value for the money" say those who know this "quiet" New French bistro in a "slightly anonymous" spot in the 8th; a few find the "small" dining room "needs refreshing", but the "gentle prices" and "discreet" service prevail.

Grenier de Notre Dame (Le) **S**   ▽ 18 | 17 | 16 | 32
18, rue de la Bûcherie, 5ᵉ (Maubert-Mutualité/St-Michel), 01 43 29 98 29; fax 01 43 29 98 29
◪ Macrobiotic mavens migrate toward this "nice little Vegetarian spot" with a "great location" in Saint-Michel, marveling over the "highly nourishing" fare and "pretty" surroundings with a plethora of potted plants; but critics carp about being "packed in like sardines" to feed on "casseroles that are all the same."

Griffonnier (Le)   ▽ 16 | 10 | 18 | 39
8, rue des Saussaies, 8ᵉ (Champs-Elysées/ Miromesnil), 01 42 65 17 17
◼ "Serious cholesterol in several wonderful forms" is the take on the "tasty" cooking of this "very chic" wine bar in the heart of the 8th; "it's only open for dinner on Thursdays", but this "very good address" is definitely worth discovering at noon; just be prepared for "a bit of a crush."

Grille (La)   ▽ 20 | 12 | 18 | 62
80, rue du Faubourg Poissonnière, 10ᵉ (Poissonnière), 01 47 70 89 73
◼ For most, the major memories of this "good and pleasant" bistro in the 10th are of "the turbot, which is magic", and the "effusive personality of the owner"; the "kitschy decor" surrounds a "meal that's amusing – until the check comes."

Grille Montorgueil (La) ◐**S**   ▽ 13 | 13 | 11 | 35
50, rue Montorgueil, 2ᵉ (Etienne-Marcel), 01 42 33 21 21; fax 01 42 33 21 21
◼ "One of the prettiest zinc bars" in Paris highlights the cute "old-fashioned setting" of this Traditional French bistro in the 2nd; "good food", including an "excellent steak tartare", and modest prices pull a lively young clientele.

Gualtiero Marchesi   – | – | – | E
Hôtel Lotti, 7, rue de Castiglione, 1ᵉʳ (Concorde/Palais Royal-Musée du Louvre), 01 42 60 40 62; fax 01 42 60 55 03
Owner Gualtiero Marchesi, the maestro of Milano, flies his flag at this slick yearling in the Hôtel Lotti; prices take a cue from the fancy jewelers in the Place Vendôme nearby – they're *molto caro*, caro – but this hasn't stopped a well-heeled crowd of Parisian pastaphiles from parking themselves on the white-canvas chairs and partaking of the kitchen's playful, inventive modern riff on Italian cooking.

Guilvinec (Le) **S**   ▽ 16 | 15 | 15 | 43
34, cour St-Emilion, 12ᵉ (Cour St-Emilion), 01 44 68 01 35; fax 01 44 68 08 17
◼ With a handsome and "calm setting" in one of the old stone wine warehouses of the pedestrian-only Cour Saint-Emilion, this "quality place" serves "sublime fish"; some

find it "a little expensive", but most are content with this catch, "especially on nice days."

Guinguette de Neuilly (La) ⑤   13 | 18 | 14 | 39
12, bd Georges Seurat, Neuilly-sur-Seine (Porte de Champerret), 01 46 24 25 04; fax 01 47 38 20 49
■ "A table overlooking the Seine", "old-fashioned ambiance and lots of charm" are the lures at this Classic French on the Ile de la Jatte in Neuilly; you "accept the mediocre cooking" and "the slightly inflated prices" "for the setting", especially "on a pretty summer night."

Guirlande de Julie (La) ⑤   ▽ 14 | 18 | 16 | 44
25, pl des Vosges, 4ᵉ (Bastille/St-Paul), 01 48 87 94 07; fax 01 48 87 01 22
◪ Owned by the Terrail family, which also runs La Tour d'Argent and L'Escargot Montorgueil, this "restaurant benefits from the attraction of the Place des Vosges", but if some find it "classic and reasonable", others call it "a tourist trap" with "slow service"; the consensus, though, is "correct."

GUY SAVOY, RESTAURANT   26 | 22 | 25 | 126
18, rue Troyon, 17ᵉ (Charles de Gaulle-Etoile/Ternes), 01 43 80 40 61; fax 01 46 22 43 09
■ "Guy Savoy's attentiveness, combined with outstanding cuisine, makes the evening go much too quickly" at his "serious but fun" New French in the 17th; "truly exceptional food", including "artichoke soup to die for", is "served with grace and pride" (and augmented by "the chef-owner making several passes through the dining room"); depending on your taste, the revamped decor is either "elegant and modern" or "somber and stifling", but overall, this is "a place you want to come back to"; P.S. "single diners welcome."

Hangar (Le) ◕⇥   17 | 11 | 15 | 32
12, impasse Berthaud, 3ᵉ (Rambuteau), 01 42 74 55 44
■ "It certainly lives up to its reputation for the chocolate cake, and the foie gras is the best" sigh surveyors over the signature dishes of this little New French "lost in a dead-end street near the Centre Pompidou"; admittedly the "setting's sad" and it's "a nuisance that they don't take credit cards", but it's an "agreeable" experience – and "an excellent buy."

Hédiard   16 | 16 | 15 | 51
21, pl de la Madeleine, 8ᵉ (Madeleine), 01 43 12 88 99; fax 01 43 12 88 98
■ Located "upstairs from the [celebrated] gourmet food shop", this eatery offers "tasty", though "predictable", Traditional French cuisine; still, the "tables are well spaced", the "prices are honest" and overall, it's well "worth a stop if you're near the Madeleine" or "for lunch with a girlfriend."

HÉLÈNE DARROZE

21 | 17 | 16 | 85

4, rue d'Assas, 6e (Sèvres-Babylone), 01 42 22 00 11;
fax 01 42 22 25 40

☑ "Sometimes you're enchanted and sometimes you're disappointed" at this highly publicized spot in the 6th run by a rising young chef from a gourmet dynasty; while admirers hail her "Haute Cuisine of the Southwest" as "creative and challenging" and served by a "friendly, non-obtrusive staff", detractors dismiss as "all hype and no substance" the "horribly expensive" food that's "fair at best" and slam the service as "very slow"; all agree you should "avoid it in hot weather" (room's "uncomfortably warm").

Higuma 🆂

▽ 16 | 5 | 11 | 20

32 bis, rue Ste-Anne, 1er (Pyramides), 01 47 03 38 59

■ Though the "depressing decor is worthy of a barracks in Vladivostok", most fans of this Nipponese near the Opéra Garnier ignore it in favor of the "excellent cooking" for "very reasonable prices"; "the dumplings are fantastic, and the cooks work in front of you, Japanese style"; just don't be disappointed that "they don't serve sushi."

Hippopotamus 🆂

9 | 7 | 8 | 27

29, rue Berger, 1er (Les Halles), 01 45 08 00 29;
fax 01 40 41 98 63 🕐

1, bd des Capucines, 2e (Opéra), 01 47 42 75 70;
fax 01 42 65 23 08 🕐

1, bd Beaumarchais, 4e (Bastille), 01 44 61 90 40;
fax 01 48 87 84 67 🕐

9, rue Lagrange, 5e (Maubert-Mutualité), 01 43 54 13 99;
fax 01 44 07 18 20 🕐

119, bd du Montparnasse, 6e (Vavin), 01 43 20 37 04;
fax 01 43 22 68 95 🕐

42, av des Champs-Elysées, 8e (Franklin D. Roosevelt),
01 53 83 94 50; fax 01 53 83 94 51

20, rue Quentin Bauchart, 8e (George V), 01 47 20 30 14;
fax 01 47 20 95 31 🕐

68, bd du Montparnasse, 14e (Montparnasse-Bienvenüe),
01 40 64 14 94; fax 01 43 21 46 10

CNIT, 2, pl de la Défense, Puteaux (La Défense-Grande
Arche), 01 46 92 13 75; fax 01 46 92 13 69

8, bd Saint Denis, 10e (Strasbourg-St-Denis),
01 53 38 80 28; fax 01 53 38 80 26 🕐

☑ "Tough steaks and tougher waitresses" tells the story at this "unavoidable (alas)" carnivore's chain with locations all over Paris; though those who think these terminals "tacky" and "noisy" rule the day, a minority maintains they offer "good meat" and frites at "reasonable prices" and "'round the clock" (many branches serve until 5 AM).

Hiramatsu

– | – | – | E

7, quai Bourbon, 4^e (Pont Marie), 01 56 81 08 80; fax 01 56 81 08 81

Tucked away in a tiny (only 18 covers) home on the Ile Saint-Louis, star Japanese chef Hiroyuki Hiramatsu offers his own take on French Haute Cuisine with dishes like thin strips of pigeon covering warm foie gras and a garnish of Savoy cabbage; a chic contempo decor adorns a beamed-ceiling, exposed-stone-wall room with frosted glass and black slate; be prepared for muscular checks.

Huîtrier (L') ⑤ | 17 | 11 | 14 | 46 |
16, rue Saussier-Leroy, 17ᵉ (Ternes), 01 40 54 83 44; fax 01 40 54 83 86
■ No one much cares for the airline-office decor and "crowded" setting of this seafooder in the 17th, but that doesn't stop most from coming anyway, since "the oysters are gorgeous" and the "fish is very fresh"; many mourn "the mounting prices."

I Golosi ◐ | 18 | 11 | 13 | 42 |
6, rue de la Grange-Batelière, 9ᵉ (Richelieu-Drouot), 01 48 24 18 63
■ Located behind the Drouot auction rooms, this modern Italian offers "attentive service" and an "inventive" menu of "copious dishes", like the signature "delicious risotto", that keep it busy, even if it's "a little expensive."

Il Baccello | ▽ 20 | 11 | 17 | 45 |
33, rue Cardinet, 17ᵉ (Wagram), 01 43 80 63 60; fax 01 43 80 63 65
◪ Young Italian chef Raphael Bembaron trained at Joia, the famous meatless restaurant in Milan, and this past experience makes his intimate storefront in the 17th "an excellent choice for vegetarians who love contemporary Italian cooking"; a minority mumbles this Med's "mediocre" and "pretentious", but most enjoy the "original" experience.

Il Barone ◐⑤ | 17 | 9 | 17 | 37 |
5, rue Léopold Robert, 14ᵉ (Raspail/Vavin), 01 43 20 87 14; fax 01 43 20 87 14
■ According to its many fans, this "very good trattoria" in Montparnasse has "smiling service" and "reasonable prices" along with "authentic", "well-prepared Italian standards"; yes, the surroundings get "smoky" and "noisy", but for most "it's a nice surprise"; P.S. "the back room is the best" place to be seated.

Il Cortile | 20 | 18 | 18 | 69 |
Hôtel Castille, 37, rue Cambon, 1ᵉʳ (Concorde/Madeleine), 01 44 58 45 67; fax 01 44 58 45 69
■ "Ah, that patio!" – "one meal in the garden and you'll think you're in Italy" avow *amici* of this hotel "sophisticate" in the 1st, where "very nice servers" dish up "incredible", "innovative" cuisine; a few fuss it's a "fine Italian place that's been Ducasse-ed into an Italianate French place" (chef Alain Ducasse is culinary consultant), but for most it's "the best [of The Boot] in Paris" and even a "good buy" at lunch, assuming the waiter "presents you with the prix fixe menu."

Ile (L') ◑ S

12	20	11	42

170, quai de Stalingrad, Parc de l'Ile St-Germain, Issy-les-Moulineaux (RER Issy-Val de Marne), 01 41 09 99 99; fax 01 41 09 99 19

◪ "Perfect for seeing and being seen" if you're part of the "TV and advertising crowd", this "hangar-like" Classic French in Issy-les-Moulineaux serves food "that's not particularly original" but is "pretty good for a fashion restaurant"; the terrace on the water's edge is "pleasant, especially for brunch"; just be prepared for a "noisy" buzz and to "play spot-the-waiter" when you need service.

Il Etait une Oie dans le Sud-Ouest

15	9	13	32

8, rue Gustave Flaubert, 17ᵉ (Ternes/Villiers), 01 43 80 18 30; fax 01 43 80 99 50

■ "*Vive* the cassoulet" and all the other "good regional specialties" (duck confit, foie gras) that have won this "genial" Southwesterner near the Place des Ternes a happy following among those who "don't watch the cholesterol"; it's also "a great buy" and there's a "friendly welcome", even if "the service is a little slow."

Il Palazzo

–	–	–	E

Hôtel Normandy, 7, rue de l'Echelle, 1ᵉʳ (Palais Royal-Musée du Louvre/Pyramides), 01 42 60 91 20; fax 01 42 60 45 81

The striking decor, a mix of Napoleon III and Milano modern, as in white curtains hanging from a seventeen-foot ceiling, perfectly reflects the cooking of chef Thierry Barot, whose Classic French menu speaks with an Italian accent; the Hôtel Normandy crowd is similarly cosmopolitan.

Il Ristorante

17	14	16	57

22, rue Fourcroy, 17ᵉ (Wagram), 01 47 54 91 48; fax 01 47 63 34 00

◪ To its admirers, this Italian not far from the Place des Ternes is "a good one" for "delicious" "dishes prepared as they should be" and a "warm welcome"; but gripers grumble about the "austere" decor and suggest "the boss should have another look at the quality of the service, which is neither amiable or efficient."

Il Sardo

19	12	17	42

11, rue Treilhard, 8ᵉ (Miromesnil), 01 45 61 09 46; fax 01 42 89 11 14

■ "Bravo" surveyors say to this "friendly and genuine" Sardinian (as the name translates) in the 8th; most feel that its move from a rue de Clichy storefront to a larger, quieter and more comfortable dining room "hasn't changed a thing", since the "pasta is [still] exquisite" and the service remains "personalized, smiling and efficient."

Il Viaggio

–	–	–	E

34, rue de Bourgogne, 7ᵉ (Varenne), 01 45 55 80 75; fax 01 47 05 34 47

The terra-cotta colored walls of this intimate young enclave serve as the backdrop to some elegant contemporary Italian cooking by young chef Giovanni Perrone; popular with politicians from the nearby Assemblée Nationale by day, it pulls dressed-up locals in the evening.

Il Viccolo ∣ − ∣ − ∣ − ∣ M ∣
34, rue Mazarine, 6ᵉ (Odéon), 01 43 25 01 11
Chef Angelo Procopio once had a very popular Italian restaurant by the same name in the Marais, and now he runs this reasonably priced place in Saint-Germain (rapidly becoming the gastronomic Little Italy of Paris); dishes like squid-and-red-bean salad or homemade spaghetti with zucchini and baby clams have made this enclosed-sidewalk cafe a happily noisy home both for old friends and new.

Impala Lounge ●S ∣ 10 ∣ 15 ∣ 11 ∣ 36 ∣
2, rue de Berri, 8ᵉ (George V), 01 43 59 12 66; fax 01 43 59 24 64
◪ Those seeking "a safari on the Champs-Elysées" should seek out this "trendy" spot in the 8th, whose "pretty decor" boasts leopard-print fabric and high-backed wooden chairs; however, the "great atmosphere and excellent music" ("jazz during Sunday brunch") are the high points of the hunt, since antagonists avow there's "nothing especially African about the food" – and "no culinary interest" either.

Impatient (L') ∣ 17 ∣ 11 ∣ 13 ∣ 36 ∣
14, passage Geffroy Didelot, 17ᵉ (Rome/Villiers), 01 43 87 28 10; fax 01 43 87 28 10
◼ "A really great surprise" exclaim those who've just discovered this little New French where "old bathtubs planted with flowers" line the terrace set on "a pedestrian street" in the 17th; what they rave about is the "refined and innovative cooking" for "unbeatable prices"; only, was the name inspired by the "smiling" but "very slow service"?

Improviste (A l') ∇ ∣ 14 ∣ 8 ∣ 13 ∣ 36 ∣
21, rue Médéric, 17ᵉ (Courcelles/Monceau), 01 42 27 86 67
◪ Advocates are "never disappointed" in this "good neighborhood bistro" in the 17th because it offers "a great set-price menu that includes wine" and Classic French dishes made with "fresh foodstuffs"; but critics counter that the 30-seat dining room is "too small" and "rather ugly" and the food is "badly served", despite the "client-loving owner."

Inagiku ∣ 14 ∣ 11 ∣ 15 ∣ 40 ∣
14, rue de Pontoise, 5ᵉ (Maubert-Mutualité), 01 43 54 70 07; fax 01 40 51 74 44
◼ "A perfect place to introduce Japanese cooking to your children" profess pleased parents about this "reasonably priced" address in the Latin Quarter; "the decor's cold and without originality", but "the owner's nice" and "it's always a diversion", since most of the food preparation is done in front of you on "heated tabletops."

Indiana Café ●⑤
8 | 7 | 8 | 25

7, bd des Capucines, 2ᵉ (Opéra), 01 42 68 02 22
1, pl de la République, 3ᵉ (République), 01 48 87 82 35
130, bd St-Germain, 6ᵉ (Odéon), 01 46 34 66 31
235-237, rue du Faubourg St-Honoré, 8ᵉ (Ternes), 01 44 09 80 00
79, bd de Clichy, 9ᵉ (Place de Clichy), 01 48 74 42 61
14, pl de la Bastille, 11ᵉ (Bastille), 01 44 75 79 80
72, bd du Montparnasse, 14ᵉ (Montparnasse-Bienvenüe),
01 43 35 02 34; fax 01 43 35 07 25
◪ "Is there really a cook in the kitchen?" query querulous customers of this "hamburger and Tex-Mex" chain; a few defenders – maybe "homesick Americans" – say "it's a sure bet for a burger" "after the movies" and a "good buy for the money", but the majority maintains that given "the noise" and "poor service", "there's no reason to try" these places.

Indra
16 | 16 | 14 | 47

10, rue du Commandant Rivière, 8ᵉ (St-Philippe-du-Roule),
01 43 59 46 40; fax 01 42 25 00 32
◪ "Hot food and a cool welcome" sums up the mixed reaction to this veteran Brahmin in the 8th; while converts contend it's "one of the few Indian restaurants that actually serves Indian" cuisine and admire the "refined" ambiance, the less-content contend that the "surly" service makes the experience seem "not as good."

Iode (L')
– | – | – | M

48, rue d'Argout, 2ᵉ (Etienne Marcel/Sentier), 01 42 36 46 45
Tucked away in a fashionable pedestrian street on the northern edge of Les Halles, this new seafooder is a hit with the locals, as well as other young fish fans who've heard about the simply cooked, first-rate marine fare; service is rather rapid, perhaps reflecting the beat of the loud background music.

ISAMI ⑤
24 | 13 | 17 | 50

4, quai d'Orléans, 4ᵉ (Pont-Marie), 01 40 46 06 97
■ There's "no contest" – "the best sushi in Paris" is found at this small Japanese on the Ile St-Louis, which is "absolutely worth trying" for "fish like you find in Tokyo"; "it's a little expensive, but that's normal for flavors that are unlike anything you've ever tasted."

Isard (L')
– | – | – | M

14, rue St-Augustin, 2ᵉ (Quatre Septembre), 01 42 96 00 26;
fax 01 42 96 10 06
Though it's unlikely you'll spot an isard – a species of Pyrenean mountain stag – in the vaulted basement of this bistro, chef-owner Victor Brisebois maintains a decidedly Southwestern tone on his menu, which includes a variety of Basque and Bearnais dishes; situated in the 2nd, not far from the Opéra Garnier, the dining room fills with a mix of theatergoers and bargain-hunting tourists by night, more of a business crowd by day.

Isse
22 | 13 | 15 | 65

56, rue Ste-Anne, 2ᵉ (Pyramides/Quatre Septembre),
01 42 96 67 76; fax 01 42 96 82 63

■ "Expensive, but justifiably so", this 2nd arrondissement Asian "offers an experience equal to the best restaurants in Japan" declare disciples of its "delicious" sushi and sashimi, among other dishes; refurbished with a fresh take on its signature minimalist style (possibly unreflected in the Decor score), it's frequented by a stylish crowd, including "the designer Kenzo", which finds "it's best to be at the bar."

JACQUES CAGNA
23 | 22 | 22 | 97

14, rue des Grands-Augustins, 6ᵉ (Odéon/St-Michel),
01 43 26 49 39; fax 01 43 54 54 48

☑ Admirers applaud the "great" "Traditional" French food and "lovely service" at chef Jacques Cagna's eponymous establishment with a "charming setting" in a "16th-century house" not far from the Odéon; though a cluster of critics carp that a "clientele that's mostly tourists" doesn't notice it "lacks creativity" and has grown "very expensive", it remains a "warm and comfortable" "old favorite" for many.

JAMIN
25 | 22 | 24 | 103

32, rue de Longchamp, 16ᵉ (Trocadéro), 01 45 53 00 07;
fax 01 45 53 00 15

☑ This "lovely, cozy" New French in the 16th attracts a lot of "wealthy, air-kissing Americans" for the "magnificent cooking" of chef-owner Benoît Guichard, "a protégé" of retired star chef Joël Robuchon, and "impeccable service"; of course "memories of past glories" leave longtimers feeling "let down", but for most, this "time capsule" remains "a little marvel" that's not only good "for business" but "perfect for a romantic dinner."

Jardin (Le)
21 | 20 | 22 | 77

Hôtel Royal Monceau, 37, av Hoche, 8ᵉ (Charles de Gaulle-Etoile), 01 42 99 98 70; fax 01 42 99 89 90

■ "A most pleasant surprise", this "charming place" in the Hôtel Royal Monceau near the Arc de Triomphe rouses applause for the "excellent", "light" Med–New French cooking of chef Hervé Galidie, as well as the "attentive service" and "beautiful decor" – the dining room overlooks an interior garden, with "a lovely terrace"; prices are hefty, but the "international clientele" doesn't complain.

Jardin des Cygnes Ⓢ
▽ 23 | 27 | 24 | 85

Hôtel Prince de Galles, 33, av George V, 8ᵉ (George V),
01 53 23 78 50; fax 01 53 23 78 82

■ "One of the best places for a business lunch" or "an excellent Sunday brunch", this dining room just off the Champs-Elysées is also recommended for a "romantic dinner", especially in summer, when they serve on the courtyard terrace, "a wonderful setting"; "service is attentive but not overbearing", and though "expensive", it's "among the better hotel restaurants" in Paris for "delicious" Classic French cooking.

Jardins de Bagatelle (Les) S — 13 | 21 | 14 | 56

Route de Sèvres à Neuilly, 16ᵉ (Pont-de-Neuilly), 01 40 67 98 29; fax 01 40 67 93 04

■ Most say the "enchanting setting" of this Classic French overlooking the "beautiful" Bois de Boulogne's Bagatelle gardens makes up for the "mediocre food", "exasperatingly slow service" and "absurd prices"; it's "perfect for a romantic evening" when your mind's not on eating anyway.

Jarrasse S — 16 | 10 | 14 | 70

4, av de Madrid, Neuilly-sur-Seine (Pont-de-Neuilly), 01 46 24 07 56; fax 01 40 88 35 60

■ "Very good but too expensive" is the prevailing judgment on this "familial fish house" with "soigné service" in Neuilly that "definitely knows its subject – seafood"; perhaps the "classic", if slightly "unoriginal", preparations make it seem pricey "for what you're eating"; certainly an "antiquated setting" doesn't help.

Je Thé . . . Me — – | – | – | M

4, rue d'Alleray, 15ᵉ (Convention/Vaugirard), 01 48 42 48 30; fax 01 48 42 48 30

Though not well known, this "very pleasant" neighborhood tearoom in the 15th delights its regulars with "a relaxed family style atmosphere" in a dining room with "superb decor" created by the intact interiors of a landmarked 19th-century grocery store; "the kitchen has a real way with fish" and other light New French dishes and offers "good value for the money" too.

Joe Allen ◑ S — 13 | 14 | 14 | 35

30, rue Pierre Lescot, 1ᵉʳ (Etienne-Marcel), 01 42 36 70 13; fax 01 42 36 90 80

◪ "If you're tired of nose-in-the-air Parisian waiters, this just might be the place for you" suggest surveyors who like the "good service" and "authentic New York ambiance" at this Les Halles branch of a Manhattan theater-district restaurant; no one raves about the American cuisine, but it's "practical, and not bad in the hamburger-and-cheesecake genre", although several find it "expensive for what it is."

Jo Goldenberg ◑ S — 10 | 8 | 10 | 35

7, rue des Rosiers, 4ᵉ (St-Paul), 01 48 87 20 16; fax 01 48 87 20 16

◪ "Oy, don't bother!" cry critics, whose kveching about this 1920s "classic Eastern European deli's" "declining cuisine", less-than-pristine surroundings and "slapdash service" are confirmed by a slip in scores; a few find there's "terrific matzo-ball soup" and perhaps "the potato pancake is worth a visit", but most go only for "the great history of the [old] Jewish quarter" of the Marais.

Joséphine "Chez Dumonet"

20 | 14 | 15 | 60

117, rue du Cherche-Midi, 6ᵉ (Duroc/Falguière), 01 45 48 52 40;
fax 01 42 84 06 83

■ Near Montparnasse, this "gem" of a "neighborhood bistro" with belle epoque decor is "the type of restaurant foreigners incorrectly assume abounds in Paris"; would that it were true, since they serve "great food" from the Landes region, including "mille-feuille of pigeon" and "truffles in season"; P.S. "sit outside, weather permitting."

JULES VERNE S

22 | 27 | 21 | 99

Tour Eiffel, 2nd level, 7ᵉ (Bir-Hakeim), 01 45 55 61 44;
fax 01 47 05 29 41

◪ "You must go at least once", since the "dream setting" of this eatery perched on the second level of the Eiffel Tower offers a "grand experience"; but once past that "magic" panorama of Paris, "responses are less elevated": though fans find the Classic French eats "exceptional" and the staff "warm", skeptics snap "the fish was tough, and so was the maitre d'"; still, that "gorgeous view" leaves most "high on meals" here.

Jumeaux (Les)

▽ 17 | 13 | 16 | 36

73, rue Amelot, 11ᵉ (Chemin Vert), 01 43 14 27 00

■ Though few know it, those who do would agree that this tiny New French run by "adorable" twin brothers near the Cirque d'Hiver in the 11th is "a real treasure" with "careful, original cooking", including the "magic foie gras starter"; the small dining room strikes some as "slightly sad", but others (maybe fans of the modern art on the walls) say it's "sort of elegant"; undisputed is the fact that it's "a great buy."

Juveniles

15 | 12 | 17 | 35

47, rue de Richelieu, 1ᵉʳ (Bourse/Palais Royal-Musée du Louvre),
01 42 97 46 49; fax 01 42 60 31 52

■ "If you want to find English-speaking people in Paris, go here" recommend regulars of this "casual" bar à vins in the 1st; Scottish owner "Tim Johnston is a hoot", and he creates a "convivial" ambiance of "such charm" that fans overlook the "too small" dining room and "slightly expensive" prices for the pleasure of Mediterranean "dishes washed down well" with "very good foreign" and French wines.

Kaïten ◑

– | – | – | M

63, rue Pierre Charron, 8ᵉ (George V), 01 43 59 78 78;
fax 01 43 59 71 51

This conveyor-belt sushi place has instantly picked up a large and fashionable following in the 8th; take a seat at either the counter or a table and pick from a revolving assortment of raw fish that's priced according to the color of the dish it's served on; tabs are moderate unless you opt for one of the hot main courses (served only at tables).

Kambodgia
18 | 20 | 16 | 47

15, rue de Bassano, 16ᵉ (George V), 01 47 23 31 80; fax 01 47 20 41 22

■ With "soft lighting" and "very pretty", if "somber", decor of wood and bamboo, this Asian in the 16th is "pleasant for a romantic night out"; the kitchen produces an "excellent" array of "refined" Cambodian, Laotian and Vietnamese dishes; the hitch: it's "expensive", given the "small portions."

Khun Akorn 🅂
∇ 21 | 16 | 16 | 39

8, av de Taillebourg, 11ᵉ (Nation), 01 43 56 20 03; fax 01 40 09 18 44

■ Intrepid explorers of the 11th say this relatively unknown Thai near the Place de la Nation "should be discovered" for its "original" dishes like 'tiger tears' (grilled fillet of beef marinated in herbs and honey) and gentle prices; simple but attractive decor, including several framed travel posters vaunting the home country, add to the appeal.

Kim Anh 🅂
∇ 20 | 15 | 18 | 50

49, av Emile Zola, 15ᵉ (Charles Michels), 01 45 79 40 96; fax 01 40 59 49 78

■ Tucked away in the 15th, this "sophisticate" in a slightly snug location gets raves for its "heavenly Vietnamese" food ("the best I've ever tried, except for my mother-in-law's"), "attentive but not intrusive" service and "charming owner"; it's not cheap, but most vow they'll "be back."

KINUGAWA
24 | 15 | 17 | 71

9, rue du Mont Thabor, 1ᵉʳ (Tuileries), 01 42 60 65 07; fax 01 42 60 45 21
4, rue St-Philippe-du-Roule, 8ᵉ (St-Philippe-du-Roule), 01 45 63 08 07; fax 01 42 60 45 21

■ "First class" – in terms of both the "imaginative", "delicious" food and the prices ("the same ones you find in Tokyo") – is how devotees describe these two "true" Japanese in the 1st and the 8th where "the best sushi in Paris" and "divine tempura" delight the Franco-Nipponese crowds; despite discord over the decor ("sophisticated" vs. "unattractive"), most agree about the "very good service."

Kiosque (Le) 🅂
14 | 13 | 13 | 37

1, pl de Mexico, 16ᵉ (Trocadéro), 01 47 27 96 98; fax 01 45 53 89 79

◪ Run by a former journalist, this "interesting theme restaurant" in the 16th offers its "trendy" clientele a large range of regional dailies and magazines to peruse; however, the Classic French fare is the subject of warring editorials, with some advocating the "good food at good prices" and others arguing "go here to read, not eat" (unless you like "small portions" served by "unpleasant personnel").

Lac-Hong
22 | 11 | 14 | 42

67, rue Lauriston, 16ᵉ (Boissière/Victor Hugo), 01 47 55 87 17

◪ "Some of the best Asian food in Paris" draws disciples to this Sino-Vietnamese in the 16th; unfortunately, the "fine flavors" don't distract from the "slow, sullen service", "high cost" and drab decor; P.S. the best bet is to "let the owner order for you."

LADURÉE
17 | 20 | 14 | 41

21, rue Bonaparte, 6ᵉ (St-Sulpice), 01 44 07 64 87;
fax 01 44 07 64 93 ◗ 🆂
75, av des Champs-Elysées, 8ᵉ (Franklin D. Roosevelt),
01 40 75 08 75; fax 01 40 75 06 75 ◗ 🆂
16, rue Royale, 8ᵉ (Concorde/Madeleine), 01 42 60 21 79;
fax 01 49 27 01 95 ◗ 🆂
Printemps, 64, bd Haussmann, 9ᵉ (Havre-Caumartin),
01 42 82 40 10; fax 01 42 82 62 00

◪ "A sweet heaven" can be found at this quartet of "quintessential Parisian tea and pastry" rooms, known for their "exquisite" florid interiors (the 1862 "original on the Rue Royale is the loveliest"); except for the "sublime pastries" ("I'd sell my soul to the devil for the mille-feuilles and éclairs"), alas, "neither the [Classic French] food nor service matches the decor"; but with "an abundance of delicacies that boggles the mind", you'll have a "frolicking good time" anyway.

Lalqila ◗ 🆂
– | – | – | M

88, av Emile Zola, 15ᵉ (Charles Michels), 01 45 75 68 40;
fax 01 45 79 68 61

The rather "arresting" and "amusing" setting– "a copy of the Lal Qila Palace built by the Moghul Emperor Shahjehan" animated by "video clips of Indian films" – causes most of the comment at this quiet corner of the 15th; the tandoori-oriented cuisine gets nods, though be advised that as with "most Indian restaurants in Paris, 'very hot' only means that food is well-flavored with interesting spices"; service can be "slow."

Languedoc (Le) 🆂
17 | 12 | 16 | 25

64, bd de Port-Royal, 5ᵉ (Les Gobelins), 01 47 07 24 47

◪ "Real Traditional French cooking" is on offer at this bistro in the 5th arrondissement that pulls in a "neighborhood crowd of regulars"; friends name it a "fabulous find" for "good portions" and gentle prices, but foes say the "conservative" cuisine "lacks surprises" ("should be in a museum") and service "unpleasant"; still, the majority holds that the Languedoc "region is on the way up, and this restaurant is following it."

Lao Siam 🆂
▽ 20 | 7 | 10 | 25

49, rue de Belleville, 19ᵉ (Belleville/Pyrénées),
01 40 40 09 68

◼ This "excellent Thai is surely one of the best in the capital" – "it's frequented by a large number of Asians", as well as others willing to overlook the "drab decor" and make the trek up to Belleville; with such "delicious" food, it's "often packed", so definitely reserve.

Lao Tseu S ▽ 18 | 13 | 18 | 39

209, bd St-Germain, 7ᵉ (Rue du Bac), 01 45 48 30 06; fax 01 45 50 36 38

■ In the 7th, this "neighborhood Chinese" wins praises for its "excellent", "remarkably reasonably priced dishes" (perhaps a bit "short on vegetarian" options) and "extremely efficient service" that makes it "a great place when your evening involves more than eating"; dim sum at "Sunday brunch" is also fun, even though "it's too crowded" then.

LAPÉROUSE 19 | 24 | 19 | 87

51, quai des Grands-Augustins, 6ᵉ (Pont-Neuf/St-Michel), 01 43 26 90 14; fax 01 43 26 99 39

◪ Though it seems as though this place with a long and delicious history (opened in 1766) overlooking the Seine in the 6th has been on a "culinary roller coaster" for some time, the ride's gotten smoother since chef Alain Hacquard (ex Chiberta and Grand Véfour) took over; ratings and reviewers confirm the Classic French "cuisine and the service have improved considerably"; "let's hope it continues", so the only appeal won't be the "old world charm" of the "adorable little dining rooms."

LASSERRE 25 | 26 | 25 | 122

17, av Franklin D. Roosevelt, 8ᵉ (Franklin D. Roosevelt), 01 43 59 02 13; fax 01 45 63 72 23

■ "What's not to like?" about this veteran in the 8th; you go "from the private elevator to a stunning dining room whose sliding glass roof provides views of the sky"; now overseen by Jean-Louis Nomicos (ex Grande Cascade), "the Haute Cuisine's divine", and "even with 15 staff members on the floor at once the service isn't cloying"; admittedly the crowd's a tad "touristy" and the scene a bit "pompous", but that's par for the course at what's practically "the last of the great Classic French" establishments.

LAURENT 23 | 26 | 24 | 115

41, av Gabriel, 8ᵉ (Champs-Elysées-Clémenceau), 01 42 25 00 39; fax 01 45 62 45 21

■ With a "beautiful" belle epoque pavilion overlooking the gardens of the Champs-Elysées in the 8th, this "romantic" and "very, very Paris" place offers an "exceptional" experience ("irreproachable service", "exquisite" Haute Cuisine), especially if you come during the summer "for a table on the shady terrace with a fountain"; some spoilsports snap "don't be seduced by the setting, the food's mediocre", but for most the only flaw is that it's "madly expensive."

Lavinia – | – | – | M

3-5, bd de la Madeleine, 8ᵉ (Madeleine), 01 42 97 20 20; fax 01 42 97 54 50

Located in what's billed as Europe's largest wine store (with some 6,500 selections from around the world), this sleek lunch-only spot in the 8th offers a eclectic range of Classic

French dishes to accompany the substantial selection by the glass or bottle (the latter priced at retail).

LEDOYEN
22 | 24 | 23 | 101

1, av Dutuit, 8ᵉ (Concorde), 01 53 05 10 01; fax 01 47 42 55 01

☑ The Second Empire–style "dream-making" decor by star designer Jacques Grange wins raves at this restaurant with a "great location" in the gardens of the Champs-Elysées, while Christian Le Squer's "luscious" Haute Cuisine "rates praise" as well; some squawk over the service – while "attentive and professional", it creates an "arm's-length" atmosphere that's "a little stuffy" – and many ask if the overall experience is "worth the expense", but for most, this century-old stop remains "elegance personified."

Léna et Mimile
▽ 9 | 15 | 10 | 37

32, rue Tournefort, 5ᵉ (Censier-Daubenton), 01 47 07 72 47

☑ "Fun and reasonably priced", this 1937 vintage bistro has "an absolutely charming perched terrace" that many claim is the prettiest in the Latin Quarter; "it's too bad the [Alsatian-oriented] cooking isn't as good as the setting" – a fact that causes critics to caution you to come "just for the folklore."

Léon de Bruxelles
8 | 7 | 9 | 25

120, rue Rambuteau, 1ᵉʳ (Les Halles), 01 42 36 18 50; fax 01 42 36 27 50 S

3, bd Beaumarchais, 4ᵉ (Bastille), 01 42 71 75 55; fax 01 42 71 75 56 ◖S

131, bd St-Germain, 6ᵉ (Mabillon/Odéon), 01 43 26 45 95; fax 01 43 26 47 02 ◖S

63, av des Champs-Elysées, 8ᵉ (Franklin D. Roosevelt/George V), 01 42 25 96 16; fax 01 42 25 95 42 ◖S

1-3, place Pigalle, 9ᵉ (Pigalle), 01 42 80 28 33; fax 01 42 80 27 72 ◖S

8, pl. de la République, 11ᵉ (République), 01 43 38 28 69; fax 01 43 38 33 41 ◖S

64, av des Gobelins, 13ᵉ (Les Gobelins/Place d'Italie), 01 47 07 51 07; fax 01 47 07 89 04 S

82 bis, bd du Montparnasse, 14ᵉ (Montparnasse-Bienvenüe/ Vavin), 01 43 21 66 62; fax 01 43 21 66 76

349, rue de Vaugirard, 15ᵉ (Convention), 01 55 76 99 72; fax 01 55 76 99 71 ◖S

95, bd Gouvion St Cyr, 17ᵉ (Porte Maillot), 01 55 37 95 30; fax 01 55 37 95 35 ◖S

☑ "The Mickey D's of musseldom", this Belgian brasserie chain gets dissed for its "industrial cooking" and "deplorable service"; but a few fans retort "this is what fast food should be" – "fun for the kids" and "just right for emergency rations"; overall, "what you see is what you get."

Lescure
17 | 15 | 16 | 32

7, rue de Mondovi, 1ᵉʳ (Concorde), 01 42 60 18 91

■ "Good food at reasonable prices" has kept this family-owned bistro near the Place de la Concorde "packed like a sardine" can ever since it opened in 1919; "efficient, amiable service" and Traditional French and Limousin favorites like "great pickled herring" and "terrific ham and asparagus" make this place "an experience"; while the sidewalk seating is "great on a nice day", some say it's "best in the winter when there are no tourists."

Lina's
10 | 9 | 9 | 15

UGC Forum des Halles, Place de la Rotonde, 1er (Les Halles), 01 42 21 36 64; fax 01 42 21 35 74 🆂
50, rue Etienne Marcel, 2e (Etienne Marcel/Sentier), 01 42 21 16 14; fax 01 42 33 78 03
47, rue des Francs-Bourgeois, 4e (St-Paul), 01 44 78 95 00; fax 01 44 78 95 01 🆂
22, rue des Saints Pères, 7e (St-Germain-des-Prés), 01 40 20 42 78; fax 01 40 20 42 79
8, rue Marbeuf, 8e (Alma-Marceau), 01 47 23 92 33; fax 01 47 23 93 09
105, rue du Faubourg-St-Honoré, 8e (Miromesnil), 01 42 56 42 57; fax 01 42 89 93 01 ◑⊟
30, bd des Italiens, 9e (Opéra), 01 42 46 02 06; fax 01 42 46 02 40 🆂
2, rue Henri Desgrange, 12e (Bercy), 01 43 40 42 42; fax 01 43 40 65 11
23, av de Wagram, 17e (Charles de Gaulle-Etoile/Ternes), 01 45 74 76 76; fax 01 45 74 76 77
156, av Charles de Gaulle, Neuilly-sur-Seine (Pont-de-Neuilly), 01 47 45 60 60; fax 01 47 45 34 68 ◑
■ A "good packaging" concept – "fresh sandwiches" "in a stylish setting" – has caused this "convenient" chain to mushroom during the past few years; a few regret the "typically Parisian attitude toward customers" and say "it's expensive for what it is", but for most the "consistent" fare is "always a standby when in a hurry."

Livingstone ◑🆂
17 | 22 | 15 | 38

106, rue St-Honoré, 1er (Louvre-Rivoli), 01 53 40 80 50; fax 01 53 40 80 51
■ A "trendy but cozy" interior that blends African accents with vintage colonial objects characterizes this Thai that offers a "warm welcome" near Les Halles; and if many presume that "the food isn't as good as the decor", the "magical" "mix of styles" provides "a nice change of pace" to "thirtysomethings who are too old for bars but still want to have fun."

Loir dans la Théière (Le) 🆂
14 | 16 | 16 | 25

3, rue des Rosiers, 4e (St-Paul), 01 42 72 90 61
■ "Service that's young, friendly and nice" and a "very pleasant atmosphere" make this Marais tearoom a highly "congenial" spot say surveyors happily snuggling into "big leather armchairs to eat pretty good savory tarts" and "excellent pastries" that "aren't expensive"; though

"more than crowded" on weekends, it's a "very good address for brunch" too.

Lô Sushi ◑Ⓢ
| 12 | 17 | 10 | 38 |

8, rue de Berri, 8ᵉ (George V), 01 45 62 01 00; fax 01 45 62 01 10
◪ A large part of the "fun" of this "self-service" sushi spot in the 8th (with "hip" Andrée Putman–designed minimalist decor) is the "instant gratification – you see something you want and you take it off the conveyor belt" that circles the bar ("choo-choo sushi!"); to fans, it's "the ultimate fast food and very pleasant", but foes fume "it's a scandal for anyone who really knows and appreciates Japanese" cuisine – and furthermore, "the bill is often hefty."

Lozère (La)
▽ | 19 | 15 | 18 | 29 |

4, rue Hautefeuille, 6ᵉ (St-Michel), 01 43 54 26 64; fax 01 44 07 00 43
◼ Specializing in the cooking of Auvergne's Lozère region, this "rustic" little spot "in an alley" near Saint-Michel serves up "nourishing and authentic" dishes like *aligot* (a mixture of whipped potatoes, cheese curds and garlic) and sausage; and if the "large portions" make it "a little on the heavy side", the prices remain relatively lightweight, and the service "couldn't be nicer."

LUCAS CARTON
| 27 | 26 | 25 | 131 |

9, pl de la Madeleine, 8ᵉ (Concorde/Madeleine), 01 42 65 22 90; fax 01 42 65 06 23
◪ Managing what may be "the most beautiful restaurant in Paris" for its "museum-quality" art nouveau decor, chef-owner Alain Senderens stuns with his "always marvelous" Haute Cuisine, with "the matching of food with wines" "unparalleled"; the staff garners many compliments too for its "impeccable" efforts; some go away "disappointed" by the "Russian service, i.e. indifferent to frigid", and argue that even if the food's "spectacular", it doesn't merit "stratospheric prices"; still, "a must-do" for most.

Luna (La)
| 20 | 13 | 16 | 69 |

69, rue du Rocher, 8ᵉ (Villiers), 01 42 93 77 61; fax 01 40 08 02 44
◪ Located in a "quiet, petit-bourgeois area behind the Gare Saint-Lazare" in the 8th, this "excellent fish place" with "attentive but homey" service is patronized by "lots of business types", who presumably don't mind the sturdy prices; "the setting's ghastly", but "who cares about decor when the food's this good?"

Lyonnais (Aux) ◑
| – | – | – | M |

32, rue St-Marc, 2ᵉ (Bourse/Richelieu-Drouot), 01 42 96 65 04; fax 01 42 97 42 95
◪ Recently taken under the wings of chef-entrepreneur Alain Ducasse and Chez L'Ami Louis owner Thierry de la Brosse, this century-old bistro near the old stock exchange now has a new lease on life; a sensitive renovation of the

magnificent Majorelle interior, decorated with art nouveau tiles, and an appealing, reasonable menu of judiciously modernized classics from Lyon and the surrounding Beaujolais region have made it a hit with *le tout* Paris, supplemented by a sprinkling of tourists.

Ma Bourgogne ●ⓈⱫ   15 | 14 | 14 | 41

19, pl des Vosges, 4ᵉ (Bastille/St-Paul), 01 42 78 44 64; fax 01 42 78 19 37

☑ If some find this Classic French bistro "very good for a drink or snack in the Place des Vosges" (a "location that can't be beat"), others complain that the "prices are going up and the service is coming down"; follow the regulars' recommendations, though – "have the steak tartare" and, weather permitting, "sit outside under the vaulted arcade" – and you'll be happy here.

Macéo   18 | 17 | 18 | 51

15, rue des Petits-Champs, 1ᵉʳ (Bourse/Palais Royal-Musée du Louvre), 01 42 97 53 85; fax 01 47 03 36 93

☑ This "comfortable, pleasant" belle epoque room in the 1st seems to be the setting for disparate dining experiences: one camp finds the "service friendly with plenty of nice touches" and the New French food "delicious", especially the "unusual vegetarian selections"; the opposition dubs the cuisine "very disappointing" and "the waiter a caricature of French rudeness"; "at least you can drink from the long wine list" (the owner is vinophile Mark Williamson, also of Willi's Wine Bar nearby).

Madonina (La)   – | – | – | M

10, rue Marie et Louise, 10ᵉ (République), 01 42 01 25 26

The delicious pastas served at this vest-pocket Italian just steps from the Canal Saint-Martin have won it a following of hip young regulars; they also like the convivial ambiance, warm, family-style service and moderate prices, which make it easy to overlook the nondescript decor.

Magnolias (Les)   ▽ 25 | 18 | 21 | 47

48, av de Bry, Perreux-sur-Marne (RER Nogent-sur-Marne), 01 48 72 47 43; fax 01 48 72 22 28

■ "The revelation of the year" say supporters of this "sophisticated", "soigné" location where "passionate" young chef-owner Jean Chauvel's "sublime cooking" and "wonderfully subtle flavors" warrant the half-hour trip to suburban Perreux-sur-Marne; the "modest prices for such high-quality" New French fare and "excellent, if slow", service mean most would "love to come back."

Maharajah (Le) ●Ⓢ   ▽ 15 | 10 | 14 | 37

72, bd St-Germain, 5ᵉ (Maubert-Mutualité/St-Michel), 01 43 54 26 07; fax 01 40 46 08 18

■ Claiming to be Paris' oldest Indian restaurant, this Saint Michel outpost of the Subcontinent offers "delicious" food (including numerous vegetarian dishes) "at a fair price"; most agree that you "can't go wrong" here, even if the carved-wood decor could use some freshening up.

MAISON BLANCHE ⑤   19 | 23 | 17 | 89

15, av Montaigne, 8ᵉ (Alma-Marceau), 01 47 23 55 99; fax 01 47 20 09 56

◪ With a "panoramic view of Paris and the Seine" from its perch atop the Théâtre des Champs-Elysées in the 8th, this dramatic dining room pleases with its "pretty" black-and-white decor; however, the great expectations aroused by the advent of the Pourcel twins haven't yet been met: even though their New French–Southern cooking is "intelligent" and "inventive", "somehow something is missing"; "service is spotty" too, and the "prices aren't justified"; overall view: "give this one some time."

Maison Courtine (La)   ▽ 18 | 16 | 17 | 47

157, av de Maine, 14ᵉ (Alésia), 01 45 48 08 04; fax 01 45 45 91 35

◪ Near the Porte d'Orléans, this Classic French "with strong Southwestern influences" serves some "remarkable" fare and "a very intelligent wine list" in a "spacious", "well-decorated" setting, supporters say; but critics carp a meal here would be more of a treat if "the service were less stiff" and if, "instead of wandering about the dining room, the chef would stay in the kitchen so that dishes don't arrive lukewarm."

MAISON DE L'AMÉRIQUE LATINE   16 | 24 | 16 | 58

217, bd St-Germain, 7ᵉ (Rue du Bac/Solférino), 01 49 54 75 10; fax 01 40 49 03 94

◼ "Excellent during the summer, middling during the winter" is the consensus on this "classy" Left Banker in a 1700s townhouse; for although the well-bred "traditional clientele" delights in the "delicious garden" while seated on "one of Paris' most beautiful terraces", the "refined" New French cooking is "sometimes fussy" and the service "stuffy."

Maison du Caviar (La) ●⑤   19 | 15 | 17 | 77

21, rue Quentin Bauchart, 8ᵉ (George V), 01 47 23 53 43; fax 01 47 20 87 26

◼ "Judging by the chic women [here], caviar can't be fattening" speculates one surveyor (incorrectly) about the main gastronomic attraction at this "very exclusive" "jet-set canteen" in the 8th just off the Champs-Elysées; "super service", "movie-set decor" (that a few find "austere") and Russian snacks like "perfect salmon" and "the best borsch in Paris" to go along with those fish eggs make it a crowd-pleaser despite "the smoke" and "the noise."

Maison du Jardin (La)   – | – | – | I

27, rue de Vaugirard, 6ᵉ (Rennes), 01 45 48 22 31

Just steps from the Luxembourg Gardens, this understated but friendly new modern bistro is the second Left Bank address of restaurateurs Francis Vandenhande and Denise Fabre of La Ferme Saint-Simon; chef Philippe Marquis does an interesting and original market-oriented menu at such modest prices that this pale yellow and bordeaux–colored dining room has become a big hit with pennywise-but-picky locals.

Maison Prunier

– | – | – | E

16, av Victor Hugo, 16ᵉ (Charles de Gaulle/Etoile), 01 44 17 35 85; fax 01 44 17 90 10

One of the prettiest places in Paris (the art deco interior alone is worth the trip), this beloved seafood veteran in the 16th has become a caviar bar under the auspices of Pierre Bergé, co-founder of Yves Saint Laurent; it offers a short menu of simple international luxury foods like Bellota-Bellota ham from Spain or Joe's Stone Crabs from Florida; they also feature the little fish eggs, so don't make the scene without plenty of green.

Maison Rouge (La) ●🅂

– | – | – | M

13, rue des Archives, 4ᵉ (Hôtel-de-Ville), 01 42 71 69 69; fax 01 42 71 04 08

While the name means Red House, this trendy new Marais brasserie boasts an almost all-white interior, with window walls on three sides – a rarity in Parisian establishments; the soft pink lighting flatters the faces of the arty young crowd that gathers to dine on Contemporary French cuisine that runs to grills, salads and pasta.

Mandarin de Neuilly

▽ 20 | 13 | 17 | 35

148, av Charles de Gaulle, Neuilly-sur-Seine (Pont-de-Neuilly), 01 46 24 11 80

■ Suburban surveyors kowtow to this mandarin, "the best Chinese restaurant in Neuilly", which offers "good value" in the "dependable quality" of its eats (try the "turbot for two"); while the interior is "nice", locals laud the sidewalk seats as "the most beautiful outdoor dining in the city."

Man Ray ●🅂

12 | 21 | 11 | 52

34, rue Marbeuf, 8ᵉ (Franklin D. Roosevelt), 01 56 88 36 36; fax 01 42 25 36 36

◪ A "pretty crowd" that creates "quite a scene some nights" ("Fridays are the best") and the "exotic" East-meets-West setting of this movie-star-financed spot off the Champs don't make up for the fact that it's also "attitude city" because of "sour-faced servers" who are "slow" about delivering "so-so", "overpriced" Asian–Classic French food.

Mansouria

18 | 16 | 14 | 41

11, rue Faidherbe, 11ᵉ (Faidherbe-Chaligny), 01 43 71 00 16; fax 01 43 71 01 58

◪ Most maintain this Moroccan between the Bastille and Place de la Nation serves up "original", "always refined" dishes from "a battery of [North African] women's recipes" that "are worth the wait", thanks to the "pleasant setting"; however, cynics suggest "it's nothing close to the hype."

Manufacture (La)   18 | 17 | 16 | 43

20, esplanade de la Manufacture, Issy-les-Moulineaux (Corentin-Celton), 01 40 93 08 98; fax 01 40 93 57 22

◼ Installed in an attractively recycled tobacco factory in suburban Issy-les-Moulineaux, this is one "très marketing"-oriented spot, both in the sense of its advertising and media clientele and its "menu with a lot of originality" that mixes classic favorites with "inventive" New French bistro dishes; the "very good service" makes folks feel "like family."

Maoh Noodles Bar ◗   – | – | – | I

6, rue du Cdt-Pilot, Neuilly-sur-Seine (Les Sablons), 01 47 47 19 94

In the bustling shopping section of Neuilly, this sizeable noodle bar serves a wide array of healthy Asian-inspired specialties such as dumplings, miso soups and, of course, oodles of you-know-what, fresh from the wok; the dimly lit, Zen decor is ideal for quiet, intimate tête-à-têtes.

MARÉE (LA)   24 | 17 | 21 | 96

1, rue Daru, 8ᵉ (Ternes), 01 43 80 20 00; fax 01 48 88 04 04

◼ "Just short of world-class" profess patrons of this "very fine, classic" seafooder near the Place de Ternes in the 8th that caters with "superb service" to a clientele of "bankers and government ministers" (style: "gentlemen's club in London or Paris"); most maintain the "marvelous cooking" (which features "wonderful turbot") is "worth the prices" – although a few fret "they're starting to become prohibitive."

Marée de Versailles   19 | 14 | 14 | 48

22, rue au Pain, Versailles (Versailles Rive Droite), 01 30 21 73 73; fax 01 39 49 98 29

◪ Boasting a boat-like setting, this Versailles seafooder is popular with trendy "bobos [French for funky yuppies] from the western edge of Paris and suburbs"; critics carp it's "a bit expensive" and service can be "offhand", but if you crave "very good fish", it's "definitely worth a visit outside" the city limits.

Mariage Frères ⑤   15 | 18 | 14 | 31

30, rue du Bourg-Tibourg, 4ᵉ (Hôtel-de-Ville), 01 42 72 28 11; fax 01 42 74 51 68
13, rue des Grands-Augustins, 6ᵉ (St-Michel), 01 40 51 82 50; fax 01 44 07 07 52
260, rue du Faubourg St-Honoré, 8ᵉ (Ternes), 01 46 22 18 54; fax 01 42 67 18 54

◼ "Travel to the past" with this "Indian colonial"-style mini-chain of "simply charming" upmarket tearooms that's "highly recommended" to connoisseurs of a perfect cuppa – not just for the brew but for "inventive cooking" and "very good pastries" that suit most people to, well, a T; some scold the "slow service", but the majority loves coming to "the temple of tea in Paris", especially since "it's a good buy"; P.S. "delightful brunch" on weekends.

Marius
19 | 13 | 16 | 64

82, bd Murat, 16ᵉ (Porte de St-Cloud), 01 46 51 67 80; fax 01 47 43 10 24

■ As if some of "the best bouillabaisse in Paris" isn't reason enough to journey here, fin fans also heap praise upon the salt-encrusted sea bream and other "fish delights" at this "remarkable seafooder" in the 16th; despite a complaint or two about "slow service", it's a "very cozy place" "where it feels good to be with friends."

Marius et Janette ⑤
20 | 15 | 16 | 76

4, av George V, 8ᵉ (Alma-Marceau), 01 47 23 84 36; fax 01 47 23 07 19

☑ This nautically decorated fish house near the Pont de l'Alma definitely has its "ups and downs", with positives praising the "excellent seafood, simply prepared", and negatives nattering about "tables that are too, too tight" and "out-of-sight prices"; still, for over 40 years there's "always [been] a crowd" here; P. S. the "pretty terrace" is a special plus.

Market ◐⑤
– | – | – | E

15, av Matignon, 8ᵉ (Champs Elysées/Clémenceau), 01 56 43 40 90; fax 01 63 59 10 87

After opening establishments everywhere from New York to Las Vegas to London, French-born chef Jean-Georges Vongerichten comes home to Christie's Paris headquarters in the 8th; his loftily priced, patented East-meets-West fusion fare, including spicy sea bream en crôute and coconut-milk panna cotta, is unveiled amid somber Asian-inspired decor by designer Christian Liaigre.

Marlotte (La)
14 | 14 | 14 | 45

55, rue du Cherche-Midi, 6ᵉ (Sèvres-Babylone/St-Placide), 01 45 48 86 79; fax 01 45 44 34 80

■ On the Left Bank not far from the Bon Marché department store, this "unpretentious", "reliable neighborhood" Classic French changed owners a while ago, but a "congenial staff" still offers "a warm welcome" and "good bourgeois cooking" to a well-heeled "crowd of locals" and tourists in a candlelit dining room.

Maroc (Le) ◐⑤
– | – | – | I

9, rue Danielle Casanova, 1ᵉʳ (Pyramides), 01 42 61 38 83; fax 01 42 60 49 33

Though few surveyors know this North African veteran near the Opéra Garnier, those who do praise the "typical Moroccan copper-toned decor", "reasonable prices" and perhaps "the best couscous in Paris"; the "mechoui [roasted lamb] is a must" and a "charming welcome" greets you, so what are you waiting for?

Marsagny (Le)   _ | _ | _ | M
73, av Parmentier, 11ᵉ (Parmentier), 01 47 00 94 25
Chef-owner Francis Bonfillou, veteran of several hotel restaurants (George V, the Intercontinental), has now opened this upbeat traditional bistro not too far from Place de la République; he brings a modern Haute Cuisine touch (but lowdown prices) to the grandmotherly classics that compose the constantly revised chalkboard menu.

Martel (Le) ☉   _ | _ | _ | M
3, rue Martel, 10ᵉ (Château d'Eau), 01 47 70 67 56
Anyone asking for proof that the once-woebegone 10th is surfing a new wave of hip need look no further than this French-Algerian packing in the fashionistas, fashion professionals and wanna-bes night after night; decorated with globe lamps, framed photos, soft lighting and bare wooden tables and floors, this newcomer (run by a former waiter at Chez Omar, the original Gallic-African hybrid) features smiling servers and prices moderate enough to make anyone a regular.

Marty ☉S   15 | 15 | 16 | 51
20, av des Gobelins, 5ᵉ (Les Gobelins), 01 43 31 39 51;
fax 01 43 37 63 70
◪ A long-running (since 1913) favorite in the Gobelins neighborhood, this fish specialist had its "pretty" "art deco interior" refurbished with contemporary touches, to the dismay of nostalgists who find the dining room "noisy since the transformation" and the cuisine "more and more disappointing" as "prices have risen"; but modernists insist the "well-polished" decor now "shines as much as" the "fine brasserie cooking" and enjoy "attentive service."

Mascotte (La)   ▽ 17 | 10 | 16 | 32
270, rue du Faubourg St-Honoré, 8ᵉ (Ternes), 01 42 27 75 26;
fax 01 40 31 15 06
■ "For serious eaters", this little Auvergnat bistro near the Place des Ternes is "very simple, but one is never disappointed by its fine cuts of meat", including the huge côte du boeuf; popular with "business types" at noon, it fills up with carnivorous locals in the evening, attracted by one of the best buys in the neighborhood.

Mathusalem (Le)   15 | 11 | 14 | 32
5 bis, bd Exelmans, 16ᵉ (Exelmans), 01 42 88 10 73;
fax 01 42 88 42 43
■ Thanks to "a nice owner who continues to do a great job after many years", this "pleasant neighborhood" place "near the Parc des Ormes" maintains "a warm bistro atmosphere" and remains an "unbeatable value for the money"; the signature "*croustillant* de Camembert is a

must", and the rest of the Classic French menu is "always good" – which is why "you always have to book ahead."

Matsuri   – | – | – | M

36, rue de Richelieu, 1ᵉʳ (Pyramides), 01 42 61 05 73;
fax 01 42 33 10 38
2, rue de Passy, 16ᵉ (Passy), 01 42 24 96 85;
fax 01 42 24 14 54 ●S

Though they were recently renovated, the big attraction of these two sushi siblings remains their central conveyor belts, which display masterful preparations of raw fish, as well as other Japanese specialties, on color-coded plates; while the seating on high bar stools is slightly precarious, the prices are quite comfortable – and affordable, given the central locations near the Palais Royal and the Trocadéro; N.B. they also do a booming delivery biz.

Maupertu (Le)   20 | 17 | 21 | 42

94, bd de La Tour-Maubourg, 7ᵉ (Ecole Militaire/
La Tour-Maubourg), 01 45 51 37 96; fax 01 45 50 26 70
■ "Owner Sophie Canton is a jewel", and the "warm welcome and absolutely fabulous food" she offers attract a crowd of regulars, plus a sprinkling of tourists, to her "very pleasant" Classic French in the 7th; blessed with a pretty view of the dome of the Invalides, the recently "expanded space works well", and the "perfect dinner" is capped off by being a "fine value for the money."

Mauzac (Le)   ▽ 14 | 10 | 14 | 33

7, rue de l'Abbé de l'Epée, 5ᵉ (Luxembourg), 01 46 33 75 22
■ Some "wanted to keep this address to themselves", but more altruistic advocates say try this wine bar/"real Parisian bistro in the 5th and you will be satisfied" by the "plain, tasty food"; perhaps "the decor's sad", but an "unforgettable welcome by the owner" ensures "nice" ambiance, and the Luxembourg Gardens are nearby for a walk after lunch.

Mavrommatis S   18 | 13 | 16 | 44

42, rue Daubenton, 5ᵉ (Censier-Daubenton), 01 43 31 17 17;
fax 01 43 36 13 08
☑ Even Hellenes hail this "pretty" taverna as "the best Greek in Paris"; there are quibbles about "inefficient service" and some think "they should vary the menu", but if you want "delicious hors d'oeuvres" and "excellent moussaka" at "a good buy", "this is where you should go."

Maxence (Le) S   19 | 14 | 18 | 74

9 bis, bd du Montparnasse, 6ᵉ (Duroc), 01 45 67 24 88;
fax 01 45 67 10 22
☑ "Montparnasse needed something like this" say supporters of this small spot where "discreet" young chef-owner David Van Laer offers "well thought-out" Classic French cuisine laced with "inventive" nods to his native Flanders and northern France; but despite the

decor's "warm colors", detractors declare the place "cold" and "scandalously expensive" for "not memorable" food; still, given the much-improved "sweet service", it might be "worth a visit."

MAXIM'S
17 | 25 | 19 | 102

3, rue Royale, 8ᵉ (Madeleine/Concorde), 01 42 65 27 94; fax 01 42 65 30 26
Aérogare Orly Ouest, Orly (Orly Ouest par liaison OrlyVal), 01 49 75 16 78; fax 14 46 87 05 39
☑ "You feel like Gigi" (or one of her escorts) amid the "fabulous decor" of this "elegant" belle epoque "classic" on the Rue Royale; while the arrival of chef Bruno Stril (ex Biarritz's Laporte) has improved the Haute Cuisine score (especially "good for luncheon" some say), the irritated insist this landmark "gets by on name only" and find the service "royal but cold" "unless you're a somebody"; P.S. if nowhere near as grand as the mother ship, "the branch at Orly" is still an improvement over most airport options.

Méditerranée (La) S
15 | 18 | 14 | 56

2, pl de l'Odéon, 6ᵉ (Odéon), 01 43 26 02 30; fax 01 43 26 18 44
☑ An "elegant", "spacious" setting that provides a "view over the Odéon" (both the Place and the Theater) makes this World War II veteran "worth a trip"; once one of Paris' most celebrated poisson palaces, it still serves "very nice seafood" supporters say (special mention: "the gazpacho with avocado, crab and ginger"), while dissenters deem some "dishes delicious, others less so"; the "considerate" service can get "slow and rude when the place is packed."

Mekong Bar
– | – | – | M

38, rue de Vaugirard, 6ᵉ (Odéon), 01 43 26 74 64; fax 01 46 38 67 72
Despite the lack of decor, this new Vietnamese in the heart of Saint-Germain is still more comfortable (not to mention convenient) than the usual Formica-clad, neon-lit quick-eats Asians in the 13th; and if not quite as authentic as they, it still advances the standards of Paris' Indochine cuisine for students, editors, musicians and anyone else who appreciates relatively gentle prices and servers who manage to combine coddling with efficiency.

Mellifère (Le) ❶
▽ 18 | 12 | 18 | 36

8, rue Marigny, 2ᵉ (Quatre Septembre), 01 42 61 21 71; fax 01 42 61 31 71
■ While few have found this boisterous bistro in the 2nd adorned with framed posters and cartoons, those who have appreciate its "personal service and satisfying food" (technically Classic French, though the kitchen's capable of being "original, with an irreproachable technique"); it's "very good for after the theater" – not surprising, since it's near the Opéra Comique.

Mère Agitée (La)   ▽ 15 | 13 | 17 | 28

21, rue Campagne-Première, 14ᵉ (Raspail), 01 43 35 56 64; fax 01 43 35 56 64

◪ Reactions to "restless" ('agitée') owner Valérie Delahaye (a presence difficult to ignore, since she both cooks and waits table) tend to determine how much visitors like this "really original" Traditional French bistro in Montparnasse; most enjoy the "homey" cooking from her very limited menu – she serves a single main course daily – but some delicately suggest it could "perhaps be a bit difficult for tourists who don't speak French."

MEURICE (LE) ⑤   23 | 26 | 24 | 102

Hôtel Meurice, 228, rue de Rivoli, 1ᵉʳ (Concorde/Tuileries), 01 44 58 10 55; fax 01 44 58 10 76

◪ A "magnificent, practically royal, setting" – a tour de force of ormolu, marble, mirrors and crystal chandeliers – creates an impression of "luxury, space and comfort" at this New French where "the service is pure ballet"; though cranks carp the "cuisine doesn't reach the same heights" as the setting or staff (or "elevated prices"), they're outvoted by supporters who say it's "superb"; and overall, "everything is in perfect taste" – exactly what you'd expect of a dining "room at the Meurice."

MICHEL ROSTANG   27 | 22 | 25 | 118

20, rue Rennequin, 17ᵉ (Pereire/Ternes), 01 47 63 40 77; fax 01 47 63 82 75

◼ Surveyors scurry for superlatives to describe this "excellent [establishment] with enormous class" in the 17th; the game-oriented New French cuisine offers a "wonderful combination of tradition and originality" (don't miss the "truffle sandwich" that's "beyond belief" or the "extraordinary duck in a sauce of its own blood"), served by the "best, friendliest" staff amid "very refined decor"; of course, "prices are high", but every Euro is merited when you're a "marvel that never goes out of style."

Mirama ⑤   19 | 3 | 8 | 26

17, rue St-Jacques, 5ᵉ (Maubert-Mutualité/St-Michel), 01 43 54 71 77; fax 01 43 25 37 63

◼ At this "Chinese hole-in-the-wall", the "only thing that counts is the food", which includes such "outstanding", "inexpensive" dishes as the signature "flavorful, meaty roast duck"; the decor may be "old" and "sad" and the "arrogant", "expressionless" waiters are "easily the most disagreeable in Paris", but most are willing to grin and bear it since its Latin Quarter locale "is always full."

Moissonnier   17 | 14 | 17 | 46

28, rue des Fossés St-Bernard, 5ᵉ (Cardinal Lemoine/Jussieu), 01 43 29 87 65

◼ This "authentic Lyonnais bistro in the heart of Paris" (more precisely, the 5th) serves up "gargantuan portions" of "hearty and rich" classics like "marinated roast beef at honest prices in a simple setting"; it's been "successfully taken over" by a "very amiable couple", causing some to claim there's "no better mom-and-pop restaurant in town."

Monde des Chimères (Le) S ▽ | 19 | 18 | 22 | 38
69, rue St-Louis-en-l'Ile, 4ᵉ (Pont-Marie), 01 43 54 45 27; fax 01 43 29 84 88

■ "One of the island's loveliest surprises", this "tiny" Classic French bistro with "stone walls and flowers" on the Ile Saint-Louis offers "great food, excellent service" and "very comfortable and hospitable" atmosphere, established by the indefatigable "eightysomething owner Cécile Ibane" and her daughter; so, no surprise, you "need reservations."

Monsieur Lapin S | 20 | 17 | 20 | 48
11, rue Raymond Losserand, 14ᵉ (Gaîté), 01 43 20 21 39; fax 01 43 21 84 86

■ The name of this "very pleasant theme restaurant" tells the whole story – there are "rabbits on the menu and rabbits everywhere in the decor", which feels like "someone's home" (maybe Beatrix Potter's) in Montparnasse; its clientele consists of "local families with a serious attitude toward food", plus the odd "solo diner", who often gets babied by the "incredibly helpful chef-owner."

Montalembert (Le) S | 15 | 17 | 16 | 56
Hôtel Montalembert, 3, rue de Montalembert, 7ᵉ (Rue du Bac), 01 45 49 68 03; fax 01 45 49 69 49

◪ "More of a cafe/lunch place" than a dinner destination, this hotel dining room in the 7th offers "attentive service", "simple cuisine and minimalist decor" to a crowd of fashion types, book editors and boutique owners who like the "very calm atmosphere"; contented customers call the New French fare "innovative", but hungry types huff the "model-size portions" "lack personality" and "passion."

Montparnasse 25 (Le) | 22 | 18 | 21 | 71
Le Méridien-Montparnasse, 19, rue du Cdt. René Mouchotte, 14ᵉ (Montparnasse-Bienvenüe), 01 44 36 44 25; fax 01 44 36 49 03

■ Although "everything is excellent", "Paris' most gorgeous cheese trolley" steals the show at this "cosmopolitan" New French named for its neighborhood; naturally the *fromager* is "a master", but all the service is "attentive", directed by "a head maitre d' who's a real pro"; the somewhat "sad" art deco–style decor dampens some, but most say this Méridien dining room is "grand hotel" all the way.

Moulin à Vent "Chez Henri" (Au) | 19 | 12 | 17 | 60
20, rue des Fossés St-Bernard, 5ᵉ (Jussieu), 01 43 54 99 37; fax 01 40 46 92 23

■ "A kingdom of copper and Châteaubriand" sums up this well-liked, pot-adorned spot, known for "exceptional meat", "sautéed frogs' legs" and other "Classic French dishes" offered by "adorable servers"; the stingy snap "you can find as good for less money elsewhere", but for most, this "bistro experience of yesteryear" "should be protected."

Moulin de la Galette ◐S − | − | − | M

83, rue Lepic, 18ᵉ (Abbesses/Blanche), 01 46 06 84 77; fax 01 47 58 11 91

This venerable Montmartre spot has been revamped substantially; it now offers Contemporary French cuisine in an equally modern, bright setting – clean lines, minimalist furniture and jewel-toned banquettes; happily, the historic mill overhead and the garden patio remain intact.

Murat (Le) ◐S 13 | 14 | 11 | 53

1, bd Murat, 16ᵉ (Porte d'Auteuil), 01 46 51 33 17; fax 01 53 17 88 54

◪ To the "livelier" members of the public, this Costes brothers' brasserie is "very welcome in this neighborhood" (Porte d'Auteuil), offering "a pleasant indoor terrace" and, as with all the boys' efforts, a "trendy" scene; as usual too, the cooking is "mediocre" at best and the service "dreadful" ("to each his own profession – models don't know how to wait table"); if you come, try to be "young and fashionable", since "there's not too much welcome for non-anorexics."

Muscade − | − | − | M

36, rue Montpensier, 1ᵉʳ (Bourse/Palais Royal-Musée du Louvre), 01 42 97 51 36; fax 01 42 97 51 36

"A pretty terrace overlooking the gardens" is the main lure of this tearoom in the Palais Royal, "especially in the summer", when outdoor seating makes it triple in size; "the good salads" are standouts of the "pleasant" cuisine that's considerably less expensive than other restaurants on the palatial grounds.

MUSES (LES) 23 | 17 | 23 | 73

Hôtel Scribe, 1, rue Scribe, 9ᵉ (Opéra), 01 44 71 24 26; fax 01 44 71 24 64

◼ "It's true that this place is hidden in a basement, but the high-class cooking is worth the effort to find the entrance" muse mavens of this Haute Cuisine haven in the 9th; the "original" fare and "beautiful setting" provide a "magical", if formal, evening (there's "very much a temple-of-gastronomy atmosphere, with the staff acting as priests"); just bear in mind that "with drinks and wine, the bill climbs quickly."

Natacha ◐ 14 | 12 | 12 | 42

17 bis, rue Campagne Première, 14ᵉ (Raspail), 01 43 20 79 27; fax 01 43 22 93 97

◼ Newer trendies come and go, but this bi-level old-timer in Montparnasse holds its own in the "stylish" sweepstakes; "frequented by rock stars" and other celebrities, it's also "ideal for a dinner with friends" and actually charges comparatively moderate prices for its French fare; just be sure to "sit on the ground floor, not near the toilets downstairs", to get the best of the people-watching for which it's famous; N.B. a recent switch to a New Bistro menu may outdate the Food score.

Natachef
17 | 17 | 15 | 40

9, rue Duban, 16ᵉ (La Muette), 01 42 88 10 15; fax 01 42 88 10 15
☑ "Run by the wife of" Apicius chef Jean-Pierre Vigato, this "smart little restaurant" may "still be being broken in", but "it's well worth following", since the Classic French "menu is short, simple, fresh" – tailor-made for the "chatty bourgeois women of the 16th" who are its biggest fans; additional pluses are Nathalie, the "nice owner" herself, and the "low prices"; N.B. they also offer cooking lessons and a table d'hôte for those going solo.

Nemrod (Le)
12 | 9 | 14 | 27

51, rue du Cherche-Midi, 6ᵉ (Sèvres-Babylone/St-Placide), 01 45 48 17 05; fax 01 45 48 17 83
☑ Near the Bon Marché department store, this "well-situated" "corner bistro" with an Auvergnat tint is extolled by enthusiasts as one of the rare places in Paris where "you can get a real salad" that's "good enough for an entire meal", as well as "quality beef"; though it's been redecorated, dissenters say the dining room remains "too noisy" and "too crowded" for "nothing special" fare.

New Jawad ●🅂
15 | 15 | 19 | 32

12, av Rapp, 7ᵉ (Alma-Marceau), 01 47 05 91 37; fax 01 45 50 31 27
■ "The fine flower of the bourgeoisie of the 7th can't resist coming" to this "Indo-Pakistani" place with "a pretty dining room", "smiling service" and "well-executed" dishes; the "reasonable prices" are appreciated, and if the "portions are a bit small", "apéritifs and digestifs are on the house", so all in all, "you're never disappointed."

New Nioullaville ●🅂
14 | 9 | 10 | 27

32-34, rue de l'Orillon, 11ᵉ (Belleville), 01 40 21 96 18; fax 01 40 21 96 58
■ Perhaps "the most Chinese of all the Chinese" places in Paris, this enormous establishment offers an "amusing Hong Kong–like experience" where "dim sum carts provide munchies while you decide what to order from the 18-page menu" ("which can be difficult to decipher"); if "not exactly refined", it's ideal for "a truly transporting" meal.

NOBU ●
23 | 19 | 20 | 78

15, rue Marbeuf, 8ᵉ (Franklin D. Roosevelt), 01 56 89 53 53; fax 01 56 89 53 54
☑ "If you're beautiful, rich and famous, you're going to love" this outpost of the famed Japanese chef-owner's empire, already dubbed "the best 'in' restaurant in town"; acolytes attest the food's "just as good in Paris as it is in

NYC", which is to say "delicious", "fabulous", "sublime"; for the record, reviewers note it's "noisy", the "service needs a bit of breaking in" and "too bad it's so expensive" – "but it's all worth it."

Noces de Jeannette (Les) S
14	13	15	35

14, rue Favart, 2ᵉ (Richelieu-Drouot), 01 42 96 36 89; fax 01 47 03 97 31

■ "Affordable prices", "four different reception rooms" and a convenient location near the Salle Favart concert hall make this Traditional French "an excellent place for visiting groups"; "it's a good solid bistro with Parisian flair, even if the food is not the greatest."

Note de Frais (La)
–	–	–	M

47, rue de Bourgogne, 7ᵉ (Invalides/Varennes), 01 45 55 15 35; fax 01 56 89 85 86

Its name possibly a tongue-in-cheek reference to much of its Assemblée Nationale clientele lunching on the public pocket (*la note de frais* is an expense-account receipt), this vest-pocket–size New French is run by a bright young kitchen team; their training at Michel Guérard's and Alain Ducasse's establishments shows in the light, well-executed dishes that are heavy on the fresh herbs, light on the fat and cream, and served amid a streamlined but colorful decor.

Noura/Noura Pavillon ● S
16	12	14	39

121, bd du Montparnasse, 6ᵉ (Vavin), 01 43 20 19 19; fax 01 43 20 05 40
21, av Marceau, 16ᵉ (Alma-Marceau), 01 47 20 33 33; fax 01 47 20 60 31

◪ "Authentic" and "delicious Lebanese food" keeps this pair in the 6th and 16th "packed"; of the two, the Pavilion is "more expensive", and some "prefer the younger brother" in Montparnasse, "which is livelier" and has a "pretty and pleasant interior garden"; otherwise, the settings are "rather uninteresting" in both, and they also suffer from "the same crummy service" ("even if you speak Arabic"); but if you're hankering for hummus, these are "favorite places."

Nouveau Village Tao-Tao ● S
▽ | 14 | 11 | 9 | 32 |
|---|---|---|---|

159, bd Vincent Auriol, 13ᵉ (Nationale), 01 45 86 40 08; fax 01 45 86 46 21

■ "In a city without [many] wonderful Chinese restaurants", this "noisy, crowded" Sino-Thai in the 13th ranks "slightly above average"; the "plausible" options include the "very good Peking duck" and "mussels with basil"; "too bad the servers' amiability doesn't match the quality of the food."

O à la Bouche (L') ●
17	13	15	42

124, bd du Montparnasse, 14ᵉ (Vavin), 01 56 54 01 55; fax 01 43 21 07 87

◪ A "total success – except for the chairs" diners decree about this "delightful place" in Montparnasse; furniture aside, what pleases patrons is chef Franck Paquier's "original" New French–Southwest cooking and the "soigné service"; and if the kitchen has an occasional "indigestible" miss, the "setting's pleasant" and "the ambiance too."

Obélisque (L') S   20 | 19 | 21 | 67

Hôtel de Crillon, 4, rue Boissy-d'Anglas, 8ᵉ (Concorde), 01 44 71 15 15; fax 01 44 71 15 02

■ Technically, it's the "less formal dining [option] in the Crillon", but this place still possesses a pretty "plummy atmosphere" as well-heeled locals mix with an international crowd, enjoying "a view of the Place de la Concorde from certain tables"; the menu "shines with modern presentations of Classic French dishes, beautifully served" by a "courteous and knowledgeable" staff; just bear in mind that in a luxury hotel, even a "poor cousin" charges "high prices."

Oeillade (L')   15 | 11 | 14 | 44

10, rue de St-Simon, 7ᵉ (Rue du Bac/Solférino), 01 42 22 01 60

☑ "Down-home cooking, generously served" and "fair prices" continue to fill this Classic French bistro in the 7th with "red-and-white-checked tablecloths"; however, a fair number of surveyors say "it's not as good as it was a few years ago" and boo the "banal" decor.

Oenothèque (L')   ▽ 21 | 14 | 17 | 54

20, rue St-Lazare, 9ᵉ (Notre-Dame-de-Lorette), 01 48 78 08 76; fax 01 40 16 10 27

■ They must be doing something right at this "small" Classic French near the Gare Saint-Lazare, since it's maintained "high-level standards for 18 years"; fans extol the "simply delicious cooking", served with "wonderful wines" in a "convivial" setting; though not cheap, the experience still equals "good value for the money"; P.S. the oenophile owner will share "his cave's treasures – if you strike his fancy."

Oïshi ● S   – | – | – | I

106, rue de Richelieu, 2ᵉ (Richelieu-Drouot), 01 42 96 45 94; fax 01 42 96 43 58

Not far from the franchise-infested Grands Boulevards, this young Japanese, with an airy decor of peach-painted walls and gray tile floors, has become a word-of-mouth hit thanks to its extremely reasonable range of classic dishes, from sushi to tempura; the lunchtime clientele of journalists, bankers and brokers appreciates the prompt service.

Olivades (Les)   18 | 12 | 14 | 44

41, av de Ségur, 7ᵉ (Ségur), 01 47 83 70 09; fax 01 42 73 04 75

☑ With the advent of a new chef post-*Survey*, this very popular bistro in the 7th now offers Tradtional French cooking along with Provençal fare that brings "a little sunshine to Paris"; but opponents warn about "badly organized" "overtaxed staffers" and add this spot's "not for the claustrophobic", since the "tables are jammed" (often with tourists) and it's "noisy"; despite all that, many vow "we will return."

Orangerie (L') ● S   20 | 22 | 20 | 70
28, rue St-Louis-en-L'Ile, 4ᵉ (Pont Marie), 01 46 33 93 98
☑ Tucked away on the Ile Saint-Louis, this "very refined" veteran (gentlemen, jackets please) filled with "superb bouquets of flowers" is a long-running hit for actor-owner Jean-Claude Brialy, even though the original jet-set clientele has mostly moved on; the "serious" "Classic French food" "never disappoints" (but never surprises, either) and the service is "prompt", if sometimes "pretentious"; the only real gripe is over the "very tightly spaced tables", which tend to trip up the otherwise "romantic" atmosphere.

Orenoc (L') ● S   ▽ 21 | 22 | 22 | 56
Le Méridien Etoile, 81, bd Gouvion St-Cyr, 17ᵉ (Porte Maillot), 01 40 68 30 40; fax 01 40 68 30 81
■ The few who have found their way to this Haute Cuisine hideout at the Porte Maillot say "it's an excellent surprise" for its "splendid decor" of precious woods and leather, "chic and professional service" and the "tastes-of-the-world" menu conceived by consulting chef Michel Rostang; ideal "for a spicy night on the town", it adds "another pearl to the necklace of fine restaurants"; it's not cheap, but then there's only one pearl to every oyster too.

Orient-Extrême   18 | 12 | 15 | 42
4, rue Bernard Palissy, 6ᵉ (St-Germain-des-Prés), 01 45 48 92 27; fax 01 45 48 20 94
■ Tucked away in the heart of Saint-Germain, this "most refined of Japanese" restaurants offers "sublime sashimi" and sushi; the "decor's rather worn and needs to be refreshed", but that doesn't stop those who come for "excellent, if a little expensive", fare and people-watching the "jet-setty and intellectual clientele", even if it "causes the servers to behave a bit pretentiously."

Ormes (Les)   ▽ 19 | 12 | 18 | 41
8, rue Chapu, 16ᵉ (Exelmans), 01 46 47 83 98; fax 01 46 47 83 98
■ Though the dining room is "microscopic", it's worth traveling deep into the 16th to sample the "top-flight cooking" of "ambitious" young chef Stéphane Molé, "who trained at Jamin"; add in the "pleasant service" and "gentle prices", and most readily forgive the postage-stamp-size space of this Classic French.

Os à Moelle (L') ●   21 | 12 | 17 | 43
3, rue Vasco de Gama, 15ᵉ (Lourmel), 01 45 57 27 27; fax 01 45 57 27 27
■ Except for dessert, there are no options on the single Classic French menu that "inventive" chef-owner Thierry

Faucher creates each day, but "with food this good, who needs choices?" demand devotees who have taken "the trouble" of finding their way to "the outer reaches of the 15th"; the service "is both friendly and competent", and if the setting is "banal, it nevertheless corresponds to a certain idea of Parisian restaurants that foreigners love."

OSTÉRIA (L')
24 | 13 | 16 | 52

10, rue de Sévigné, 4ᵉ (St-Paul), 01 42 71 37 08; fax 01 48 06 27 71
■ Shhh . . . "don't reveal this secret address" in the Marais, a "tiny" Italian that offers "the ideal combo of ambiance and food" – especially "delicious pasta" and "great risotto"; "the dining room is very crowded" ("make friends with your neighbor's plate"), but folks don't mind, since it's packed with "well-known types from the worlds of TV, architecture and fashion", which probably explains the "steep tabs"; patrons put up with it, though, for the privilege of being "in the club."

Oulette (L')
22 | 15 | 19 | 57

15, pl Lachambeaudie, 12ᵉ (Cour St-Emilion/Dugommier), 01 40 02 02 12; fax 01 40 02 04 77
■ Connoisseurs have long said chef/co-owner Marcel Baudis "deserves to be better known", and now that the Cour Saint-Emilion is hot, greater numbers are going "out of the way" for his "superbly inventive and tasty cooking"; the "service is good" as well, and if the decor reads "hotel restaurant" ("chic but impersonal"), no one cares when such "wonderful Southwestern cuisine" is involved.

Oum el Banine
19 | 13 | 16 | 45

16 bis, rue Dufrenoy, 16ᵉ (Porte Dauphine/Rue de la Pompe), 01 45 04 91 22; fax 01 45 03 46 26
■ "The lightest couscous in Paris", along with "detour-worthy b'steeya and mechoui [roasted lamb]", attract fans to this "very good Moroccan" in the 16th; the "movie-set"-like setting is "a bit cramped" and they "don't give the food away", but overall it's "a treat."

Pachyderme 🆂
– | – | – | M

2 bis, bd St-Martin, 10ᵉ (République), 01 42 06 32 56; fax 01 42 40 58 59
Standing out amid the chain restaurants and fast-food places that dominate the Place de la République, this upmarket singles spot offers a crackling bar scene and a moderately priced International menu custom-made for its fashionable young clientele; the mock colonial-African decor (including several wood carvings of elephants) glows with candles and subdued lights.

Palanquin (Le)
∇ 15 | 13 | 15 | 37

12, rue Princesse, 6ᵉ (Mabillon/St-Germain-des-Prés), 01 43 29 77 66
■ "Excellent food and friendly ambiance" make this tiny Vietnamese with exposed-stone walls and soft lighting in

Saint-Germain popular; if some find portions "frugal", prices are equally so; hence, many vote it "worth a visit" "when you need a change of pace."

Palenque (El) ⊅ | 20 | 10 | 13 | 33 |
5, rue de la Mont. Ste-Geneviève, 5ᵉ (Maubert-Mutualité), 01 43 54 08 99; fax 01 64 38 09 84

■ A place many describe as *the* Argentine in Paris, a title warranted by over 30 years on the Left Bank, rounds up a happily carnivorous crowd with imported "meat to dream about", empanadas, "interesting wines" and *dulce de leche* for dessert; while the pampas gets "cramped", "it's great value for the money", so "reservations are indispensable."

Pamphlet (Le) ● | 18 | 12 | 16 | 41 |
38, rue Debelleyme, 3ᵉ (Filles-du-Calvaire), 01 42 72 39 24; fax 01 42 72 12 53

■ "Lost near the Place de la République", this "superb auberge" is worth a stop proclaim pamphleteers who vaunt chef-owner Alain Carrère's "inventive", "eclectic Basque cuisine" at "gentle prices"; bearing a "heavy" "provincial" look, "the decor's not very jolly", but the "welcome's warm" and the "service friendly", making this place "a true Parisian find."

Paolo Petrini | 20 | 10 | 16 | 56 |
6, rue du Débarcadère, 17ᵉ (Argentine/Porte Maillot), 01 45 74 25 95; fax 01 45 74 12 95

◪ "Very good cooking" snags a high Food score for this Italian in the 17th, even though vocal opponents opine it's "overrated" and "finally, too French"; perhaps their letdown stems from the "disappointing setting", which a majority agrees is "rather sad"; still, "the service is warm" and a wine list laden with "Barolos and Chiantis" makes it worthwhile if you don't mind the "pretentious" prices.

Paparazzi ● | 15 | 10 | 10 | 25 |
7 bis, rue Geoffroy-Marie, 9ᵉ (Grands-Boulevards), 01 48 24 59 39; fax 01 42 74 54 68

■ Though "the dining room could stand a coat of paint", that doesn't keep the "young" crowds away from this "lively" Italian in the 9th, best known for its "gargantuan" "fantastic pizzas" (so big, they're "served on two plates!"); there's "good pasta" too, plus it's an "excellent value for the money."

Parc aux Cerfs (Le) S | 18 | 13 | 15 | 38 |
50, rue Vavin, 6ᵉ (Vavin), 01 43 54 87 83; fax 01 43 26 42 86

◪ Perfectionists pout there's "nothing very exciting on the menu", but most find this "friendly" Mediterranean–New French "satisfying" and "a good choice for well-behaved children" who can "amuse themselves with the colored pencils" while their parents "dine at leisure"; overall, it provides "a very pleasant table" – something "rare in Montparnasse."

Paris (Le) ▽ 20 | 19 | 19 | 93

Hôtel Lutétia, 23, rue de Sèvres, 6ᵉ (Sèvres-Babylone),
01 49 54 46 90; fax 01 49 54 46 00

■ With an "elegant" art deco "ocean-liner-like room" created by Sonia Rykiel, this "chic restaurant in the Hôtel Lutétia" on the Left Bank is a "refined" favorite of those who admire its "very good" "contemporary" twists on Classic French cuisine (the 'everything chocolate' dessert is a "don't miss"); "prices are high, but you leave feeling satisfied."

Paris Brest – | – | – | E

131, rue St-Dominique, 7ᵉ (École Militaire),
01 44 18 37 55

Boasting a cheerful decor of blue and black tiles and comfortable, dark-wood club chairs, this stylish and intimate newcomer in the 7th hints at its specialties with its name; Brest is a premier city of Brittany, the source of many a bivalve presented on the shellfish-oriented menu; the place also features a fine Paris-Brest, the cream-filled pastry created to celebrate a bicycle race between the two towns; the prices reflect the quality of the comestibles served by a friendly staff.

Paris Main d'Or ▽ 18 | 10 | 18 | 33

133, rue du Faubourg St-Antoine, 11ᵉ (Ledru-Rollin),
01 44 68 04 68; fax 01 44 68 04 68

■ You'll "fall in love with Corsica" after a visit to this intimate outpost in the 11th, which offers the "real" thing – "roast baby goat, Corsican cheeses and remarkable wines" – at Napoleon-size prices; the "smoky" setting's not much, but "a nice welcome" makes it "a delightful discovery."

Paris Seize (Le) – | – | – | M

18, rue des Belles Feuilles, 16ᵉ (Trocadéro),
01 47 04 56 33

In a busy section of the 16th, this cozy enclave resembles an upscale take on a sports cafe, with small tables and themed decorations showcasing rugby, football and tennis players; run by the successful Dumant brothers, Jérôme and Stéphane, this old-timer serves Franco-Italian fare (sautéed scampi and filet Rossini, beef topped off with foie gras) at reasonable prices that attract yuppies at lunchtime and locals in the evening.

Park (Le) – | – | – | E

Hyatt Paris Vendôme, 3-5, rue de la Paix, 2ᵉ (Opéra),
01 58 71 12 34

Infused with elegant Zen-like decor by Amanresorts decorator Ed Tuttle, this hotel grill just steps from the Place Vendôme features an open kitchen manned by chef Christophe David, whose Australian experience shows in the Asian flavorings in his Classic French cuisine, as well as seasonal and organic produce (which may help explain the rather robust checks).

Passiflore
16 | 15 | 17 | 53

33, rue de Longchamp, 16ᵉ (Boissière/Trocadéro), 01 47 04 96 81;
fax 01 47 04 32 27

◪ The name means 'passion flower', and followers of chef-owner Roland Durand (ex Pré Catelan) get pretty passionate, saying his Classic French cooking with its signature spicy Asian influences "should not be missed"; feelings are a little cooler over the interior ("pretty" vs. "mediocre") and "the service is still sorting itself out", but overall, this "affordable" address in the 16th is "off to a good start."

Passy Mandarin ⑤
18 | 15 | 15 | 45

6, rue d'Antin, 2ᵉ (Opéra), 01 42 61 25 52; fax 01 42 60 33 92 ◑
6, rue Bois-le-Vent, 16ᵉ (La Muette), 01 42 88 12 18;
fax 01 45 24 58 54

■ "One of the best Chinese tables in Paris" actually has two locations, next to the Place de la Opéra and in Passy, and both are lauded for their "very good steamed dumplings", "Peking duck" and other "authentic" dishes in "elegant settings"; service is generally "attentive", if not always cheerful, and reviewers recommend them "all-around", even though the calculating criticize the "expensive prices" as indicative of "pretentious profit margins."

Patrick Goldenberg ⑤
12 | 9 | 13 | 39

69, av de Wagram, 17ᵉ (Ternes), 01 42 27 34 79;
fax 01 40 53 02 45

■ "The rendezvous of Slavs in the 17th", this small spot is a "classic in the category" of Jewish delis, serving "fine and exotic" (for Paris, anyway) pastrami and cheesecake that are "perfect for lunch", especially when partnered with some Israeli wine; the decor may be a little "tacky", but you can always sit out "on the terrace in the sun."

Paul Chêne
19 | 13 | 18 | 66

123, rue Lauriston, 16ᵉ (Trocadéro/Victor Hugo), 01 47 27 63 17;
fax 01 47 27 53 18

■ Even "my grandmother didn't cook better" than this 16th arrondissement old-timer, a "classic" for its "sincere French bourgeois cooking" that includes "the best crêpes suzettes in Paris"; some snap that the "1950s decor" hasn't changed while the "expensive" prices definitely have, but the "always friendly greeting, like [you're] returning home", seals its status as "a little corner of delight."

Paul, Restaurant ⑤
16 | 14 | 15 | 32

75, pl Dauphine, 1ᵉʳ (Pont Neuf), 01 43 54 21 48;
fax 01 56 24 94 09

■ "If Caveau du Palais is closed, go next door" to this veteran Classic French on the Ile de la Cité; it's a "restaurant you can count on" for such mainstays as veal stew and baba au rhum; indoors there's typical old-time bistro decor, but outside, the sidewalk seating offers Seine-side views in summer.

Pavillon des Princes 🅂

16 | 17 | 15 | 72

69, av de la Porte d'Auteuil, 16ᵉ (Porte d'Auteuil), 01 47 43 15 15; fax 01 46 51 16 94

■ "After a run in the woods" (the nearby Bois de Boulogne), well-heeled clients cool down at this "nice and relaxed" Classic French; while the "straightforward cooking" is "agreeable" enough, it's the number of "well-spaced tables", especially on the popular terrace, that particularly pleases the princes and princesses of the 16th.

Pavillon Montsouris

18 | 23 | 16 | 56

20, rue Gazan, 14ᵉ (Cité-Universitaire), 01 45 88 38 52; fax 01 45 88 63 40

■ It's all "charm" at this special-occasion address with a "beautiful setting" on the edge of the Parc Montsouris, especially when one sits outside, overlooking all of the immaculately groomed greenery; the belle epoque pavilion where Mata Hari once sat has a "corporate" decor today, but most are delighted to come to a place where there's a combination of "honorable" Traditional French and "rather original cooking", proffered by "agreeable servers."

Pavillon Puebla

18 | 22 | 14 | 58

Parc des Buttes-Chaumont, 19ᵉ (Buttes-Chaumont/Pyrénées), 01 42 08 92 62; fax 01 42 39 83 16

■ "The most spectacular park in Paris" – the carefully crafted and perfectly groomed "wilderness" of the Buttes de Chaumont – makes a "marvelous setting" for this Classic French–Spaniard, particularly during the summer, when you can dine outside; if some suggest that the belle epoque pavilion needs to be "freshened up", the "well-prepared, sophisticated cooking" and "amiable service" just round out "the dream" for most.

Per Bacco

▽ 19 | 7 | 12 | 37

10, rue Lambert, 18ᵉ (Château Rouge), 01 42 52 22 40; fax 01 42 52 22 40

■ According to admirers, "the best Neapolitan cooking in Paris", along with other "excellent" seasonal dishes from all over The Boot, is found at this snug, simple eatery on a quiet little street in Montmartre; admittedly, "the decor is nothing" and the service can be "inefficient", but "the cuisine saves it."

Père Claude (Le) 🅂

14 | 10 | 12 | 39

51, av de La Motte-Picquet, 15ᵉ (La Motte-Picquet-Grenelle), 01 47 34 03 05; fax 01 40 56 97 84

■ "A place to go when you don't feel like cooking for yourself", this "very pleasant" Classic French rotisserie near the Ecole Militaire serves a stylish clientele "copious" quantities of "good meats and chicken"; "the decor is more or less insignificant", but who cares when there's "a warm atmosphere", a "set-price menu that's a great buy" and an owner who's something of a "picturesque" character.

Pergolèse (Le)   19 | 18 | 17 | 71

40, rue Pergolèse, 16ᵉ (Porte Dauphine/Porte Maillot),
01 45 00 21 40; fax 01 45 00 81 31

■ It's slightly more animated at lunch than dinner, but at any hour a meal at this "quality neighborhood" New French in the 16th leaves "remarkable memories" behind – primarily of "inventive cooking, impeccable service" and a "pretty, bon-bon–like decor"; oh, and let's not forget the "chatty owner"; N.B. it just birthed a baby bistro next door.

Perraudin ⊭   14 | 11 | 15 | 25

157, rue St-Jacques, 5ᵉ (Luxembourg), 01 46 33 15 75

■ This "canteen-style restaurant for students" in the Latin Quarter is "always up to its own standards" of providing "good Classic French food" at a "great value"; despite the vintage 1903 facade, it's a lively scene – if you can get a seat, which isn't easy, given that it's also "always full."

Perron (Le)   16 | 10 | 15 | 42

6, rue Perronet, 7ᵉ (St-Germain-des-Prés),
01 45 44 71 51

■ To some eyes, this "small neighborhood restaurant" in the 7th arrondissement may look "slightly sad", but an army of amici see it as a "really nice" "Roman trattoria", with "tasty" Italian cooking that includes "custom-made risottos, including one with squid's ink"; just be warned their "interesting wines" (like the "Sardinian Turriga") "can cause the bill to explode."

Petit Bofinger ●Ⓢ   12 | 11 | 12 | 34

6, rue de la Bastille, 4ᵉ (Bastille), 01 42 72 05 23;
fax 01 42 72 04 94
20, bd Montmartre, 9ᵉ (Richelieu-Drouot), 01 47 70 91 35;
fax 01 42 47 08 99
46, bd du Montparnasse, 14ᵉ (Montparnasse), 01 45 48 49 16;
fax 01 45 44 92 05
10, pl Maréchal Juin, 17ᵉ (Pereire), 01 56 79 56 20;
fax 01 56 79 56 21

☒ "You never risk being disappointed – or astounded" by this slightly "impersonal" string of Traditional French bistros, masters of the middle road – as in "middling cooking, middling bill, middling satisfaction"; many consider them "good value for the money", though, even if "the chain-restaurant tone ruins [some of] the pleasure" ("there's not much family resemblance to the original Bofinger").

Petit Colombier (Le)   20 | 16 | 18 | 66

42, rue des Acacias, 17ᵉ (Argentine/Charles de Gaulle-Etoile),
01 43 80 28 54; fax 01 44 40 04 29

■ Near the Etoile, this "little corner of Provence" is a "pleasant" spot, serving "quality" "bourgeois cooking" and "specializing in game"; fans also laud the "genial service", though a few have found the welcome less than warm; still, for most, "there's nothing to say, but 'perfect.'"

Petite Chaise (à la) S   14 | 14 | 14 | 37
36, rue de Grenelle, 7ᵉ (Sèvres-Babylone/St-Germain-des-Prés), 01 42 22 13 35; fax 01 42 22 33 84
■ "One of the oldest restaurants in Paris", this "very quaint" Classic French has been serving Saint-Germain since 1680; "happily redecorated", it remains popular today for its "unpretentiously" "good cooking" and "service that's full of gentility"; obviously, it's "a tourist find" – and plenty of "Americans have found it" – but even locals love this "institution that endures."

Petite Cour (La)   16 | 18 | 15 | 46
8, rue Mabillon, 6ᵉ (Mabillon/St-Germain-des-Prés), 01 43 26 52 26; fax 01 44 07 11 53
■ "All tour guides lead" to this Traditional French table "with a certain charm" "in the heart of Saint-Germain"; the big appeal is the patio, "a real haven of peace", though the cooking also garners "good" comments, as does the "fast" service; all told, a most "pleasant experience."

Petite Sirène de Copenhague (La)   19 | 12 | 19 | 37
47, rue Notre Dame de Lorette, 9ᵉ (St-Georges), 01 45 26 66 66
■ "You can hear the North Sea" at this "charming bistro" in the 9th where the Danish dishes (including "the best smoked salmon in Paris") are so good they "could incite you to catch the next plane to Copenhagen"; ah, but then you'd miss meeting "truly adorable" chef-owner Peter Thulstrup, whose training at the Crillon and La Tour d'Argent shows through in the "smiling, friendly service."

Petite Tour (La)   15 | 12 | 15 | 61
11, rue de la Tour, 16ᵉ (Passy), 01 45 20 09 31; fax 01 45 20 09 31
◪ For a "French village feel in the big city", head to this "quaint" place in Passy, which offers "refined" versions of such Classic French favorites as calf's head and flambéed peaches; the "welcome can be uncertain, depending on the owner's mood", but the real hesitation for some habitués is that it's "become so expensive."

Petit Laurent (Le)   ▽ 20 | 16 | 18 | 55
38, rue de Varenne, 7ᵉ (Rue du Bac), 01 45 48 79 64; fax 01 45 44 15 95
■ "Classy, quiet, lovely" reads the dossier on this diplomats' and "politicians' favorite" located in an embassy- and ministry-laden section of the 7th and adorned with a "men's club atmosphere"; but "the talent of a grand" restaurant and "the prices of a lesser one" also make it a people's choice for a Classic French menu that emphasizes (some say "is too restricted to") fish.

Petit Lutétia (Au) S   16 | 17 | 17 | 38
107, rue de Sèvres, 6ᵉ (Vaneau), 01 45 48 33 53; fax 01 45 48 74 59
■ Armed with "a landmarked setting" (circa 1915) and "efficient service", this midsize brasserie makes "a

sure-value" stop for solid seafood ("oysters are the best here") while shopping or strolling on the Left Bank; the fact that it's "not as noisy as the big guys" is a plus too.

Petit Marché (Le) S — | — | — | M

9, rue de Béarn, 3ᵉ (St-Paul), 01 42 72 06 67

Recently relaunched by the Costes brothers, this popular little place a few steps north of the Place des Vosges has retained its cozy decor and plate-glass windows, but now boasts a New French menu of moderately priced, casual eats like salads and grills; the sought-after sidewalk tables offer good views of the passing parade of the Marais.

Petit Marguery (Au) S — | — | — | M

(aka La Pizzeria d'Auteuil)

81, rue la Fontaine, 16ᵉ (Michel Ange/Auteuil), 01 42 88 00 86; fax 01 47 05 92 21

Adding a third jewel to their double crown (which includes Auberge Bressane and Paris Seize), the Dumant brothers have taken over this small traditional Italian in the quiet residential area of Auteuil; designed to look like a 1950s Venetian tavern, it serves a wide array of pasta and fresh seafood, as well as pizzas with extra flair, baked in a special refractor oven imported from Italy.

Petit Marguery (Le) 20 | 14 | 18 | 50

9, bd de Port-Royal, 13ᵉ (Les Gobelins), 01 43 31 58 59; fax 01 43 36 73 34

■ This "exceptional" spot near Les Gobelins is admired as an "authentic Parisian bistro" where you can count on "super Lyonnais" cooking and also "have a very good time"; the "traditional atmosphere" makes a "warm" backdrop against which to sample "remarkable game" and mushrooms (in season) while being babied by "avuncular service"; in fact, there's "nothing 'petit' about this place – except the prices."

Petit Niçois (Le) S 15 | 11 | 15 | 44

10, rue Amélie, 7ᵉ (La Tour-Maubourg), 01 45 51 83 65; fax 01 47 05 77 46

☑ "Stepping inside took me from a winter's night in Paris to a summer afternoon in Antibes" enthuses one eloquent surveyor of this 41-year-old Provençal table in the 7th; other supporters say the signature "bouillabaisse is still great", as are the "delicious desserts"; but a slipping Food score sides with critics who carp "the cooking is less good and more expensive since the change in owners"; even so, many maintain it remains "a good buy."

Petit Poucet (Le) ● S 13 | 18 | 12 | 41

4, rd-pt Claude Monet, Levallois-Perret (Pont-de-Levallois), 01 47 38 61 85; fax 01 47 38 20 49

☑ It's "the superb terrace at water's edge" that lures locals to this Contemporary French bistro on the Ile de la Jatte, since most agree that "the cooking's without interest" and the service is "nonexistent" – in fact, some "really wonder why it has any customers"; well, perhaps it's because the "young, trendy crowd" of advertising and media folk, the "good value for the money" and that "verdant Seine-side setting" all make "you feel like you're on vacation."

Petit Prince de Paris (Le) ◗⑤ | 21 | 18 | 20 | 36 |
12, rue de Lanneau, 5ᵉ (Maubert-Mutualité), 01 43 54 77 26; fax 01 43 54 36 77

■ An atmosphere of "sweetness and tolerance" explains the long reign of this little prince, "a quiet oasis in Saint-Germain"; if groupies gush that the Classic French "food has consistently been fantastic", it's the "cheery service", "plush setting" and fact that it's "not expensive" that seal the place's popularity; "come as a couple", of any stripe, since the scene "is gay in all meanings of the word."

Petit Rétro (Le) | 14 | 16 | 13 | 38 |
5, rue Mesnil, 16ᵉ (Victor Hugo), 01 44 05 06 05; fax 01 44 05 06 05
■ The tiled art nouveau decor of this Classic French in the 16th creates an "appealing" atmosphere in which to enjoy a "non-fussy" "menu that's both traditional and original" and "a wonderful value for the money"; a bit of a *vieille France bistro* (one that offers old-fashioned courtesy), it's an especially "good place to bring foreigners."

Petit Riche (Au) ◗ | 14 | 19 | 15 | 47 |
25, rue Le Peletier, 9ᵉ (Le Peletier/Richelieu-Drouot), 01 47 70 68 68; fax 01 48 24 10 79
■ The "sumptuous" 19th-century decor of frosted, engraved windows, brass lamps (once gas, now electric) and wood paneling delights devotees of this Classic French in the 9th that's served "after-theater suppers" since 1880; most feel that "it's a very good buy" for "Loire Valley wines" and "hyperclassic bourgeois dishes", but critics chastise the "cavalier" service and find the kitchen "much overrated"; tip: "best to go in the evening, when the [business-lunching] bankers have gone home."

Petits Marseillais (Les) ◗⑤ | – | – | – | I |
72, rue Vieille-du-Temple, 3ᵉ (Hôtel-de-Ville), 01 42 78 91 59; fax 01 42 78 91 59
On the northern fringes of the Marais, this Lilliputian but lively Provençal run by two boyhood friends (one gay, one straight, about the same ratio as the clientele) from Marseille pulls a hip, young crowd that enjoys the "modest but pleasant" chalkboard menu; the "tables are regrettably too crowded" – though the proximity leads to conversation.

Petit St. Benoît (Le) ⌀ | 11 | 13 | 14 | 29 |
4, rue St-Benoît, 6ᵉ (St-Germain-des-Prés), 01 42 60 27 92
◪ If some snap this Saint-Germain stalwart's a "tourist trap" that's "finally off my list after 30 years because of

grubby, insipid food, could-care-less service" and a decor that's "time-worn, to say the least", the more forgiving find "you excuse the mistakes" because of the "plain, honest Classic French fare" and "anti-slick atmosphere"; either way, it's "unbeatable for anyone trying to do Paris on a budget", which explains why it's "always full."

Petit Théâtre (Au)   − | − | − | M

15, pl du Marché St-Honoré, 1ᵉʳ (Pyramides/Tuileries), 01 42 61 00 93; fax 01 47 03 31 64
If you agree with the old French saying that 'everything's good from a pig', then you'll enjoy this quaint rustic bistro overlooking the sleek Ricardo Bofill building in this intimate square in the 1st; not only does pork – in many guises – occupy pride of place on the moderately priced menu, the decor features a variety of paintings, faience and ceramics with a porcine theme.

Petit Victor Hugo (Le) ●   12 | 11 | 12 | 38

143, av Victor Hugo, 16ᵉ (Rue de la Pompe/Victor Hugo), 01 45 53 02 68; fax 01 44 05 13 46
◪ "Well-frequented" by "the bourgeois of the 16th", this brasserie's "buzzy atmosphere" is as much of an attraction as "the reasonable prices"; aside from "excellent seafood", the cooking's "without great culinary interest" and the service sometimes seems "too speedy"; still, it's a "sure value" and a good place to "bring your aged mother if she lives nearby."

Petit Zinc (Le) ●S   15 | 16 | 14 | 48

11, rue St-Benoît, 6ᵉ (St-Germain-des-Prés), 01 42 86 61 00; fax 01 42 86 61 09
◪ "I know it's touristy, but I still like it" sums up the slightly defiant sentiment about this "Contemporary French" brasserie "off the Boulevard Saint-Germain" in the 6th celebrated for its "charming art nouveau decor"; the fact that it "belongs to the Frères Blanc chain" naturally arouses some ire about "chain-style cooking", but most surveyors find the "food unexpectedly decent"; bottom line: if this place is "not wonderful, it's a reliable" Paris trademark, so "take your visitors."

Petrossian   22 | 18 | 19 | 74

18, bd de La Tour-Maubourg, 7ᵉ (La Tour-Maubourg), 01 44 11 32 32; fax 01 44 11 32 35
■ "An explosion of flavors" awaits at this "excellent" seafooder with a restful beluga-gray "modern decor" in the 7th; expect "sublime" and "very original" dishes like smoked salmon with white-salmon sorbet, along with "unforgettable desserts", and since they like to layer ingredients and serve "in glasses", the concoctions are "a festival for the eyes as well" as the palate; service is "hospitable", if a bit "too ceremonial" for some, and prices aren't so ruinous that you'll rue your roe.

Pétrus 🅂
19 | 15 | 16 | 75

12, pl du Maréchal Juin, 17ᵉ (Pereire), 01 43 80 15 95;
fax 01 47 66 49 86

☑ Depending on your view, the aquarium is half-full or half-empty at this 7th arrondissement veteran: while "too expensive, it's a classic that never disappoints" with its "exquisite fish" – "you must taste the oysters" – and "refined service" according to admirers; antagonists admit the seafood's "excellent" but argue the "standard decor" and "snooty" "servers don't justify the prices" unless you're a "masochistic, anorexic spendthrift."

Pharamond
– | – | – | M

24, rue de la Grande Truanderie, 1ᵉʳ (Etienne Marcel/Les Halles),
01 40 28 45 18; fax 01 40 28 45 87

Parisians heaved a sigh of relief when this old-timer, a favorite of the late President François Mitterrand, re-opened in Les Halles; still equipped with its stunning interior of art nouveau tiles, it now reflects its new owner's roots in the Cantal region, with good grills and dishes like pig's feet with shallots – but a few of the old Normandy standbys (like tripes *à la mode de Caen*) remain, all served by amiable staffers.

Pichet de Paris (Le)
18 | 12 | 14 | 61

68, rue Pierre Charron, 8ᵉ (Franklin D. Roosevelt),
01 43 59 50 34; fax 01 42 89 68 91

☑ This seafooder just off the Champs-Elysées catches a crowd of actors and athletes who don't seem to mind "paying fortunes" for some of "the best fish" ("try the Dover sole in lobster sauce") in town; however, "it's best to be a celebrity here, since otherwise" you can wind up with a table by the door; P.S. a post-*Survey* renovation may outdate the Decor score.

Pied de Chameau (Au) ◑🅂
14 | 18 | 12 | 35

20, rue Quincampoix, 4ᵉ (Hôtel-de-Ville), 01 42 78 35 00;
fax 01 42 78 00 50

☑ "Just as kitsch as can be", this Moroccan in the Marais distracts diners from their couscous or tagines with "belly dancers (good idea!)" and overblown Arabian Nights decor; most like the setting more than the "middling", if "correct", cuisine, but one way or another, a "transporting evening" is guaranteed once the live music starts.

Pied de Cochon (Au) ◑🅂
14 | 16 | 14 | 47

6, rue Coquillière, 1ᵉʳ (Châtelet-Les Halles), 01 40 13 77 00;
fax 01 40 13 77 09

☑ This famous "classic" brasserie for "night owls" (it's open 24 hours a day, seven days a week) and "tourists of all nationalities" in Les Halles has theatrical decor (down to the brass pig's-trotter front door handles) that makes it a "fun" place for "onion soup at 5 AM"; it's "a bit of a factory", with food that's not much more than "decent" and service that can be "nonexistent"; still, it's "convivial" and "lively"; just be forewarned that the namesake "pigs' feet are definitely an acquired taste."

Pied de Fouet (Au) ⌐∄   ▽ | 16 | 12 | 15 | 25 |
45, rue de Babylone, 7ᵉ (St-François-Xavier), 01 47 05 12 27
■ Though it's perhaps "the cheapest restaurant in the 7th, it's good anyway" chirp cheerful cost-cutters about this long-running Traditional French bistro once frequented by André Gide; you "sit elbow-to-elbow in the happy humor" that prevails here and dine on "simple" "homestyle dishes"; just don't plan on lingering, since service is brisk and if you want coffee after your meal, you'll drink it standing at the bar.

"Pierre" à la Fontaine Gaillon ● | 16 | 16 | 16 | 61 |
1, pl Gaillon, 2ᵉ (Opéra/Quatre Septembre), 01 42 65 87 04; fax 01 47 42 63 22
☒ The observation that "time stopped in the middle of the '50s" applies to the "good, classic cooking", "luxurious decor" and "elegant service" at this "Traditional" French business-lunch favorite in a Mansard-style townhouse near the Opéra Garnier; one thing that hasn't stood still, though, are the prices, which many find "expensive for the quality" of the cuisine; P.S. "for small, special occasions, ask for the private room."

Pierre au Palais Royal ● | 18 | 15 | 18 | 60 |
10, rue Richelieu, 1ᵉʳ (Palais Royal-Musée du Louvre), 01 42 96 09 17; fax 01 47 96 09 62
☒ If some rave that this restaurant next to the Palais-Royal is "a treasure, with superb food and great personal service", dissenters find the decor rather "grandmotherly" and the Classic French cuisine "uneven" and "maybe a little overpriced"; passing through the little flower shop at the entrance, though, is a "royal" experience.

PIERRE GAGNAIRE ⓢ | 27 | 22 | 25 | 143 |
Hôtel Balzac, 6, rue Balzac, 8ᵉ (Charles de Gaulle-Etoile/ George V), 01 58 36 12 50; fax 01 58 36 12 51
■ "The summit of Haute Cuisine" lies in the "exceptional creativity" and "sheer artistry" of the eponymous chef-owner of this establishment in the 8th (swallow "a mouthful signed Gagnaire, and tears of emotion come to your eyes"); kudos, too, to his wife, who oversees the "very attentive but not stiff service" in the "cleanly elegant" dining room; a few gripe the "outrageously expensive" gastronomic imaginings "don't always work", but most merely marvel at "the most dazzling high-wire act" in town.

Pitchi Poï ⓢ | 10 | 10 | 11 | 35 |
7, rue Caron, 4ᵉ (St-Paul), 01 42 77 46 15; fax 01 42 77 75 49
■ "One of the last of its kind", this Eastern European specialist in the Marais is "like eating at your grandmother's

house", assuming that grandma was from Krakow or Budapest, of course; if few folks actually get passionate about the pastrami, they still agree that this place is "a pleasant detour to the lands of Yiddish" cooking, best passed on the "nice terrace."

Place (La) — | — | — | E

Radisson SAS Hotel Champs-Elysées, 78, av Marceau, 8ᵉ (Charles de Gaulle-Etoile), 01 53 23 43 63; fax 01 53 23 43 44
Tucked away on the main floor of the new Radisson Champs-Elysées, this tiny dining room – already popular with the fashion and advertising crowds – has a sleek contemporary look and a Southern French–Med menu designed by chef Jean-André Charial (of L'Oustau de Baumanière in Provence) and a staff overseen by Vinny Mazzara, ex sommelier at the Hôtel Bristol; weather permitting, try for a table in the miniscule open-air garden.

Planet Hollywood ⬤ 🅂 5 | 12 | 7 | 33

78, av des Champs-Elysées, 8ᵉ (Franklin D. Roosevelt/ George V), 01 53 83 78 27; fax 01 45 63 02 84
☑ "Proof that you can actually get a bad meal in Paris" cry critics of this Champs-Elysées outpost of this International movie-memorabilia chain, which is also "too noisy", "too expensive" and suffering from "service that does not exist"; diehards deem the "burgers good", but aside from taking the "the kids, who love it", few care to orbit this planet.

PLAZA-ATHÉNÉE, RESTAURANT 27 | 26 | 27 | 132

(aka Alain Ducasse)
Hôtel Plaza-Athénée, 25, av Montaigne, 8ᵉ (Alma-Marceau/ Franklin D. Roosevelt), 01 53 67 65 00; fax 01 53 67 65 12
◼ "Three cheers for the star of Parisian cuisine": "Alain Ducasse gets it right again and again" at his "elegant", if "surprisingly modern", home in the ultra-fashionable Plaza-Athénée, delighting the delirious with "heavenly" New French food ("every morsel teases the palate") and service so "remarkable" that southpaws are served with "the coffee cup handle facing left"; "decadent in every aspect", this *haut lieu* of Haute Cuisine rates as "one of the world's – not just Paris' – best", but "my God, the prices!"

Polidor 🅂 ⌿ 12 | 13 | 13 | 27

41, rue Monsieur-le-Prince, 6ᵉ (Luxembourg/Odéon), 01 43 26 95 34; fax 01 43 26 22 79
☑ "To rediscover your student life" or "if you want to feel like" Jack Kerouac, Richard Ford or "a starving Hemingway in the '20s", head for this "typical", "cheap" Traditional French bistro in the – where else – Latin Quarter; though a soft touch cites the "satisfying" cuisine, "plentiful" is the best most can say, and there's almost "no decor and no service" either; still, Parisians have been patronizing this "picturesque" place since 1845, and sentimentalists "hope my children will go" here too.

Poquelin (Le)   ▽ 16 | 15 | 17 | 49
*17, rue Molière, 1ᵉʳ (Palais Royal-Musée du Louvre),
01 42 96 22 19; fax 01 42 96 05 72*
■ "Close to the Comédie Française" (the decor celebrates
the theater and Molière), this well-established Auvergnat
wins applause for the "very good quality" of the cooking
("the veal was mouth watering"), "good service" and the
owners, a husband-and-wife team who clearly "love their
métier"; given that, and the "very good price-value ratio",
this is a show "to be recommended."

Port Alma   20 | 15 | 19 | 70
*10, av de New York, 16ᵉ (Alma-Marceau), 01 47 23 75 11;
fax 01 47 20 42 92*
■ "Call ahead for a table with a view of the Eiffel Tower"
(only a few are available) from this "pleasantly bourgeois"
"pricey fish house" "along the quay" in the 16th, and you'll
join well-heeled regulars who appreciate the "charming
welcome" and "precisely cooked" seafood, which includes
rare seasonal specialties like ormer from the Channel
Islands; decorators describe the "calm" dining room as
"sad", but most say the place "merits its muscular prices."

Potager du Roy (Le) 🅂   21 | 15 | 17 | 49
*1, rue du Maréchal-Joffre, Versailles (RER Versailles-
Rive Gauche), 01 39 50 35 34; fax 01 30 21 69 30*
■ "An institution in Versailles", this Classic French serves
"good bourgeois cooking", along with "interesting vegetable
dishes", like carrot and sautéed squid salad, inspired by
proximity to the royal kitchen gardens; come here for "an
extremely pleasant, good-value lunch", especially on
Sundays, or in the evening to relax with a crowd that ranges
from local – "this is an address that the Versaillais keep to
themselves" – to international; only the "old-fashioned
decor" gives some pause.

Pouilly Reuilly   ▽ 18 | 12 | 18 | 48
*68, rue André Joineau, Le Pré-St-Gervais (Hoche),
01 48 45 14 59; fax 01 48 45 93 93*
◪ Owner "Christian Millet has redone the kitchens without
changing the perfectly classic dishes that issue from them
one iota" at this French bistro with vintage '50s decor;
many think it's "worth the trip" to suburban Le Pré-Saint-
Gervais for platters of calf's head and kidneys that "prove
the value of tradition" – even if a few find it's "touristy"
and pout about paying prices of the present for provender
of the past.

Poule au Pot (La) 🅂   16 | 15 | 15 | 45
*9, rue Vauvilliers, 1ᵉʳ (Châtelet-Les Halles/Louvre-Rivoli),
01 42 36 32 96; fax 01 40 91 90 64*
■ Late-nighters and gourmets gravitate toward this "very
French" Classic for its "warm welcome" and "robust
cooking" (including the namesake "specialty, whose

authenticity can't be beat, except at your grandmother's")
that makes "no concessions to modern cuisine"; it also
provides a great dose of "the old atmosphere of Les Halles",
and even if it didn't, "what else is there at 4 AM?"

Pravda ◑🅂   – | – | – | M |

49, rue Jean-Pierre Timbaud, 11ᵉ (Parmentier), 01 48 06 19 76
With Soviet-inspired decor (think vintage posters and
minimalist decor with red-painted accents), this 11th
arrondissment hipster serves modernized Russian dishes,
along with vodka by the carafe and Georgian wines; a young
neighborhood crowd appreciates the party line that includes
easygoing prices and a communal atmosphere.

PRÉ CATELAN (LE) 🅂   23 | 25 | 21 | 103 |

*Bois de Boulogne, route de Suresnes, 16ᵉ (Porte Dauphine),
01 44 14 41 14; fax 01 45 24 43 25*
■ Surveyors swoon over the "beautiful location in the
Bois de Boulogne" of this "romantic" legend with an
atmosphere that's "homey if you live in a chateau"; chef
Frédéric Anton does some "fabulous cooking" in the Haute
Cuisine kitchen – "pity the portions are microscopic" –
and despite some "warm and friendly" examples, "it's too
bad the service isn't up to the level of the rest" too; still, no
one would argue that this destination isn't "a dream in
spring" – or "paradise on earth in summer."

Pressoir (Au)   ▽ 21 | 16 | 20 | 97 |

*257, av Daumesnil, 12ᵉ (Michel Bizot), 01 43 44 38 21;
fax 01 43 43 81 77*
■ While only an intrepid few have found their way to this
comfortable Traditional French table on the edge of town in
the 12th, those who have cry "long live Henri!" in homage
to chef-owner Henri Seguin, who does "definitely very
good work" with such rich dishes as truffle mille-feuille,
lobster pot-au-feu and game in season; one of eastern
Paris' plusher places, it pulls a business crowd at noon and
those celebrating special occasions at night.

Prima Donna ◑   – | – | – | M |

*29, bd d'Algerie, 19ᵉ (Danube), 01 40 18 56 23;
fax 01 40 18 56 27*
In a quiet, almost bucolic corner of the 19th, this simple
Italian trattoria lures locals with hearty, home-cooked dishes
at easy prices; a mix of long-time residents and the arty
types who are waking up this corner of the city fill the small
dining room, enjoying the friendly, if occasionally chaotic,
family-style service.

Procope (Le) ◑🅂   13 | 20 | 14 | 46 |

*13, rue de l'Ancienne Comédie, 6ᵉ (Odéon), 01 40 46 79 00;
fax 01 40 46 79 09*
◪ Voltaire, Thomas Jefferson and Benjamin Franklin would
probably be surprised to hear their old hangout near the

Odéon called "flashy and fun", but that's what this famous 1686 literary cafe has become, thanks to an "attractive", if rather zealously renovated, setting by the Frères Blanc chain; somewhat less amusing is the "brasserie-style cuisine" ("overpriced tourist food") and the "perfunctory" service, but nostalgists note "it's no worse than others in the area, and it's more historic", too.

P'tit Troquet (Le)   18 | 15 | 19 | 38

28, rue de l'Exposition, 7ᵉ (Ecole-Militaire), 01 47 05 80 39; fax 01 47 05 80 39

■ "One word suffices – yum!" to describe this New French bistro with "charming" 1920s-vintage decor; but if that's not enough, patrons also praise the "simply wonderful service" and "gentle prices" charged for a "memorable meal" of "updated traditional fare"; the cozy setting can get "smoky" and "stuffy", but "if you're in the 7th", odds are you too will be "so happy you found this sweet little restaurant."

Pure Café   – | – | – | M

14, rue Jean-Macé, 11ᵉ (Faidherbe-Chaligny), 01 43 71 47 22

Bistro-lovers are beating tracks to this new example of a threatened local genus in a gentrifying part of the 11th; swift and saucy servers, easygoing prices and a roster of expertly executed International dishes means that this good-looking place with a horse-shoe shaped bar is packed nightly with young professionals – so be sure to book ahead.

Quai Ouest ●S   12 | 17 | 11 | 41

1200, quai Marcel Dassault, Saint-Cloud (Pont-de-St-Cloud), 01 46 02 35 54; fax 01 46 02 33 02

◪ "Trendy, but good" insist mateys of this large barge-restaurant moored in Saint-Cloud; from among the Eclectic fare, regulars recommend the "excellent salads" and "decent brunch", while less-enthused landlubbers say the "cooking's alright but the noise is intolerable" and "the service could be improved"; luckily, "the terrace with its view of the Seine helps you forget the slightly high prices"; P.S. "if you don't like children, don't go."

404 (Le) ●S   19 | 22 | 16 | 43

69, rue des Gravilliers, 3ᵉ (Arts-et-Métiers), 01 42 74 57 81; fax 01 42 74 03 41

◪ A "hip, hip, hip crowd of models, movie stars and moguls" frequents this Moroccan with a "magnificent dining room" of carved stone that "makes you feel you're in a *ryad* [a house built around a garden courtyard]" instead of the 3rd; the menu offers "delicious dishes", especially the "excellent couscous"; on the downside, the service "leaves more and more to be desired" and it's also "hard to have a conversation because the music is too loud", but happily "both the food and the setting take you away."

Quincy (Le) ⌨   ▽ 20 | 13 | 18 | 48
28, av Ledru-Rollin, 12ᵉ (Gare de Lyon/Quai de la Rapée),
01 46 28 46 76; fax 01 46 28 46 76
■ Located in the 12th, this "great small place" is clearly a force to be reckoned with, as is its "colorful" owner Michel Bosshard, who likes to banter; what really makes the regulars happy here, though, is the "fabulous" Classic French fare from several provinces, including Burgundy (the escargots), Berry and the Ardèche.

Quinson (Le)   ▽ 15 | 10 | 12 | 40
5, pl Etienne Pernet, 15ᵉ (Commerce/Félix-Faure),
01 45 32 48 54; fax 01 44 19 73 18
■ While the 15th is bristling with new eateries, this post-World War II veteran soldiers on; the young team that's taken over from the namesake Quinsons works in a Mediterranean register, serving not only the "specialty bouillabaisse" but salt cod and swordfish tartare; "even if you live far away, you'll be back for the freshness of the foodstuffs and the charming simplicity" of the setting.

R.   – | – | – | M
8, rue de la Cavalerie, 15ᵉ (La Motte Picquet-Grenelle),
01 45 67 06 85
Occupying the former Morot-Gaudry penthouse space, this hip young table specializes in views of the Eiffel Tower, striking minimalist decor by Christophe Pillet and New French fare served to fashionistas and mediaphiles, who don't usually venture to this quiet residential quarter.

R'Aliment ●   – | – | – | M
57, rue Charlot, 3ᵉ (Filles du Calvaire/République), 01 48 04 88 28;
fax 01 48 04 88 28
Polyurethane chairs, aluminum tables and other sleek features (courtesy of Reso Design, packaging and image specialists) draw a trendy crowd to this hip novice in the northern Marais; the kitchen's concept is inventive organic cooking, which runs to lots of unusually garnished pasta, grain and vegetable dishes, at good old moderate prices.

Ravi   – | – | – | E
50, rue de Verneuil, 7ᵉ (Rue du Bac), 01 42 61 17 28
In "a city not known for Indian cuisine", this "tiny restaurant serves up big flavors" – possibly the "best in Paris" – though fire-eaters suggest the cuisine "is perhaps toned down for delicate French palates"; the "only drawback is that the one waiter is overtaxed" – but at least "the wait gives you time to enjoy" the "cossetting, comfortable space."

Récamier (Le)   20 | 17 | 19 | 70
4, rue Récamier, 7ᵉ (Sèvres-Babylone), 01 45 48 86 58;
fax 01 42 22 84 76
☑ Owner Martin Cantegrit has ceded the reins of this "bustling" little Burgundian in a cul-de-sac in the 7th to

his son, and fans (book editors, cabinet ministers) say everything remains the same, with "traditional" specialties like boeuf bourguignon and "mushrooms in season" and a lavish wine list; complainers claim the food's "too staid" and the "decor smells dusty" ("it would be good to give it a coat of paint" too), but all agree that while "the terrace is heaven, the check is hell."

Rech (Le) ❷⑤ 　　　17 | 10 | 14 | 63

62, av des Ternes, 17ᵉ (Charles de Gaulle-Etoile/Ternes), 01 45 72 29 47; fax 01 45 72 41 60

☑ This "venerable" brasserie in the 17th has been serving since 1925; while *amis* applaud the quality "traditional cooking", which emphasizes "fish and seafood" and an "oyster bar", the less-nostalgic say it's pretty "pricey for what it is", particularly given the "aging decor"; overall, though, it remains "true to itself", which is what you'd expect from "a good old classic" like this one.

Réconfort (Le) 　　　∇ 16 | 19 | 16 | 36

37, rue de Poitou, 3ᵉ (St-Sébastien-Froissart), 01 49 96 09 60; fax 01 49 96 09 62

■ At this Marais bistro, the "very colorful" and vaguely "baroque" (as in over the top) decor "enchants" its clientele of local hipsters from the fashion industry, even as they savor Provençal fare that's "light and original"; continuing the Mediterranean theme, the "welcome is warm", even if the service is "a tad cold", and prices are easily digested.

RÉGALADE (LA) ❷ 　　　22 | 12 | 15 | 46

49, av Jean Moulin, 14ᵉ (Alésia), 01 45 45 68 58; fax 01 45 40 96 74

■ "The cooking is just simply exceptional" at chef-owner Yves Camdeborde's bistro "off the beaten path" in the 14th; the problem is, everyone knows it, making it "hard to get a reservation" and creating a rugged dining experience – multiple seatings make the "knowledgeable" "servers stressed and high-strung"; you also sit "on top of each other, but it's worth it" for such "magnificent" Classic French food ("be prepared for the frequent and fantastic use of organ meats") "at very fair prices."

Relais d'Auteuil "Patrick Pignol" 　　　22 | 15 | 20 | 88

31, bd Murat, 16ᵉ (Michel-Ange Molitor/Porte d'Auteuil), 01 46 51 09 54; fax 01 40 71 05 03

■ Chef-owner Patrick Pignol's "chic but relaxed" spot may be "small", but it's decidedly grand to devotees delighted by "every detail", from the "superb food" (try "the sea bass in peppered pastry") to Mme. Pignol's "warm welcome" to the "thoughtful and multilingual service"; a few find the prices "exorbitant" and some feel it has "decidedly high pretensions for a place that's not much more than a glassed-in cafe", but most maintain it's "without doubt one of the best tables in Auteuil."

Relais de l'Entrecôte (Le) ◑ ⑤   17 | 12 | 17 | 32
20 bis, rue St-Benoit, 6ᵉ (St-Germain-des-Prés), 01 45 49 16 00; fax 01 45 49 29 75
15, rue Marbeuf, 8ᵉ (Franklin D. Roosevelt), 01 49 52 07 17; fax 01 47 23 34 98
■ "The sauce is the secret weapon" at these two "major classics" – one in Saint-Germain, the other off the Champs-Elysées – that do a "very good" job "diligently" serving nothing but steak with frites (so "don't come for the fish"); you "simply can't beat the value" either, which makes up for the fact that their interiors will never make the cover of *Elle Decor*.

Relais de Venise (Le) ◑ ⑤   18 | 12 | 16 | 36
271, bd Pereire, 17ᵉ (Porte Maillot), 01 45 74 27 97
■ At this Porte Maillot cow palace, "there's no surprise, since they only serve one dish" – "great steak", the star of a set menu that includes a walnut-garnished salad, frites and a "famous secret sauce" that has a Pavlovian effect on patrons; service can be "machine-gun-like", there's "lots of waiting" for seats and "it's a little cramped" at table, but none of this deters disciples from "a sure bet" and a good buy, to boot.

Relais Louis XIII   22 | 21 | 19 | 85
8, rue des Grands-Augustins, 6ᵉ (Odéon/St-Michel), 01 43 26 75 96; fax 01 44 07 07 80
☑ Located in a medieval Saint-Germain manse that's "magic itself", this "luxurious" table serves an "interesting" blend of "classic and inventive" French fare created by chef Manuel Martinez (ex Tour d'Argent); but if there's "food to make Louis XIII himself jealous", "it's too bad the service isn't at the same level" ("were the waiters hired that day?") – a sentiment that leaves many "expecting more for these prices."

Relais Plaza (Le) ◑ ⑤   17 | 20 | 21 | 69
Hôtel Plaza-Athénée, 21, av Montaigne, 8ᵉ (Alma-Marceau/ Franklin D. Roosevelt), 01 53 67 64 00; fax 01 53 67 66 66
☑ "The food's standard, but there's a strong message of luxury" emanating from this upscale brasserie, thanks to a "prestigious setting" (the Plaza Athenée) and "beautiful" art deco decor; not surprisingly, the "quite stiff prices" and "impeccable service" attract "an older crowd" comprised, to quote one alliterative wit, of "painted ladies pushing lettuce leaves around their plates."

Réminet ⑤   21 | 14 | 20 | 46
3, rue des Grands Degrés, 5ᵉ (Maubert-Mutualité), 01 44 07 04 24; fax 01 44 07 17 37
■ This "sweet little bistro" in the Latin Quarter is "a real find", thanks to the "exceptional, really superb" New French cooking of chef-owner Hugues Gournay and his "charming" wife (who speaks excellent English); "the only thing bad

about this place is its lack of space", though "opening onto the sidewalk in summer" helps ease the squeeze.

Rendez-vous des Camionneurs (Au) ≠   – | – | – | I

34, rue des Plantes, 14ᵉ (Alésia/Plaisance), 01 45 40 43 36
Existing in an endearing 1950s time warp – think Yves Montand and Simone Signoret – this "likable" locale deep in the 14th offers a menu reminiscent of the "familiar" food to be found in cafe-restaurants along the national highways: sausage sandwiches, fried baby sole and apple tart; utterly "unpretentious", it's an ideal pit stop for small budgets.

Rendez-vous des Chauffeurs (Au) S   – | – | – | I

11, rue des Portes Blanches, 18ᵉ (Marcadet-Poissonniers), 01 42 64 04 17; fax 01 42 52 75 68
With a name that refers to its past as a rendezvous for cab drivers having a quick bite between shifts, this "amusing" spot in the 18th is now "for students", bargain-hunters and "enthusiastic regulars coming home for real food" (think Classic French dishes like pot-au-feu, boeuf bourguignon and "the best pommes frites in the world").

Renoma Café Gallery ●❙S   15 | 15 | 13 | 53

32, av George V, 8ᵉ (George V), 01 56 89 05 89; fax 01 47 20 23 77
☑ With "avant-garde New York–style decor", this yearling just off the Champs features "an appealing atmosphere" of exhibits of photos and paintings; but while some applaud the "surprisingly good Classic French food" (supplemented with some contemporary offerings post-*Survey*), others suggest the kitchen is "not yet broken in" and mutter "bring your credit card – this is a cafe in name only."

Repaire de Cartouche (Le)   20 | 11 | 16 | 43

99, rue Amelot, 11ᵉ (St-Sébastien-Froissart), 01 47 00 25 86
■ "Happy are those who find their way" to young chef-owner Rodolphe Paquin's Classic French bistro, occupying a duplex in the 11th; not only does he offer "great country cooking", he does so at a "good buy" ("surprised it wasn't more expensive"); a few scold him for "spending too much time in the dining room", but most say it's "a great address"; now if only they'd redo that somewhat "sinister decor."

Restaurant de la Tour   ▽ 17 | 13 | 14 | 39

6, rue Desaix, 15ᵉ (Dupleix), 01 43 06 04 24; fax 01 44 49 05 66
■ Perched on "the border between the 7th and 15th" sits this "unsung hero" of a Classic French where "chef-owner Cédric Robert is a wizard in the kitchen, turning out luscious dishes at bistro prices"; "widely spaced seating is a plus" as well, and when augmented by "charming" servers, "it's the perfect place to relax after a busy day."

Restaurant du Marché ▽ 17 | 11 | 12 | 47

59, rue de Dantzig, 15ᵉ (Porte de Versailles), 01 48 28 31 55; fax 01 48 28 18 31

■ Observe the chef through the window between the kitchen and the dining room at this small bistro deep in the 15th and you'll see a truly passionate cook turning out both original dishes like vinegar-roasted chicken and "solid" "Southwestern classics" like a crispy confit de canard; it's not "light", but it's "good food overall", and "charming service" augments the "appealing atmosphere."

Restaurant du Musée d'Orsay ⑤ 14 | 22 | 14 | 33

Musée d'Orsay, 1, rue de Légion d'Honneur, 7ᵉ (Solférino), 01 45 49 47 03; fax 01 42 22 34 12

■ This "magical spot", "a jewel in the crown" of the Musée d'Orsay, delights culture vultures with an "ornate dining room" – think crystal chandeliers, parquet and ormolu – and a Classic French "buffet lunch" that's not only "reasonably priced" but "delicately prepared"; if the culinary art doesn't rival the masterpieces on the walls, "it's very good for a museum restaurant", with helpful, multilingual service.

Restaurant du Palais Royal 18 | 21 | 16 | 56

110, Galerie de Valois, 1ᵉʳ (Bourse/Palais Royal-Musée du Louvre), 01 40 20 00 27; fax 01 40 20 00 82

☑ With a "magnificent" space in a corner of the arcade that runs around the Palais-Royal, this Classic French–Med makes "a great place for a special celebration"; but while royalists rave over the "fresh and light" cuisine and "sincere welcome", revolutionaries rail that "using the pretext of a prestigious setting, they serve neither-here-nor-there food to tourists"; no one denies, though, that the "garden views" from the "outstanding patio" make it "a must in summer."

Restaurant les Dolomites 17 | 13 | 16 | 36

38, rue Poncelet, 17ᵉ (Ternes), 01 47 66 38 54; fax 01 47 27 39 57

■ The "decor's average but the food delights" at this Classic French ensconced in a "not so lively" neighborhood of the 17th, which offers up a signature duck ravioli and mushrooms along with daily market specialties; some say it's lost a little soul since a change in owners, but most maintain it's "a place that makes you want to linger."

Restaurant W ▽ 22 | 13 | 19 | 75

Hôtel Warwick, 5, rue de Berri, 8ᵉ (George V), 01 45 61 82 08; fax 01 45 63 75 81

■ The rather "claustrophobic" dining room of the Hôtel Warwick just off the Champs-Elysées will never tempt anyone with its decor, but chef Franck Charpentier is "a major talent in the making", concocting a New French menu that ranges from "great small surprises" in the starters to "wonderful" mains; it's served by a "maître d'hôtel who loves what he does and shares it beautifully" says the mostly expense-account clientele that doesn't mind the substantial prices.

Riad (Le) S
– | – | – | M

47, av Charles de Gaulle, Neuilly-sur-Seine (Les Sablons/ Porte Maillot), 01 46 24 42 61; fax 01 46 40 19 91
Meander into Morocco when you sink into the comfortable cushions of this small North African haven that's a hop, skip and a jump from the Porte Maillot; the authentic couscous and other specialties – including a soothing, traditional mint tea – satisfy just as much as the very reasonable bill.

Ribe S
▽ 13 | 13 | 12 | 43

15 av de Suffren, 7ᵉ (Bir-Hakeim), 01 45 66 53 79; fax 01 45 66 53 79
■ "Charming" chant clients about this belle epoque baby (born 1909) in the 7th that welcomes "lots of foreigners" due to its "nice location" near the Hilton Hotel and Eiffel Tower; it's a "good Parisian brasserie", with Classic French prix fixes to provide "value for the money."

River Café S
13 | 19 | 13 | 42

146, quai de Stalingrad, Issy-les-Moulineaux (RER Issy Plaine), 01 40 93 50 20; fax 01 41 46 19 45
◤ For "a change of pace within Paris", surveyors set a course for this riverside barge in Issy-les-Moulineaux, whose "trendy atmosphere" is "popular with a young advertising crowd"; while foes fume "it's a factory" with "too many people and not enough servers", the more forgiving find the Classic French "cuisine is honest, but it's primarily for the setting that you come" – "the terrace in summer, the fireplace in winter."

Robe et le Palais (La)
– | – | – | M

13, rue de Lavandières-Ste-Opportune, 1ᵉʳ (Châtelet-Les Halles), 01 45 08 07 41; fax 01 45 08 07 41
Outside its regular following from the nearby Palais de Justice, this bistro à vins is surprisingly little-known; chef-owner Patrice Gras, who trained with Alain Dutournier, offers such imaginative dishes as risotto with baby squid and date mousse, and augmenting his "attractive food" is "courteous but friendly service" from the "funny guys" who preside here.

Robert et Louise ⌿
– | – | – | M

64, rue Vieille-du-Temple, 3ᵉ (Rambuteau), 01 42 78 55 89
A meal at this very old-fashioned auberge in the Marais, complete with long wooden tables and a fire in the hearth, is like dinner with that nice older couple that lives next door to your country house: you start with charcuterie or maybe celery rémoulade, and then move on to the pièce de résistance, a big steak grilled over an open fire; it's an "authentic" provincial experience, but while "the meat's good", some cosmopolites are put off by "having to pay too-high prices in cash."

Roi du Pot-au-Feu (Le)
14 | 10 | 13 | 34

34, rue Vignon, 9ᵉ (Madeleine), 01 47 42 37 10

■ Make no bones about it, though bones figure prominently at this 1930s Traditional French bistro near the Madeleine: "this place is great at what they do, which is to serve one dish [guess what?] and one wine in rustic surroundings"; some find the vino "mediocre", but most rate the pot-au-feu as "superb", especially "during the winter", and though it fills you up, it doesn't empty your wallet.

Romantica (La)
20 | 14 | 15 | 57

73, bd Jean Jaurès, Clichy (Mairie-de-Clichy), 01 47 37 29 71; fax 01 47 37 76 32

◪ To experience "Italy just two steps from Paris", head to this Clichy cucina, where converts cheer "long live the wheel of Parmesan", from which many of the "bellissimo" pastas are served ("quite a show and a brilliant idea"); pessimists pout about "pompous" service and "heavy", "too expensive" eats, but even they agree this place definitely "merits its name", as it's "perfect for dining both in summer, outside in a lovely garden, and in winter, around the log fire."

Rosimar
▽ 19 | 12 | 20 | 40

26, rue Poussin, 16ᵉ (Michel-Ange Auteuil/Porte d'Auteuil), 01 45 27 74 91; fax 01 45 20 75 05

■ "Paris' best paella, without a doubt – even in Spain it's not this good" attest amigos of this "smiling" Spaniard near the Porte d'Auteuil; the only rain falling on this plain is the "hallucinogenic" "mirrored decor", but that's "quickly forgotten" given the "high-quality cuisine"; and with prices this moderate, there's no point in waiting for an olé before you charge; P.S. the paella "must be ordered when you make your reservation."

Rôtisserie d'Armaillé
16 | 13 | 15 | 48

6, rue d'Armaillé, 17ᵉ (Charles de Gaulle-Etoile), 01 42 27 19 20; fax 01 40 55 00 93

■ Not far from the Etoile, this "classic rotisserie" is "dependable" and "especially good for finicky American visitors" who crave meat and potatoes; it's one of chef Jacques Cagna's trio of spit-roasted spots, which explains the slightly "chic" (read: "snob") atmosphere and "pleasant" but "relatively austere" decor.

Rôtisserie d'en Face (La)
19 | 15 | 19 | 50

2, rue Christine, 6ᵉ (Odéon/Pont Neuf/St-Michel), 01 43 26 40 98; fax 01 43 54 22 71

◪ It's "like eating in California" to attend Jacques Cagna's original rotisserie in Saint-Germain: not only "has it become frequented largely by Americans", but much of the simple "grilled" menu (with a signature "roast chicken") could hail from the Napa Valley too; if fans find the "food is all it professes to be" (the "chocolate cake is extraordinary"), skeptics say "any of a dozen Left Bank bistros are better" and this is so "expensive, you might as well go *en face*" to the chef-owner's main restaurant 'facing' this one.

Rôtisserie du Beaujolais (La) 🆂 | 18 | 15 | 17 | 42 |
19, quai de la Tournelle, 5ᵉ (Jussieu/Pont Marie), 01 43 54 17 47; fax 01 56 24 43 71
☑ Converts call come to Claude Terrail's (La Tour d'Argent) "festive" riverside rotisserie in the Latin Quarter for Lyonnais-like "homestyle dishes like we ate when we were children", along with "special cuts and odd meats like wild boar and other game"; but naysayers claim it's "nothing exceptional and the prices are too high", especially given the "crowded-together" digs.

Rôtisserie Monsigny (La) | 14 | 12 | 14 | 41 |
1, rue Monsigny, 2ᵉ (Quatre Septembre), 01 42 96 16 61; fax 01 42 97 40 97
☑ On the Right Bank near the Bourse, the largest of chef Jacques Cagna's rotisseries rouses the least enthusiasm – "no surprises, neither good nor bad, in a rather sterile setting"; however, its location makes it "perfect for a working lunch" or "before the theater" (several are nearby).

Rotonde ⬤🆂 | 14 | 17 | 16 | 45 |
105, bd du Montparnasse, 6ᵉ (Vavin), 01 43 26 48 26; fax 01 46 34 52 40
◼ "Man Ray and Henry Miller are all that's missing" from this "quintessential Montparnasse brasserie" (both were patrons back in the neighborhood's artistic and intellectual glory days); thanks to the "really good food and service", "one feels at ease" here – at least until the check comes, since it's gotten "very expensive"; "avoid the busiest times of the day, since the staff is quickly overwhelmed."

Rouge Vif (Le) | 17 | 13 | 18 | 36 |
48, rue de Verneuil, 7ᵉ (Musée d'Orsay/Solférino), 01 42 86 81 87
◼ "Beautiful people from a beautiful neighborhood in a beautiful little find of a bistro" bay boosters of this "fun, casual" address near the Assemblée Nationale; owner Pascal Rousseau, "a very warm type", animates the dining room, while "the quality cooking delights all palates", from Classic French to Filipino; the only negative thing anyone has to say is that "it can be noisy during the day."

Rubis (Le) ⊘ | 15 | 13 | 16 | 22 |
10, rue du Marché St Honoré, 1ᵉʳ (Tuileries), 01 42 61 03 34
◼ "Still the best wine bar in Paris" opine oenophiles about this "Place du Marché Saint Honoré neighborhood" "institution"; "a must on the night when the Beaujolais Nouveau comes out", it's also a traditional "bistro like you don't find in Paris anymore", with "simple, authentic cooking" ("trust the plat du jour"); "always a pleasure for a quick lunch on your feet", it's also "unbeatable for bringing foreign friends."

Rucola (La) — | — | — | M

198, bd Malesherbes, 17ᵉ (Wagram), 01 44 40 04 50; fax 01 44 40 04 50

Catering mostly to bankers and brokers, this smart, stylish newcomer near the Place de Wagram woos the well-heeled with soft lighting, wood paneling and a divinely diverse Italian menu – The Boot-spanning specialties travel from Naples to Rome to Milan.

Rue Balzac ❶ S | 16 | 17 | 14 | 58

3-5, rue Balzac, 8ᵉ (George V), 01 53 89 90 91; fax 01 53 89 90 94

◪ This "upbeat" and "very New Yorky" "airy space" just off the Champs is a collaboration between chef Michel Rostang, restaurateur Claude Bouillon and singer Johnny Hallyday; many find the brasserie-style eats "an agreeable surprise" for such a "showbiz" scene, though antagonists aver "I had my doubts about Hallyday's culinary talents and I still have them" and also slam the "slow, put-you-to-sleep" service, the majority rule finds it "pretty good", even if "you pay for the buzz."

Rughetta (La) | 14 | 9 | 13 | 34

41, rue Lepic, 18ᵉ (Abbesses/Blanche), 01 42 23 41 70; fax 01 42 23 41 70

■ "Good pizzas and a trendy crowd" are the lures of this locale on a winding street in Montmartre; the showbiz locals dub it a "true Italian" for its "simple, effective" eats and "incredibly friendly" staff that make it a "good place to attend with amici"; P.S. the tiny terrace is "very pleasant during the summer."

Saint Amarante (Le) — | — | — | M

4, rue Biscornet, 12ᵉ (Bastille), 01 43 43 00 08

Christophe Dupire, who trained at Ledoyen and the Ritz, is the "competent chef" installed after an ownership change at this "nice", moderately priced little bistro by the Opéra Bastille; so far his New French fare seems "very good"; now, if only they could spruce the place up some, since surveyors swear by all the saints "it's ugly."

Saint Vincent (Le) ▽ 16 | 15 | 16 | 34

26, rue de la Croix-Nivert, 15ᵉ (Cambronne), 01 47 34 14 94; fax 01 45 66 46 58

■ Come to this cozy little Lyonnaise-oriented bistro near the Ecole Militaire for a "great selection of Beaujolais to go with the quality cooking" of classics like lamb cooked for seven hours; busy with UNESCO types and government workers at noon, it's much quieter in the evening.

Salle à Manger (La) S — | — | — | E

Hôtel Raphaël, 17, av Kléber, 16ᵉ (Kléber), 01 53 64 32 11; fax 01 53 64 32 02

"Like the Hôtel Raphaël [where it's located], this place is non-ostentatious", which is why it remains "a hidden gem off the Champs-Elysées"; chef Philippe Delahaye delights discreet devotees with innovative updates on Traditional French dishes, including shellfish-stuffed squid and rabbit with girolle mushrooms; "evenings are an event" here, marred only by "the need for light and a little music."

Salon d' Hélène
18 | 19 | 16 | 49

4, rue d' Assas, 6ᵉ (Sèvres-Babylone), 01 42 22 00 11; fax 01 42 22 25 40

☑ Chef-owner Hélène Darroze had the "excellent idea" to allocate the ground floor of her high-end restaurant in the 7th for a more "casual" – and less costly – bistro serving her "delicious" brand of Southwestern fare; if expansive appetites find the Basque/Spanish-inspired tapas too "minimal for maximal prices" and a few regret that "service is not on par with the food", friends consider the little plates and "laid-back ambiance" "ideal for get-togethers."

Sardegna a Tavola
– | – | – | M

1, rue de Cotte, 12ᵉ (Ledru-Rollin), 01 44 75 03 28; fax 01 44 75 03 28

Though a "recent discovery" for reviewers, this table in a quiet, arty part of the 12th is already becoming a "favorite" for "exceptional Sardinian cooking" ("almost too copious"), Italian handicrafts–heavy decor and an "excellent price-value ratio"; it's attracting a growing crowd, so book, and be prepared to be dispatched to the back room until you become known.

Sarladais (Le)
19 | 15 | 18 | 52

2, rue de Vienne, 8ᵉ (St-Augustin), 01 45 22 23 62; fax 01 45 22 23 62

■ In the 8th, not far from where the great gourmand Curnonsky once lived, this "calm", well-regarded veteran offers "all of the excellence of the Périgord – food, human warmth and decor – in one place"; and if the kitchen is "very classic", it's also "very reliable" in its "evocation of the flavors and scents" of the Southwest – "a good example of provincial cuisine that never pales, even in Paris."

Sasso
– | – | – | I

36, rue Raymond Losserand, 14ᵉ (Pernety), 01 42 18 00 38

In a quiet Montparnasse neighborhood, this venture from the team behind the hit Les Cailloux is lasso-ing locals (plus people from other parts of town) with its range of freshly made pastas and other Italian classics; low lighting, plain wooden tables with lacquered tops and cheerful, multi-lingual waiters set a relaxed mood.

Saudade
▽ 16 | 14 | 16 | 39

34, rue des Bourdonnais, 1ᵉʳ (Châtelet-Les Halles), 01 42 36 03 65; fax 01 42 36 27 77

■ Amigos agree that this Les Halles Lusitanian sets "the best Portuguese table in Paris", though a few suggest the very "classic" menu be "renovated" with "simpler cod dishes and other fish as well"; still, with plenty of "attentive servers" to keep pouring the Porto, this "restful" dining room decorated with blue-and-white *azueloes* (hand-painted tiles) is a "pleasure."

Sauvignon (Au)   11 | 12 | 12 | 33

80, rue des Saints-Pères, 7ᵉ (Sèvres-Babylone), 01 45 48 49 02; fax 01 45 49 41 00

☑ A "super site, especially the terrace" has made this Left Bank wine bar one of the most stylish "addresses in the quarter"; admirers attest it's an "adorable" place, offering "a very good opportunity to taste cheeses or foie gras" with "good French wines by the glass", but the sour-grapes sort snap it's "too expensive for sandwiches."

Sawadee   18 | 10 | 15 | 39

53, av Emile Zola, 15ᵉ (Charles-Michels), 01 45 77 68 90; fax 01 45 77 57 78

☑ This Thai "off the beaten track" in the 15th may not have much in the way of decor – it's mostly an aquarium and a few potted plants – but its "very refined" cooking makes it "extremely recommendable" to curry-cravers; surveyors split over the service, with some sad that "it's not warmer (a smile, please)" and others finding it "pleasantly personalized"; reasonable prices rule.

Scheffer (Le)   15 | 10 | 14 | 36

22, rue Scheffer, 16ᵉ (Trocadéro), 01 47 27 81 11

■ Okay, so it's "noisy" and "you're packed in like sardines", but these are the only beefs against this "traditional bistro" in the 16th, where young execs, bargain-loving local gourmets and well-advised tourists delight in French fare composed of "quality ingredients" ("like you used to make at home for yourself" when you still had time to cook); "framed posters and waxed-canvas tablecloths" give it an "authentic", "neighborhood restaurant" feel.

Sébillon ●🅂   15 | 12 | 14 | 48

20, av Charles de Gaulle, Neuilly-sur-Seine (Porte Maillot), 01 46 24 71 31; fax 01 46 24 43 50

☑ While this "classic" 91-year-old Neuilly brasserie may strike you as stuck-up ("the staff is like the clientele – snobby"), most put up with the "haughty expressions of certain waiters" for the endless portions of "leg of lamb, sliced tableside"; regulars, however, recommend that you stick to that and the "superb" "seafood and nothing else" – otherwise, it's "boredom down to the bottom of the plate."

Sébillon Élysées ●🅂   16 | 14 | 14 | 46

66, rue Pierre Charron, 8ᵉ (Franklin D. Roosevelt), 01 43 59 28 15; fax 01 43 59 30 00

■ The same "clever formula" – "all-you-can-eat" servings of roasted leg of lamb and white beans from a tableside trolley – patented by its Neuilly parent pleases patrons of this "agreeable brasserie" in the 8th; some sniff the "glitzy" "decor needs to be redone" and "the service is often overwhelmed", but overall, "one eats here with pleasure."

Seize au Seize ─|─|─| E
(fka Ghislaine Arabian)
16, av Bugeaud, 16ᵉ (Victor Hugo), 01 56 28 16 16; fax 01 56 28 16 78
In the 16th arrondissment space once occupied by chef-owner Ghislaine Arabian, the team she left behind has created a stylish, Contemporary French table whose cooking and dressy decor (they've kept the gold-leaf trimmings) have already made it a hit, despite prices that are rather stiff.

16 Haussmann (Le) ◐ 16|17|15| 44
Hôtel Ambassador, 16, bd Haussmann, 9ᵉ (Chaussée d'Antin/Richelieu-Drouot), 01 44 83 40 58; fax 01 48 00 06 38
■ "An unexpected oasis of calm near the big department stores" in the 9th, this "refreshingly different" dining room pleases with its "pretty contemporary decor" of ochre and blue walls and Philippe Starck furniture; the kitchen sends out "agreeable dishes" in an intelligently inventive register – prawn ravioli in basil cream and perch sautéed with treviso, for example – and most find it "deserves to be better known."

Senso ◐ S ─|─|─| M
Hôtel de la Trémoille, 16, rue de la Trémoille, 8ᵉ (Alma-Marceau), 01 56 52 14 14; fax 01 56 52 14 13
Sir Terence Conran's second Paris brasserie (Alcazar's the other) occupies a long narrow space with an ebony-stained parquet floor and dove-gray walls in the recently renovated Hôtel de la Trémoille, which is tucked away on a quiet street in the 'Golden Triangle' of luxury shopping; the kitchen sends out a mix of New French dishes, along with a selection of International favorites like Cesar salad.

Senteurs de Provence (Aux) ▽ 15|9|12| 45
295, rue Lecourbe, 15ᵉ (Lourmel), 01 45 57 11 98; fax 01 45 58 66 84
◪ Following a "change of hands", it seems as though there now are as many cloudy days as sunny ones at this Provençal in the 15th; if some maintain that it's still "a nice little address with good fish dishes" and "sweet service", others detect "problems in the kitchen", since the signature "bouillabaisse isn't good" anymore ("excessively salty" and "peppery", "it's not Provence, it's Algeria"); the decor's downright "dusty" too.

7ème Sud Grenelle ◐ S ─|─|─| M
159, rue de Grenelle, 7ᵉ (La Tour-Maubourg), 01 44 18 30 30
Popular with well-heeled locals, this 7th arrondissement spot may be "small", but it spans the Mediterranean with specialties that range from Southern France to North

Africa; a "warm and intimate" atmosphere pervades the dining rooms – one of which doubles as the wine cellar – abetted by "waiters and waitresses who practice their English on you."

Sept Quinze (Le)   19 | 12 | 18 | 33

29, av Lowendal, 15ᵉ (Cambronne), 01 43 06 23 06; fax 01 45 67 14 11

■ On a "quiet avenue near the Ecole Militaire", this "island of conviviality" offers "amazing value" for its Eclectic array of "extraordinary cooking" (described as "California style" by several) – which, along with "incredibly cordial service", explains why "it's always full"; "the only downside is that the tables are a little cramped", making it "noisy"; even so, "everyone you bring returns" to this "happening place."

Shozan   20 | 20 | 16 | 68

11, rue de La Trémoille, 8ᵉ (Alma-Marceau/George V), 01 47 23 37 32; fax 01 47 23 67 30

■ Equipped with a "refined" and "restful Zen setting" by designer Christian Liaigre (a rarity for à la mode tables in the 8th arrondissement), this "unusual and sophisticated" "Franco-Japanese" conducts an "East-West dialogue at its best", sending out "passionate", "incredible" hybrid dishes like "truffled foie gras sushi"; it's "a little expensive", but partisans pay gladly to visit "a trendy place that, for once, serves original and excellent food" (strange, but true).

Si   – | – | – | M

14, rue Charlot, 3ᵉ (Filles du Calvaire), 01 42 78 02 31

Tucked away on an increasingly trendy street on the northern edges of the Marais, this attractive new spot pulls in an *au courant* crowd of gallery owners, media types and fashionistas with an eclectic menu that touches down in France, Italy and Asia; the setting boasts a sleek-but-warm contemporary Italian influence.

Sinago (Le)   – | – | – | I

17, rue de Maubeuge, 9ᵉ (Cadet), 01 48 78 11 14

"Good Cambodian cooking", a rarity in Paris, causes food fans to find their way to this tiny (22-seat) spot in the 9th near the Gare du Nord; though the setting is "cramped" and "service can be slow", it's a great buy for unusual and generously served homestyle dishes like a large crêpe stuffed with diced pork and vegetables.

6 New York   – | – | – | M

6, av de New York, 16ᵉ (Alma-Marceau), 01 40 70 03 30; fax 01 40 70 04 77

Flanking the Seine in the 16th, this New French table with a decor of dark woods and jewel-toned upholstery attracts a hip, well-heeled young crowd to an otherwise rather sedate neighborhood; chef Jérôme Gangneux trained with co-owner Jean-Pierre Vigato at Apicius, a background reflected in the fusion fare that features both first-rate ingredients and his technical talent.

Sizin
_ | _ | _ | M

47, rue St-Georges, 9ᵉ (Notre-Dame-de-Lorette), 01 44 63 02 28
Popular with media and fashion types who live nearby in the stylish St. Georges quarter of the 9th, this tempting Turk with a simple decor serves authentic and generous portions of classic dishes from all over that country; meals may begin with a complimentary *raki* (anise-flavored aperitif), but what's really memorable is the short but fine list of native wines, which will see you through meze like *imam baildi* (eggplant stuffed with vegetables) all the way to the dessert pastries.

70 (Le)
_ | _ | _ | M

Parc des Princes, 24, rue du Cdt-Guilbaud, 16ᵉ (Porte de St-Cloud), 01 45 27 05 70; fax 01 40 50 11 18
Fans of chef Yves Camdeborde (who owns La Régalade) can sample the well-priced, modern Southwestern French food of his protégé, Sylvain Danière, at this rather remote spot in the 16th (within the Parc des Princes football stadium) that's decked out with '70s decor, and named for the birth-year of Paris' soccer team; a large terrace has already made this neophyte a popular address in good weather, and if it's busy at noon, it's usually quiet at night.

Sole d'Italia ◐Ⓢ
_ | _ | _ | I

10, av de Trudaino, 9ᵉ (Anvers), 01 44 53 91 33
Just a small passel of pasta eaters knows this tiny place, but with a variety of "original dishes, a charming setting and nice service", it's the sole spot many choose for an Italian evening, especially since this neighborhood near the Place d'Anvers doesn't abound with good eats; P.S. "the spaghetti with shellfish and the panna cotta are to die for."

Soleil (Le) Ⓢ
_ | _ | _ | M

109, av Michelet, Saint-Ouen (Porte de Clignancourt), 01 40 10 08 08; fax 01 40 10 16 85
Located in the middle of the Porte de Clignancourt flea market, this little New French bistro is usually packed with antique hounds and the occasional famous chef; two very friendly waiters and a cozy, cafe-front-style dining room with twig window shades and soft lighting create a relaxed, stylish ambiance in which to enjoy simple fare (foie gras and green bean salad, steak in wine sauce, baba au rhum) from a chalkboard menu that changes daily.

Sologne (La)
▽ 20 | 16 | 20 | 53

164, av Daumesnil, 12ᵉ (Daumesnil), 01 43 07 68 97; fax 01 43 44 66 23
■ Its slightly remote location in the 12th may explain why this "classic bourgeois" French table, decorated with "beautiful silverware settings", is relatively little known; a

menu that highlights "game in season and fish" for relatively "moderate prices" (especially on the "good set menu") makes the habitués, older couples and executives happy.

Sormani　　　22 | 17 | 20 | 79
4, rue du Général Lanrezac, 17ᵉ (Charles de Gaulle-Etoile), 01 43 80 13 91; fax 01 40 55 07 37

◪ It's a toss-up as to what's mentioned most often when it comes to this establishment near the Champs-Elysées – the "delicious", "creative" "Italian cuisine as seen by a talented Frenchman" or the "astronomical" prices; suffice to say that many reviewers are resigned to paying the latter to get the former, especially since the "setting is pretty" and the service is "charming"; a few rebels roar it's "très overrated", but for most "it's superb."

Soufflé (Le)　　　20 | 14 | 18 | 46
36, rue du Mont-Thabor, 1ᵉʳ (Concorde), 01 42 60 27 19; fax 01 42 60 54 98

■ Boosters are blown away by this "original" old-timer near the Tuileries that "has perfected the art of" – you guessed it – "out-of-this-world soufflés", both sweet ("the raspberry's worth the trip") and savory (the "asparagus is a must"); the "slightly shabby" decor's a bit deflating, but the "service is incredibly kind"; and while the prices aren't as airy as the namesake dish, no one's complaining at this "convivial" corner.

Souletin (Le)　　　▽ 17 | 15 | 18 | 38
6, rue La Vrillière, 1ᵉʳ (Bourse/Châtelet-Les Halles), 01 42 61 43 78; fax 01 42 61 43 78

◪ Pay a visit to Southwestern France when you visit this "pretty", if "somewhat old-fashioned", bistro in the 1st, patronized by discreet regulars from the Banque de France and nearby boutiques; if most contentedly consume such "good" regional fare as Bayonne ham and *confit de canard*, plus a nice selection of Irouléguys, a few foes find the "cuisine uneven"; N.B. a post-*Survey* renovation may outdate the Decor score.

Soun 🅂　　　▽ 19 | 14 | 17 | 43
192, av Victor Hugo, 16ᵉ (Henri Martin), 01 45 04 04 31

■ Located in the 16th, this "chic Chinese doesn't shock", but it does offer some "interesting" eats, including a "competitively priced Peking duck menu" and Thai treats, to a well-heeled clientele; "the very '70s decor" (unchanged since the previous tenant) is a bit "strange", so aim for the "lovely garden in the back" if weather permits.

Soupière (La)　　　16 | 11 | 15 | 45
154, av de Wagram, 17ᵉ (Wagram), 01 46 22 80 10; fax 01 46 22 27 09

◪ Friends of fungi flock to this compact Classic French, since the chef is a champion of champignon who proposes "many excellent menus featuring mushrooms" and other "high-level" dishes, served by an "exceptionally friendly" staff; detractors' appetites are dampened by the "somewhat sad setting", but on a happier note, "it's not expensive at all!"

Sousceyrac (A) 　　　　　18 | 12 | 16 | 55
35, rue Faidherbe, 11ᵉ (Charonne/Faidherbe-Chaligny), 01 43 71 65 30; fax 01 40 09 79 75
■ This "grand classic" offers "unfussy French food at old-fashioned prices" – "excellent" "Southwestern cuisine and game in season" (including an "exceptional" hare *à la royale*); despite the "simple" but "charming" decor and "attentive service", a few sentimentalists sigh "it's known better days", but they're overwhelmed by optimists who acclaim it for maintaining a taste of "Old Paris" in the 11th.

Spicy Restaurant ●⑤ 　　　11 | 13 | 11 | 36
8, av Franklin D. Roosevelt, 8ᵉ (Franklin D. Roosevelt/ St-Philippe-du-Roule), 01 56 59 62 59; fax 01 56 59 62 50
◪ Serving up "fusion" fare "fashionable" enough to pull trendies in off the Champs, this Eclectic is "fun" "for dinner after the show" say supporters sweet on the rosy-hued decor (not to mention "the outfits worn by the waitresses"); but cynics snap the "glorified fast food" "is not spicy and is not good", and neither is the "assembly-line service."

SPOON, FOOD & WINE 　　　20 | 18 | 18 | 66
Sofitel Hôtel Marignan, 14, rue de Marignan, 8ᵉ (Franklin D. Roosevelt), 01 40 76 34 44
■ "Iconoclasts" unite at Alain Ducasse's "experiment" in Eclectic cuisine in the 8th, where "the interactive menu empowers patrons" to create their own combinations using "novel ingredients"; the "audacity works" according to those duly impressed by the "pretty, minimalist" decor and "vast" selection of international wines; and despite claims of "over-hype" and "scandalous" prices, most like challenging what's "acceptable in the world of Haute Cuisine."

Square Trousseau (Le) ● 　　15 | 17 | 15 | 39
1, rue Antoine Vollon, 12ᵉ (Bastille/Ledru-Rollin), 01 43 43 06 00; fax 01 43 43 00 66
■ There's "no reason to deprive yourself" say self-indulgers of this Traditional French bistro that serves "honest", "so good" food on an "adorable square" near the Bastille; the same are also enthusiastic about the "handsome setting" and coveted "terrace" tables; if a few deem the cooking just "average", they don't dispute the "chic" appeal or the need to "reserve, since it's always full."

Stella Maris 　　　　　　22 | 14 | 19 | 84
4, rue Arsène Houssaye, 8ᵉ (Charles de Gaulle-Etoile), 01 42 89 16 22; fax 01 42 89 16 01
■ "Refined and delicious" effuse enthusiasts who "enjoyed every second" of their meal at this Contemporary French

near the Arc de Triomphe, where chef-owner Tateru Yoshino puts a Japanese spin on Haute Cuisine; connoisseurs claim the dishes are "works of art" (even if a few austere palates say they'd "be perfect if less precious"); some say the ambiance "could be nicer", but overall, it's worth "keeping an eye on this one."

Stéphane Martin
▽ 19 | 8 | 12 | 41

67, rue des Entrepreneurs, 15ᵉ (Charles Michels/Commerce), 01 45 79 03 31; fax 01 45 79 44 69

■ "If you live in the neighborhood, you'll find yourself eating here as often as you can" proclaim local partisans of this "small, unpretentious" New French in the 15th; "passionate" chef-owner Stéphane Martin has "a few tricks up his sleeve", producing "inventive", if occasionally "off-kilter", dishes at gentle prices; subtract the "anonymous" decor but factor in an "ample wine selection" and you'll wonder "how long can such a good value last?"

Stresa (Le)
18 | 13 | 16 | 68

7, rue Chambiges, 8ᵉ (Alma-Marceau), 01 47 23 51 62

■ A veritable "jet-setter hangout", this Italian off the Avenue Montaigne caters to bold-faced names ("Mick Jagger dined at the next table") who come to "see and be seen" over platefuls of the "best pasta in Paris" at Concorde-level prices; the decor can't compete with the "spectacular" people-watching, but given the "showbiz and show-off" milieu, it's not surprising that "reservations are difficult" to come by if "you're not well known."

Studio (The) ◐ S
10 | 16 | 11 | 28

41, rue du Temple, 4ᵉ (Hôtel-de-Ville/Rambuteau), 01 42 74 10 38; fax 01 42 41 50 34

■ Set in the "magnificent" courtyard of the Marais Dance Center, this Tex-Mex–Californian pulls in a "young, hip" clientele with such gringo favorites as fajitas; while the food might be a bit "banal", the tabs are affordable and the environs so "pleasant" that amigos can "feel good here."

Sud (Le)
15 | 20 | 14 | 46

91, bd Gouvion St Cyr, 17ᵉ (Porte Maillot), 01 45 74 02 77; fax 01 45 74 35 36

◪ The "sunny" Southern fare and "transporting" setting – complete with olive trees and crickets – at this place near the Porte Maillot prompt some patrons to fancy themselves on "vacation in Provence"; "too bad the cuisine falls short of the fabulous decor" opine those miffed by "inexperienced" servers and "heavy" tabs, but they're outvoted by optimists who say grab "a Pastis" and let yourself be transported.

Table d'Anvers (La) ◐
20 | 14 | 17 | 79

2, pl d'Anvers, 9ᵉ (Anvers), 01 48 78 35 21; fax 01 45 26 66 67

■ "A pure delight" exclaim epicures of this Montmartre-area Contemporary French where chef-owner Christian

Conticini's "perfectly presented", "light, inventive cuisine" takes center stage; a few gripe it's "overpriced", with service that's "too ceremonial" for the surrounding, but the only real criticism is that the decor is not "up to par with the culinary sophistication", which is well suited to "special occasions."

Table de Lucullus (La)   ∇ 21 | 6 | 16 | 41

129, rue Legendre, 17ᵉ (Brochant/La Fourche), 01 40 25 02 68; fax 01 40 25 02 68

■ Those who've heard the buzz about this Contemporary French in the quiet 17th have only accolades for young chef Nicolas Vagnon and his "creative" cuisine based on "high-quality foodstuffs"; they also appreciate his "enthusiasm" and appearances in the dining room to "present his menus"; and while the "sad" decor could definitely use an upgrade, the gentle prices can stay just as they are.

Table du Baltimore (La) ⑤   – | – | – | E

Sofitel Demeure Hôtel Baltimore, 88, bis av Kléber, 16ᵉ (Kléber), 01 44 34 54 34; fax 01 44 34 54 44

An upscale crowd convenes at this elegant New French that's housed in the Sofitel Demeure Hôtel Baltimore; chef Jean Philippe Peyrol's novel takes on classic dishes are "quite good", and selections from the impressive wine cellar help lubricate business dinners and discreet rendezvous; the prix fixe lunch offers a less-pricey alternative; N.B. the Food score doesn't reflect a recent switch to an all-seafood menu.

Table Oliviers & Co.   – | – | – | I

Oliviers & Co., 8, rue de Levis, 17ᵉ (Villiers), 01 53 42 18 04; fax 01 53 42 18 15

Located in a branch of the olive-oriented boutique chain, this 17th arrondissement table d'hôte makes a nice light lunch option, especially for vegetarians; the Mediterranean menu runs to dishes made with the products sold here – creamed salted cod with Greek olive oil, eggplant with Croatian oil, etc.; diners select two or three offerings, which are served in little terra-cotta plates that fit into a wooden tray.

TAILLEVENT   28 | 27 | 28 | 130

15, rue Lamennais, 8ᵉ (Charles de Gaulle-Etoile/George V), 01 44 95 15 01; fax 01 42 25 95 18

■ "Forget trying to figure out what heaven's like and just call here for a reservation" say smitten souls who've voted this Haute Cuisine "ne plus ultra" near the Etoile No. 1 for Food, Service and Popularity; now executed by Alain Solivérès (ex Elysées du Vernet), the "sublime" "food is the star", and the wine list one that "Louis XIV would envy", but "consummate host" Jean-Claude Vrinat and "unparalleled service" "steal the show"; it's an "unforgettable" meal that should be experienced at least "once in a lifetime."

Taïra 🅂
21 | 11 | 14 | 62

10, rue des Acacias, 17ᵉ (Argentine), 01 47 66 74 14;
fax 01 47 66 74 14

■ If "exceptionally" fresh fish is what you crave, then this seafooder with "wonderful Japanese overtones" is "worth the detour" to the 17th; its "nice, small" setting is conducive to a pleasant meal, and while perceptions of prices vary ("not expensive" vs. "a bit high"), there's a prix fixe option.

Taka
– | – | – | E

1, rue Véron, 18ᵉ (Abbesses), 01 42 23 74 16

"Excellent" but little-known, this Japanese above Pigalle in the 18th pulls in a funky mix of locals who satisfy their yen for sushi and sashimi in a pared-down setting devoid of "chichi" airs; given the room's bento-box proportions, it's not a bad idea to "reserve in advance"; N.B. dinner only.

Tan Dinh ⊭
22 | 14 | 20 | 65

60, rue de Verneuil, 7ᵉ (Rue du Bac/Solférino),
01 45 44 04 84; fax 01 45 44 36 93

■ This "gracious" family-run Vietnamese near the Musée d'Orsay is an "old favorite", serving "delicious and flavorful" cuisine that's among the "best" of its kind in Paris; the "real surprise" here is the truly "exceptional" wine list ("one of the sons is a wine fanatic"); if there are some complaints about "dismal decor" and big prices for "small portions", they don't diminish the fact that the "tables are always full."

Tang
21 | 16 | 19 | 69

125, rue de la Tour, 16ᵉ (Rue de la Pompe), 01 45 04 35 35;
fax 01 45 04 58 19

■ "You can't go wrong" at this "haute" Chinese serving "excellent" Cantonese fare with some "Thai influences"; the "well-spaced tables and serene decor" impart a "relaxed ambiance", and the service is generally "first class"; a few frown about prices that seem "high", but more find them "moderate for such luxe" in the upscale 16th.

Tanjia ●🅂
12 | 20 | 11 | 51

23, rue de Ponthieu, 8ᵉ (Franklin D. Roosevelt), 01 42 25 95 00;
fax 01 42 25 95 02

◪ This "très à la mode" Moroccan from the Les Bains gang snares a "hip" clientele with its "dreamy" interior evoking a sumptuous Maghrebian home and with "beautiful belly dancers" who gyrate on weekends; alternately described as "authentic" and "ordinary and expensive", the cuisine seems secondary to the "nightclubby" atmosphere, and the "good looking" staff could use some polish; but despite how "dark" it is, the "people-watching" here is prime.

Tante Jeanne
17 | 14 | 15 | 50

116, bd Pereire, 17ᵉ (Pereire), 01 43 80 88 68; fax 01 47 66 53 02

■ The junior of the late Bernard Loiseau's three 'tantes' ('aunts'), this Classic French in the 17th turns out "delicious"

Gallic standards enhanced by a "limited" but "expertly chosen" wine list; the setting is "inviting", if a bit prim, and while the service may be "slow" sometimes, most nieces and nephews still profess the warmest appreciation for "this good aunt."

Tante Louise   18 | 15 | 16 | 53
41, rue Boissy-d'Anglas, 8ᵉ (Concorde/Madeleine), 01 42 65 06 85; fax 01 42 65 28 19
☑ This Classic French in the 8th is the oldest of "the three Parisian showcases of Bernard Loiseau" (who sadly died post-*Survey*), and if most say the "traditional food" is "refined" and "hearty", the tart-tongued retort that it's all about "marketing", i.e. "decent but not very original"; opinions also vary on the "old-fashioned" decor, but overall, this is "tops among the three Tantes."

Tante Marguerite   16 | 14 | 16 | 60
5, rue de Bourgogne, 7ᵉ (Assemblée Nationale/Invalides), 01 45 51 79 42; fax 01 47 53 79 56
■ Located near the Assemblée Nationale, the late Bernard Loiseau's 'tante' dispenses Traditional French cuisine that famished ministers and deputies declare "excellent for a business lunch"; the "cosseting" wood-paneled setting and "discreet" service also make it conducive to "leisurely discussions"; if a few edgy types wish the fare were less "banal", devotees belt out "bravo!"

TASTEVIN S   23 | 21 | 19 | 92
9, av Eglé, Maisons-Laffitte (RER Maisons-Laffitte), 01 39 62 11 67; fax 01 39 62 73 09
■ This Classic French in Maisons-Laffitte pairs "excellent bourgeois" cuisine with a "very good" and lengthy wine list; it also features a "pleasant setting" (fireplace in the winter, garden dining in the summer) and a private room that's well suited for "family parties"; a few sigh that "service could be improved" and that tabs are "outrageously expensive", but loyalists counter "the refined cuisine, the quality of the decor and the reception" merit the prices.

Taverne de Maître Kanter ●S   11 | 13 | 11 | 35
16, rue Coquillière, 1ᵉʳ (Châtelet-Les Halles/Louvre-Rivoli), 01 42 36 74 24; fax 01 42 21 42 31
☑ A "handy solution" for a "late" supper near Les Halles, this brasserie can be counted on for "excellent shellfish" platters, "ok" choucroute and, as the word 'tavern' suggests, "good beer"; service ranges from "stressful" to "courteous", and while the decor is nothing to rave about, most concede the "price is right", particularly for "large families."

Taverne Henri IV ⊄   ▽ 15 | 15 | 11 | 40
13, pl du Pont-Neuf, 1ᵉʳ (Pont-Neuf), 01 43 54 27 90
■ Quite "fabulous" proclaim patrons of this bar à vins sweetly situated on the Ile de la Cité that marries "excellent,

affordable wines" – including numerous ones by the glass – with "marvelous" platters of "country cheeses, hams and breads"; despite service that might be "as crusty" as a baguette, a meal here is "a delightful experience."

Taverne "L'Esprit Boulevard" ● S — | — | — | M

24, bd des Italiens, 9ᵉ (Opéra/Richelieu-Drouot), 01 55 33 10 00; fax 01 55 33 10 09

Those looking for a fitting place to "rest their feet and have a simple meal and a beer" near the Opéra Garnier could do worse than tuck into this "large, noisy brasserie" owned by the Frères Blanc chain; the choucroute and shellfish platters are a "good value" and fortifying on a "blustery winter day", and the atmosphere is particularly "lively at night", when an after-show crowd troops in.

Télégraphe (Le) ● 13 | 20 | 13 | 51

41, rue de Lille, 7ᵉ (Rue du Bac), 01 42 92 03 04; fax 01 42 92 02 77

■ Set in an old dorm for telegraph operators behind the Musée d'Orsay, this Classic French appeals to "tourists" and locals with its "superb" belle epoque interior, "beautiful patio" and a bar that's a "cozy" backdrop for "after-dinner drinks and cigars"; the food, however, "disappoints" and, according to veterans, "used to be better"; still, it remains "charming for brunch" before viewing the Impressionists.

Temps des Cerises (Le) ● 10 | 12 | 14 | 25

18, rue de la Butte-aux-Cailles, 13ᵉ (Place d'Italie), 01 45 89 69 48

■ Opened by a workers' cooperative, this Butte-aux-Cailles Classic French–Eclectic feeds the masses with "simple" eats in a "congenial", informal setting where comrades "*tutoie* (use the familiar 'tu' rather than the formal 'vous') each other"; and while you can't expect anything *haut* about the "so-so" fare, you're sure to have "fun" here.

Terminus Nord ● S 16 | 19 | 16 | 43

23, rue de Dunkerque, 10ᵉ (Gare du Nord), 01 42 85 05 15; fax 01 40 16 13 98

■ "Perfect" for a "rapid meal" before "darting off to Brussels" or London say travelers to this "straightforward brasserie" by the Gare du Nord; the "magnificent" 1920s decor and "splendid" shellfish platters may make some late for their trains, while foes sniff the food's "standard" stuff that's best "when you know what to order"; still, loyalists insist this "faithful fixture" is "irreproachable."

Terrasse (La) S ▽ 10 | 23 | 11 | 46

Hôtel Terrass, 12, rue Joseph de Maistre, 18ᵉ (Blanche/ Place de Clichy), 01 44 92 34 00; fax 01 42 52 29 11

■ This Classic French off the Place Clichy has a "wonderful view over Paris"; it's "ideal in the summer" for drinks on the namesake terrace say fans, who regret that "what's on your plate" is less spectacular than the vista; still, the prix fixe menus are "handy and affordable" and the milieu (with a piano player at night) hard to beat for romance.

Terroir (Le)   ▽ 19 | 10 | 18 | 43
11, bd Arago, 13ᵉ (Les Gobelins), 01 47 07 36 99;
fax 01 42 72 52 20
■ A jovial clientele "of regulars and friends" frequents this Classic French in the 15th serving country-style fare "prepared with excellent ingredients"; loyalists laugh that this place takes "familial" to far extremes with an owner who "nearly sits down with you and eats off your plate" – but, of course, that's all part of the charm.

Thanksgiving 🄢   ▽ 16 | 13 | 13 | 38
20, rue St-Paul, 4ᵉ (St-Paul), 01 42 77 68 28;
fax 01 42 77 70 83
🄩 Whether or not surveyors give thanks for the Cajun fare at this American in the Marais depends on who you talk to: those pining for a bit of bayou say it's "original and good" and dig the "great background music", while the ungrateful grumble about skimpy portions and the "nonexistent" welcome at the gate; at the least it can be "a perfect stop for Yanks who've been away from home too long."

Thierry Burlot   – | – | – | M
8, rue Nicolas Charlet, 15ᵉ (Pasteur), 01 42 19 08 59;
fax 01 45 67 09 13
Rising star Thierry Burlot (ex the late Le Caffe) attempts to relight the fires of fashionableness with this spot in the 15th, the site of the old Olympe; the slick ambiance – cocoa-colored walls, black-and-white still-life food photos and a perpetual dance-music soundtrack – indicates the clientele he's catering to; but the disco-averse can enjoy the New French menu, which also shows off the chef-owner's skill with Italian entrees and dishes from his native Brittany.

Thiou/Petit Thiou   18 | 13 | 15 | 52
49, quai d'Orsay, 7ᵉ (Invalides), 01 40 62 96 50; fax 01 40 62 97 30
3, rue Surcouf, 7ᵉ (Invalides), 01 40 62 96 50; fax 01 40 62 96 70
■ Hipsters and fashionistas seeking something "spicy" and "exotic" sashay over to chef Thiou's eponymous Thai near Les Invalides where the food is "as delicate as she is"; the elegant surrounds can get "smoky" and too "noisy" for a "peaceful tête-à-tête" but don't necessarily distract from what some consider "the best" Siamese in Paris; N.B. the newer branch in the 7th is unrated.

Thoumieux ●🄢   13 | 14 | 13 | 39
Hôtel Thoumieux, 79, rue St-Dominique, 7ᵉ (Invalides/
La Tour-Maubourg), 01 47 05 49 75; fax 01 47 05 36 96
🄩 For "copious" portions of Southwestern favorites like "duck confit" and stick-to-your-ribs "cassoulet", this "tried-and-true" brasserie overlooking the Invalides doesn't disappoint and is especially "nourishing in winter"; while the

"snippy service" is something of a bête noire, the "bustling", "convivial" atmosphere offers a taste of "old Paris", as do the "affordable" yesteryear prices.

Timbre (Le) – – – M

3 rue Ste-Beuve, 6ᵉ (Notre-Dame-des-Champs/Vavin), 01 45 49 10 40

'Le timbre' translates as 'stamp', and that's about the size of this little Left Banker; nevertheless, the kitchen offers Traditional French Bistro cooking, plus top-shelf British cheeses from Neale's Yard in London; the friendly ambiance, accompanied by a Chet Baker soundtrack, draws a hip crowd, including Marianne Faithful, all of whom appreciate the discreet staff – and the gentle bill too.

Timgad (Le) 🇸 19 19 16 54

21, rue Brunel, 17ᵉ (Argentine), 01 45 74 23 70; fax 01 40 68 76 46

■ "Two hours at Timgad is like a weekend in Marrakech" exclaim arm-chair travelers of this Moroccan in the 17th that has such "nice atmosphere" compared with the "more casual" ones of its ilk – not to mention couscous and tagines that rank among "the best in Paris"; "too bad it's a bit expensive" – though definitely cheaper than a Royal Air Maroc ticket.

Tire-Bouchon (Le) 21 12 19 41

62, rue des Entrepreneurs, 15ᵉ (Charles-Michels), 01 40 59 09 27; fax 01 40 59 09 27

■ The "energetic but small husband-and-wife team offers a big performance" at this "charming" Classic French in the 15th; "excellent" food, including an "innovative" tasting menu and "great desserts", as well as "thoughtful" service is the reason that regulars "frequently return"; their only suggestion: the "bland decor" could use "some spunk."

T.M. Café – – – M

54, bd de La Tour Maubourg, 7ᵉ (La Tour-Maubourg), 01 47 05 89 86; fax 01 45 56 03 84

In the place of Paul Minchelli – a very pricey fish house that was popular with celebrities and movie stars – this new seafooder harpoons a more bourgeois 7th arrondissement crowd with a traditionally prepared catch-of-the-day menu at considerably more reasonable prices; the decor by restaurant designer Slavik has been updated with a vivid new apricot-colored paint job.

Tong Yen ◗🇸 18 12 18 56

1 bis, rue Jean Mermoz, 8ᵉ (Franklin D. Roosevelt), 01 42 25 04 23; fax 01 45 63 51 57

◪ Owner "Thérèse [Luong] welcomes presidents and VIPs" to her 31-year-old Chinese off the Champs, where they relish the "calm, comfortable" setting and "warm" service; those who don't count themselves among "her faithful" report that the menu's "conventional" and that "you don't come here for the cuisine" but for the "people" – a fact that fails to tarnish this "classic."

Tonkinoise (La) 🇸⊄   _ | _ | _ | I

20, rue Philibert Lucot, 13ᵉ (Maison Blanche),
01 45 85 98 98
Perhaps the neon-and-Formica setting lacks allure, but this small storefront deep in the 13th is pulling crowds with some of the best and most authentic Vietnamese cooking (such as dill-seasoned monkfish and shrimp cakes), economically priced and briskly served.

Tonnelle Saintongeaise (La)   16 | 15 | 17 | 46

32, bd Vital Bouhot, Neuilly-sur-Seine (Pont-de-Levallois),
01 46 24 43 15; fax 01 46 24 36 33
■ On a fine "summer" day, there's little that beats a "meal under the arbor" at this "charming" Classic French that lures even die-hard urbanites to the upscale Ile de la Jatte in Neuilly; fans cite the "sophisticated cuisine" with signature seafood offerings, which make up for the fact that, although "agreeable", the place is "not right on the water."

Toque (La)   ▽ 21 | 15 | 18 | 45

16, rue de Tocqueville, 17ᵉ (Villiers), 01 42 27 97 75;
fax 01 47 63 97 69
■ Savvy citizens of the 17th call chef-owner Jacky Joubert's Contemporary French "a very good address to know", lauding the "fresh foodstuffs" at the base of dishes that marry "tradition and novelty"; some protest that the "provincial" decor could use a boost, but the "unobtrusive and charming" service and easy-to-swallow prices make this "one worth recommending."

Totem (Le) ◗🇸   9 | 21 | 10 | 40

Musée de l'Homme, 17, pl du Trocadéro, 16ᵉ (Trocadéro),
01 47 27 28 29; fax 01 47 27 53 01
■ "A tête à tête with the Eiffel Tower" is what beckons diners to the terrace of this Classic French in the Musée de l'Homme; alas, the "fabulous view" has little to compete with, as the food is plainly "forgettable" and the service often "arrogant"; but those looking for a little "Parisian magic" simply turn their backs to the kitchen, look out over the Trocadéro plaza and treat themselves to "a drink."

Toupary (Le) ◗   11 | 22 | 12 | 44

La Samaritaine, 2, quai du Louvre, 1ᵉʳ (Pont-Neuf),
01 40 41 29 29; fax 01 42 33 96 79
■ At this rooftop Classic French in Samaritaine, "you pay for the view, not the bland cuisine" – but what a "sumptuous view" it is say surveyors who find "watching the sunset over Paris is worth" putting up with not only the "average" eats but "slow service"; also, "walking through a closed department store to dinner is unexpectedly decadent."

TOUR D'ARGENT (LA) S
23 | 28 | 24 | 116

*17, quai de la Tournelle, 5ᵉ (Cardinal Lemoine/Pont Marie),
01 43 54 23 31; fax 01 44 07 12 04*

☑ "Sure, it's full of tourists", but this "Vatican" of Haute Cuisine remains a "tour de force" for the "novelty of the numbered pressed duck" as well as the "divine" setting "overlooking Notre Dame"; however, while "the view can't be improved, the food can" carp critics, who also find the "formal service" "overly stuffy"; still, even those who lament it's "living on its reputation" concede "you have to dine" at this grande dame "at least once" (which "might be all you can afford"); P.S. "visit the wine cellar, an absolute fantasy."

Tournesol (Le)
15 | 15 | 15 | 39

*2, av de Lamballe, 16ᵉ (Passy), 01 45 25 95 94;
fax 01 45 25 43 09*

■ "Bright and cheerful" is the take on this Traditional French bistro in the 16th near Passy pulling in the "young and dynamic" with its "good food and good fun"; there's a "lovely terrace above the Seine, but the best thing to look at is the beautiful people" who keep this address "always busy."

TRAIN BLEU (LE) S
15 | 27 | 16 | 59

*Gare de Lyon, 12ᵉ (Gare de Lyon), 01 43 43 09 06;
fax 01 43 43 97 96*

■ Dining in this "grandiose" belle epoque salon in the Gare de Lyon is like "returning to the days of yesteryear when train travel was first class"; the "stunning setting" solicits sighs of admiration, yet the "Traditional French cuisine", "though good", "doesn't match" the "step-back-in-time" Second Empire–style splendor; still, patrons are willing to overlook that and the "insolent prices" for the pleasure of experiencing "one of Paris' most beautiful decors."

Tricotin S
▽ 19 | 9 | 13 | 24

*15, av de Choisy, 13ᵉ (Porte de Choisy), 01 45 84 74 44;
fax 01 45 85 17 54*

☑ In a "good location for browsing Chinatown" (the edge of the 13th) lies this large eatery that features "fresh, beautifully prepared vegetables" and "wonderful noodle dumpling soups" in its mélange of "Chinese, Thai and Vietnamese cuisines"; though not "without its faults" – the "rustic, Asian-style" ambiance "is rather unromantic" – it remains "popular" "for a cheap, rapid meal."

Triporteur (Le)
– | – | – | M

4, rue de Dantzig, 15ᵉ (Convention), 01 45 32 82 40

With a collection of miscellaneous bibelots referring to the 1957 French film of the same name, this young bistro on the outskirts of the 15th has won a loyal following with a carefully executed selection of old-fashioned Gallic classics and solicitous service; popular with a TV and advertising crowd at noon, it pulls in diverse locals in the evening with its relaxed atmosphere and prices.

TROIS MARCHES (LES)   24 | 25 | 23 | 103
Hôtel Trianon Palace, 1, bd de la Reine, Versailles
(RER Versailles Rive Droite), 01 39 50 13 21; fax 01 30 21 01 25
■ "After a visit to Versailles", memorable dining awaits you in the Hôtel Trianon Palace; the "fabulous views" of the gardens, "delicate, sophisticated" New French cuisine and "waiting-on-you-hand-and-foot service" all "come close to perfection"; sure, this "elegant experience" is "very expensive", but who wouldn't pay for "a table in paradise"?

Troquet (Le)   19 | 10 | 17 | 35
21, rue François Bonvin, 15ᵉ (Sèvres-Lecourbe/Volontaire), 01 45 66 89 00; fax 01 45 66 89 83
■ "It's worth the effort to find" this "good, little" New French bistro in the 15th, whose "simple set menu" makes diners "feel like they've been invited to the chef's house for dinner"; but while the "tender, succulent" bill of fare here "changes daily, the quality and hospitality remain constant" – and have even improved by a score-boosting renovation.

Trou Gascon (Au)   21 | 15 | 19 | 74
40, rue Taine, 12ᵉ (Daumesnil), 01 43 44 34 26; fax 01 43 07 80 55
■ "Keeps the spirit of Southwestern cuisine burning high" declare devotees of chef-owner Alain Dutournier's dressed-down version of his famed Carré des Feuillants; though the 12th arrondissement locale's a touch "inconvenient", "it's worth the trip to the back of beyond" for such "excellent Gascon" fare ("oh, that cassoulet"); would-be designers dis the renovated, "modern decor that doesn't fit with the food", but "aside from that, it's reassuringly" the same.

Troyon (Le)   16 | 11 | 16 | 49
4, rue Troyon, 17ᵉ (Charles de Gaulle-Etoile), 01 40 68 99 40; fax 01 40 68 99 57
■ Just "steps away from the Etoile, this affordable" New French bistro ("as unpretentious as a place can be") woos gastronomes with a "serious" menu that changes daily; "friendly service" makes it popular, despite "tables that are too close (a vice you find in two out of three places in Paris)."

Truffe Noire (La)   18 | 12 | 15 | 70
2, pl Parmentier, Neuilly-sur-Seine (Porte Maillot), 01 46 24 94 14; fax 01 46 24 94 60
☑ Takes on this Neuilly truffle-laced table are mixed: hedonists hunt it down for its "refined" New French fare, but cynics sniff "everything's outmoded", from the "bland cuisine" to the "provincial atmosphere"; still, this can be "the place to take La Défense–based contacts to lunch."

Truffière (La) 🅂   19 | 20 | 18 | 56
4, rue Blainville, 5ᵉ (Cardinal Lemoine/Place Monge), 01 46 33 29 82; fax 01 46 33 64 74
■ Reviewers root for this romance-friendly Latin Quarter address where the Southwest specialties are laced with

the fabulously fleshy fungi ("at last, a whole truffle!"); the "first-class food" is served "in a warm, cozy atmosphere", a 17th-century building with fireplace and arched-ceiling cellar; unhappy hounds howl it's "très touristy" and the service swings from "pushy" to "professional", but most have nothing but "sweet memories" of their experience here.

Trumilou (Le) 🇸   16 | 10 | 15 | 26

84, quai de l'Hôtel-de-Ville, 4ᵉ (Hôtel-de-Ville/Pont-Marie), 01 42 77 63 98; fax 01 48 04 91 89

■ The budget-minded migrate to this Seine-sider near the Hôtel-de-Ville for "real Auvergnat cuisine" served in a "congenial, unpretentious" atmosphere; it may be "nothing special", but it's so "affordable" you just can't complain, and when you take along "a band of buddies" it's a downright "fun place."

Tsé-Yang 🌑🇸   18 | 20 | 17 | 72

25, av Pierre 1er de Serbie, 16ᵉ (Alma-Marceau/léna), 01 47 20 70 22; fax 01 49 52 03 68

☑ This "pillar of Chinese cuisine in Paris" (with a cousin column in New York) draws a chic set to its "exotic" locale in the upscale 16th; while all agree about "superb decor", patrons part over the food – "delicious" vs. "exorbitantly priced for what's on hand"; still, most habitués happily pay the price for such "reliable high quality."

Tsukizi 🇸   19 | 9 | 15 | 38

2 bis, rue des Ciseaux, 6ᵉ (Mabillon/St-Germain-des-Prés), 01 43 54 65 19

■ It may be "small and unattractive"; nevertheless, this "real Japanese" turns out "excellent sushi" that keeps a well-heeled Saint-Germain clientele returning; praise goes not only to the "fresh" provisions but to the "charming" service, causing possessive patrons to whisper "thankfully, it's not very well known – for now."

Ty Coz   16 | 10 | 15 | 51

35, rue St-Georges, 9ᵉ (St-Georges), 01 48 78 42 95

☑ While owner Marie-Françoise Lachaud no longer mans the helm of this "Brittany-inspired" seafooder in the 9th, loyalists still simply "love this place" for its "exceptional fruits de mer platters" and "friendly people"; but "alas, the price is high" – "unjustifiably so" some mutter.

Vache Acrobate (La)   – | – | – | M

77, rue Amelot, 11ᵉ (Chemin Vert/Filles du Calvaire), 01 47 00 49 42; fax 01 47 00 49 09

Founded by four friends from Armagnac, this noisy, jovial bistro has been a hit almost from the day it opened in the 11th; what the arty locals love is creatively updated, regional Ardèche cooking, generously served at very fair prices; the green, pink and brick-red–colored decor and prompt, well-informed young servers add to the fun.

Vagenende ●⑤
13 | 20 | 15 | 43

142, bd St-Germain, 6ᵉ (Mabillon/Odéon), 01 43 26 68 18; fax 01 40 51 73 38

■ It's "a tad touristy" perhaps, but this "reliable Left Bank brasserie" (founded in 1904) at Saint-Germain transports patrons "to another era" with its "genuine fin de siècle" decor; even if it doesn't work the same "magic" as the setting, the "solid" bourgeois cuisine rates as "good"; and "since they don't build them like this anymore", "it's a must if you're in the 6th", especially since "the staff graciously encourages you to stay late."

Van Gogh
18 | 17 | 17 | 62

2, quai Aulagnier, Asnières-sur-Seine (Mairie de Clichy), 01 47 91 05 10; fax 01 47 93 00 93

■ Partisans of this New French fish specialist in Asnières just north of Paris recommend it "for a business lunch in summer" on the "fabulous terrace" right on "the banks of the Seine"; prices are somewhat "expensive", but the "very good cuisine", riverside setting and "client-stroking service" make it "a class act."

Vaudeville (Le) ●⑤
14 | 17 | 14 | 46

29, rue Vivienne, 2ᵉ (Bourse), 01 40 20 04 62; fax 01 49 27 08 78

■ "Across from the stock exchange" and surrounded by theaters (hence the name), this "bustling art deco"–style brasserie fills up with show-goers, off-duty actors and tourists who find it a "reliable" choice both early and late in the evening; the service may be "indifferent", but the "solid, traditional cuisine", including "seafood platters that are everything one would want", inspires reviewers to rate it as a "sure value."

Vendanges (Les)
▽ 17 | 13 | 15 | 47

40, rue Friant, 14ᵉ (Porte d'Orléans), 01 45 39 59 98; fax 01 45 39 74 13

◪ Near the Porte d'Orléans, this small French cooks up classics such as cassoulet and Grand Marnier soufflé to accompany an impressive (400 vintage strong) variety of Bordeaux; but while friends show faith in the food and enthuse you "feel like you're in the provinces", not everyone is keen on traipsing so far down south for "extremely disappointing" eats served by staffers they "don't dare pose questions to."

Verre Bouteille (Le) ●⑤
13 | 10 | 14 | 33

5, bd Gouvion St Cyr, 17ᵉ (Porte de Champerret), 01 47 63 39 99; fax 01 47 63 07 02
85, av des Ternes, 17ᵉ (Porte Maillot), 01 45 74 01 02; fax 01 47 63 07 02

■ Consumers can count on "informal food and good service" – not to mention "a rather nice choice of wines by the glass" – at these "slightly expensive" twin bars à vins in the 17th; among the Traditional French bistro eats, the "excellent chopped-by-knife steak tartare" is popular with the "young, dynamic executive types" who flock here for a "quick, efficient" meal, "even at 4 in the morning" (for the Porte Maillot branch).

Verre Volé (Le) S　　　　　–|–|–|I
67, rue de Lancry, 10ᵉ (Jacques Bonsergent/République), 01 48 03 17 34; fax 01 68 03 17 36
This bar à vins in the increasingly trendy Canal Saint-Martin area offers "tasty" pork sausages and "cheese and charcuterie platters" that go perfectly with the "well-furnished wine selection" – either on the "miniscule" premises or *chez vous*; it's the kind of spot that locals laud for its "extremely congenial ambiance" and "simplicity."

Viaduc Café (Le) ❷S　　　10|14|10|34
43, av Daumesnil, 12ᵉ (Bastille/Gare de Lyon), 01 44 74 70 70; fax 01 44 74 70 71
■ "Great for lunch" after roller skating, "walking or jogging down the Promenade des Plantes", this cafe "under the arches of an old railway viaduct near the Bastille" draws in a "young, hip clientele" (with or without blades) with its "ideal" terrace and "jazzy Sunday brunch"; and while some say the New French bistro fare is no better than "blasé", the fact that it's "always packed" suggests it agrees with most.

Vieille Fontaine Rôtisserie (La) S　15|19|14|45
8, av Grétry, Maisons-Laffitte (RER Poissy), 01 39 62 01 78; fax 01 39 62 13 43
■ The "enchanting setting" – a "tastefully decorated" villa with "a terrace overlooking a beautiful garden" – of this New French in Maisons-Laffitte enchants enthusiasts, while the "inventive cuisine" and "well-balanced wine list" add to the charm without offending the budget; indeed, this "excellent value" "deserves to be better known."

Vieux Bistro (Le) S　　　19|15|16|47
14, rue du Cloître Notre-Dame, 4ᵉ (Cité/St-Michel), 01 43 54 18 95; fax 01 44 07 35 63
■ Though the location alongside Notre Dame might lead one to think otherwise, this thirtysomething spot is "not a tourist trap" state those who savor the "wonderful" "Traditional French bistro food" – including what some deem "the best steaks in Paris" – and "a superb wine list"; admittedly the "attentive, but not particularly warm service" deflates, but add to the list of lauds "all the ambiance you could possibly want" and you can see why it offers "really excellent value all-around."

Villa Corse (La) ❷　　　–|–|–|M
164, bd de Grenelle, 15ᵉ (Cambronne/La Motte Picquet-Grenelle), 01 53 86 70 81; fax 01 53 86 90 73
This new annex of the popular Casa Corsa brings the rich cooking of Corsica to a quiet residential corner of the 15th;

warm Mediterranean colors and wooden book shelves create a cozy atmosphere, despite the fact that the space seats roughly 140 souls; surprisingly cheerful and efficient service (given the volume) and moderate prices keep everyone in a good mood, too.

Village d'Ung et Li Lam ⦿S | 19 | 16 | 19 | 42 |
10, rue Jean Mermoz, 8ᵉ (Franklin D. Roosevelt),
01 42 25 99 79; fax 01 42 25 12 06
■ "Good Sino-Thai food" and "always attentive, smiling" servers add up to admiration for this "luxury" Chinese off the Champs; the amorous offer it a "good address" "for a first date": what better conversation-starter than the "aquarium above your head" on the ceiling?

Villa Mauresque (La)   ▽ | 19 | 21 | 19 | 37 |
5-7, rue du Cdt. Rivière, 8ᵉ (St-Philippe du Roule),
01 42 25 16 69; fax 01 42 56 37 05
■ Those seeking an exotic experience are enchanted by the "warm", "agreeable" Arabian Nights atmosphere (complete with native dancing) of this 8th arrondissement villa; "the food isn't at the same level as the decor", but fans still favor the "original idea" of mixing "refined" Moroccan and Med fare; the "graciousness of [owner] Fatima Abouayoub" surmounts sometimes "nonchalant" service.

Villaret (Le) ⦿ | 21 | 12 | 18 | 46 |
13, rue Ternaux, 11ᵉ (Parmentier/Oberkampf), 01 43 57 89 76;
fax 01 43 57 89 69
■ "Simple" and "savory" sums up this "sincere bisto" that "stays the course when it comes to reasonable prices"; it's "a great local find" for both "fresh", "remarkably well-executed" Traditional French food in a culinary desert of the 11th and late hours that offer "night owl" appeal; decor may be "nonexistent", but "you never regret coming here."

Vinci (Le) | 17 | 12 | 17 | 55 |
23, rue Paul Valéry, 16ᵉ (Boissière/Victor Hugo), 01 45 01 68 18;
fax 01 45 01 60 37
■ "Close your eyes and you're in Italy" exclaim dreamy devotees of this coat-and-tie customer by the Arc de Triomphe; its "sophisticated" and "original dishes" and "quiet", hush-hush atmosphere make it a "pleasant", if *petit,* "place to take a client" or a romantic prospect; plus it's "an excellent value."

Vin des Rues (Au) | – | – | – | M |
21, rue Boulard, 14ᵉ (Denfert-Rochereau), 01 43 22 19 78;
fax 01 43 27 74 11
"Great ambiance is guaranteed" at this wine bar in the 14th, "especially when the Beaujolais Nouveau comes out"; the "simple" but "excellent" Lyonnaise cuisine and "warm welcome" ensure its "popularity" on the four nights a week it serves dinner.

Vinea Café (Le) ◖🅂

| 10 | 14 | 11 | 31 |

26-28, Cour St-Emilion, 12ᵉ (Cour St-Emilion), 01 44 74 09 09;
fax 01 44 74 06 66

☑ The 19th-century "Cour Saint-Emilion is an agreeable" locale, and so a turn on the terrace can be "pleasant" at this large cafe; unfortunately, the Med-oriented meals are at best "middling", though they're perhaps "the best [bet] near the Bercy cinema."

Vin et Marée 🅂

| 17 | 12 | 14 | 42 |

71, av de Suffren, 7ᵉ (La Motte-Picquet-Grenelle),
01 47 83 27 12; fax 01 43 06 62 35
276, bd Voltaire, 11ᵉ (Nation), 01 43 72 31 23; fax 01 40 09 05 24
108, av du Maine, 14ᵉ (Gaîté), 01 43 20 29 50;
fax 01 43 27 84 11 ◖
183, bd Murat, 16ᵉ (Porte St-Cloud), 01 46 47 91 39;
fax 01 46 47 69 07

■ Fin fans unite at these "unpretentious", "dependable" seafooders serving up "excellent fish of remarkable freshness" ("ordered from a chalkboard"), plus "the house pride", a baba au rhum that's "big enough for two or three"; service is always "efficient" and sometimes even "friendly", and while the "banal decor" "slows down" some spirits, the "terrific value" prices work well for dinners *en famille.*

Vin sur Vin

| 20 | 14 | 19 | 58 |

20, rue de Montdessuy, 7ᵉ (Alma-Marceau), 01 47 05 14 20

■ Near the Eiffel Tower, this tiny New French woos wine buffs and gourmets alike with "exquisite" vintages and "quality cuisine" "presented in a creative manner"; the "decor might seem a bit austere", but the overall "great experience" makes this "sweet place" "an address connoisseurs" can't pass up.

VIOLON D'INGRES (LE)

| 23 | 18 | 21 | 88 |

135, rue St-Dominique, 7ᵉ (Ecole-Militaire), 01 45 55 15 05;
fax 01 45 55 48 42

☑ Chef-owner Christian Constant cooks up "celestial cuisine" at his "club-like" Haute Southwestern; his "wife Catherine, the quintessential hostess", leads a "staff that goes out of its way to assure satisfaction", and those who found the "decor average" will appreciate the redo that's made it "very pretty" now; there are "too many English speakers" (even according to Americans) and "prices are a little high" – "but we are in the 7th" after all, and so "merci, Mr. Constant" is the majority's motto.

Virgin Café ◖🅂

| 9 | 10 | 8 | 29 |

Virgin Megastore, 52-60, av Champs-Elysées, 8ᵉ
(Franklin D. Roosevelt), 01 42 56 15 96; fax 01 49 53 03 76

☑ "Convenient for a break" from CD shopping, this Classic French cafe in the Virgin Megastore serves up "surprisingly" "pleasant" fare for a "fast" fix loyal listeners say; nitpickers complain the "pre-fab" eats are "average" and there's "no interest whatsoever in the decor"; but both camps concede the "view overlooking the Champs" is "beautiful" and it's a "moderate" option in an otherwise expensive neighborhood.

Voltaire (Le) | 19 | 20 | 19 | 63 |
27, quai Voltaire, 7ᵉ (Rue du Bac), 01 42 61 17 49
■ Boasting an "exceptional atmosphere", this husband-and-wife-run "landmark" located Seine-side in Saint-Germain "joyously spoils all Paris and New York" with "incomparable service" and "marvelous traditional food" (ironic that the "most bourgeois restaurant in the 7th [is named] for the anti-establishment libertine philosopher" who once lived here); it's "expensive, but oh so French", and that makes it "a don't-miss."

Wadja | 17 | 15 | 18 | 39 |
10, rue de la Grande Chaumière, 6ᵉ (Vavin), 01 46 33 02 02
■ "In the heart of Montparnasse, this neighborhood bistro" offers "original" Contemporary French fare, accompanied by numerous "very good wines by the glass"; "affordable prices", along with a "not too stuffy" (e.g. "noisy") ambiance explain why it's a favorite stomping ground among "students, professors" and artistic types.

Waknine   ▽ | 14 | 16 | 16 | 34 |
9, av Pierre-1er de Serbie, 16ᵉ (Iéna), 01 47 23 48 18; fax 01 47 23 87 33
☑ "A personalized welcome" greets stylish regulars at this Classic French–International, whose offerings range from a crayfish-and-crab cake to chocolate *délice*; adorned with tissue-paper-shaded ceiling lamps and off-white walls, the setting is streamlined and so, some scoff, are the portions ("for anorexics!"); still, it's surprisingly affordable for the 16th.

Wally Le Saharien | 18 | 17 | 16 | 49 |
36, rue Rodier, 9ᵉ (Anvers), 01 42 85 51 90; fax 01 45 86 08 35
■ Try to overlook the "sex shops and closed boutiques" surrounding this veteran in the 9th to concentrate on "frankly delicious" cuisine, including the signature Saharan-style (i.e. dry) "airy couscous", "professionally" served amid a "transporting Maghreban-furnished decor"; at night, "there's only one menu, so you better like it" – but since it's been "one of Paris' best" North Africans since 1980, odds are you will.

Wepler ●S | 14 | 15 | 14 | 46 |
14, pl de Clichy, 18ᵉ (Place de Clichy), 01 45 22 53 24; fax 01 44 70 07 50
■ "Oysters rule!" at this "typical bustling brasserie" ("one of the last" ones "that hasn't given in to a chain") that's "wonderful" as long as you "stick to the seafood" (other "dishes are middling"); founded in 1892, the "place has aged", but at least this "*sans* chichi" spot remains "the real deal", down to the turn-of-the-century decor.

Willi's Wine Bar   18 | 15 | 17 | 45

13, rue des Petits-Champs, 1er (Bourse/Palais Royal-Musée du Louvre), 01 42 61 05 09; fax 01 47 03 36 93

■ "Vive le vin!" opine the oenophiles at this "foreigner-friendly" wine bar near the Place des Victoires; naturally "one goes for the huge international menu" of "amazing" – even "to die for" – varietals, "but stick around to eat": the "ambitious" kitchen turns out "delicious", "inventive" Med meals that are "a bargain", according to the "lively crowd" that hangs here; though "nice", service can be "slow" – but in such a "laid-back" ambiance, who wants to be rushed?

Wok Restaurant   ▽ 12 | 12 | 11 | 29

25, rue des Taillandiers, 11^e (Bastille/Voltaire), 01 55 28 88 77; fax 01 55 28 88 78

☒ This Asian in the 11th arrondissement offers a "playful concept": clients get to choose the toppings for their noodle-based stir-fry supper; but while converts call it "creative cooking in a Zen-like setting", the wok-wary warn the "whimsy wears off" and "the service slows down when there are lots of people."

Xu ◐   13 | 16 | 13 | 48

19, rue Bayard, 8^e (Franklin D. Roosevelt), 01 47 20 82 24; fax 01 47 20 20 21

☒ DJ-spun "music and Pop Art"–inspired surroundings set the stage at this "I'm-so-trendy" "restaurant/bar" in the upscale 8th; but while the "hip space" appeals to adherents, adversaries argue "avoid it" – the Eclectic "model food" "varies in quality" (to put it mildly) and the crowd's more "wanna-be" than with-it.

Yen   – | – | – | E

22, rue St-Benoît, 6e (St-Germain-des-Prés), 01 45 44 11 18; fax 01 45 44 19 48

Run by the Kashiyama fashion group, this "newly discovered gem" in Saint-Germain serves up "excellent", "authentic Nipponese cuisine", including "very fresh" homemade soba and an assortment of "remarkable" tempuras; not surprising, "it's always filled with Japanese" visitors, as well as affluent, adventuresome locals.

Yvan ◐   18 | 18 | 18 | 59

1 bis, rue Jean Mermoz, 8^e (Franklin D. Roosevelt), 01 43 59 18 40; fax 01 42 89 30 95

☒ "It's not only in the magazines" that this New French off the Champs "looks marvelous" – "the beautiful flower bouquets" and "nicely spaced tables" create a "romantic ambiance" in real life too; while many think the decor "marvelously matches" the "tasty cooking", others mutter "the quality of the meal depends" on whether "gallivanting" owner "Yvan the adorable" is in residence, and the same goes for the "slightly dilettante" service; for most, though, it's "still a favorite."

Yvan, Petit (Le) ◐
16 | 14 | 15 | 41

*1 bis, rue Jean Mermoz, 8ᵉ (Franklin D. Roosevelt),
01 42 89 49 65; fax 01 42 89 30 95*

■ Seems like it's perpetually "party time" (down to "dancing on the tables" sometimes) at this neighboring "antechamber of the great Yvan" in the 8th; while the "elbow-to-elbow" ambiance "isn't always agreeable" and the "charming servers get stressed (have pity, they're overworked)", the Traditional French bistro fare is "fine and affordable" and overall, "a good evening's assured."

Yves Quintard
▽ 20 | 16 | 19 | 52

99, rue Blomet, 15ᵉ (Vaugirard), 01 42 50 22 27; fax 01 42 50 22 27

■ Run by a husband-and-wife team, this "cozy" New French in the 15th attracts staunch loyalists with its "elaborate", "inventive cuisine" and "candy-store decor"; led by the "charming" Mme. Quintard, the staff offers "thoughtful service" – the finishing touch for fans who feel, "though not well-known, it's one of the greats."

Zebra Square ◐S
12 | 16 | 11 | 40

*3, pl Clément-Ader, 16ᵉ (Mirabeau), 01 44 14 91 91;
fax 01 45 20 46 41*

☑ "Trendy but faded" is the take on this 16th arrondissement "rendezvous for the media" crowd near the Maison de la Radio; fans still tune in for the "pretty", "high-tech", zebra-style decor, the multiple "versions of tartare" and the "nice brunch" on weekends; but it gets lots of static from skeptics who slam the Classic French cuisine as "very middling" and the "waitresses who worry more about their looks than service."

Ze Kitchen Galerie
– | – | – | M

4, av des Grands-Augustins, 6ᵉ (St-Michel), 01 44 32 00 32; fax 01 44 32 00 33

A few steps from the Seine in Saint-Germain, this New French has become a hit with an attractive gallery-like setting and light eats from its oh-so-modern menu, trendily divided into four gastronomic themes – soups, 'raw' (as in tuna tartare), pastas and grills; it's the baby of chef William Ledeuil, part-owner of the neighboring Les Bookinistes.

Zéphyr (Le)
14 | 17 | 15 | 38

1, rue du Jourdain, 20ᵉ (Jourdain), 01 46 36 65 81

■ "Original, tasty and very reasonable", this "trendy" New French bistro in the "out-of-the-way" 19th is "worth the detour" for its "art deco ambiance" and "imaginative combinations of tastes"; a few fault its more ambitious attempts, but most salute it as "a good value."

Zeyer (Le) ◐S
12 | 12 | 12 | 41

62, rue d'Alésia, 14ᵉ (Alésia), 01 45 40 43 88; fax 01 45 40 64 51

☑ Maybe this "classic" brasserie in the 14th arrondissement lacks "originality" ("neither the decor, nor the cuisine, nor the staff seems to have changed since its opening"), but its "varied menu" "satisfies" "when you don't feel like cooking", which – since it's open from "noon till midnight nonstop" – can be anytime.

Zinc-Zinc ∇ 12 | 12 | 14 | 38
209, av Charles de Gaulle, Neuilly-sur-Seine (Pont de Neuilly), 01 40 88 36 06; fax 01 47 38 16 21
☑ This "noisy" Neuilly native is a "chic" bistro for such Traditional French classics as Bresse chicken; some find the food a bit "so-so", but others respectfully "recognize that the formula is efficient and with-it."

Zo ◉ 🆂 ∇ 14 | 15 | 13 | 36
13, rue Montalivet, 8ᵉ (Champs-Elysées/Clémenceau), 01 42 65 18 18; fax 01 42 65 10 91
■ In an area near the Elysées Palace where eateries are "few and far between", this "cool" late-night table is a much welcomed fixture; nearby embassy workers, along with financial and fashion types, flock here for a "nice mixture" of Japanese and Mediterranean fare in a "calm", lounge-like ambiance, offered by pleasantly "casual servers" at equally easygoing prices.

Zygomates (Les) ∇ 18 | 13 | 15 | 36
7, rue de Capri, 12ᵉ (Daumesnil/Michel Bizot), 01 40 19 93 04; fax 01 44 73 46 63
■ "Gourmets mustn't miss" this Classic French in the 12th where "succulent cuisine with innovative flavors" is served in a locale "small enough" to seem like a "real Lyonnais bistro" (though it's really a 1920s butcher shop); admittedly, the "decor's austere, but the fare makes up for it."

Indexes

CUISINES
LOCATIONS
SPECIAL FEATURES

Indexes list the best of many within each category.

CUISINES

African
African Grill (10ᵉ)
Entoto (13ᵉ)
Impala Lounge (8ᵉ)

American
Buffalo Grill (3ᵉ, 5ᵉ, 9ᵉ, 10ᵉ, 13ᵉ,
    14ᵉ, 15ᵉ, 17ᵉ, 19ᵉ)
Chicago Pizza Pie (8ᵉ)
Coffee Parisien (6ᵉ, 16ᵉ)
Diable des Lombards (1ᵉʳ)
Joe Allen (1ᵉʳ)
Planet Hollywood (8ᵉ)
Studio (4ᵉ)
Thanksgiving (4ᵉ)

Argentinean
Anahï (3ᵉ)

Armenian
Diamantaires (9ᵉ)

Asian
Asian (8ᵉ)
Baan-Boran (1ᵉʳ)
Blue Elephant (11ᵉ)
Buddha Bar (8ᵉ)
China Town Olympiades (13ᵉ)
Coin des Gourmets (5ᵉ)
Djakarta Bali (1ᵉʳ)
Erawan (15ᵉ)
Foc Ly (Neuilly)
Kambodgia (16ᵉ)
Lac-Hong (16ᵉ)
Maoh Noodles Bar (Neuilly)
Soun (16ᵉ)
Tan Dinh (7ᵉ)
Tang (16ᵉ)
Tricotin (13ᵉ)
Village d'Ung et Li Lam (8ᵉ)
Wok Restaurant (11ᵉ)

Belgian
Bouillon Racine (6ᵉ)
Graindorge (17ᵉ)
Léon de Bruxelles (1ᵉʳ, 4ᵉ, 6ᵉ, 8ᵉ,
    9ᵉ, 11ᵉ, 13ᵉ, 14ᵉ, 15ᵉ, 17ᵉ)

British/Irish
Carr's (1ᵉʳ)

Cajun/Creole
Flamboyant (14ᵉ)

Cambodian
Coin des Gourmets (5ᵉ)
Sinago (9ᵉ)

Caribbean
Flamboyant (14ᵉ)

Central European
Patrick Goldenberg (17ᵉ)

Chinese
Chen (15ᵉ)
Chez Ngo (16ᵉ)
Chez Vong (1ᵉʳ)
China Club (12ᵉ)
China Town Olympiades (13ᵉ)
Davé (1ᵉʳ)
Délices de Szechuen (7ᵉ)
Elysées Hong Kong (16ᵉ)
Foc Ly (Neuilly)
Lao Tseu (7ᵉ)
Mandarin de Neuilly (Neuilly)
Mirama (5ᵉ)
New Nioullaville (11ᵉ)
Nouveau Village Tao-Tao (13ᵉ)
Passy Mandarin (2ᵉ, 16ᵉ)
Tong Yen (8ᵉ)
Tsé-Yang (16ᵉ)

Danish
Copenhague (8ᵉ)
Flora Danica (8ᵉ)

Eastern European
Chez Marianne (4ᵉ)
Jo Goldenberg (4ᵉ)
Pitchi Poï (4ᵉ)

Eclectic/International
Ailleurs (8ᵉ)
Auberge du Clou (9ᵉ)
Auberge Nicolas Flamel (3ᵉ)
Bains (3ᵉ)
Barramundi (9ᵉ)
B*fly (8ᵉ)
Bon (16ᵉ)
Café des Délices (6ᵉ)
Chamarré (7ᵉ)
Chez Prune (10ᵉ)
Costes (1ᵉʳ)
Cou de la Girafe (8ᵉ)
Doobie's (8ᵉ)
Epicure 108 (17ᵉ)
Flora (8ᵉ)
Fumoir (1ᵉʳ)
Georges (4ᵉ)
Man Ray (8ᵉ)
Market (8ᵉ)
Pachyderme (10ᵉ)
Pure Café (11ᵉ)
Quai Ouest (St-Cloud)

Rouge Vif (7ᵉ)
Sept Quinze (15ᵉ)
Si (3ᵉ)
Spicy Rest. (8ᵉ)
Spoon, Food & Wine (8ᵉ)
Temps des Cerises (13ᵉ)
Waknine (16ᵉ)
Xu (8ᵉ)
Zo (8ᵉ)

Ethiopian
Entoto (13ᵉ)

French Bistros (Contemporary)
Absinthe (1ᵉʳ)
Affriolé (7ᵉ)
Ardoise (1ᵉʳ)
Avant Goût (13ᵉ)
Beurre Noisette (15ᵉ)
Bistro d'Hubert (15ᵉ)
Bistrot de Breteuil (7ᵉ)
Bistrot de l'Etoile Lauriston (16ᵉ)
Bistrot de l'Etoile Niel (17ᵉ)
Bistrot des Capucins (20ᵉ)
Bouchons de Fr. Clerc (5ᵉ, 8ᵉ, 15ᵉ, 17ᵉ)
Butte Chaillot (16ᵉ)
Café Beaubourg (4ᵉ)
Café Bleu (8ᵉ)
Café d'Angel (17ᵉ)
Café de la Jatte (Neuilly)
Café de la Musique (19ᵉ)
Café de l'Esplanade (7ᵉ)
Café Faubourg (8ᵉ)
C'Amelot (11ᵉ)
Casa Olympe (9ᵉ)
Chez Jean (9ᵉ)
Coude Fou (4ᵉ)
Durand Dupont (Neuilly)
Epi Dupin (6ᵉ)
Maison du Jardin (6ᵉ)
Manufacture (Issy-les-Moulineaux)
Marsagny (11ᵉ)
Natacha (14ᵉ)
Nemrod (6ᵉ)
Parc aux Cerfs (6ᵉ)
Paris Seize (16ᵉ)
Petit Poucet (Levallois)
Petit Prince de Paris (5ᵉ)
P'tit Troquet (7ᵉ)
Régalade (14ᵉ)
Relais Louis XIII (6ᵉ)
Réminet (5ᵉ)
Rue Balzac (8ᵉ)
Salon d' Hélène (6ᵉ)
Soleil (St-Ouen)
Stéphane Martin (15ᵉ)

Table de Lucullus (17ᵉ)
Troquet (15ᵉ)
Troyon (17ᵉ)
Viaduc Café (12ᵉ)
Wadja (6ᵉ)
Zéphyr (20ᵉ)

French Bistros (Traditional)
A et M Le Bistrot (16ᵉ)
Agape (15ᵉ)
Allard (6ᵉ)
Ami Pierre (11ᵉ)
AOC (5ᵉ)
Aristide (17ᵉ)
Assiette (14ᵉ)
Assis au Neuf (13ᵉ)
Astier (11ᵉ)
Babylone (7ᵉ)
Baracane (4ᵉ)
Bar des Théâtres (8ᵉ)
Béarn (1ᵉʳ)
Beaujolais d'Auteuil (16ᵉ)
Benoît (4ᵉ)
Bistro 121 (15ᵉ)
Bistro de Gala (9ᵉ)
Bistro de la Grille (6ᵉ)
Bistro de l'Olivier (8ᵉ)
Bistro des Deux Théâtres (9ᵉ)
Bistro du 17ème (17ᵉ)
Bistro Melrose (17ᵉ)
Bistrot d'à Côté (17ᵉ, Neuilly)
Bistrot d'Albert (17ᵉ)
Bistrot d'Alex (6ᵉ)
Bistrot d'André (15ᵉ)
Bistrot de Breteuil (7ᵉ)
Bistrot de l'Université (7ᵉ)
Bistrot de Paris (7ᵉ)
Bistrot des Dames (17ᵉ)
Bistrot d'Henri (6ᵉ)
Bistrot du Peintre (11ᵉ)
Bistrot Mélac (11ᵉ)
Bistrot Paul-Bert (11ᵉ)
Bistrot St. Ferdinand (17ᵉ)
Bistrot St. James (Neuilly)
Bistrot Vivienne (1ᵉʳ)
Bombis (12ᵉ)
Bon Accueil (7ᵉ)
Boulangerie (20ᵉ)
Café Charbon (11ᵉ)
Café de Flore (6ᵉ)
Café de l'Industrie (11ᵉ)
Café de Mars (7ᵉ)
Café Indigo (8ᵉ)
Café Louis Philippe (4ᵉ)
Café Max (7ᵉ)
Canal Café (10ᵉ)
Carpe Diem (Neuilly)
Cartet Restaurant (11ᵉ)
Cave de l'Os à Moelle (15ᵉ)

Cuisine Index

Cave Drouot (9ᵉ)
Caves Pétrissans (17ᵉ)
Chardenoux (11ᵉ)
Charpentiers (6ᵉ)
Chavignol (17ᵉ)
Chez André (8ᵉ)
Chez Catherine (8ᵉ)
Chez Denise (1ᵉʳ)
Chez Diane (6ᵉ)
Chez Fred (17ᵉ)
Chez Georges (2ᵉ)
Chez Gérard (Neuilly)
Chez Germaine (7ᵉ)
Chez Jacky (13ᵉ)
Chez Janou (3ᵉ)
Chez L'Ami Louis (3ᵉ)
Chez la Vieille (1ᵉʳ)
Chez Léon (17ᵉ)
Chez Maître Paul (6ᵉ)
Chez Marcel (6ᵉ)
Chez Michel (10ᵉ)
Chez Nenesse (3ᵉ)
Chez Paul (11ᵉ, 13ᵉ)
Chez Pauline (1ᵉʳ)
Chez René (5ᵉ)
Chez Savy (8ᵉ)
Chez Toutoune (5ᵉ)
Clémentine (2ᵉ)
Cloche d'Or (9ᵉ)
Clovis (1ᵉʳ)
Clown Bar (11ᵉ)
Comédiens (9ᵉ)
Crus de Bourgogne (2ᵉ)
D'Chez Eux (7ᵉ)
De La Garde (15ᵉ)
Dos de la Baleine (4ᵉ)
Driver's (16ᵉ)
Ebauchoir (12ᵉ)
Epi d'Or (1ᵉʳ)
Escargot Montorgueil (1ᵉʳ)
Filoche (15ᵉ)
Fontaine de Mars (7ᵉ)
Fontaines (5ᵉ)
Gauloise (15ᵉ)
Gavroche (2ᵉ)
Gourmets des Ternes (8ᵉ)
Grille (10ᵉ)
Grille Montorgueil (2ᵉ)
Improviste (17ᵉ)
Joséphine "Chez Dumonet" (6ᵉ)
Languedoc (5ᵉ)
Lescure (1ᵉʳ)
Ma Bourgogne (4ᵉ)
Marsagny (11ᵉ)
Martel (10ᵉ)
Mathusalem (16ᵉ)
Mère Agitée (14ᵉ)
Moulin à Vent (5ᵉ)
Noces de Jeannette (2ᵉ)

Oeillade (7ᵉ)
Perraudin (5ᵉ)
Petit Bofinger (4ᵉ, 9ᵉ, 14ᵉ, 17ᵉ)
Petite Chaise (7ᵉ)
Petite Cour (6ᵉ)
Petite Tour (16ᵉ)
Petit Marguery (13ᵉ)
Petit St. Benoît (6ᵉ)
Petit Théâtre (1ᵉʳ)
Pied de Fouet (7ᵉ)
Polidor (6ᵉ)
Pouilly Reuilly (Le
  Pré-St-Gervais)
Poule au Pot (1ᵉʳ)
Quincy (12ᵉ)
Régalade (14ᵉ)
Rendez-vous/Camionneurs (14ᵉ)
Rendez-vous/Chauffeurs (18ᵉ)
Renoma Café Gallery (8ᵉ)
River Café (Issy-les-Moulineaux)
Robert et Louise (3ᵉ)
Roi du Pot-au-Feu (9ᵉ)
Rouge Vif (7ᵉ)
Saint Amarante (12ᵉ)
Scheffer (16ᵉ)
Square Trousseau (12ᵉ)
Timbre (6ᵉ)
Tire-Bouchon (15ᵉ)
Tournesol (16ᵉ)
Triporteur (15ᵉ)
Verre Bouteille (17ᵉ)
Vieux Bistro (4ᵉ)
Villaret (11ᵉ)
Vin et Marée (7ᵉ)
Virgin Café (8ᵉ)
Voltaire (7ᵉ)
Yvan, Petit (8ᵉ)
Zinc-Zinc (Neuilly)

French Brasseries

Alcazar (6ᵉ)
Alsace (8ᵉ)
Arbuci (6ᵉ)
Auberge Dab (16ᵉ)
Ballon des Ternes (17ᵉ)
Bœuf sur le Toit (8ᵉ)
Bofinger (4ᵉ)
Brasserie Balzar (5ᵉ)
Brasserie de la Poste (16ᵉ)
Brasserie de l'Ile St. Louis (4ᵉ)
Brasserie du Louvre (1ᵉʳ)
Brasserie Flo (10ᵉ)
Brasserie Julien (10ᵉ)
Brasserie Lipp (6ᵉ)
Brasserie Lorraine (8ᵉ)
Brasserie Lutétia (6ᵉ)
Brasserie Mollard (8ᵉ)
Brasserie Munichoise (1ᵉʳ)
Café de la Paix (9ᵉ)

Café de l'Esplanade (7ᵉ)
Café du Commerce (15ᵉ)
Café Marly (1ᵉʳ)
Café Ruc (1ᵉʳ)
Café Runtz (2ᵉ)
Cap Vernet (8ᵉ)
Chez Francis (8ᵉ)
Chez Georges-Porte Maillot (17ᵉ)
Chez Jenny (3ᵉ)
Chien qui Fume (1ᵉʳ)
Congrès (17ᵉ)
Coupole (14ᵉ)
Dagorno (19ᵉ)
Editeurs (6ᵉ)
Flandrin (16ᵉ)
Flore en l'Ile (4ᵉ)
Gallopin (2ᵉ)
Garnier (8ᵉ)
Gauloise (15ᵉ)
Grand Café (9ᵉ)
Grand Colbert (2ᵉ)
Grandes Marches (12ᵉ)
Maison Rouge (4ᵉ)
Marty (5ᵉ)
Murat (16ᵉ)
Petit Lutétia (6ᵉ)
Petit Victor Hugo (16ᵉ)
Petit Zinc (6ᵉ)
Pied de Cochon (1ᵉʳ)
Procope (6ᵉ)
Rech (17ᵉ)
Rotonde (6ᵉ)
Sébillon (Neuilly)
Sébillon Élysées (8ᵉ)
Taverne de Maître Kanter (1ᵉʳ)
Taverne "L'Esprit Boulevard" (9ᵉ)
Terminus Nord (10ᵉ)
Thoumieux (7ᵉ)
Vagenende (6ᵉ)
Vaudeville (2ᵉ)
Wepler (18ᵉ)
Zeyer (14ᵉ)

French (Classic)

Aiguière (11ᵉ)
Allobroges (20ᵉ)
Altitude 95 (7ᵉ)
Ampère (17ᵉ)
Anacréon (13ᵉ)
Androuet (7ᵉ)
Angle du Faubourg (8ᵉ)
Appart' (8ᵉ)
Armand au Palais Royal (1ᵉʳ)
Atelier Maître Albert (5ᵉ)
Aub. du Champ de Mars (7ᵉ)
Auberge Nicolas Flamel (3ᵉ)
Bar Vendôme (1ᵉʳ)
Basilic (7ᵉ)
BE (17ᵉ)

Beauvilliers (18ᵉ)
Berkeley (8ᵉ)
Bermuda Onion (15ᵉ)
Beudant (17ᵉ)
Biche au Bois (12ᵉ)
Bistro des Deux Théâtres (9ᵉ)
Bistrot d'à Côté (5ᵉ, 17ᵉ, Neuilly)
Bistrot d'Alex (6ᵉ)
Bistrot d'André (15ᵉ)
Bistrot de l'Etoile Lauriston (16ᵉ)
Bistrot des Capucins (20ᵉ)
Bistrot du Sommelier (8ᵉ)
Bistrot Papillon (9ᵉ)
Bistrot St. James (Neuilly)
Bon Saint Pourçain (6ᵉ)
Boucholeurs (1ᵉʳ)
Bouclard (18ᵉ)
Bûcherie (5ᵉ)
Café Flo (9ᵉ)
Café Les Deux Magots (6ᵉ)
Café Terminus (8ᵉ)
Café Véry (1ᵉʳ)
Caméléon (6ᵉ)
Camélia (Bougival)
Camille (3ᵉ)
Canard (17ᵉ)
Cap Seguin (Boulogne)
Catounière (Neuilly)
Caveau du Palais (1ᵉʳ)
Caves Pétrissans (17ᵉ)
C . . . Comme Cochons (12ᵉ)
Chai 33 (12ᵉ)
Chalet des Iles (16ᵉ)
Champ de Mars (7ᵉ)
Chartier (9ᵉ)
Chez Clément (2ᵉ, 4ᵉ, 6ᵉ, 8ᵉ, 14ᵉ, 15ᵉ, 17ᵉ, Boulogne)
Chez Fabrice (1ᵉʳ)
Chez Françoise (7ᵉ)
Chez Gégène (Joinville)
Chez Jenny (3ᵉ)
Chez Toutoune (5ᵉ)
Christine (6ᵉ)
Cigale (7ᵉ)
Cloche d'Or (9ᵉ)
Closerie des Lilas (6ᵉ)
Clos Saint-Honoré (1ᵉʳ)
Coconnas (4ᵉ)
Coq/Maison Blanche (St-Ouen)
Costes (1ᵉʳ)
Cou de la Girafe (8ᵉ)
Coupe-Chou (5ᵉ)
Dame Tartine (4ᵉ, 12ᵉ)
Deux Canards (10ᵉ)
Drouant (2ᵉ)
Editeurs (6ᵉ)
Entracte (18ᵉ)
Epicure 108 (17ᵉ)
Etoile (8ᵉ)

Etrier (18e)
Faugeron (16e)
Ferme de Boulogne (Boulogne)
Ferme des Mathurins (8e)
Ferme St-Simon (7e)
Fermette Marbeuf 1900 (8e)
Fernandises (11e)
Fins Gourmets (7e)
Florimond (7e)
Fouquet's (8e)
Fous d'en Face (4e)
Gamin de Paris (4e)
Gare (16e)
Gastroquet (15e)
Gitane (15e)
Gourmet de l'Isle (4e)
Grande Armée (16e)
Grande Rue (15e)
Grand Louvre (1er)
Guinguette de Neuilly (Neuilly)
Guirlande de Julie (4e)
Hédiard (8e)
Ile (Issy-les-Moulineaux)
Il Palazzo (1er)
Jacques Cagna (6e)
Jardin des Cygnes (8e)
Jardins de Bagatelle (16e)
Jules Verne (7e)
Kiosque (16e)
Ladurée (6e, 8e, 9e)
Lapérouse (6e)
Lavinia (8e)
Léna et Mimile (5e)
Maison Courtine (14e)
Marlotte (6e)
Maupertu (7e)
Maxence (6e)
Mellifère (2e)
Monde des Chimères (4e)
Monsieur Lapin (14e)
Natachef (16e)
Obélisque (8e)
Olivades (7e)
Orangerie (4e)
Ormes (16e)
Os à Moelle (15e)
Paris (6e)
Park (2e)
Passiflore (16e)
Paul Chêne (16e)
Paul, Restaurant (1er)
Pavillon des Princes (16e)
Pavillon Montsouris (14e)
Père Claude (15e)
Petit Colombier (17e)
Petit Laurent (7e)
Petit Prince de Paris (5e)
Petit Rétro (16e)
Petit Riche (9e)

Pharamond (1er)
"Pierre" à la Fontaine (2e)
Pierre au Palais Royal (1er)
Potager du Roy (Versailles)
Pressoir (12e)
Relais d'Auteuil "Patrick Pignol" (16e)
Relais Plaza (8e)
Repaire de Cartouche (11e)
Restaurant les Dolomites (17e)
Rest. de la Tour (15e)
Rest. du Musée d'Orsay (7e)
Rest. du Palais Royal (1er)
Ribe (7e)
Salle à Manger (16e)
16 Haussmann (9e)
Sologne (12e)
Soufflé (1er)
Soupière (17e)
Tante Jeanne (17e)
Tante Marguerite (7e)
Tastevin (Maisons-Laffitte)
Télégraphe (7e)
Terrasse (18e)
Terroir (13e)
Tire-Bouchon (15e)
Tonnelle Saintongeaise (Neuilly)
Totem (16e)
Toupary (1er)
Train Bleu (12e)
Vendanges (14e)
Waknine (16e)
Zebra Square (16e)
Ze Kitchen Galerie (6e)

French (Haute Cuisine)

Ambassadeurs (8e)
Ambroisie (4e)
Apicius (17e)
Arpège (7e)
Bristol (8e)
Carré des Feuillants (1er)
Céladon (2e)
Cinq (8e)
Elysées du Vernet (8e)
Espadon (1er)
Faugeron (16e)
Gérard Besson (1er)
Grand Véfour (1er)
Guy Savoy (17e)
Hiramatsu (4e)
Lasserre (8e)
Laurent (8e)
Ledoyen (8e)
Lucas Carton (8e)
Maxim's (8e, Orly)
Michel Rostang (17e)
Muses (9e)
Orenoc (17e)

Cuisine Index

Pierre Gagnaire (8e)
Plaza-Athénée (8e)
Pré Catelan (16e)
Taillevent (8e)
Tour d'Argent (5e)

French (New)

Ambassadeurs (8e)
Amognes (11e)
Amphyclès (17e)
Amuse Bouche (14e)
Argenteuil (1er)
Astor (8e)
Astrance (16e)
Atelier Berger (1er)
Atelier Gourmand (17e)
Avenue (8e)
Bamboche (7e)
Baptiste (17e)
Bar Vendôme (1er)
Bath's (8e)
Béatilles (17e)
Bélier (6e)
Bistro de Gala (9e)
Bistro d'Hubert (15e)
Bon 2 (2e)
Bookinistes (6e)
Bouchons de Fr. Clerc (5e, 8e,
    15e, 17e)
Bourdonnais/Cantine (7e)
Braisière (17e)
Bristol (8e)
Café M (8e)
Carré (8e)
Carré des Feuillants (1er)
Cartes Postales (1er)
Cave Gourmande (19e)
Cazaudehore La Forestière
    (St-Germain-en-Laye)
Céladon (2e)
Chez Catherine (8e)
Chez Jean (9e)
Chez Michel (10e)
Chiberta (8e)
Cinq (8e)
59 Poincaré (16e)
Clos des Gourmets (7e)
Clos Morillons (15e)
Clovis (Le) (8e)
Coco et sa Maison (17e)
Communautés (Puteaux)
Comte de Gascogne (Boulogne)
Contre-Allée (14e)
Cottage Marcadet (18e)
Dédicace Café (6e)
Doobie's (8e)
En Vue (8e)
Etienne Marcel (2e)
Excuse (4e)

Faucher (17e)
Feuilles Libres/Entrées (Neuilly)
Fontaine d'Auteuil (16e)
Fumoir (1er)
Glénan (7e)
Grande Cascade (16e)
Grange Batelière (9e)
Grenadin (8e)
Guy Savoy (17e)
Hangar (3e)
Hélène Darroze (6e)
Il Baccello (17e)
Impatient (17e)
Jamin (16e)
Jardin (8e)
Jumeaux (11e)
Luna (8e)
Macéo (1er)
Magnolias (Perreux-sur-Marne)
Maison Blanche (8e)
Maison/l'Amérique Latine (7e)
Maison Rouge (4e)
Meurice (8e)
Michel Rostang (17e)
Montalembert (7e)
Montparnasse 25 (14e)
Moulin de la Galette (18e)
Note de Frais (7e)
O à la Bouche (14e)
Pergolèse (16e)
Petit Marché (3e)
Plaza-Athénée (8e)
R. (15e)
Relais Louis XIII (6e)
Renoma Café Gallery (8e)
Restaurant W (8e)
Seize au Seize (16e)
Senso (8e)
Shozan (8e)
6 New York (16e)
Stella Maris (8e)
Table d'Anvers (9e)
Table du Baltimore (16e)
Thierry Burlot (15e)
Toque (17e)
Trois Marches (Versailles)
Truffe Noire (Neuilly)
Van Gogh (Asnières)
Vieille Fontaine Rôtiss.
    (Maisons-Laffitte)
Yvan (8e)
Yves Quintard (15e)

French (Regional)

Alsace/Jura

Alsace (8e)
Alsaco (9e)
Bofinger (4e)
Brasserie Lipp (6e)

Café Runtz (2e)
Chez Jenny (3e)
Chez Maître Paul (6e)
Editeurs (6e)
Epicure 108 (17e)
Fabrique (11e)
Forge (15e)
Léna et Mimile (5e)

Auvergne
Ambassade d'Auvergne (3e)
Bath's (8e)
Chantairelle (5e)
Chez Savy (8e)
Clovis (1er)
Lozère (6e)
Mascotte (8e)
Nemrod (6e)
Poquelin (1er)
Trumilou (4e)

Aveyron
Auberge Aveyronnaise (12e)
Bistrot Mélac (11e)

Basque
Auberge Etchégorry (13e)
Bascou (3e)
Casa Alcalde (15e)
Chez L'Ami Jean (7e)
Pamphlet (3e)

Brittany
Cagouille (14e)
Chez Michel (10e)
Crêperie de Josselin (14e)
Divellec (7e)
Dôme du Marais (4e)
Guilvinec (12e)
Ty Coz (9e)

Burgundy
Bourguignon du Marais (4e)
Crus de Bourgogne (2e)
Ferme des Mathurins (8e)
Ma Bourgogne (4e)
Récamier (7e)
Tante Jeanne (17e)
Tante Louise (8e)
Tante Marguerite (7e)

Corsica
Alivi (4e)
Casa Corsa (6e)
Cosi (Le) (5e)
Paris Main d'Or (11e)
Villa Corse (15e)

Lyon
Assiette Lyonnaise (8e)
Auberge Bressane (7e)
Aub. Pyrénées Cévennes (11e)
Bellecour (7e)
Bistrot d'Alex (6e)

Bons Crus (1er)
Cartet Restaurant (11e)
Chez Fred (17e)
Chez Marcel (6e)
Chez René (5e)
Lyonnais (2e)
Moissonnier (5e)
Moulin à Vent (5e)
Petit Marguery (13e)
Rôtisserie du Beaujolais (5e)
Saint Vincent (15e)
Vin des Rues (14e)
Zygomates (12e)

Mediterranean/Provence
Aimant du Sud (13e)
Angle du Faubourg (8e)
Bastide Odéon (6e)
Bistro de l'Olivier (8e)
Bistrot d'Alex (6e)
Bistrot des Dames (17e)
Casa Olympe (9e)
Chez Janou (3e)
Coco et sa Maison (17e)
Elysées du Vernet (8e)
Fish La Boissonnerie (6e)
Il Baccello (17e)
Jardin (8e)
Languedoc (5e)
Marius (16e)
Parc aux Cerfs (6e)
Petit Colombier (17e)
Petit Niçois (7e)
Petits Marseillais (3e)
Quinson (15e)
Réconfort (3e)
Rest. du Palais Royal (1er)
Senteurs de Provence (15e)
7ème Sud Grenelle (7e)
Sud (17e)
Table Oliviers & Co. (17e)
Vache Acrobate (11e)
Vinea Café (12e)
Willi's Wine Bar (1er)

Normandy
Fernandises (11e)
Pharamond (1er)

Southwest
Ambassade du Sud-Ouest (7e)
Aub. Pyrénées Cévennes (11e)
Bacchantes (9e)
Baracane (4e)
Bascou (3e)
Bistrot des Capucins (20e)
Café Faubourg (8e)
Café Max (7e)
Cazaudehore La Forestière
   (St-Germain-en-Laye)
Chez Toutoune (5e)

Comte de Gascogne (Boulogne)
Dagorno (19ᵉ)
Dauphin (1ᵉʳ)
D'Chez Eux (7ᵉ)
Domaine de Lintillac (9ᵉ)
Espace Sud-Ouest (8ᵉ, 10ᵉ, 14ᵉ, 15ᵉ)
Fermette du Sud-Ouest (1ᵉʳ)
Fins Gourmets (7ᵉ)
Florimond (7ᵉ)
Fontaine de Mars (7ᵉ)
Hélène Darroze (6ᵉ)
Il Etait une Oie (17ᵉ)
Isard (2ᵉ)
Joséphine "Chez Dumonet" (6ᵉ)
Maison Blanche (8ᵉ)
O à la Bouche (14ᵉ)
Oulette (12ᵉ)
Pavillon Puebla (19ᵉ)
Place (8ᵉ)
Rest. du Marché (15ᵉ)
Salon d' Hélène (6ᵉ)
Sarladais (8ᵉ)
70 (16ᵉ)
Souletin (1ᵉʳ)
Sousceyrac (11ᵉ)
Thoumieux (7ᵉ)
Trou Gascon (12ᵉ)
Truffière (5ᵉ)
Violon d'Ingres (7ᵉ)

French (Seafood)

Aristippe (1ᵉʳ)
Augusta (17ᵉ)
Bar à Huîtres (3ᵉ, 5ᵉ, 14ᵉ)
Bistrot d'à Côté (5ᵉ, Neuilly)
Bistrot d'Albert (17ᵉ)
Bistrot de Marius (8ᵉ)
Bistrot du Dôme (4ᵉ, 14ᵉ)
Boucholeurs (1ᵉʳ)
Cagouille (14ᵉ)
Cap Vernet (8ᵉ)
Charlot - Roi/Coquillages (9ᵉ)
Comptoir du Saumon (15ᵉ, 17ᵉ)
Dédicace Café (6ᵉ)
Dessirier (17ᵉ)
Divellec (7ᵉ)
Dôme (14ᵉ)
Duc (14ᵉ)
Espadon Bleu (6ᵉ)
Filoche (15ᵉ)
Fish La Boissonnerie (6ᵉ)
Frégate (12ᵉ)
Garnier (8ᵉ)
Gaya, L'Estaminet (1ᵉʳ)
Gaya Rive Gauche (7ᵉ)
Glénan (7ᵉ)
Goumard (1ᵉʳ)
Guilvinec (12ᵉ)
Huîtrier (17ᵉ)

Iode (2ᵉ)
Jarrasse (Neuilly)
Luna (8ᵉ)
Maison Prunier (16ᵉ)
Marée (8ᵉ)
Marée de Versailles (Versailles)
Marius (16ᵉ)
Marius et Janette (8ᵉ)
Méditerranée (6ᵉ)
Petit Lutétia (6ᵉ)
Petit Niçois (7ᵉ)
Pétrus (17ᵉ)
Pichet de Paris (8ᵉ)
Port Alma (16ᵉ)
Quinson (15ᵉ)
Sébillon (Neuilly)
Taïra (17ᵉ)
T.M. Café (7ᵉ)
Tonnelle Saintongeaise (Neuilly)
Ty Coz (9ᵉ)
Van Gogh (Asnières)
Vaudeville (2ᵉ)
Vin et Marée (7ᵉ, 11ᵉ, 14ᵉ, 16ᵉ)
Wepler (18ᵉ)

French (Shellfish)

Alcazar (6ᵉ)
Alsace (8ᵉ)
Arbuci (6ᵉ)
Auberge Dab (16ᵉ)
Ballon des Ternes (17ᵉ)
Bar à Huîtres (3ᵉ, 5ᵉ, 14ᵉ)
Bistrot de Marius (8ᵉ)
Brasserie Lorraine (8ᵉ)
Brasserie Lutétia (6ᵉ)
Brasserie Mollard (8ᵉ)
Charlot - Roi/Coquillages (9ᵉ)
Chez Clément (2ᵉ, 4ᵉ, 6ᵉ, 8ᵉ, 14ᵉ, 15ᵉ, 17ᵉ, Boulogne)
Chez Francis (8ᵉ)
Chien qui Fume (1ᵉʳ)
Congrès (17ᵉ)
Dessirier (17ᵉ)
Dôme (14ᵉ)
Garnier (8ᵉ)
Gildas Delamer (2ᵉ, 5ᵉ)
Grand Café (9ᵉ)
Huîtrier (17ᵉ)
Jarrasse (Neuilly)
Marius et Janette (8ᵉ)
Marty (5ᵉ)
Méditerranée (6ᵉ)
Paris Brest (7ᵉ)
Petit Lutétia (6ᵉ)
Pétrus (17ᵉ)
Pichet de Paris (8ᵉ)
Port Alma (16ᵉ)
Rech (17ᵉ)
Taverne de Maître Kanter (1ᵉʳ)

Taverne "L'Esprit Boulevard" (9e)
Ty Coz (9e)
Wepler (18e)

French (Specialty Cheeses)
Ambassade d'Auvergne (3e)
Androuet (7e)
Astier (11e)
Ferme St-Hubert (8e)
Montparnasse 25 (14e)
Verre Volé (10e)

French (Steakhouses)
Bœuf Couronné (19e)
Charpentiers (6e)
Dagorno (19e)
DeVèz (Le) (8e)
Gavroche (2e)
Gourmets des Ternes (8e)
Hippopotamus (1er, 2e, 4e, 5e, 6e,
    8e, 10e, 14e, Puteaux)
Mascotte (8e)
Relais de l'Entrecôte (6e, 8e)
Relais de Venise (17e)
Robert et Louise (3e)
Rôtisserie d'Armaillé (17e)
Rôtisserie d'en Face (6e)
Rôtisserie du Beaujolais (5e)
Rôtisserie Monsigny (2e)

French (Tearooms)
Angelina (1er)
A Priori Thé (2e)
Arbre à Cannelle (2e, 5e)
Bernardaud (8e)
Cour de Rohan (6e)
Dalloyau (4e, 6e, 7e, 8e, 9e, 15e,
    Boulogne)
Deux Abeilles (7e)
Je Thé . . . Me (15e)
Ladurée (8e, 9e)
Loir dans la Théière (4e)
Mariage Frères (4e, 6e, 8e)
Muscade (1er)

French (Wine Bars/Bistros)
Bacchantes (9e)
Baron Rouge (12e)
Bistrot Mélac (11e)
Bons Crus (1er)
Bouchons de Fr. Clerc (5e, 8e,
    15e, 17e)
Bourguignon du Marais (4e)
Café du Passage (11e)
Chavignol (17e)
Cloche des Halles (1er)
Dix Vins (15e)
Ecluse (6e, 8e, 11e, 17e)
Enoteca (4e)
Griffonnier (8e)

Juveniles (1er)
Mauzac (5e)
Oenothèque (9e)
Robe et le Palais (1er)
Rubis (1er)
Sauvignon (7e)
Taverne Henri IV (1er)
Verre Volé (10e)
Vin des Rues (14e)
Vin sur Vin (7e)
Willi's Wine Bar (1er)

German
Brasserie Munichoise (1er)

Greek
Délices d'Aphrodite (5e)
Diamantaires (9e)
Mavrommatis (5e)

Hamburgers
Café Bleu (8e)
Coffee Parisien (16e)
Joe Allen (1er)

Health Food
Bon (16e)
Ferme (1er)
Grenier de Notre Dame (5e)
R'Aliment (3e)

Indian
Annapurna (8e)
Indra (8e)
Lalqila (15e)
Maharajah (5e)
New Jawad (7e)
Ravi (7e)

Indonesian
Djakarta Bali (1er)

Italian
Amici Mei (4e)
Bartolo (6e)
Bauta (6e)
Beato (7e)
Bel Canto (4e, 14e)
Bellini (16e)
B4 (1er)
Ca d'Oro (1er)
Cafetière (6e)
Caffé Toscano (7e)
Cailloux (13e)
Carpaccio (8e)
Casa Bini (6e)
Casa Vigata (11e)
Cherche Midi (6e)
Chez Gildo (7e)
Chez Livio (Neuilly)

Pakistani
New Jawad (7ᵉ)

Pizza
Amici Mei (4ᵉ)
Bartolo (6ᵉ)
Chicago Pizza Pie (8ᵉ)
Paparazzi (9ᵉ)
Petit Marguery (16ᵉ)
Rughetta (18ᵉ)

Portuguese
Chez Albert (6ᵉ)
Saudade (1ᵉʳ)

Russian
Cantine Russe (16ᵉ)
Caviar Kaspia (8ᵉ)
Daru (8ᵉ)
Dominique (6ᵉ)
Maison du Caviar (8ᵉ)
Petrossian (7ᵉ)
Pravda (11ᵉ)

Sandwich Shops
BE (17ᵉ)
Café Véry (1ᵉʳ)
Cosi (6ᵉ)
Dame Tartine (4ᵉ, 12ᵉ)
Ferme (1ᵉʳ)
Lina's (1ᵉʳ, 2ᵉ, 4ᵉ, 7ᵉ, 8ᵉ, 9ᵉ, 12ᵉ, 17ᵉ, Neuilly)

Scandinavian
Café des Lettres (7ᵉ)
Comptoir du Saumon (4ᵉ, 8ᵉ, 15ᵉ, 17ᵉ)
Copenhague (8ᵉ)
Flora Danica (8ᵉ)
Petite Sirène/Copenhague (9ᵉ)

Seychelles
Coco de Mer (5ᵉ)

Spanish
Bellotta-Bellotta (7ᵉ)

Casa Alcalde (15ᵉ)
Casa Tina (16ᵉ)
Catalogne, Maison (6ᵉ)
Fogón Saint Julien (5ᵉ)
Pavillon Puebla (19ᵉ)
Rosimar (16ᵉ)

Tex-Mex
Indiana Café (2ᵉ, 3ᵉ, 6ᵉ, 8ᵉ, 9ᵉ, 11ᵉ, 14ᵉ)
Studio (4ᵉ)

Thai
Baan-Boran (1ᵉʳ)
Chez Diep (8ᵉ)
Chez Ngo (16ᵉ)
Chieng Mai (5ᵉ)
Erawan (15ᵉ)
Khun Akorn (11ᵉ)
Lao Siam (19ᵉ)
Livingstone (1ᵉʳ)
Nouveau Village Tao-Tao (13ᵉ)
Sawadee (1ᵉʳ)
Thiou/Petit Thiou (7ᵉ)

Turkish
Sizin (9ᵉ)

Vegetarian
Bon (16ᵉ)
Grenier de Notre Dame (5ᵉ)

Vietnamese
Baie d'Ha Long (16ᵉ)
Chez Diep (8ᵉ)
Davé (1ᵉʳ)
Kambodgia (16ᵉ)
Kim Anh (15ᵉ)
Lac-Hong (16ᵉ)
Mekong Bar (6ᵉ)
Palanquin (6ᵉ)
Tan Dinh (7ᵉ)
Tonkinoise (13ᵉ)
Tricotin (13ᵉ)

LOCATIONS

PARIS

subscribe to zagat.com

OUTLYING AREAS

Levallois-Perret
Petit Poucet

Maisons-Laffitte
Tastevin
Vieille Fontaine Rôtiss.

Neuilly-sur-Seine
Bistrot d'à Côté
Bistrot St. James
Café de la Jatte
Carpe Diem
Catounière
Chez Gérard
Chez Livio
Durand Dupont
Feuilles Libres/Entrées
Foc Ly
Guinguette de Neuilly
Jarrasse
Lina's
Mandarin de Neuilly
Maoh Noodles Bar
Riad
Sébillon
Tonnelle Saintongeaise

Truffe Noire
Zinc-Zinc

Orly
Maxim's

Perreux-sur-Marne
Magnolias

Puteaux
Communautés
Hippopotamus

Saint-Cloud
Quai Ouest

Saint-Germain-en-Laye
Cazaudehore La Forestière

Saint-Ouen
Coq/Maison Blanche
Soleil

Versailles
Marée de Versailles
Potager du Roy
Trois Marches

SPECIAL FEATURES

Additions

Abazu (6e)
Amici Mei (4e)
Androuet (7e)
Andy Whaloo (3e)
AOC (5e)
Assis au Neuf (13e)
Barroco (6e)
BE (17e)
Béarn (1er)
Bellotta-Bellotta (7e)
Bistrot Paul-Bert (11e)
Bistrot Vivienne (1er)
Bon 2 (2e)
B4 (1er)
Canal Café (10e)
Cantine Russe (16e)
Chai 33 (12e)
Chamarré (7e)
Chaumière Massyle (10e)
Chavignol (17e)
Cosi (Le) (5e)
Dédicace Café (6e)
De La Garde (15e)
Dell Orto (9e)
DeVèz (Le) (8e)
Domaine de Lintillac (9e)
Dôme du Marais (4e)
Elysées Hong Kong (16e)
En Vue (8e)
Etienne Marcel (2e)
Feuilles Libres/Entrées (Neuilly)
Fleurs de Thym (4e)
Flora (8e)
Gildas Delamer (2e, 5e)
Grande Rue (15e)
Gualtiero Marchesi (1er)
Il Palazzo (1er)
Il Viaggio (7e)
Iode (2e)
Isard (2e)
Kaïten (8e)
Lavinia (8e)
Madonina (10e)
Maison du Jardin (6e)
Maison Rouge (4e)
Maoh Noodles Bar (Neuilly)
Marsagny (11e)
Martel (10e)
Matsuri (1er, 16e)
Mekong Bar (6e)
Note de Frais (7e)
Oïshi (2e)
Pachyderme (10e)

Paris Brest (7e)
Paris Seize (16e)
Park (2e)
Petit Marché (3e)
Petit Marguery (16e)
Petit Théâtre (1er)
Pharamond (1er)
Place (8e)
Pravda (11e)
Prima Donna (19e)
Pure Café (11e)
R. (15e)
R'Aliment (3e)
Riad (Neuilly)
Rucola (17e)
Sasso (14e)
Seize au Seize (16e)
Senso (8e)
Si (3e)
6 New York (16e)
Sizin (9e)
70 (16e)
Thierry Burlot (15e)
Timbre (6e)
T.M. Café (7e)
Tonkinoise (13e)
Triporteur (15e)
Vache Acrobate (11e)
Villa Corse (15e)

Breakfast

(See also Hotel Dining)
Alsace (8e)
Angelina (1er)
Avenue (8e)
Bernardaud (8e)
Bistro de la Grille (6e)
Brasserie Balzar (5e)
Brasserie Mollard (8e)
Bristol (8e)
Café Beaubourg (4e)
Café de Flore (6e)
Café de la Musique (19e)
Café de l'Esplanade (7e)
Café Les Deux Magots (6e)
Café Marly (1er)
Café Ruc (1er)
Cave Drouot (9e)
Chalet des Iles (16e)
Cloche des Halles (1er)
Closerie des Lilas (6e)
Congrès (17e)
Coupole (14e)

Special Feature Index

Dalloyau (4e, 6e, 7e, 8e, 9e, 15e,
  Boulogne)
Deux Abeilles (7e)
Dôme (14e)
Editeurs (6e)
Flore en l'Ile (4e)
Fontaines (5e)
Fouquet's (8e)
Grand Café (9e)
Grande Armée (16e)
Jardins de Bagatelle (16e)
Ladurée (8e, 9e)
Loir dans la Théière (4e)
Mauzac (5e)
Murat (16e)
Nemrod (6e)
Pied de Cochon (1er)
Planet Hollywood (8e)
Renoma Café Gallery (8e)
Sauvignon (7e)
Taverne de Maître Kanter (1er)
Terminus Nord (10e)
Terrasse (18e)
Vaudeville (2e)
Vinea Café (12e)
Virgin Café (8e)
Wepler (18e)
Zebra Square (16e)

Brunch

Alcazar (6e)
A Priori Thé (2e)
Arbre à Cannelle (2e, 5e)
Asian (8e)
Barrio Latino (12e)
Berkeley (8e)
Bermuda Onion (15e)
Café Beaubourg (4e)
Café Charbon (11e)
Café de la Musique (19e)
Café de Mars (7e)
Café des Lettres (7e)
Chez Prune (10e)
Cour de Rohan (6e)
Dalloyau (4e, 6e, 8e, 9e, 15e,
  Boulogne)
Diable des Lombards (1er)
Durand Dupont (Neuilly)
Flore en l'Ile (4e)
Fumoir (1er)
Grand Café (9e)
Jardin des Cygnes (8e)
Joe Allen (1er)
Kiosque (16e)
Loir dans la Théière (4e)
Mauzac (5e)
Nemrod (6e)

Pied de Cochon (1er)
Quai Ouest (St-Cloud)
Viaduc Café (12e)
Vinea Café (12e)
Virgin Café (8e)
Wepler (18e)
Zebra Square (16e)

Business Dining

Amphyclès (17e)
Angle du Faubourg (8e)
Argenteuil (1er)
Armand au Palais Royal (1er)
Astrance (16e)
Bistrot d'à Côté (5e)
Bistrot de l'Etoile Lauriston (16e)
Bistrot de l'Etoile Niel (17e)
Bistrot St. Ferdinand (17e)
Bœuf Couronné (19e)
Bœuf sur le Toit (8e)
Bon 2 (2e)
Bourdonnais/Cantine (7e)
Café de l'Esplanade (7e)
Café Faubourg (8e)
Cap Vernet (8e)
Caves Pétrissans (17e)
Céladon (2e)
Chez André (8e)
Chez L'Ami Louis (3e)
Chez Pauline (1er)
Chez Savy (8e)
Chiberta (8e)
Clos des Gourmets (7e)
Communautés (Puteaux)
Copenhague (8e)
Costes (1er)
Dessirier (17e)
Divellec (7e)
Dôme (14e)
Dôme du Marais (4e)
Drouant (2e)
Duc (14e)
Flora (8e)
Flora Danica (8e)
Fontaine d'Auteuil (16e)
Fouquet's (8e)
Gaya, L'Estaminet (1er)
Gaya Rive Gauche (7e)
Gérard Besson (1er)
Glénan (7e)
Goumard (1er)
Graindorge (17e)
Grandes Marches (12e)
Gualtiero Marchesi (1er)
Guilvinec (12e)
Guy Savoy (17e)
Hélène Darroze (6e)

Caviar

Caviar Kaspia (8ᵉ)
Comptoir du Saumon (4ᵉ, 8ᵉ, 15ᵉ, 17ᵉ)
Daru (8ᵉ)
Flora Danica (8ᵉ)
Maison du Caviar (8ᵉ)
Maison Prunier (16ᵉ)
Petrossian (7ᵉ)

Celebrity Chefs

(* Indicates consultant role)
Ambroisie (4ᵉ), *Bernard Pacaud*
Apicius (17ᵉ), *Jean-Pierre Vigato*
Arpège (7ᵉ), *Alain Passard*
Astor (8e), *Eric Lecerf;*
    Joël Robuchon*
Bélier (6ᵉ), *Jean-Pierre Vigato**
Bistrot d'à Côté (5ᵉ, 17ᵉ, Neuilly),
    Michel Rostang
Bookinistes (6ᵉ), *Guy Savoy*
Bristol (8ᵉ), *Eric Fréchon*
Butte Chaillot (16ᵉ), *Guy Savoy*
Cap Vernet (8ᵉ), *Guy Savoy*
Carré des Feuillants (1ᵉʳ),
    Alain Dutournier
Cinq (8ᵉ), *Philippe Legendre*
59 Poincaré (16ᵉ), *Alain Ducasse**
Dessirier (17ᵉ), *Michel Rostang*
Elysées du Vernet (8ᵉ),
    Eric Briffard
Espadon (1ᵉʳ), *Michel Roth*
Espadon Bleu (6ᵉ),
    Jacques Cagna
Gérard Besson (1ᵉʳ),
    Gérard Besson
Grand Véfour (1ᵉʳ), *Guy Martin*
Gualtiero Marchesi (1ᵉʳ),
    Gualtiero Marchesi
Guy Savoy (17ᵉ), *Guy Savoy*
Hélène Darroze (6ᵉ),
    Hélène Darroze
Hiramatsu (4ᵉ),
    Hiroyuki Hiramatsu
Il Cortile (1ᵉʳ), *Alain Ducasse**
Jacques Cagna (6ᵉ),
    Jacques Cagna
Jamin (16ᵉ), *Benoît Guichard*
Lasserre (8ᵉ), *Jean-Louis Nomicos*
Ledoyen (8ᵉ), *Christian Le Squer*
Lucas Carton (8ᵉ), *Alain Senderens*
Market (8ᵉ), *Jean-Georges*
    Vongerichten
Michel Rostang (17ᵉ),
    Michel Rostang
Nobu (8ᵉ), *Nobuyuki Matsuhisa*
Orenoc (17ᵉ), *Michel Rostang**

Pierre Gagnaire (8ᵉ),
    Pierre Gagnaire
Plaza-Athénée (8ᵉ),
    Alain Ducasse
Régalade (14ᵉ), *Yves*
    Camdeborde
Rôtisserie d'Armaillé (17ᵉ),
    Jacques Cagna
Rôtisserie d'en Face (6ᵉ),
    Jacques Cagna
Rôtisserie Monsigny (2ᵉ),
    Jacques Cagna
Rue Balzac (8ᵉ), *Michel Rostang**
Salon d' Hélène (6ᵉ),
    Hélène Darroze
Spoon, Food & Wine (8ᵉ),
    Alain Ducasse
Taillevent (8ᵉ), *Alain Solivérès*
Trou Gascon (12ᵉ),
    Alain Dutournier
Violon d'Ingres (7ᵉ),
    Christian Constant

Child-Friendly

Altitude 95 (7ᵉ)
Ay!! Caramba!! (19ᵉ)
Buffalo Grill (3ᵉ, 5ᵉ, 9ᵉ, 10ᵉ, 13ᵉ,
    14ᵉ, 15ᵉ, 17ᵉ, 19ᵉ)
Café Véry (1ᵉʳ)
Chalet des Iles (16ᵉ)
Chez Clément (2ᵉ, 4ᵉ, 6ᵉ, 8ᵉ, 14ᵉ,
    15ᵉ, 17ᵉ, Boulogne)
Chicago Pizza Pie (8ᵉ)
Coffee Parisien (6ᵉ, 16ᵉ)
Dame Tartine (4ᵉ, 12ᵉ)
Epi d'Or (1ᵉʳ)
Espace Sud-Ouest (8ᵉ, 10ᵉ, 14ᵉ, 15ᵉ)
Hippopotamus (1ᵉʳ, 2ᵉ, 4ᵉ, 5ᵉ, 6ᵉ,
    8ᵉ, 10ᵉ, 14ᵉ, Puteaux)
Ile (Issy-les-Moulineaux)
Indiana Café (2ᵉ, 3ᵉ, 6ᵉ, 8ᵉ, 9ᵉ, 11ᵉ,
    14ᵉ)
Joe Allen (1ᵉʳ)
Léon de Bruxelles (1ᵉʳ, 4ᵉ, 6ᵉ, 8ᵉ,
    9ᵉ, 11ᵉ, 13ᵉ, 14ᵉ, 15ᵉ, 17ᵉ)
Lina's (1ᵉʳ, 2ᵉ, 4ᵉ, 7ᵉ, 8ᵉ, 9ᵉ, 12ᵉ,
    17ᵉ, Neuilly)
Ma Bourgogne (4ᵉ)
Marty (5ᵉ)
Petit Rétro (16ᵉ)
Planet Hollywood (8ᵉ)
Quai Ouest (St-Cloud)
Sarladais (8ᵉ)
Sébillon Élysées (8ᵉ)
Spicy Rest. (8ᵉ)
Taverne de Maître Kanter (1ᵉʳ)
Terrasse (18ᵉ)

Thoumieux (7ᵉ)
Toupary (1ᵉʳ)
Trumilou (4ᵉ)
Vagenende (6ᵉ)
Vaudeville (2ᵉ)
Viaduc Café (12ᵉ)
Virgin Café (8ᵉ)
Wally Le Saharien (9ᵉ)
Wepler (18ᵉ)
Wok Restaurant (11ᵉ)

Critic-Proof
(Get lots of business, despite so-so food)
Alcazar (6ᵉ)
Alsace (8ᵉ)
Angelina (1ᵉʳ)
Appart' (8ᵉ)
Avenue (8ᵉ)
Bar des Théâtres (8ᵉ)
Barrio Latino (12ᵉ)
B*fly (8ᵉ)
Bœuf sur le Toit (8ᵉ)
Brasserie Balzar (5ᵉ)
Brasserie Lorraine (8ᵉ)
Brasserie Lutétia (6ᵉ)
Buddha Bar (8ᵉ)
Café de Flore (6ᵉ)
Café de la Paix (9ᵉ)
Café Les Deux Magots (6ᵉ)
Café Marly (1ᵉʳ)
Chez Clément (2ᵉ, 4ᵉ, 6ᵉ, 8ᵉ, 14ᵉ, 15ᵉ, 17ᵉ, Boulogne)
Chez Livio (Neuilly)
Costes (1ᵉʳ)
Coupole (14ᵉ)
Fermette Marbeuf 1900 (8ᵉ)
Fouquet's (8ᵉ)
Fumoir (1ᵉʳ)
Gare (16ᵉ)
Georges (4ᵉ)
Hippopotamus (1ᵉʳ, 2ᵉ, 4ᵉ, 5ᵉ, 6ᵉ, 8ᵉ, 10ᵉ, 14ᵉ, Puteaux)
Léon de Bruxelles (1ᵉʳ, 4ᵉ, 6ᵉ, 8ᵉ, 9ᵉ, 11ᵉ, 13ᵉ, 14ᵉ, 15ᵉ, 17ᵉ)
Lina's (1ᵉʳ, 2ᵉ, 4ᵉ, 7ᵉ, 8ᵉ, 9ᵉ, 12ᵉ, 17ᵉ, Neuilly)
Man Ray (8ᵉ)
Pied de Cochon (1ᵉʳ)
Procope (6ᵉ)
Thoumieux (7ᵉ)

Dancing
Chez Clément (17ᵉ)
Chez Gégène (Joinville)
Coupole (14ᵉ)

Tanjia (8ᵉ)
Zebra Square (16ᵉ)

Dining Alone
(Other than hotels)
Abazu (6ᵉ)
Aimant du Sud (13ᵉ)
Alcazar (6ᵉ)
Alsace (8ᵉ)
Ampère (17ᵉ)
Amuse Bouche (14ᵉ)
Anacréon (13ᵉ)
Aristide (17ᵉ)
Arpège (7ᵉ)
Assiette (14ᵉ)
Auberge Bressane (7ᵉ)
Ballon des Ternes (17ᵉ)
Bar des Théâtres (8ᵉ)
Bar à Huîtres (3ᵉ, 5ᵉ, 14ᵉ)
Bistrot d'Alex (6ᵉ)
Bistrot de Marius (8ᵉ)
Bistrot du Peintre (11ᵉ)
Bistrot Mélac (11ᵉ)
Bœuf sur le Toit (8ᵉ)
Bouchons de Fr. Clerc (5ᵉ, 8ᵉ, 15ᵉ, 17ᵉ)
Bouillon Racine (6ᵉ)
Bourguignon du Marais (4ᵉ)
Brasserie de l'Ile St. Louis (4ᵉ)
Buffalo Grill (3ᵉ, 5ᵉ, 9ᵉ, 10ᵉ, 13ᵉ, 14ᵉ, 15ᵉ, 17ᵉ, 19ᵉ)
Ca d'Oro (1ᵉʳ)
Café Beaubourg (4ᵉ)
Café de Flore (6ᵉ)
Café de l'Industrie (11ᵉ)
Café des Lettres (7ᵉ)
Café du Commerce (15ᵉ)
Café du Passage (11ᵉ)
Café Les Deux Magots (6ᵉ)
Café Marly (1ᵉʳ)
Caméléon (6ᵉ)
Camille (3ᵉ)
Cap Vernet (8ᵉ)
Carr's (1ᵉʳ)
Cartet Restaurant (11ᵉ)
Cave de l'Os à Moelle (15ᵉ)
Charlot - Roi/Coquillages (9ᵉ)
Charpentiers (6ᵉ)
Chartier (9ᵉ)
Chez Catherine (8ᵉ)
Chez Georges (2ᵉ)
Chez Germaine (7ᵉ)
Chez Jean (9ᵉ)
Chez Jenny (3ᵉ)
Chez la Vieille (1ᵉʳ)
Chez Maître Paul (6ᵉ)
Chez Marcel (6ᵉ)

Entertainment

(Call for days, times and performers)

Chez L'Ami Jean (7e) (Basque)
Chicago Pizza Pie (8^e) (DJ)
China Club (12^e) (jazz)
China Town (13^e) (karaoke)
Closerie des Lilas (6^e) (piano)
Diamantaires (9^e) (musicians)
Djakarta Bali (1er) (Balinese dancing)
Fabrique (11e) (DJ/jazz)
Georges (4e) (DJ)
Impala Lounge (8e) (DJ)
Maroc (1er) (dancers)
Meurice (1er) (musicians)
Orenoc (17e) (jazz)
Pied de Chameau (4e) (Oriental dancing)
Planet Hollywood (8e) (DJ)
Spicy Rest. (8e) (jazz)
Studio (4e) (salsa)
Viaduc Café (12e) (jazz)
Xu (8e) (DJ)

Family Appeal

Aimant du Sud (13e)
Alivi (4e)
Allard (6e)
Allobroges (20e)
Ambassade d'Auvergne (3e)
Ampère (17e)
Ardoise (1er)
Aristide (17e)
Aub. Pyrénées Cévennes (11e)
Babylone (7e)
Baracane (4e)
Bartolo (6e)
Bascou (3e)
Biche au Bois (12e)
Bistro 121 (15e)
Bistro des Deux Théâtres (9e)
Bistrot d'Alex (6e)
Bistrot du Peintre (11e)
Bistrot Mélac (11e)
Bon Accueil (7e)
Bouillon Racine (6e)
Ca d'Oro (1er)
Café du Commerce (15e)
Café du Passage (11e)
Cafetière (6e)
Caméléon (6e)
Camille (3e)
Cartet Restaurant (11e)
Casa Corsa (6e)
Chardenoux (11e)
Charpentiers (6e)
Chez André (8e)
Chez Catherine (8e)
Chez Denise (1er)

Chez Georges (2e)
Chez Georges-Porte Maillot (17e)
Chez Germaine (7e)
Chez Jean (9e)
Chez la Vieille (1er)
Chez Maître Paul (6e)
Chez Marcel (6e)
Chez Michel (10e)
Chez Paul (11e)
Coconnas (4e)
Coude Fou (4e)
Epi d'Or (1er)
Espace Sud-Ouest (8e, 10e, 14e, 15e)
Etrier (18e)
Fabrique (11e)
Fermette du Sud-Ouest (1er)
Fins Gourmets (7e)
Flore en l'Ile (4e)
Fogón Saint Julien (5e)
Fontaine de Mars (7e)
Gallopin (2e)
Hippopotamus (1er, 2e, 4e, 5e, 6e, 8e, 10e, 14e, Puteaux)
Joséphine "Chez Dumonet" (6e)
Languedoc (5e)
Lescure (1er)
Lyonnais (2e)
Maison Courtine (14e)
Marlotte (6e)
Marty (5e)
Mauzac (5e)
Mellifère (2e)
Moulin à Vent (5e)
Noces de Jeannette (2e)
Pamphlet (3e)
Perraudin (5e)
Petit Colombier (17e)
Petite Chaise (7e)
Petit Prince de Paris (5e)
Petit Rétro (16e)
Pied de Fouet (7e)
Poule au Pot (1er)
Régalade (14e)
Rendez-vous/Camionneurs (14e)
Rendez-vous/Chauffeurs (18e)
Repaire de Cartouche (11e)
Roi du Pot-au-Feu (9e)
Sarladais (8e)
Sousceyrac (11e)
Square Trousseau (12e)
Taverne de Maître Kanter (1er)
Terminus Nord (10e)
Terroir (13e)
Thoumieux (7e)
Toupary (1er)
Train Bleu (12e)
Trumilou (4e)

Vagenende (6e)
Vaudeville (2e)
Vieux Bistro (4e)
Vin des Rues (14e)
Wally Le Saharien (9e)
Wepler (18e)
Wok Restaurant (11e)
Zéphyr (20e)

Fireplaces

Atelier Maître Albert (5e)
Auberge du Clou (9e)
Bon (16e)
Bûcherie (5e)
Carr's (1er)
Cazaudehore La Forestière
    (St-Germain-en-Laye)
Chalet des Iles (16e)
China Club (12e)
Coq/Maison Blanche (St-Ouen)
Costes (1er)
Coupe-Chou (5e)
Diamantaires (9e)
Grande Cascade (16e)
Ile (Issy-les-Moulineaux)
Il Palazzo (1er)
Iode (2e)
Jarrasse (Neuilly)
Je Thé . . . Me (15e)
Montalembert (7e)
Orangerie (4e)
Pavillon Montsouris (14e)
Per Bacco (18e)
Petit Colombier (17e)
Petit Poucet (Levallois)
Petit Victor Hugo (16e)
Pré Catelan (16e)
Quai Ouest (St-Cloud)
River Café (Issy-les-Moulineaux)
Robert et Louise (3e)
Romantica (Clichy)
Sud (17e)
Tastevin (Maisons-Laffitte)
Truffière (5e)
Van Gogh (Asnières)

Game in Season

Affriolé (7e)
Allobroges (20e)
Ambassadeurs (8e)
Ambroisie (4e)
Amognes (11e)
AOC (5e)
Apicius (17e)
Armand au Palais Royal (1er)
Assiette (14e)
Avant Goût (13e)

Bacchantes (9e)
Baptiste (17e)
Bascou (3e)
Béatilles (17e)
Benoît (4e)
Biche au Bois (12e)
Bistro d'Hubert (15e)
Bistrot d'à Côté (5e)
Bistrot d'Henri (6e)
Bistrot du Peintre (11e)
Bistrot Paul-Bert (11e)
Bon Saint Pourçain (6e)
Brasserie de l'Ile St. Louis (4e)
Café Runtz (2e)
Chez Pauline (1er)
Cinq (8e)
Cosi (Le) (5e)
Crus de Bourgogne (2e)
Dôme du Marais (4e)
Elysées du Vernet (8e)
Espadon (1er)
Faucher (17e)
Ferme St-Simon (7e)
Fermette Marbeuf 1900 (8e)
Fernandises (11e)
Flora (8e)
Graindorge (17e)
Grande Cascade (16e)
Grand Véfour (1er)
Guy Savoy (17e)
Hélène Darroze (6e)
Iode (2e)
Jacques Cagna (6e)
Jamin (16e)
Lapérouse (6e)
Lasserre (8e)
Lavinia (8e)
Ledoyen (8e)
Lucas Carton (8e)
Maison Courtine (14e)
Marsagny (11e)
Maxence (6e)
Meurice (1er)
Michel Rostang (17e)
Monsieur Lapin (14e)
Montparnasse 25 (14e)
Muses (9e)
Note de Frais (7e)
Ormes (16e)
Oulette (12e)
Pachyderme (10e)
Pamphlet (3e)
Petit Colombier (17e)
Petit Marguery (13e)
Petit Théâtre (1er)
Pharamond (1er)
Pierre au Palais Royal (1er)

1914 Sébillon (Neuilly)
1918 Daru (8ᵉ)
1919 Chez Marcel (6ᵉ)
1919 Lescure (1ᵉʳ)
1920 Closerie des Lilas (6ᵉ)
1920 Grange Batelière (9ᵉ)
1920 Zéphyr (20ᵉ)
1922 Café du Commerce (15ᵉ)
1923 Sousceyrac (11ᵉ)
1923 Thoumieux (7ᵉ)
1924 Bristol (8ᵉ)
1924 Chez L'Ami Louis (3ᵉ)
1925 Biche au Bois (12ᵉ)
1925 Guinguette de Neuilly
       (Neuilly)
1925 Salle à Manger (16ᵉ)
1925 Terminus Nord (10ᵉ)
1925 Vaudeville (2ᵉ)
1927 Caviar Kaspia (8ᵉ)
1927 Coupole (14ᵉ)
1928 Cloche d'Or (9ᵉ)
1928 Dominique (6ᵉ)
1929 Diamantaires (9ᵉ)
1929 Petit Colombier (17ᵉ)
1929 Tante Louise (8ᵉ)
1930 Allard (6ᵉ)
1930 Garnier (8ᵉ)
1930 Roi du Pot-au-Feu (9ᵉ)
1930 Totem (16ᵉ)
1930 Trumilou (4ᵉ)
1932 Bœuf Couronné (19ᵉ)
1932 Chiberta (8ᵉ)
1932 Crus de Bourgogne (2ᵉ)
1932 Jarrasse (Neuilly)
1935 Epi d'Or (1ᵉʳ)
1935 Poule au Pot (1ᵉʳ)
1936 Cartet Restaurant (11ᵉ)
1936 Relais Plaza (8ᵉ)
1939 Voltaire (7ᵉ)
1940 Chez Catherine (8ᵉ)
1940 Flandrin (16ᵉ)
1942 Lasserre (8ᵉ)
1942 Méditerranée (6ᵉ)
1945 Chez Fred (17ᵉ)
1945 Clovis (1ᵉʳ)
1945 Ferme des Mathurins (8ᵉ)
1945 Pied de Cochon (1ᵉʳ)
1946 Chez Maître Paul (6ᵉ)
1946 Taillevent (8ᵉ)
1947 Babylone (7ᵉ)
1947 Moulin à Vent (5ᵉ)
1948 Cave Drouot (9ᵉ)
1948 Chez la Vieille (1ᵉʳ)
1950 Chez Jean (9ᵉ)
1950 Deux Canards (10ᵉ)
1954 Chez Germaine (7ᵉ)
1954 Coconnas (4ᵉ)

1957 Chez René (5ᵉ)
1962 Caméléon (6ᵉ)
1963 Chez Denise (1ᵉʳ)

Hotel Dining

Four Seasons George V
   Cinq (8ᵉ)
Grand Hôtel Inter-Continental
   Café de la Paix (9ᵉ)
Hôtel Ambassador
   16 Haussmann (9ᵉ)
Hôtel Astor
   Astor (8ᵉ)
Hôtel Balzac
   Pierre Gagnaire (8ᵉ)
Hôtel Bristol
   Bristol (8ᵉ)
Hôtel Castille
   Il Cortile (1ᵉʳ)
Hôtel Concorde St-Lazare
   Café Terminus (8ᵉ)
Hôtel Costes
   Costes (1ᵉʳ)
Hôtel de Crillon
   Ambassadeurs (8ᵉ)
   Obélisque (8ᵉ)
Hôtel de la Bourdonnais
   Bourdonnais/Cantine (7ᵉ)
Hôtel de la Trémoille
   Senso (8ᵉ)
Hôtel du Louvre
   Brasserie du Louvre (1ᵉʳ)
Hôtel El Dorado
   Bistrot des Dames (17ᵉ)
Hôtel Hyatt
   Café M (8ᵉ)
Hôtel Le Parc
   59 Poincaré (16ᵉ)
Hôtel Lotti
   Gualtiero Marchesi (1ᵉʳ)
Hôtel Lutétia
   Brasserie Lutétia (6ᵉ)
   Paris (6ᵉ)
Hôtel Meurice
   Meurice (1ᵉʳ)
Hôtel Montalembert
   Montalembert (7ᵉ)
Hôtel Normandy
   Il Palazzo (1ᵉʳ)
Hôtel Novotel Tour Eiffel
   Benkay (15ᵉ)
Hôtel Plaza Athénée
   Plaza-Athénée (8ᵉ)
   Relais Plaza (8ᵉ)
Hôtel Prince de Galles
   Jardin des Cygnes (8ᵉ)

Special Feature Index

Hôtel Raphaël
   Salle à Manger (16ᵉ)
Hôtel Ritz
   Espadon (1ᵉʳ)
Hôtel Royal Monceau
   Carpaccio (8ᵉ)
   Jardin (8ᵉ)
Hôtel Scribe
   Muses (9ᵉ)
Hôtel Terrass
   Terrasse (18ᵉ)
Hôtel Thoumieux
   Thoumieux (7ᵉ)
Hôtel Trianon Palace
   Trois Marches (Versailles)
Hôtel Vernet
   Elysées du Vernet (8ᵉ)
Hôtel Warwick
   Restaurant W (8ᵉ)
Hôtel Westminster
   Céladon (2ᵉ)
Hyatt Paris Vendôme
   Park (2ᵉ)
Le Méridien Etoile
   Orenoc (17ᵉ)
Le Méridien-Montparnasse
   Montparnasse 25 (14ᵉ)
L'Hôtel
   Bélier (6ᵉ)
Radisson SAS
   Place (8ᵉ)
Sofitel Arc de Triomphe
   Clovis (Le) (8ᵉ)
Sofitel Demeure Hôtel Baltimore
   Table du Baltimore (16ᵉ)
Sofitel Hôtel Marignan
   Spoon, Food & Wine (8ᵉ)
Sofitel Le Faubourg
   Café Faubourg (8ᵉ)

"In" Places

Alcazar (6ᵉ)
Anahï (3ᵉ)
Andy Whaloo (3ᵉ)
Angle du Faubourg (8ᵉ)
Appart' (8ᵉ)
Arpège (7ᵉ)
Astor (8ᵉ)
Astrance (16ᵉ)
Auberge du Clou (9ᵉ)
Avant Goût (13ᵉ)
Avenue (8ᵉ)
Bains (3ᵉ)
Bar des Théâtres (8ᵉ)
Barramundi (9ᵉ)
Barrio Latino (12ᵉ)
Bélier (6ᵉ)

Benoît (4ᵉ)
Beurre Noisette (15ᵉ)
B*fly (8ᵉ)
Bistrot de l'Etoile Lauriston (16ᵉ)
Bistrot des Dames (17ᵉ)
Bistrot du Peintre (11ᵉ)
Bon (16ᵉ)
Bookinistes (6ᵉ)
B4 (1ᵉʳ)
Brasserie Balzar (5ᵉ)
Brasserie de la Poste (16ᵉ)
Brasserie Lipp (6ᵉ)
Buddha Bar (8ᵉ)
Butte Chaillot (16ᵉ)
Café Beaubourg (4ᵉ)
Café Charbon (11ᵉ)
Café d'Angel (17ᵉ)
Café de Flore (6ᵉ)
Café de la Jatte (Neuilly)
Café de l'Esplanade (7ᵉ)
Café des Délices (6ᵉ)
Café du Passage (11ᵉ)
Café Marly (1ᵉʳ)
Café Ruc (1ᵉʳ)
Café Runtz (2ᵉ)
Cailloux (13ᵉ)
Carré (8ᵉ)
Cave Gourmande (19ᵉ)
C . . . Comme Cochons (12ᵉ)
Cherche Midi (6ᵉ)
Chez L'Ami Louis (3ᵉ)
Chez Michel (10ᵉ)
Chez Omar (3ᵉ)
Chez Paul (11ᵉ)
Chez Prune (10ᵉ)
Chez Vong (1ᵉʳ)
Chieng Mai (5ᵉ)
China Club (12ᵉ)
Cigale (7ᵉ)
Cinq (8ᵉ)
Clos des Gourmets (7ᵉ)
Coco et sa Maison (17ᵉ)
Coin des Gourmets (5ᵉ)
Colette (1ᵉʳ)
Comptoir Paris-Marrakech (1ᵉʳ)
Contre-Allée (14ᵉ)
Costes (1ᵉʳ)
Cou de la Girafe (8ᵉ)
Deux Abeilles (7ᵉ)
Dix Vins (15ᵉ)
Durand Dupont (Neuilly)
Editeurs (6ᵉ)
Emporio Armani Caffé (6ᵉ)
Espadon (1ᵉʳ)
Etienne Marcel (2ᵉ)
Etoile (8ᵉ)
Fabrique (11ᵉ)

Fish La Boissonnerie (6ᵉ)
Flandrin (16ᵉ)
Flora Danica (8ᵉ)
Fontaine d'Auteuil (16ᵉ)
Fontaine de Mars (7ᵉ)
Fouquet's (8ᵉ)
Fumoir (1ᵉʳ)
Gare (16ᵉ)
Garnier (8ᵉ)
Georges (4ᵉ)
Gli Angeli (3ᵉ)
Grande Armée (16ᵉ)
Grandes Marches (12ᵉ)
Guy Savoy (17ᵉ)
Hangar (3ᵉ)
Hélène Darroze (6ᵉ)
Hiramatsu (4ᵉ)
Il Cortile (1ᵉʳ)
Ile (Issy-les-Moulineaux)
Il Sardo (8ᵉ)
Il Viccolo (6ᵉ)
Isami (4ᵉ)
Isse (2ᵉ)
Joséphine "Chez Dumonet" (6ᵉ)
Jumeaux (11ᵉ)
Kiosque (16ᵉ)
Ladurée (8ᵉ, 9ᵉ)
Magnolias (Perreux-sur-Marne)
Maison Blanche (8ᵉ)
Maison Prunier (16ᵉ)
Man Ray (8ᵉ)
Manufacture (Issy-les-Moulineaux)
Mariage Frères (4ᵉ, 6ᵉ, 8ᵉ)
Market (8ᵉ)
Martel (10ᵉ)
Mavrommatis (5ᵉ)
Maxence (6ᵉ)
Méditerranée (6ᵉ)
Montalembert (7ᵉ)
Natacha (14ᵉ)
Natachef (16ᵉ)
Nobu (8ᵉ)
Orangerie (4ᵉ)
Ormes (16ᵉ)
Ostéria (4ᵉ)
Pamphlet (3ᵉ)
Passiflore (16ᵉ)
Petite Sirène/Copenhague (9ᵉ)
Petits Marseillais (3ᵉ)
Petrossian (7ᵉ)
Pierre au Palais Royal (1ᵉʳ)
Pierre Gagnaire (8ᵉ)
404 (3ᵉ)
Régalade (14ᵉ)
Relais Plaza (8ᵉ)
Renoma Café Gallery (8ᵉ)
River Café (Issy-les-Moulineaux)

Rughetta (18ᵉ)
Salon d' Hélène (6ᵉ)
Sardegna a Tavola (12ᵉ)
Sauvignon (7ᵉ)
Sept Quinze (15ᵉ)
Shozan (8ᵉ)
Soleil (St-Ouen)
Sormani (17ᵉ)
Spoon, Food & Wine (8ᵉ)
Square Trousseau (12ᵉ)
Stresa (8ᵉ)
Table de Lucullus (17ᵉ)
Table Oliviers & Co. (17ᵉ)
Taillevent (8ᵉ)
Taka (18ᵉ)
Tan Dinh (7ᵉ)
Tanjia (8ᵉ)
Tante Louise (8ᵉ)
Tante Marguerite (7ᵉ)
Télégraphe (7ᵉ)
Thiou/Petit Thiou (7ᵉ)
Tong Yen (8ᵉ)
Totem (16ᵉ)
Tour d'Argent (5ᵉ)
Vin des Rues (14ᵉ)
Vin sur Vin (7ᵉ)
Voltaire (7ᵉ)
Xu (8ᵉ)
Zebra Square (16ᵉ)
Ze Kitchen Galerie (6ᵉ)
Zo (8ᵉ)

Jacket/Tie Required

Ambassadeurs (8ᵉ)
Ambroisie (4ᵉ)
Apicius (17ᵉ)
Arpège (7ᵉ)
Astor (8ᵉ)
Bar Vendôme (1ᵉʳ)
Benkay (15ᵉ)
Bristol (8ᵉ)
Carré des Feuillants (1ᵉʳ)
Cinq (8ᵉ)
Divellec (7ᵉ)
Drouant (2ᵉ)
Espadon (1ᵉʳ)
Faugeron (16ᵉ)
Gérard Besson (1ᵉʳ)
Grande Cascade (16ᵉ)
Grand Véfour (1ᵉʳ)
Guy Savoy (17ᵉ)
Jamin (16ᵉ)
Jules Verne (7ᵉ)
Lapérouse (6ᵉ)
Lasserre (8ᵉ)
Ledoyen (8ᵉ)
Lucas Carton (8ᵉ)

Maxim's (8ᵉ, Orly)
Mekong Bar (6ᵉ)
Meurice (1ᵉʳ)
Michel Rostang (17ᵉ)
Muses (9ᵉ)
Orangerie (4ᵉ)
Plaza-Athénée (8ᵉ)
Pré Catelan (16ᵉ)
Récamier (7ᵉ)
Salle à Manger (16ᵉ)
Taillevent (8ᵉ)
Tour d'Argent (5ᵉ)
Trois Marches (Versailles)
Vieille Fontaine Rôtiss.
    (Maisons-Laffitte)

July/August Dining

(July and August are the
traditional vacation months
for Parisian restaurants.
Below is a partial list of
places open during this
period. As dates may change,
call in advance to confirm.)
Absinthe (1ᵉʳ)
Alcazar (6ᵉ)
Ambassadeurs (8ᵉ)
Amphyclès (17ᵉ)
Arpège (7ᵉ)
Avenue (8ᵉ)
Beauvilliers (18ᵉ)
Bœuf sur le Toit (8ᵉ)
Bofinger (4ᵉ)
Bourdonnais/Cantine (7ᵉ)
Brasserie Balzar (5ᵉ)
Brasserie du Louvre (1ᵉʳ)
Brasserie Lipp (6ᵉ)
Bristol (8ᵉ)
Bûcherie (5ᵉ)
Buddha Bar (8ᵉ)
Café Marly (1ᵉʳ)
Café Ruc (1ᵉʳ)
China Club (12ᵉ)
Cinq (8ᵉ)
Closerie des Lilas (6ᵉ)
Colette (1ᵉʳ)
Coupole (14ᵉ)
Divellec (7ᵉ)
Dôme (14ᵉ)
Emporio Armani Caffé (6ᵉ)
Espadon (1ᵉʳ)
Fouquet's (8ᵉ)
Gérard Besson (1ᵉʳ)
Grand Colbert (2ᵉ)
Grandes Marches (12ᵉ)
Il Cortile (1ᵉʳ)

Jardin (8ᵉ)
Jules Verne (7ᵉ)
Juveniles (1ᵉʳ)
Laurent (8ᵉ)
Macéo (1ᵉʳ)
Man Ray (8ᵉ)
Mansouria (11ᵉ)
Méditerranée (6ᵉ)
Meurice (1ᵉʳ)
Pavillon Montsouris (14ᵉ)
Pré Catelan (16ᵉ)
Procope (6ᵉ)
Récamier (7ᵉ)
Rest. du Palais Royal (1ᵉʳ)
Table d'Anvers (9ᵉ)
Tour d'Argent (5ᵉ)
Train Bleu (12ᵉ)
Vaudeville (2ᵉ)
Willi's Wine Bar (1ᵉʳ)

Late Dining

(Weekday closing hour;
*check locations)
Alcazar (6ᵉ) (1 AM)
Al Diwan (8ᵉ) (1 AM)
Arbuci (6ᵉ) (1 AM)
Auberge Dab (16ᵉ) (2 AM)
Bar à Huîtres (3ᵉ, 5ᵉ, 14ᵉ) (1 AM)*
Barrio Latino (12ᵉ) (2:45 AM)
Berkeley (8ᵉ) (1 AM)
B*fly (8ᵉ) (1 AM)
Bistro Melrose (17ᵉ) (1 AM)
Bœuf sur le Toit (8ᵉ) (1 AM)
Bofinger (4ᵉ) (1 AM)
Brasserie Flo (10ᵉ) (1:30 AM)
Brasserie Julien (10ᵉ) (1 AM)
Brasserie Lipp (6ᵉ) (1 AM)
Buffalo Grill (9ᵉ) (2 AM)
Café Beaubourg (4ᵉ) (1 AM)
Café de Flore (6ᵉ) (1:30 AM)
Café de l'Esplanade (7ᵉ) (2:45 AM)
Café du Passage (11ᵉ) (1 AM)
Café Marly (1ᵉʳ) (1 AM)
Café Ruc (1ᵉʳ) (1 AM)
Caviar Kaspia (8ᵉ) (1 AM)
Charlot - Roi/Coquillages (9ᵉ) (1 AM)
Chez André (8ᵉ) (1 AM)
Chez Clément (2ᵉ, 4ᵉ, 6ᵉ, 8ᵉ, 14ᵉ,
    15ᵉ, 17ᵉ, Boulogne) (1 AM)*
Chez Jenny (3ᵉ) (1 AM)
Chicago Pizza Pie (8ᵉ) (1 AM)
Chien qui Fume (1ᵉʳ) (2 AM)
China Town Olympiades (13ᵉ) (1 AM)
Cloche d'Or (9ᵉ) (4 AM)
Congrès (17ᵉ) (2 AM)
Coupe-Chou (5ᵉ) (1 AM)
Coupole (14ᵉ) (1 AM)

Diable des Lombards (1er) (1 AM)
Dominique (6e) (12 AM)
Ecluse (6e, 8e, 17e) (1 AM)*
Editeurs (6e) (2 AM)
Espace Sud-Ouest (8e, 10e, 14e, 15e) (1 AM)*
Flore en l'Ile (4e) (1:30 AM)
Gamin de Paris (4e) (2 AM)
Gavroche (2e) (2 AM)
Georges (4e) (1 AM)
Grand Colbert (2e) (1 AM)
Grande Armée (16e) (1 AM)
Grandes Marches (12e) (1 AM)
Hippopotamus (2e, 8e, 14e) (5 AM)*
Indiana Café (2e, 8e, 9e, 11e, 14e) (1 AM)*
Joe Allen (1er) (1 AM)
Léon de Bruxelles (8e, 9e) (1 AM)*
Livingstone (1er) (1 AM)
Ma Bourgogne (4e) (1 AM)
Maison du Caviar (8e) (1 AM)
Murat (16e) (1 AM)
Natacha (14e) (1 AM)
Pied de Chameau (4e) (1 AM)
Planet Hollywood (8e) (1 AM)
Poule au Pot (1er) (5 AM)
Procope (6e) (2 AM)
Rotonde (6e) (1 AM)
Taverne "L'Esprit Boulevard" (9e) (1 AM)
Terminus Nord (10e) (1 AM)
Vagenende (6e) (1 AM)
Vaudeville (2e) (1 AM)
Verre Bouteille (17e) (5 AM)
Viaduc Café (12e) (3 AM)
Wepler (18e) (1 AM)

Meet for a Drink

(Most top hotels and the following standouts)
Alcazar (6e)
Angelina (1er)
Arbuci (6e)
Bains (3e)
Bar des Théâtres (8e)
Baron Rouge (12e)
Barramundi (9e)
Bernardaud (8e)
B*fly (8e)
Bistrot du Peintre (11e)
Bistrot Mélac (11e)
Bistrot Paul-Bert (11e)
Bons Crus (1er)
Bourguignon du Marais (4e)
Brasserie Balzar (5e)
Buddha Bar (8e)
Café Beaubourg (4e)

Café Charbon (11e)
Café de Flore (6e)
Café de la Jatte (Neuilly)
Café de la Musique (19e)
Café de l'Esplanade (7e)
Café de l'Industrie (11e)
Café du Passage (11e)
Café Les Deux Magots (6e)
Café Marly (1er)
Café Ruc (1er)
Café Véry (1er)
Carr's (1er)
Cave de l'Os à Moelle (15e)
China Club (12e)
Cloche des Halles (1er)
Closerie des Lilas (6e)
Clown Bar (11e)
Comptoir Paris-Marrakech (1er)
Cosi (6e)
Coude Fou (4e)
Coupole (14e)
Cour de Rohan (6e)
Dalloyau (4e, 6e, 7e, 8e, 9e, 15e, Boulogne)
Deux Abeilles (7e)
Dix Vins (15e)
Dôme (14e)
Ecluse (6e, 8e, 11e, 17e)
Enoteca (4e)
Etoile (8e)
Excuse (4e)
Fabrique (11e)
Ferme (1er)
Fish La Boissonnerie (6e)
Fontaines (5e)
Fouquet's (8e)
Fous d'en Face (4e)
Fumoir (1er)
Gavroche (2e)
Grande Armée (16e)
Grandes Marches (12e)
Griffonnier (8e)
Impala Lounge (8e)
Indiana Café (2e, 3e, 8e, 9e, 11e, 14e)
Juveniles (1er)
Ladurée (8e, 9e)
Lina's (1er, 2e, 4e, 7e, 8e, 9e, 12e, 17e, Neuilly)
Loir dans la Théière (4e)
Ma Bourgogne (4e)
Man Ray (8e)
Mauzac (5e)
Nemrod (6e)
Oenothèque (9e)
Rest. du Palais Royal (1er)
River Café (Issy-les-Moulineaux)
Rubis (1er)

Sauvignon (7ᵉ)
Souletin (1ᵉʳ)
Taverne Henri IV (1ᵉʳ)
Viaduc Café (12ᵉ)
Vin des Rues (14ᵉ)
Vinea Café (12ᵉ)
Vin sur Vin (7ᵉ)
Virgin Café (8ᵉ)
Wepler (18ᵉ)
Willi's Wine Bar (1ᵉʳ)
Zebra Square (16ᵉ)
Zo (8ᵉ)

Non-Smoking Sections
(The following are
recommended; * entire
restaurant is non-smoking)
Affriolé (7ᵉ)
African Grill (10ᵉ)
Aiguière (11ᵉ)
Aimant du Sud (13ᵉ)
Alcazar (6ᵉ)
Al Dar (5ᵉ)
Al Diwan (8ᵉ)
Alsace (8ᵉ)
Altitude 95 (7ᵉ)
Ambassade d'Auvergne (3ᵉ)
Ambassadeurs (8ᵉ)
Ambroisie (4ᵉ)
Ampère (17ᵉ)
Anahï (3ᵉ)
Androuet (7ᵉ)
Angelina (1ᵉʳ)
AOC (5ᵉ)
Appart' (8ᵉ)
A Priori Thé (2ᵉ)*
Arbre à Cannelle (2ᵉ, 5ᵉ)
Arbuci (6ᵉ)
Aristippe (1ᵉʳ)
Arpège (7ᵉ)
Astor (8ᵉ)
Atelier Berger (1ᵉʳ)
Atelier Maître Albert (5ᵉ)
Atlas (5ᵉ)
Auberge Aveyronnaise (12ᵉ)
Auberge Dab (16ᵉ)
Auberge Etchégorry (13ᵉ)
Aub. Pyrénées Cévennes (11ᵉ)
Augusta (17ᵉ)
Avant Goût (13ᵉ)
Avenue (8ᵉ)
Baan-Boran (1ᵉʳ)
Bacchantes (9ᵉ)
Baie d'Ha Long (16ᵉ)
Ballon des Ternes (17ᵉ)
Bar à Huîtres (3ᵉ, 5ᵉ, 14ᵉ)
Barramundi (9ᵉ)

Barrio Latino (12ᵉ)
Bar Vendôme (1ᵉʳ)
Beato (7ᵉ)
Bel Canto (4ᵉ)
Bélier (6ᵉ)
Bellini (16ᵉ)
Benkay (15ᵉ)
Berkeley (8ᵉ)
Bermuda Onion (15ᵉ)
Bernardaud (8ᵉ)
Beudant (17ᵉ)
Bistro 121 (15ᵉ)
Bistro du 17ème (17ᵉ)
Bistro Melrose (17ᵉ)
Bistrot d'André (15ᵉ)
Bistrot de Breteuil (7ᵉ)
Bistrot de l'Etoile Niel (17ᵉ)
Bistrot de l'Université (7ᵉ)
Bistrot du Dôme (4ᵉ, 14ᵉ)
Bistrot Mélac (11ᵉ)
Bistrot Papillon (9ᵉ)
Bistrot St. Ferdinand (17ᵉ)
Bistrot St. James (Neuilly)
Blue Elephant (11ᵉ)
Bœuf Couronné (19ᵉ)
Bœuf sur le Toit (8ᵉ)
Bofinger (4ᵉ)
Bouchons de Fr. Clerc (8ᵉ)
Bouclard (18ᵉ)
Bouillon Racine (6ᵉ)
Bourdonnais/Cantine (7ᵉ)
Brasserie du Louvre (1ᵉʳ)
Brasserie Lorraine (8ᵉ)
Brasserie Lutétia (6ᵉ)
Brasserie Mollard (8ᵉ)
Buffalo Grill (3ᵉ, 5ᵉ, 9ᵉ, 13ᵉ, 14ᵉ,
    15ᵉ, 17ᵉ, 19ᵉ)
Butte Chaillot (16ᵉ)
Café Beaubourg (4ᵉ)
Café de Flore (6ᵉ)
Café de la Jatte (Neuilly)
Café de la Musique (19ᵉ)
Café de la Paix (9ᵉ)
Café de l'Esplanade (7ᵉ)
Café du Commerce (15ᵉ)
Café Faubourg (8ᵉ)
Café Flo (9ᵉ)
Café Indigo (8ᵉ)
Café Louis Philippe (4ᵉ)
Café M (8ᵉ)
Café Marly (1ᵉʳ)
Café Terminus (8ᵉ)
Caffé Toscano (7ᵉ)
Cagouille (14ᵉ)
Canal Café (10ᵉ)
Cap Seguin (Boulogne)
Cap Vernet (8ᵉ)

Square Trousseau (12e)
Sud (17e)
Table Oliviers & Co. (17e)
Tante Jeanne (17e)
Taverne de Maître Kanter (1er)
Taverne "L'Esprit Boulevard" (9e)
Terminus Nord (10e)
Terrasse (18e)
Thanksgiving (4e)
Timgad (17e)
Tonkinoise (13e)
Tricotin (13e)
Truffière (5e)
Tsé-Yang (16e)
Vaudeville (2e)
Vieille Fontaine Rôtiss.
   (Maisons-Laffitte)
Village d'Ung et Li Lam (8e)
Vinea Café (12e)
Vin et Marée (7e, 11e, 14e, 16e)
Violon d'Ingres (7e)
Virgin Café (8e)
Waknine (16e)
Wally Le Saharien (9e)
Wepler (18e)
Wok Restaurant (11e)
Xu (8e)
Zeyer (14e)
Zo (8e)
Zygomates (12e)

Outdoor Dining

(G=garden; P=patio;
S=sidewalk; T=terrace;
W=waterside)
Café Beaubourg (4e) (T)
Café de Flore (6e) (T)
Café de la Jatte (Neuilly) (T)
Café de la Musique (19e) (T)
Café des Lettres (7e) (P)
Café du Passage (11e) (S,T)
Café Les Deux Magots (6e) (G,T)
Café Marly (1er) (T)
Café Véry (1er) (G)
Cap Seguin (Boulogne) (T,W)
Cazaudehore La Forestière
   (St-Germain-en-Laye) (G,T)
Chalet des Iles (16e) (T,W)
Chez Françoise (7e) (T)
Chez Livio (Neuilly) (G,P)
Cinq (8e) (P)
59 Poincaré (16e) (T)
Closerie des Lilas (6e) (T)
Comte de Gascogne (Boulogne) (G)
Coq/Maison Blanche (St-Ouen) (G)
Durand Dupont (Neuilly) (G,T)
Espadon (1er) (T)

Fontaine de Mars (7e) (T)
Fouquet's (8e) (S,T)
Grande Cascade (16e) (G)
Guinguette de Neuilly (Neuilly) (T,W)
Guirlande de Julie (4e) (T)
Jardin (8e) (T)
Jardin des Cygnes (8e) (G)
Jardins de Bagatelle (16e) (T)
Laurent (8e) (T)
Maison/l'Amérique Latine (7e) (G)
Moulin de la Galette (18e) (G,S)
Pavillon des Princes (16e) (G)
Pavillon Montsouris (14e) (G,T)
Petit Poucet (Levallois) (T)
Plaza-Athénée (8e) (P)
Pré Catelan (16e) (G,T)
Quai Ouest (St-Cloud) (W)
Récamier (7e) (S)
Rest. du Palais Royal (1er) (G)
River Café
   (Issy-les-Moulineaux) (W)
Tastevin (Maisons-Laffitte) (G)
Tonnelle Saintongeaise (Neuilly) (G)
Totem (16e) (T)
Trois Marches (Versailles) (G)
Van Gogh (Asnières) (T)
Vieille Fontaine Rôtiss.
   (Maisons-Laffitte) (G)

Parking

(L= lot; V=valet)
A et M Le Bistrot (16e) (L)
Ailleurs (8e) (L)
Al Dar (5e) (L)
Ambassadeurs (8e) (L,V)
Ambroisie (4e) (L,V)
Ampère (17e) (L)
Apicius (17e) (L)
Arpège (7e) (V)
Asian (8e) (L)
Astor (8e) (L)
Auberge Bressane (7e) (L)
Avenue (8e) (L)
Bains (3e) (L)
Barrio Latino (12e) (L)
Bath's (8e) (L)
Bel Canto (14e) (L)
Benkay (15e) (L)
Benoît (4e) (V)
Berkeley (8e) (L)
B*fly (8e) (L)
Bistro 121 (15e) (L)
Bistrot d'à Côté (5e, 17e, Neuilly) (L)
Bistrot de l'Etoile Niel (17e) (L)
Bistrot de Marius (8e) (L)
Bœuf sur le Toit (8e) (L)
Bon (16e) (L)

Pré Catelan (16e)
Récamier (7e)
Relais Plaza (8e)
Renoma Café Gallery (8e)
Salon d' Hélène (6e)
Senso (8e)
6 New York (16e)
Sormani (17e)
Spoon, Food & Wine (8e)
Square Trousseau (12e)
Stresa (8e)
Taillevent (8e)
Tan Dinh (7e)
Tanjia (8e)
Thiou/Petit Thiou (7e)
Tong Yen (8e)
Tour d'Argent (5e)
Voltaire (7e)

Power Scenes

A et M Le Bistrot (16e)
Ambassadeurs (8e)
Ambroisie (4e)
Amphyclès (17e)
Apicius (17e)
Arpège (7e)
Assiette (14e)
Astor (8e)
Auberge Bressane (7e)
Augusta (17e)
Bar des Théâtres (8e)
Bastide Odéon (6e)
Beato (7e)
Beauvilliers (18e)
Bellecour (7e)
Benoît (4e)
Bistrot de l'Etoile Lauriston (16e)
Bistrot de l'Etoile Niel (17e)
Bistrot de l'Université (7e)
Bistrot de Marius (8e)
Bistrot de Paris (7e)
Bistrot d'Henri (6e)
Bon Saint Pourçain (6e)
Bouchons de Fr. Clerc (17e)
Brasserie Balzar (5e)
Brasserie Lipp (6e)
Bristol (8e)
Café de Flore (6e)
Café des Lettres (7e)
Café Faubourg (8e)
Café Marly (1er)
Cafetière (6e)
Cagouille (14e)
Cap Vernet (8e)
Carpaccio (8e)
Carré des Feuillants (1er)
Caves Pétrissans (17e)

Caviar Kaspia (8e)
Cazaudehore La Forestière
   (St-Germain-en-Laye)
Céladon (2e)
Chen (15e)
Cherche Midi (6e)
Chiberta (8e)
Clos des Gourmets (7e)
Closerie des Lilas (6e)
Comte de Gascogne (Boulogne)
Copenhague (8e)
Costes (1er)
Dessirier (17e)
Divellec (7e)
Dôme (14e)
Duc (14e)
Elysées du Vernet (8e)
Espadon (1er)
Etoile (8e)
Faucher (17e)
Faugeron (16e)
Ferme St-Simon (7e)
Fins Gourmets (7e)
Flandrin (16e)
Foc Ly (Neuilly)
Fontaine d'Auteuil (16e)
Fouquet's (8e)
Gare (16e)
Gaya, L'Estaminet (1er)
Gaya Rive Gauche (7e)
Georges (4e)
Goumard (1er)
Grande Armée (16e)
Grande Cascade (16e)
Grand Véfour (1er)
Guy Savoy (17e)
Hiramatsu (4e)
Jamin (16e)
Jardin (8e)
Jarrasse (Neuilly)
Joséphine "Chez Dumonet" (6e)
Jules Verne (7e)
Ladurée (8e)
Lasserre (8e)
Laurent (8e)
Ledoyen (8e)
Lucas Carton (8e)
Luna (8e)
Maison Blanche (8e)
Maison Prunier (16e)
Marée (8e)
Marius (16e)
Marius et Janette (8e)
Market (8e)
Marlotte (6e)
Marty (5e)
Mathusalem (16e)

Feuilles Libres/Entrées (Neuilly)
Flora (8ᵉ)
Fontaine de Mars (7ᵉ)
Fouquet's (8ᵉ)
Gaya, L'Estaminet (1ᵉʳ)
Glénan (7ᵉ)
Goumard (1ᵉʳ)
Grande Cascade (16ᵉ)
Grandes Marches (12ᵉ)
Grand Véfour (1ᵉʳ)
Guirlande de Julie (4ᵉ)
Guy Savoy (17ᵉ)
Hédiard (8ᵉ)
Isard (2ᵉ)
Jacques Cagna (6ᵉ)
Jamin (16ᵉ)
Jardin des Cygnes (8ᵉ)
Jardins de Bagatelle (16ᵉ)
Kambodgia (16ᵉ)
Khun Akorn (11ᵉ)
Kinugawa (1ᵉʳ)
Ladurée (8ᵉ)
Lao Tseu (7ᵉ)
Lapérouse (6ᵉ)
Lasserre (8ᵉ)
Laurent (8ᵉ)
Lavinia (8ᵉ)
Ledoyen (8ᵉ)
Lucas Carton (8ᵉ)
Macéo (1ᵉʳ)
Maison du Jardin (6ᵉ)
Maison/l'Amérique Latine (7ᵉ)
Maison Rouge (4ᵉ)
Man Ray (8ᵉ)
Marée (8ᵉ)
Mavrommatis (5ᵉ)
Maxim's (8ᵉ, Orly)
Méditerranée (6ᵉ)
Meurice (1ᵉʳ)
Michel Rostang (17ᵉ)
Montalembert (7ᵉ)
Montparnasse 25 (14ᵉ)
Muses (9ᵉ)
Noces de Jeannette (2ᵉ)
Note de Frais (7ᵉ)
Paris (6ᵉ)
Paul Chêne (16ᵉ)
Paul, Restaurant (1ᵉʳ)
Pavillon des Princes (16ᵉ)
Pavillon Montsouris (14ᵉ)
Petit Laurent (7ᵉ)
Petit Théâtre (1ᵉʳ)
Petrossian (7ᵉ)
Pharamond (1ᵉʳ)
Pied de Cochon (1ᵉʳ)
"Pierre" à la Fontaine (2ᵉ)
Pierre Gagnaire (8ᵉ)

Plaza-Athénée (8ᵉ)
Pravda (11ᵉ)
Procope (6ᵉ)
Récamier (7ᵉ)
Restaurant W (8ᵉ)
16 Haussmann (9ᵉ)
Senso (8ᵉ)
Shozan (8ᵉ)
Soleil (St-Ouen)
Studio (4ᵉ)
Taillevent (8ᵉ)
Thierry Burlot (15ᵉ)
T.M. Café (7ᵉ)
Tour d'Argent (5ᵉ)
Trois Marches (Versailles)
Villa Corse (15ᵉ)
Village d'Ung et Li Lam (8ᵉ)
Villa Mauresque (8ᵉ)

Quick Fix

Altitude 95 (7ᵉ)
Angelina (1ᵉʳ)
A Priori Thé (2ᵉ)
Arbre à Cannelle (2ᵉ, 5ᵉ)
Bar des Théâtres (8ᵉ)
Baron Rouge (12ᵉ)
Barrio Latino (12ᵉ)
BE (17ᵉ)
Bernardaud (8ᵉ)
Bistrot Mélac (11ᵉ)
Bons Crus (1ᵉʳ)
Buddha Bar (8ᵉ)
Buffalo Grill (3ᵉ, 5ᵉ, 9ᵉ, 10ᵉ, 13ᵉ, 14ᵉ, 15ᵉ, 17ᵉ, 19ᵉ)
Café Beaubourg (4ᵉ)
Café Bleu (8ᵉ)
Café de Flore (6ᵉ)
Café des Lettres (7ᵉ)
Café du Commerce (15ᵉ)
Café Flo (9ᵉ)
Café Les Deux Magots (6ᵉ)
Café Marly (1ᵉʳ)
Café Véry (1ᵉʳ)
Cave de l'Os à Moelle (15ᵉ)
Cave Drouot (9ᵉ)
Chez Marianne (4ᵉ)
Cloche des Halles (1ᵉʳ)
Clown Bar (11ᵉ)
Coffee Parisien (6ᵉ, 16ᵉ)
Congrès (17ᵉ)
Cosi (6ᵉ)
Cour de Rohan (6ᵉ)
Crêperie de Josselin (14ᵉ)
Dalloyau (4ᵉ, 6ᵉ, 7ᵉ, 8ᵉ, 9ᵉ, 15ᵉ, Boulogne)
Dame Tartine (4ᵉ, 12ᵉ)
Ecluse (6ᵉ, 8ᵉ, 11ᵉ, 17ᵉ)

Special Feature Index

Petit Lutétia (6ᵉ)
Petit Marguery (13ᵉ)
Petit Prince de Paris (5ᵉ)
Petit Rétro (16ᵉ)
Petrossian (7ᵉ)
Pierre au Palais Royal (1ᵉʳ)
Pierre Gagnaire (8ᵉ)
Polidor (6ᵉ)
Potager du Roy (Versailles)
Récamier (7ᵉ)
Repaire de Cartouche (11ᵉ)
Rest. du Marché (15ᵉ)
Rest. du Palais Royal (1ᵉʳ)
Roi du Pot-au-Feu (9ᵉ)
Rue Balzac (8ᵉ)
Salle à Manger (16ᵉ)
Sarladais (8ᵉ)
Saudade (1ᵉʳ)
Sébillon (Neuilly)
Sébillon Élysées (8ᵉ)
16 Haussmann (9ᵉ)
Shozan (8ᵉ)
Sologne (12ᵉ)
Soufflé (1ᵉʳ)
Stella Maris (8ᵉ)
Stresa (8ᵉ)
Taïra (17ᵉ)
Tan Dinh (7ᵉ)
Tanjia (8ᵉ)
Tante Louise (8ᵉ)
Terrasse (18ᵉ)
Thiou/Petit Thiou (7ᵉ)
Toupary (1ᵉʳ)
Trou Gascon (12ᵉ)
Tsé-Yang (16ᵉ)
Viaduc Café (12ᵉ)
Vieux Bistro (4ᵉ)
Vin des Rues (14ᵉ)
Vin et Marée (11ᵉ, 14ᵉ, 16ᵉ)
Vin sur Vin (7ᵉ)

Romantic Places
Allard (6ᵉ)
Ambassadeurs (8ᵉ)
Ambroisie (4ᵉ)
Amognes (11ᵉ)
Amphyclès (17ᵉ)
Arpège (7ᵉ)
Astor (8ᵉ)
Astrance (16ᵉ)
Bamboche (7ᵉ)
Beauvilliers (18ᵉ)
Bélier (6ᵉ)
Blue Elephant (11ᵉ)
Bookinistes (6ᵉ)
Bouillon Racine (6ᵉ)
Brasserie Flo (10ᵉ)

Brasserie Julien (10ᵉ)
Bristol (8ᵉ)
Café de Flore (6ᵉ)
Café des Délices (6ᵉ)
Café Les Deux Magots (6ᵉ)
Café Louis Philippe (4ᵉ)
Café Marly (1ᵉʳ)
Casa Olympe (9ᵉ)
Caviar Kaspia (8ᵉ)
Chalet des Iles (16ᵉ)
Chardenoux (11ᵉ)
Chez Catherine (8ᵉ)
Chez Diane (6ᵉ)
Chez Pauline (1ᵉʳ)
China Club (12ᵉ)
Closerie des Lilas (6ᵉ)
Clown Bar (11ᵉ)
Coconnas (4ᵉ)
Costes (1ᵉʳ)
Coupe-Chou (5ᵉ)
Coupole (14ᵉ)
Crus de Bourgogne (2ᵉ)
Délices d'Aphrodite (5ᵉ)
Dôme (14ᵉ)
El Mansour (8ᵉ)
Elysées du Vernet (8ᵉ)
Epi d'Or (1ᵉʳ)
Fakhr el Dine (8ᵉ, 16ᵉ)
Fontaine de Mars (7ᵉ)
Gavroche (2ᵉ)
Georges (4ᵉ)
Gourmet de l'Isle (4ᵉ)
Grande Cascade (16ᵉ)
Grand Véfour (1ᵉʳ)
Guirlande de Julie (4ᵉ)
Guy Savoy (17ᵉ)
Il Cortile (1ᵉʳ)
Isami (4ᵉ)
Jacques Cagna (6ᵉ)
Jardin (8ᵉ)
Jardins de Bagatelle (16ᵉ)
Joséphine "Chez Dumonet" (6ᵉ)
Jules Verne (7ᵉ)
Ladurée (8ᵉ, 9ᵉ)
Lapérouse (6ᵉ)
Lasserre (8ᵉ)
Laurent (8ᵉ)
Ledoyen (8ᵉ)
Ma Bourgogne (4ᵉ)
Macéo (1ᵉʳ)
Maison Blanche (8ᵉ)
Maison/l'Amérique Latine (7ᵉ)
Man Ray (8ᵉ)
Mansouria (11ᵉ)
Marty (5ᵉ)
Maxim's (8ᵉ)
Méditerranée (6ᵉ)

Escargot Montorgueil (1er) (L,D)
Ferme des Mathurins (8e) (L)
Fermette Marbeuf 1900 (8e) (L)
Finzi (8e) (L)
Flore en l'Ile (4e) (B,L)
Foc Ly (Neuilly) (L)
Fogón Saint Julien (5e) (L)
Fontaine de Mars (7e) (L)
Fouquet's (8e) (L,D)
Fumoir (1er) (L)
Gare (16e) (L,D)
Gauloise (15e) (L)
Gavroche (2e) (L)
Georges (4e) (L,D)
Grand Café (9e) (B,L)
Grand Colbert (2e) (L,D)
Grande Cascade (16e) (L)
Grand Louvre (1er) (L)
Grand Venise (15e) (L,D)
Guinguette de Neuilly (Neuilly) (L,D)
Hippopotamus (1er, 2e, 4e, 5e, 6e,
    8e, 10e, 14e, Puteaux) (L)
I Golosi (9e) (L)
Il Baccello (17e) (L)
Indiana Café (2e, 3e, 6e, 8e, 9e, 11e,
    14e) (L)
Jardins de Bagatelle (16e) (L)
Jarrasse (Neuilly) (L,D)
Joe Allen (1er) (B,L)
Jo Goldenberg (4e) (L)
Jules Verne (7e) (L)
Juveniles (1er) (L)
Ladurée (8e) (L)
Lasserre (8e) (L,D)
Ma Bourgogne (4e) (L)
Maison du Caviar (8e) (L,D)
Marius et Janette (8e) (L,D)
Méditerranée (6e) (L,D)
Moulin de la Galette (18e) (L,D)
Murat (16e) (L)
Noces de Jeannette (2e) (L)
Noura/Noura Pavillon (6e) (L,D)
O à la Bouche (14e) (L)
Orient-Extrême (6e) (L)
Os à Moelle (15e) (L)
Passy Mandarin (2e, 16e) (L)
Patrick Goldenberg (17e) (L)
Petite Sirène/Copenhague (9e) (L)
Petit Lutétia (6e) (L)
Petit Marguery (13e) (L)
Petit Riche (9e) (L)
Petrossian (7e) (L,D)
Pétrus (17e) (L,D)
Pied de Cochon (1er) (B,L)
Pierre au Palais Royal (1er) (L,D)
Planet Hollywood (8e) (L)
Polidor (6e) (L)

Pouilly Reuilly (Le
    Pré-St-Gervais) (L)
Pré Catelan (16e) (L,D)
Procope (6e) (L)
Quai Ouest (St-Cloud) (L,D)
404 (3e) (B,L)
Récamier (7e) (L)
Relais Louis XIII (6e) (L,D)
Repaire de Cartouche (11e) (L)
Rest. du Marché (15e) (L)
Saudade (1er) (L)
Square Trousseau (12e) (L)
Stéphane Martin (15e) (L)
Studio (4e) (B)
Sud (17e) (L)
Taverne de Maître Kanter (1er) (L)
Taverne "L'Esprit Boulevard" (9e) (L)
Thanksgiving (4e) (B,L)
Totem (16e) (L)
Toupary (1er) (L,D)
Tour d'Argent (5e) (L)
Train Bleu (12e) (L)
Vagenende (6e) (L)
Vaudeville (2e) (L)
Verre Bouteille (17e) (L)
Vieux Bistro (4e) (L)
Virgin Café (8e) (B,L)
Voltaire (7e) (L)
Wally Le Saharien (9e) (L)
Wepler (18e) (B,L)
Willi's Wine Bar (1er) (L)
Zebra Square (16e) (B,L)
Zeyer (14e) (L)

Sunday Dining

(B=brunch; L=lunch;
D=dinner; plus all hotels and
most Asians)
Al Dar (5e, 16e) (L,D)
Al Diwan (8e) (L,D)
Alivi (4e) (L,D)
Al Mounia (16e) (L,D)
Altitude 95 (7e) (L,D)
Ambassade d'Auvergne (3e) (L,D)
Angelina (1er) (L)
A Priori Thé (2e) (B,L)
Assiette (14e) (L,D)
Astor (8e) (L,D)
Astrance (16e) (L,D)
Atlas (5e) (L,D)
Auberge Bressane (7e) (L,D)
Auberge du Clou (9e) (L,D)
Avenue (8e) (L,D)
Bar à Huîtres (3e, 5e, 14e) (L,D)
Baron Rouge (12e) (L,D)
Barrio Latino (12e) (B,L,D)
Basilic (7e) (L,D)

Magnolias (Perreux-sur-Marne)
Mandarin de Neuilly (Neuilly)
Oenothèque (9e)
Orenoc (17e)
Paris (6e)
Petit Laurent (7e)
Pressoir (12e)
Quincy (12e)
Restaurant W (8e)
Seize au Seize (16e)
Sologne (12e)
Table de Lucullus (17e)
Toque (17e)
Yves Quintard (15e)

Special Occasions
Alcazar (6e)
Ambassadeurs (8e)
Ambroisie (4e)
Amphyclès (17e)
Apicius (17e)
Arpège (7e)
Astor (8e)
Beauvilliers (18e)
Benoît (4e)
Bristol (8e)
Carré des Feuillants (1er)
Caviar Kaspia (8e)
Cazaudehore La Forestière
   (St-Germain-en-Laye)
Céladon (2e)
Coupole (14e)
Daru (8e)
Dessirier (17e)
Divellec (7e)
Dôme (14e)
Duc (14e)
Espadon (1er)
Faucher (17e)
Faugeron (16e)
Fermette Marbeuf 1900 (8e)
Gérard Besson (1er)
Goumard (1er)
Grande Cascade (16e)
Grand Véfour (1er)
Guy Savoy (17e)
Jacques Cagna (6e)
Jamin (16e)
Jardins de Bagatelle (16e)
Jules Verne (7e)
Lapérouse (6e)
Lasserre (8e)
Laurent (8e)
Ledoyen (8e)
Lucas Carton (8e)
Macéo (1er)
Maison du Caviar (8e)

Mansouria (11e)
Michel Rostang (17e)
Orangerie (4e)
Oulette (12e)
Paris (6e)
Pavillon Montsouris (14e)
Pavillon Puebla (19e)
Petit Colombier (17e)
Pierre Gagnaire (8e)
Plaza-Athénée (8e)
Port Alma (16e)
Pré Catelan (16e)
Quai Ouest (St-Cloud)
Récamier (7e)
Relais Louis XIII (6e)
Sormani (17e)
Sousceyrac (11e)
Stella Maris (8e)
Table d'Anvers (9e)
Taillevent (8e)
Taïra (17e)
Tan Dinh (7e)
Tour d'Argent (5e)
Trois Marches (Versailles)
Violon d'Ingres (7e)
Yvan (8e)

Teen Appeal
Absinthe (1er)
Ailleurs (8e)
Alcazar (6e)
Al Dar (5e, 16e)
Altitude 95 (7e)
Anahï (3e)
Anahuacalli (5e)
Angelina (1er)
Annapurna (8e)
Appart' (8e)
Arbuci (6e)
Asian (8e)
Auberge du Clou (9e)
Avant Goût (13e)
Avenue (8e)
Ay!! Caramba!! (19e)
Bains (8e)
Baracane (4e)
Bar des Théâtres (8e)
Baron Rouge (12e)
Barramundi (9e)
Barrio Latino (12e)
Bartolo (6e)
Bascou (3e)
Berkeley (8e)
Bermuda Onion (15e)
B*fly (8e)
Bistro de la Grille (6e)
Bistrot d'André (15e)

Bistrot des Dames (17ᵉ)
Bistrot du Peintre (11ᵉ)
Bistrot Mélac (11ᵉ)
Blue Elephant (11ᵉ)
Bon (16ᵉ)
Boulangerie (20ᵉ)
Brasserie de la Poste (16ᵉ)
Brasserie de l'Ile St. Louis (4ᵉ)
Buddha Bar (8ᵉ)
Buffalo Grill (3ᵉ, 5ᵉ, 9ᵉ, 10ᵉ, 13ᵉ,
   14ᵉ, 15ᵉ, 17ᵉ, 19ᵉ)
Café Beaubourg (4ᵉ)
Café Charbon (11ᵉ)
Café de la Jatte (Neuilly)
Café de la Musique (19ᵉ)
Café de l'Esplanade (7ᵉ)
Café de l'Industrie (11ᵉ)
Café de Mars (7ᵉ)
Café des Délices (6ᵉ)
Café du Commerce (15ᵉ)
Café du Passage (11ᵉ)
Café Marly (1ᵉʳ)
Café Max (7ᵉ)
Café Ruc (1ᵉʳ)
Café Véry (1ᵉʳ)
Cailloux (13ᵉ)
C'Amelot (11ᵉ)
Carré (8ᵉ)
Carr's (1ᵉʳ)
Cave Gourmande (19ᵉ)
C . . . Comme Cochons (12ᵉ)
Chalet des Iles (16ᵉ)
Chartier (9ᵉ)
Chez Clément (2ᵉ, 4ᵉ, 6ᵉ, 8ᵉ, 14ᵉ,
   15ᵉ, 17ᵉ, Boulogne)
Chez L'Ami Jean (7ᵉ)
Chez Marianne (4ᵉ)
Chez Omar (3ᵉ)
Chez Paul (11ᵉ)
Chez Prune (10ᵉ)
Chez Vong (1ᵉʳ)
Chicago Pizza Pie (8ᵉ)
China Club (12ᵉ)
Cigale (7ᵉ)
Clown Bar (11ᵉ)
Coco de Mer (5ᵉ)
Coco et sa Maison (17ᵉ)
Coffee Parisien (6ᵉ, 16ᵉ)
Coin des Gourmets (5ᵉ)
Colette (1ᵉʳ)
Comptoir Paris-Marrakech (1ᵉʳ)
Contre-Allée (14ᵉ)
Cosi (6ᵉ)
Costes (1ᵉʳ)
Coude Fou (4ᵉ)
Coupole (14ᵉ)
Crêperie de Josselin (14ᵉ)

Délices d'Aphrodite (5ᵉ)
Diable des Lombards (1ᵉʳ)
Dix Vins (15ᵉ)
Driver's (16ᵉ)
Durand Dupont (Neuilly)
Emporio Armani Caffé (6ᵉ)
Enoteca (4ᵉ)
Entoto (13ᵉ)
Entracte (18ᵉ)
Erawan (15ᵉ)
Espace Sud-Ouest (8ᵉ, 10ᵉ, 14ᵉ, 15ᵉ)
Etoile (8ᵉ)
Etrier (18ᵉ)
Fabrique (11ᵉ)
Ferme (1ᵉʳ)
Fish La Boissonnerie (6ᵉ)
Flamboyant (14ᵉ)
Fogón Saint Julien (5ᵉ)
Fontaine de Mars (7ᵉ)
Fontaines (5ᵉ)
Forge (15ᵉ)
Fous d'en Face (4ᵉ)
Fumoir (1ᵉʳ)
Gamin de Paris (4ᵉ)
Georges (4ᵉ)
Gli Angeli (3ᵉ)
Gourmet de l'Isle (4ᵉ)
Grande Armée (16ᵉ)
Grandes Marches (12ᵉ)
Grenier de Notre Dame (5ᵉ)
Hangar (3ᵉ)
Hippopotamus (1ᵉʳ, 2ᵉ, 4ᵉ, 5ᵉ, 6ᵉ,
   8ᵉ, 10ᵉ, 14ᵉ, Puteaux)
Ile (Issy-les-Moulineaux)
Impala Lounge (8ᵉ)
Indiana Café (2ᵉ, 3ᵉ, 6ᵉ, 8ᵉ, 9ᵉ, 11ᵉ,
   14ᵉ)
Isami (4ᵉ)
Joe Allen (1ᵉʳ)
Jumeaux (11ᵉ)
Kiosque (16ᵉ)
Lao Siam (19ᵉ)
Léon de Bruxelles (1ᵉʳ, 4ᵉ, 6ᵉ, 8ᵉ,
   9ᵉ, 11ᵉ, 13ᵉ, 14ᵉ, 15ᵉ, 17ᵉ)
Lina's (1ᵉʳ, 2ᵉ, 4ᵉ, 7ᵉ, 8ᵉ, 9ᵉ, 12ᵉ,
   17ᵉ, Neuilly)
Livingstone (1ᵉʳ)
Loir dans la Théière (4ᵉ)
Lô Sushi (8ᵉ)
Ma Bourgogne (4ᵉ)
Man Ray (8ᵉ)
Mauzac (5ᵉ)
Mavrommatis (5ᵉ)
Mirama (5ᵉ)
Murat (16ᵉ)
Natacha (14ᵉ)
Natachef (16ᵉ)

Nobu (8e)
Ostéria (4e)
Petite Sirène/Copenhague (9e)
Petits Marseillais (3e)
Pied de Cochon (1er)
Planet Hollywood (8e)
Polidor (6e)
Quai Ouest (St-Cloud)
404 (3e)
Rendez-vous/Camionneurs (14e)
Rendez-vous/Chauffeurs (18e)
Renoma Café Gallery (8e)
River Café (Issy-les-Moulineaux)
Rubis (1er)
Sardegna a Tavola (12e)
Sauvignon (7e)
16 Haussmann (9e)
Sept Quinze (15e)
Shozan (8e)
Spicy Rest. (8e)
Spoon, Food & Wine (8e)
Square Trousseau (12e)
Table de Lucullus (17e)
Taka (18e)
Tanjia (8e)
Taverne de Maître Kanter (1er)
Télégraphe (7e)
Thiou/Petit Thiou (7e)
Totem (16e)
Tricotin (13e)
Trumilou (4e)
Vagenende (6e)
Vaudeville (2e)
Viaduc Café (12e)
Vinea Café (12e)
Virgin Café (8e)
Wok Restaurant (11e)
Xu (8e)
Yen (6e)
Zebra Square (16e)
Zéphyr (20e)
Zo (8e)

Theme Restaurants

Auberge Nicolas Flamel (3e)
Bar à Huîtres (3e, 5e, 14e)
Barrio Latino (12e)
Bel Canto (4e, 14e)
Bellotta-Bellotta (7e)
Bistrot d'André (15e)
Buddha Bar (8e)
Café de la Musique (19e)
Chez Clément (2e, 4e, 6e, 8e, 14e, 15e, 17e, Boulogne)
Chicago Pizza Pie (8e)
Coco de Mer (5e)
Driver's (16e)

Léon de Bruxelles (1er, 4e, 6e, 8e, 9e, 11e, 13e, 14e, 15e, 17e)
Lina's (1er, 2e, 4e, 7e, 8e, 9e, 12e, 17e, Neuilly)
Lô Sushi (8e)
Monsieur Lapin (14e)
Planet Hollywood (8e)
70 (16e)
Virgin Café (8e)
Wok Restaurant (11e)

Transporting Experiences

African Grill (10e)
Alsaco (9e)
Anahï (3e)
Annapurna (8e)
Asian (8e)
Atlas (5e)
Baie d'Ha Long (16e)
Benkay (15e)
Blue Elephant (11e)
Buddha Bar (8e)
Café de la Jatte (Neuilly)
Chalet des Iles (16e)
Chen (15e)
Chez Gégène (Joinville)
Chez Vong (1er)
China Club (12e)
Coco de Mer (5e)
Délices d'Aphrodite (5e)
Diamantaires (9e)
Djakarta Bali (1er)
Enoteca (4e)
Entoto (13e)
Erawan (15e)
Etoile Marocaine (8e)
Fakhr el Dine (8e, 16e)
Ferme St-Hubert (8e)
Flamboyant (14e)
Fogón Saint Julien (5e)
Isami (4e)
Isse (2e)
Jardins de Bagatelle (16e)
Livingstone (1er)
Lô Sushi (8e)
Man Ray (8e)
Mansouria (11e)
Mavrommatis (5e)
Monsieur Lapin (14e)
Saudade (1er)
Shozan (8e)
Soufflé (1er)
Stella Maris (8e)
Taïra (17e)
Tan Dinh (7e)
Tanjia (8e)
Timgad (17e)

Tricotin (13ᵉ)
Tsé-Yang (16ᵉ)
Wally Le Saharien (9ᵉ)
Yen (6ᵉ)

Views
Altitude 95 (7ᵉ)
Bookinistes (6ᵉ)
Café Louis Philippe (4ᵉ)
Café Marly (1ᵉʳ)
Chez Francis (8ᵉ)
Coconnas (4ᵉ)
Georges (4ᵉ)
Grand Véfour (1ᵉʳ)
Isami (4ᵉ)
Jardins de Bagatelle (16ᵉ)
Jules Verne (7ᵉ)
Lapérouse (6ᵉ)
Ledoyen (8ᵉ)
Ma Bourgogne (4ᵉ)
Maison Blanche (8ᵉ)
Maupertu (7ᵉ)
Muscade (1ᵉʳ)
R. (15ᵉ)
Rest. du Musée d'Orsay (7ᵉ)
Terrasse (18ᵉ)
Totem (16ᵉ)
Toupary (1ᵉʳ)
Tour d'Argent (5ᵉ)

Visitors on Expense Account
Ambroisie (4ᵉ)
Amphyclès (17ᵉ)
Arpège (7ᵉ)
Assiette (14ᵉ)
Augusta (17ᵉ)
Bath's (8ᵉ)
Béatilles (17ᵉ)
Beauvilliers (18ᵉ)
Benoît (4ᵉ)
Bourdonnais/Cantine (7ᵉ)
Café Faubourg (8ᵉ)
Carpaccio (8ᵉ)
Carré des Feuillants (1ᵉʳ)
Caviar Kaspia (8ᵉ)
Chen (15ᵉ)
Chez L'Ami Louis (3ᵉ)
Chez Pauline (1ᵉʳ)
Chiberta (8ᵉ)
Clovis (Le) (8ᵉ)
Copenhague (8ᵉ)
Dessirier (17ᵉ)
Divellec (7ᵉ)
Dôme (14ᵉ)
Drouant (2ᵉ)
Duc (14ᵉ)

Faucher (17ᵉ)
Ferme St-Simon (7ᵉ)
Flora Danica (8ᵉ)
Fouquet's (8ᵉ)
Frégate (12ᵉ)
Garnier (8ᵉ)
Gaya, L'Estaminet (1ᵉʳ)
Gaya Rive Gauche (7ᵉ)
Gérard Besson (1ᵉʳ)
Goumard (1ᵉʳ)
Grand Véfour (1ᵉʳ)
Grange Batelière (9ᵉ)
Guy Savoy (17ᵉ)
Hélène Darroze (6ᵉ)
Il Cortile (1ᵉʳ)
Isse (2ᵉ)
Jacques Cagna (6ᵉ)
Jamin (16ᵉ)
Jarrasse (Neuilly)
Joséphine "Chez Dumonet" (6ᵉ)
Jules Verne (7ᵉ)
Lasserre (8ᵉ)
Laurent (8ᵉ)
Ledoyen (8ᵉ)
Lucas Carton (8ᵉ)
Maison Blanche (8ᵉ)
Mansouria (11ᵉ)
Marée (8ᵉ)
Marius (16ᵉ)
Maxence (6ᵉ)
Maxim's (8ᵉ, Orly)
Michel Rostang (17ᵉ)
Muses (9ᵉ)
Natacha (14ᵉ)
Nobu (8ᵉ)
Obélisque (8ᵉ)
Orangerie (4ᵉ)
Orenoc (17ᵉ)
Oulette (12ᵉ)
Petit Colombier (17ᵉ)
Pétrus (17ᵉ)
Pierre au Palais Royal (1ᵉʳ)
Pierre Gagnaire (8ᵉ)
Pré Catelan (16ᵉ)
Pressoir (12ᵉ)
Relais Louis XIII (6ᵉ)
Relais Plaza (8ᵉ)
Restaurant W (8ᵉ)
Salle à Manger (16ᵉ)
Sousceyrac (11ᵉ)
Stella Maris (8ᵉ)
Table d'Anvers (9ᵉ)
Taillevent (8ᵉ)
Taïra (17ᵉ)
Tante Jeanne (17ᵉ)
Tante Marguerite (7ᵉ)
Tour d'Argent (5ᵉ)

Trois Marches (Versailles)
Trou Gascon (12ᵉ)

Winning Wine Lists

Ambassadeurs (8ᵉ)
Ambroisie (4ᵉ)
Amphyclès (17ᵉ)
Bistrot du Sommelier (8ᵉ)
Bistrot Paul-Bert (11ᵉ)
Bouchons de Fr. Clerc (5ᵉ, 8ᵉ,
    15ᵉ, 17ᵉ)
Bourguignon du Marais (4ᵉ)
Bristol (8ᵉ)
Café Runtz (2ᵉ)
Cagouille (14ᵉ)
Carré des Feuillants (1ᵉʳ)
Cave de l'Os à Moelle (15ᵉ)
Cave Drouot (9ᵉ)
Caves Pétrissans (17ᵉ)
Chai 33 (12ᵉ)
Chavignol (17ᵉ)
Cinq (8ᵉ)
Dessirier (17ᵉ)
Divellec (7ᵉ)
Drouant (2ᵉ)
Ecluse (6ᵉ, 8ᵉ, 11ᵉ, 17ᵉ)
Elysées du Vernet (8ᵉ)
Enoteca (4ᵉ)
Excuse (4ᵉ)
Faucher (17ᵉ)
Ferme St-Simon (7ᵉ)
Fish La Boissonnerie (6ᵉ)
Fogón Saint Julien (5ᵉ)
Gérard Besson (1ᵉʳ)
Grande Cascade (16ᵉ)
Grand Véfour (1ᵉʳ)
Grange Batelière (9ᵉ)
Guy Savoy (17ᵉ)
Hélène Darroze (6ᵉ)
Il Cortile (1ᵉʳ)
Jacques Cagna (6ᵉ)

Jamin (16ᵉ)
Jardin (8ᵉ)
Joséphine "Chez Dumonet" (6ᵉ)
Jules Verne (7ᵉ)
Lasserre (8ᵉ)
Laurent (8ᵉ)
Lavinia (8ᵉ)
Ledoyen (8ᵉ)
Lucas Carton (8ᵉ)
Macéo (1ᵉʳ)
Maison Courtine (14ᵉ)
Marée (8ᵉ)
Maxence (6ᵉ)
Maxim's (8ᵉ, Orly)
Meurice (1ᵉʳ)
Michel Rostang (17ᵉ)
Montparnasse 25 (14ᵉ)
Muses (9ᵉ)
Oenothèque (9ᵉ)
Oulette (12ᵉ)
Paris (6ᵉ)
Petit Marguery (13ᵉ)
Petrossian (7ᵉ)
Pierre au Palais Royal (1ᵉʳ)
Pierre Gagnaire (8ᵉ)
Plaza-Athénée (8ᵉ)
Pressoir (12ᵉ)
Récamier (7ᵉ)
Relais Louis XIII (6ᵉ)
Saudade (1ᵉʳ)
Sousceyrac (11ᵉ)
Spoon, Food & Wine (8ᵉ)
Stella Maris (8ᵉ)
Table d'Anvers (9ᵉ)
Taillevent (8ᵉ)
Tante Marguerite (7ᵉ)
Tour d'Argent (5ᵉ)
Trois Marches (Versailles)
Trou Gascon (12ᵉ)
Vin sur Vin (7ᵉ)

Wine Vintage Chart

This chart is designed to help you select wine to go with your meal. It is based on the same 0 to 30 scale used throughout this *Survey*. The ratings (prepared by our friend **Howard Stravitz**, a professor at the University of South Carolina) reflect both the quality of the vintage and the wine's readiness for present consumption. Thus, if a wine is not fully mature or is over the hill, its rating has been reduced. We do not include 1987, 1991–1993 vintages because they are not especially recommended for most areas.

	'85	'86	'88	'89	'90	'94	'95	'96	'97	'98	'99	'00	'01
WHITES													
French:													
Alsace	24	18	22	28	28	26	25	23	23	25	23	25	26
Burgundy	26	25	17	25	24	15	29	28	25	24	25	22	20
Loire Valley	–	–	–	–	25	23	24	26	24	23	24	25	23
Champagne	28	25	24	26	29	–	26	27	24	24	25	25	–
Sauternes	21	28	29	25	27	–	20	23	27	22	22	22	28
California (Napa, Sonoma, Mendocino):													
Chardonnay	–	–	–	–	–	22	27	23	27	25	25	23	26
Sauvignon Blanc/Semillon	–	–	–	–	–	–	–	–	24	24	25	22	26
REDS													
French:													
Bordeaux	25	26	24	27	29	22	26	25	23	24	23	25	23
Burgundy	23	–	21	25	28	–	26	27	25	22	27	22	20
Rhône	25	19	27	29	29	24	25	23	25	28	26	27	24
Beaujolais	–	–	–	–	–	–	–	–	23	22	25	25	18
California (Napa, Sonoma, Mendocino):													
Cab./Merlot	26	26	–	21	28	29	27	25	28	23	26	23	26
Pinot Noir	–	–	–	–	–	27	24	24	26	25	26	25	27
Zinfandel	–	–	–	–	–	25	22	23	21	22	24	19	24
Italian:													
Tuscany	26	–	24	–	26	22	25	20	28	24	27	26	25
Piedmont	26	–	26	28	29	–	23	26	28	26	25	24	22